Mutual Impressions

Mutual Impressions *Writers*

from

the Americas

Reading

One

Another

Edited by

Ilan Stavans

Duke University Press

Durham & London

1999

Also by Ilan Stavans

FICTION

The One-Handed Pianist and Other Stories

NONFICTION

A Cartoon History of Latinos in the U.S.
(with Lalo López Alcaráz)

The Riddle of Cantinflas:
Essays on Hispanic Popular Culture

Art & Anger: Essays on Politics and the Imagination

Bandido

The Hispanic Condition

Imagining Columbus: The Literary Voyage

EDITIONS

The Oxford Book of Jewish Stories

The Urban Muse

Tropical Synagogues

New World

Growing Up Latino: Memoirs and Stories
(co-edited with Harold Augenbraum)

The Oxford Book of Latin American Essays

TRANSLATION

Sentimental Songs, by Felipe Alfau

for Gerardo Villacrés

Mis pasos en esta calle
resuenan
   en otra calle

donde
   oigo mis pasos
pasar en esta calle
donde

Sólo es real la niebla

Octavio Paz
"Aquí"

Contents

Introduction: Coincidence and Dissidence

Ilan Stavans

> Life is for each man a solitary cell whose walls are mirrors.
> —Eugene O'Neill

This is a book about neighbors: not about who our neighbors are but about who we imagine them to be. Consequently, it is also about borders—or better, about crossing verbal and geographical borders through the most abstract of bridges: literature. The entries are all by writers from the United States, the Caribbean, and Latin America reacting to each other's views: Who are you? How did you come to be who you are? What makes your cultural habitat different from mine? How did we come to be so unlike each other? And what does literature mean for both of us?

A border, of course, is but an artificial divide, a rim delineating separate turfs, establishing their beginning and end. The most daunting border at the heart of this volume, *la frontera,* has been an obsession of mine ever since I crossed it in 1985. Or was it even before? (Mexico, my native home, more than any other Hispanic nation, lives under the spell of the United States: we are who we are by distinguishing ourselves from the *gringos.*) The actual line, the natural river dividing the Anglo-Saxon and Hispanic world into a north and a south, is less powerful than its invisible ramifications, especially as felt throughout the twentieth century: north is the English language, Protestantism, and democracy; south is Spanish and Portuguese, Catholicism, and political instability; north is utopia, whereas south is the trauma of a past not fully outgrown. All these might be large generalizations, but civilizations are based on nothing but generalizations: humans rationalize difference by basing their views on a handful of arbitrary features and beliefs.

At any rate, the Rio Grande, as it is called if one looks at it from north to south, or else el Río Bravo if from south to north, is a geographic divide that is perceived mentally from one end of the continent to the other. True, neither the north nor the south are monolithic: the United States is an immigrant society, a sum of parts;

and Mexico, or for that matter Latin America as a whole, has long been an archipelago of sovereign solitudes, often mediated by the U.S. "Distant neighbors" is the term coined by Alan Riding: different, but not quite separate, inasmuch as, since the American Revolution the United States has had a decisive influence over its southern neighbors—political, military, economic. And the opposite is also true, even though the Hispanic influence across the border has manifested itself only recently through a new Latino culture and for long decades was solely the result of penniless immigrants looking for a better life in "el Coloso del Norte." This mutual dependency is based, most often, on misconceptions: you are materialistic whereas I am an idealist; I believe in progress whereas you fear it. In short, I'm better than you. Is this measured difference at all quantifiable? Well, certainly not in literature. Literature, in fact, is the best way to see not how different we think we are but how similar we have always been.

Or have we not? Does the dictum *e pluribus unum* apply to the whole continent? For there are many other borders within it aside from *la frontera:* between the Dominican Republic and Haiti, for instance; between Canada and the United States; or between Brazil on one side and Venezuela and Colombia on the other. On both sides of these myriad borders books are written in different tongues—Spanish, Portuguese, Creole, French, and English, each an expression of a unique idiosyncrasy. Or that, at least, is the accepted view. (Should this list also include Spanglish and Portuñol? How about Dutch, German, Chinese, Yiddish, Quechua, and Nahuatl? For the region is a plurality, and immigrants from the world over have turned it into a veritable Babel of tongues, some more visible than others, obviously.) Washington Irving, in 1726, looked to Spain for inspiration, but not to Latin America because the region was still dazed by its colonial mentality and he was looking for a hero like Columbus, who could symbolize freedom and courage and adventure. His voluminous biography of Columbus is a fascinating exercise in self-deception: his mariner is a hero, a valiant explorer, a pilgrim—just the opposite view of what the Hispanic orbit had made of him since 1492: a scoundrel, an aggressor, the first colonizer. This study of opposites is at the core of the two—or shall I say the many—literatures: often the same character, the same landscape, the same dream acquires the antithetical value.

Irving established an enduring progeny. Walt Whitman, for instance, whom Emerson described as the greatest poet in the young United States, wrote in 1887 his poem "Prayer for Columbus," later included in *Leaves of Grass*, wherein he assumes the voice of the old Genoese admiral at the moment of death; his Columbus is a vulnerable individual, insecure about his own talents and achievements, goal oriented, obsessed with fame and success, a man infatuated with his own individuality. In 1892, the year of Whitman's death, the Nicaraguan *modernista* Rubén Darío, the greatest poet of *la América hispánica* according to the Uruguayan critic José Enrique Rodó, wrote "A Colón," also a poem about Columbus. But his Columbus couldn't be more different: a knave, a merciless *imperialista*. Even a superficial reading of both pieces shows how contrasting they are: Whitman celebrates courage while Darío denounces oppression and genocide; the former glorifies the mariner whereas the latter condemns him. Columbus, in the end, is nothing but a kaleidoscopic vision, a malleable ghost. Perhaps only by putting Whitman's and Darío's Columbuses side by side can we get close to a balanced picture of the real man.

American writers (I hereby refer to U.S. literati the way they do, appropriating the entire continent in the adjective *American*) have enjoyed looking for and at themselves—looking at their utopian face in the mirror—in Hispanic America and the Caribbean. For them the region symbolizes escape, chaos, barbarism: Ernest Hemingway found in Cuba the perfect landscape (after Spain) to test his manhood; Katherine Anne Porter wrote some of her more tantalizing stories about poor Mexican campesinos; John Reed, Michael Gold, and John Kenneth Turner were fascinated with the Mexican Revolution of 1910, and in particular with the mythical stature of bandits such as Pancho Villa and Emiliano Zapata; Harriet Doerr set her debut novel *Stones for Ibarra* in a tranquil Mexican town near an abandoned copper mine, quite a similar setting to Doerr's second book, *Consider This, Señora;* Jack Kerouac, William Burroughs, Allen Ginsberg, and others from the Beat generation traveled to Mexico and Cuba to experiment with drugs and test their ideological convictions; so did Ambrose Bierce, who met his fate south of the border by disappearing into immortality; Peter Matthiessen located his 1965 novel *At Play in the Fields of the Lord*, about faith and politics, in the rain forests of Bolivia and Brazil; and Paul Theroux set *The Mosquito Coast* in Central America, a habitat "where ice is an hallucination." The list goes on and on, from

Philip Freneau, Joel Barlow, and Melville to Waldo Frank and John Updike, from Elizabeth Bishop to the inevitable William H. Prescott, from Hart Crane to William Carlos Williams, Margaret Randall, W. S. Merwin, Cormac McCarthy, Robert Stone. . . . And then, of course, there is Malcolm Lowry, whose extraordinary novel *Under the Volcano,* among my own favorite books, is about a Canadian lost in Mexico.

Inspiration has also traveled the other way around: Manuel Puig's dialogue-qua-novel *Eternal Course to the Reader of These Pages* takes place in New York City; Carlos Fuentes's mythical *Old Gringo* is about Ambrose Bierce crossing the border into oblivion, and several of Fuentes's novellas, including "Constancia," take place in the U.S.; Julio Cortázar's "The Pursuer" is about saxophonist Charlie Parker in Paris and New York. Again, the list is long. And it gets even longer when one considers the Latin American authors who have switched from Spanish to English (either by writing originally in Shakespeare's tongue or by translating their own work), sometimes to experiment or, as is the case more often, to find a larger audience: Jorge Luis Borges, María Luisa Bombal, Guillermo Cabrera Infante, Rosario Ferré, Ariel Dorfman, Fuentes.

Geography, thus, is a magnet. But have American writers read seriously the literature of the region, as seriously, say, as they have read Goethe, Voltaire, and Dante? Well, not quite—at least not as attentively as Latin Americans have done with the literary production in the U.S. Porter lived in Mexico for decades and was instrumental in publishing in the United States an abbreviated English translation of what is considered to be the first Spanish-language novel in the Americas: *The Itching Parrot,* by José Joaquín Fernández de Lizardi. Scandalously, Porter claimed to have discovered it herself (I've included her lengthy prologue to the 1942 edition in this anthology). But this project fell into her lap; Porter wasn't really a reader of Mexican letters. In fact, not until the so-called literary boom of the 1960s that catapulted the generation of Gabriel García Márquez, Mario Vargas Llosa, and Cortázar to international acclaim had any Hispanic American writer been read seriously abroad, in particular north of the Rio Grande. The problem was not the unavailability of translations but of limited cultural mobility: not until the late nineteenth century was literature read outside its country of origin; this meant that an Argentine like

Esteban Echeverría, an anti-Rosas activist and the author of "The Slaughterhouse," was known only at home—during his lifetime, at least. Sor Juana Inés de la Cruz, the luminous Mexican nun responsible for *First Dream* and other poems and plays, who died in 1695, was the exception: she was known in Lima and Santiago, and was applauded in the Iberian Peninsula.* But not until the *modernista* movement, spanning from approximately 1880 to 1915, were writers like Darío and José Martí known beyond their national boundaries, when for example Darío was endorsed by Spaniards like Juan Ramón Jiménez and Juan Valera. In contrast, since the United States has often served as a political mediator between Spanish-language nations in the Southern Hemisphere, as well as nations with various verbal codes in the Caribbean, its cultural influence has been crucial: as a result, a Chilean author might be much more familiar with a Mississippian than with a Venezuelan and might read Venezuelan literature, if at all, via its acquaintance with Mississippi. (See, for example, the essay in which Alejo Carpentier reads Melville reading Peru.)

This, in part, was the result of the impact of immigration all over the Hispanic hemisphere. The *modernistas* coincided with the arrival of Jews, Asians, Germans, and other newcomers and, also, with governmental attempts to modernize the region by bringing in foreign technology and investments. Travel was more common than ever before, and the *modernista* poets, often for political reasons but also as a result of leisure and diplomatic travel, visited foreign countries at a rate higher than literati had ever done before. Still, the cadre of Spanish-language *autores* did not find an audience in the United States until after World War II, a time when the American readership was mature enough to go beyond the Good Neighbor Policy to find out who the southern neighbors really were. Goethe's concept of *Weltlitteratur* seems to have caught on in the Americas only in the twentieth century: the rise of a global mass culture, one in which the so-called Third World lives simultaneously with and not behind the industrialized countries, has forced on us the sensation that all national literatures are vulnerable to the same set of external influences. Fast, ready-made translations facilitate the expansion and osmosis of ideas

*See my introduction to *Poems, Protest, and a Dream,* by Sor Juana Inés de la Cruz (New York: Penguin Classics, 1997).

from one linguistic area to the next. High-brow readerships are no longer the properties only of major capitals such as Paris, Rome, and New York City, as was the case before 1945. With the rapid emergence of independent states in Africa, Asia, and South America, but especially because of the collective awareness of the division between rich and poor nations, of the haves and have-nots, writers such as Wole Soyinka, Milan Kundera, Salman Rushdie, and Nadine Gordimer are read everywhere at the same time, as are their U.S., Hispanic, and Caribbean counterparts.

So how have writers north and south of *la frontera* and stuck in between other regional borders read each other? With incessant curiosity and, also at times, with profound suspicion. Often the results are exhilarating and the intellectual somersaults leave the connoisseur quite surprised. In a conversation I had with Updike, published in *Diario 16*, he explained how his knowledge of Nathaniel Hawthorne, so influential in his trilogy *A Month of Sundays, Roger's Version*, and *S.*, came to him, not, as one might expect, thanks to Henry James's 1879 booklet for the series English Men of Letters, but through a lecture Borges gave in Buenos Aires in 1946, later included in *Other Inquisitions: 1936–1952*. (The lecture, frugally titled "Nathaniel Hawthorne," is included in this volume in part 1.) The reversal is extraordinary: an Argentine reminding a New England writer about his roots? Sure, just as Domingo Faustino Sarmiento's *Facundo: Civilization and Barbarism*, published in 1845, a part fictional, part realistic study of Argentine identity, is inspired by the frontier novels of James Fenimore Cooper.* Sarmiento understood the role of gauchos in the Pampas, "primitive types" he considered appealing but also as obstacles on the road to modernity, in the same fashion Cooper approached the Indians on the American frontier.

Truth is, the literary bridges across the Rio Grande and other hemispheric borders are like Borges's aleph: everywhere at once, but invisible to the naked eye. In his detective stories, Borges emulated Poe's "The Pit and the Pendulum" and "Murder in the Rue Morgue," in which August Dupin displays his logic; and so did Cortázar, whose

*I discuss Sarmiento's echoes in my opening essay in *Facundo: or, Civilization and Barbarism*, translated by Mary Peabody Mann (New York: Penguin Classics, 1998).

cuentos fantásticos—"Ligeia," "House Taken Over," etc.—have titles in homage to Poe. And it is a well-known fact that Yoknapatawpha, William Faulkner's fictional county in the American Deep South, so afflicted by the Civil War and the Depression, is replicated by García Márquez in Macondo, the imaginary Caribbean coast where *One Hundred Years of Solitude* takes place, and by Juan Carlos Onetti in Santa María, a dump of prostitutes and down-and-outs near Río de la Plata. The Colombian and Uruguayan writers saw in the Mississippi region invented by Faulkner a magnetic dimension of defeat, one overwhelmed by decades of repression and pain, and easily identified with it. After all, isn't the vision of history in Latin America very much like that in the Deep South?

And the artistic influence, after the boom of the 1960s, has been somewhat reciprocated. John Barth, in his influential essay "The Literature of Exhaustion," first published in the *Atlantic Monthly* in 1967 (it serves here as a prologue to part 2), prized Borges as one of his personal tutors. And in a 1980 sequel, "The Literature of Replenishment," he celebrated García Márquez as an unforgettable master in the tradition of the anonymous author(s) of the *Arabian Nights,* and believed, along with Susan Sontag, that Machado de Assis, Brazil's early modernist, is an unsurpassed genius in the landscape of world letters. (Sontag's essay on Machado, first published in 1990, is included also.) Plus, Updike, from his pulpit in the *New Yorker,* has served as an invaluable cataloger of Latin American fiction to English-language tastes. (See his brief representative note on Augusto Roa Bastos's encyclopedic *I, the Supreme.*) Surely the most significant name in this constellation is, of course, Borges, who has prompted by far the most admirable comments within the U.S.: from George Steiner to John Hollander, from William H. Gass—whose cerebral "Imaginary Borges and His Books" is here included—to Alfred Kazin and Updike himself: Borges is a compass, a lighthouse.

All of the entries I've selected began as *piezas de ocasión*—slight reviews, comments, conversations, lectures, and prologues. None has any ambition beyond the mere act of recording one's opinions about a figure or book the author loves or feels the need to describe. Obviously, the pieces are not designed to constitute a parallel *rezeptionsgeschichte,* a structured study of comparative responses; that is for others to accomplish. In fact, the groundwork is laid already: since the mid 1980s, scholars have been prompt to examine the multiple points of coincidence and dissidence. (Interestingly, all of them have Brazilian and Hispanic backgrounds; little of value has come from specialists in American letters. Should this be understood as a symptom of cultural parochialism?) Alfred J. MacAdam, in *Textual Confrontations*, made comparative studies of the works of W. H. Auden and Pablo Neruda; Edna Aizenberg edited *Borges and His Successors*, a book that contained an examination by Geoffrey Green of the similarities between Borges and Barth, Robert Coover, Updike, Thomas Pynchon, John Hawkes, and Don DeLillo. Lois Parkinson Zamora, in *Writing the Apocalypse*, looked at contemporary U.S. writers such as Pynchon and Walker Percy, and equated their understanding of disaster themes and techniques with those of Fuentes, Cortázar, and García Márquez. Bell Gale Chevigny and Gari Laguardia edited *Reinventing the Americas*, a volume that included essays on the correlations and bridges between Alejo Carpentier and Herman Melville, Cooper and Rosario Castellanos, Alice Walker and Elena Poniatowska, Wallace Stevens and Octavio Paz. *Do the Americas Have a Common Literature?*, edited by Gustavo Pérez-Firmat, a Cuban-American poet and academic, deals with Whitman, José Lezama Lima, and Cirilo Villaverde. *Rediscovering the New World: Inter-American Literature in a Comparative Context* by Earl E. Fitz is perhaps the most comprehensive, although not necessarily the most lucid, comparative study so far, one where Canada and the Caribbean also have a place. And there's more: a volume on Whitman's impact on Latin America, and another on Langston Hughes in the Caribbean; also, a study of José Martí in the United States, another one on Borges's interest in New England authors, and yet another on his borrowings from Poe (and those of Horacio Quiroga).

I, instead, have chosen a different route: to let the authors do what they do best—speak for themselves. Entries vary in length and depth. They are accompanied by a headnote placing the author, though not the subject, in context, offering a sampler of significant works (titles appear in translation only if the book is already available in English), and ending with the entry's original date and place of publication. All, in my eyes, are autobiographical, e.g., they are not solely, and surely not primarily, about a colleague from across the border but about the "I"—the personal eye—as classifier. Martí tells us more about Martí than about Whitman, for instance. Each piece, then, no matter how brief, is a self-portrait: *un autorretrato.* This pleases me, for the *what* and the *how* are as enticing to me as the *about whom,* but obviously the observer and observed are made to match. The volume's content is divided into two parts: south looking north, and north looking south; beyond this, their order of appearance is ruled by sheer chance.

Each part opens with a more encompassing essay, one not centered on a single figure. A word about the prologue to part 1. Pedro Henríquez Ureña, a startling essayist and among the first south of the Rio Grande to study the literature of the United States in a consistent fashion (he delivered the Charles Eliot Norton Lectures at Harvard University in 1940–41), wrote his panoramic piece in La Plata, Argentina, in 1927. It is a scintillating display of erudition (in spite of its many blind spots and contradiction), a sideboard of the kind of curiosity that literature in the United States generates throughout the Southern Hemisphere. Henríquez Ureña's objective is to explain the artistic transformation that swept American writers during two decades, from 1907 to 1927, a time of extraordinary renewal in fiction and poetry. I frankly cannot imagine a similar piece on Latin American letters—at once panoramic and extraordinarily detailed, well-informed, inclusive, and incisive—written in belletristic style by a U.S. intellectual. (Sure, foreigners such as Seymour Menton and Jean Franco, and even transposed natives like Argentine Enrique Anderson Imbert, have surveyed the literature of the Southern Hemisphere for American readers, but their products are strictly academic, and, in Franco's case, strangely misguided.) Americans, almost by definition, have an imperfect, partial knowledge of the reality south of the border. Their understanding of it is ruled by fashion, not by consistency. This also might explain why part 1 is more substantial than part 2: while the communicating vessels between the two Americas have existed for a long time, the study of "the other voice" is by far more fecund when the south looks at the north.

Dare I invoke, to conclude, the famous Spanish saying: *ni son todos lo que están, ni están todos los que son?* No quotas here, no deceitful strategies: I have reached out only to pieces I find significant and appealing, though not always congenial. My focus is the United States, Cuba, Puerto Rico, the Dominican Republic, Brazil, the Caribbean (even in its English-language vicissitudes), and the Spanish-speaking

Americas. In some cases I found too much on a single writer: Borges again, or Whitman and Poe; but, intriguingly, in spite of my effort, I unearthed nothing of interest on Emily Dickinson and Kate Chopin, for instance, perhaps because neither of them ever had a following in Spanish, where their oeuvres have fared rather poorly in translation; but I also failed to retrieve anything on Ralph Ellison, Richard Wright, or Toni Morrison, a signal perhaps of how race is played out on both sides of the Rio Grande. Had space been more elastic—and permissions fees less prohibitive—I would have included Canadians as well, such as Margaret Atwood, even though their impact in the Hispanic and Caribbean orbits is minimal; and I would have inserted also Creole- and French-speaking Caribbeans, such as Patrick Chamoiseau. I also wish I could have included pieces on Sarmiento, Delmira Agustini, Rosario Castellanos, and Juan Rulfo. Some of the contributors and themes might be deemed controversial: Julia Alvarez, for instance, born in the Dominican Republic but, strictly speaking (and like Sandra Cisneros, Judith Ortíz Cofer, or Cristina García), an American original; Lafcadio Hearn, whose "second life" as a Japanese national turned him into an intellectual icon in the Far East; Nabokov, known as a Russian émigré (I contemplated including Joseph Brodsky too, but found no comments about his friend Octavio Paz, for instance); and V. S. Naipaul, who, through endless mannerisms, pretends to be a British subject (he's Paul Theroux's Sir Vidia). These "extreme" cases, in my eyes, make the selection all the more appetizing: what is modernity about, after all, if not constant motion—verbal, physical, intellectual?

In sum, this is a book about neighbors reading each other—or, more precisely, a book of writers as readers and of readers as writers: a map to a translingual, transcultural library, one reaching across the Rio Grande. Its pages are tinted by the recurring question: *E pluribus unum?* Or should it be *e pluribus summum?* Either way, it is clear that imprisoned in each of us is another self—the mismatched I, the bordered *yo* and *je* and *ich* . . . signaling to be let out.

April 1999

I

South Reading North

Prologue: Pedro Henríquez Ureña

Born in Santo Domingo, Dominican Republic, where his father was at one time president, Pedro Henríquez Ureña (1884–1946) traveled broadly living and working in Cuba, the United States, Argentina, and Mexico. Henríquez Ureña's stay in Mexico is of particular importance since he became an integral component of that country's intellectual renewal. An early positivist and a deep admirer of Eugenio María de Hostos, Henríquez Ureña later turned toward skepticism, though he never did abandon positivism completely. Although he could not allow for the existence of any universal ideals in terms of philosophy, Henríquez Ureña believed in a global culture that has no boundaries. He was a prominent essayist and editor of anthologies (one of them in collaboration with Borges). However, he is perhaps better known as an educator. During his tenure as a professor in Argentina, he contributed to several student publications and encouraged students to militate in favor of a liberal, parliamentary, secular, anti-imperialistic, and socialist democracy. He was particularly concerned with the Spanish language and its historical tradition. Among his vast collection of published works are *Estudios de la versificación española* (1961, posthumous) and *En la orilla: Mi España* (1922). He delivered the Charles Eliot Norton Lectures at Harvard University in 1940–41, which he later published as *Literary Currents in Hispanic America* (1942). His knowledge of U.S. letters was wide, and proof of it are his essays on H. L. Mencken, T. S. Eliot, and Theodore Dreiser. But his true passion was Spanish and Hispanic civilization in all their facets. This essay was written in La Plata, Argentina, in 1927. It was first published as "Veinte años de literatura en los Estados Unidos," in *Panorama de la otra América* (Mexico City: Fondo de Cultura Económica, 1939).

I

During the twenty years from 1907 to 1927, literature has been transformed in the two Americas, the English and the Hispanic. This transformation has been bigger in the United States than in the Spanish-language Americas: a brusque and total renaissance between 1910 and

1915. Our renaissance occurred before, between 1890 and 1900. Since then we have changed a lot; we have even adopted positions that are contrary to those of 1900; but we have done so slowly, by taking small steps. In our environment there are forces capable of pushing us to a sudden acceleration and thus bringing significant change: the nationalist spirit, for instance, embraced with either an indigenous or a Creole fervor; or using style as the primary concern. But everything is still in process.

At the dawn of the new century, literature in the United States seemed stuck. It was hardly a hundred years old. After the timid beginnings of the tradition—Cooper, Irving, Bryant—a heroic cycle found its expression with Concord as its center: Emerson, Hawthorne, Lowell, Holmes, Thoreau, Longfellow, Prescott; and close to them, in rebellious zigzags, Melville, Poe, Whitman. Suddenly the North American spirit found its true expression, which in Europe was perceived as a revelation full of promises. After that, what came along was the channeling and dissemination of literary currents typical of the nineteenth century: realism, colored by a Puritanical scruple (William Dean Howells); the psychological novel (Henry James); regionalism (Bret Harte); and humor (Mark Twain).

But in 1900, the big names, the dominating names, were the ones that had emerged around 1870: Howells, James, Bret Harte, Mark Twain, José Enrique Rodó, our Uruguayan critic, described the United States in *Ariel* as follows: "For quite some time, the wings of its books have not reached the heights the whole world expected them to reach." True: aside from these four names, literature, abundant in quantity, evolved like a landscape without highlights. Short stories and novels of prudent, detailed realism were published, often exploring various regions; humor was manufactured for the masses; essays demonstrating high culture, intellectual spark, and a discreet eye appeared, but were of little consequence; theater, too, was abundant, but lacking in quality; and poetry, academic in some instances, adorned with symbolism in others (as in the easy and refined case of the Canadian author Bliss Carman), was of little substance, too: the most exciting eruptions of character—Emily Dickinson, Stephen Crane—had vanished with their premature deaths.

The best literature was in the novel and short story: Mary Wilkins,

Gertrude Atherton, Frank Norris, all young at the time, in whom one could foresee greatness; but the audience preferred light, innocuous books. And the adventurous war of 1898 had reinvigorated the mediocre genre of chivalry novels. In short, readers' tastes, when it came to the novelistic plot and development, were close to those of movie viewers. Only the gray, multifaceted Gertrude Atherton, whose disorderly talent has the aroma of the best air and bravest climate of California, would dare to accuse this literature as bourgeoisie, limited, and even "insignificant."

This lack of movement in U.S. letters was fatal: the struggle and dominion over Nature or the economic power over less mighty nations seduced the most energetic spirits; in the intellectual sphere, moral prejudices and religious taboos conquered over culture. A sense of forced optimism fell on literature as a terrible omen: the country knew everything about success, so skepticism, debate, even reflection, were considered unpatriotic sins. The mediocre tone of the intellectual elite drowned any original impulse to oppose it. The only road to salvation was rebellion. But rebels were short in coming.

Van Wyck Brooks has described with astonishing dexterity the domestication of Mark Twain: after spending his youth among his bearded compatriots in the Midwest, hiding his literary interests and believing them shameful, the poor humorist saw his oeuvre, his expression, oppressed, cut by the excessive decadence that prevailed in the cities of the Atlantic coast. His wife and his friend Howells were frightened by Twain's heavy words, his popular lingo, his uncivilized manners, and would cross out and reshape his manuscripts. And when one is forced to be introverted, the art of self-editing becomes a habit, a mania. Thus, the work of Mark Twain suffered many alterations and lost part of its freshness. The hyper-decorous atmosphere did not know how to extract the best of him. And so, during his last years, he wrote the synthesis of his ideas about the universe and society but left the book to be published posthumously, fearful that scandal would alienate his audience. But what was considered audacious in the Boston and Philadelphia of 1870 had become commonplace in the New York of 1910, a city toughened, refined by Nietzsche and Shaw.

II

What was really happening twenty years before, in 1907? Mediocrity prevailed in 1900; but it was losing control, giving room to rare outbursts of change.

William James made a loud noise with his flamboyant Pragmatism. His influential book *Pragmatism* was published exactly in 1907. It seemed as if the United States was finally giving birth to its own philosophy, the metaphysics of common sense, the theory of truth as a practical function, as a useful recourse, applying it to action and its consequences. James was abandoning the tradition of spiritual idealism—which Josiah Royce, his venerable colleague at Harvard, was still representing—and, suddenly, it appeared as if he had become the living voice of his country. If the globe was getting more and more infatuated with American materialism, in James's philosophy it could find the formula to justify that infatuation. But after a while the globe overcame the stupor of wealth and lost interest in Pragmatism, for it realized it was a mere variation of a familiar philosophical theme: the limits of human knowledge. William James was really not representing the hopes of the new generations, either by his age or by his philosophical orientation. Pragmatism is not the first philosophy of the twentieth century: it is really the last of the nineteenth century. Does all this become clear in the dedication of James's famous book to John Stuart Mill? Still, James was an admirable psychologist and a first-rate stylist, as is clear in any of his exciting, juicy pages.

George Santayana, a colleague of James in the department of philosophy at Harvard, also around 1907, was a Spaniard responsible for a vast, influential oeuvre. Until then, it was composed of poetry (*Sonnets and Other Verses*, 1894; *Lucifer: A Theological Tragedy*, 1898; *A Hermit of Carmel and Other Poems*, 1901) and philosophical treatises (*The Meaning of Beauty*, 1896; *The Life of Reason; or, The Phases of Human Progress*, 1905). As an essayist—a genre in which Santayana reaches extraordinary profundity, subtlety, and humanity—he had, at the time, published only *Interpretations of Poetry and Religion* (1900), wherein he included that much-discussed essay on the poetry of barbarism, exemplified by Browning and Whitman. Santayana had not yet written his best works, which, beginning in 1910, would be marked by his book *Three Philosophical Poets* (Lucretius, Dante, Goethe). In 1912, he moved permanently to Europe, a place he always belonged in spirit. He had been educated, in part, in America, but, as Joseph Warren Beach said, Santayana "is really a product of British and Spanish cultures; there is no definitive reflection in his work of the North American way of thinking." Nevertheless, in the five thick volumes of his *Life of Reason,* he would plant the seed of a philosophical conception that would grow and define the United States (and England) in the twentieth century: critical realism. His influence over the nation's philosophical movement has been exercised mainly from Europe; in literature, on the other hand, his imprint is hardly felt: where he is enthusiastically embraced as a writer is in England, especially among readers devoted to systematic thinking and impeccable style.

Among the young writers of 1907—or better, the "still young"— nobody was as interesting as Edith Wharton. She knew about the novel everything England and France could teach; and she handled style with astonishing mastery, combining the precision of steel with the brilliance of crystal. Among Wharton's natural qualities, one could count the control over the game of motifs that make and destroy human life, the sense of character, the art of observation, irony, and, on occasion, the power of pathos. She had two or three early novels, one of them mediocre, *The House of Mirth* (1905); and many short stories that were absolutely perfect. She then wrote novels that had an extraordinary breath of life: *The Custom of the Country* (1910) and *The Age of Innocence* (1920). But her refined intelligence, shaped at noon's light, did not prophesy the direction some obscure literary movements would take: her work is overwhelmed by an excessive loyalty to the models of her formative years (realism, psychologism) and excessive closeness to the world of the rich (as is the case with George Meredith and Henry James, Bouget and Proust). The period after 1910 has been unfair to Wharton's wonderful novelistic talent. Only the brief *Ethan Frome,* as strong and unconsoled as the most memorable Russian tales, has lasting value.

The one writer who was well aware of the artistic changes that would soon sweep his country was Henry Adams. Born in 1838 in the city of Boston—which, as he put it, meant to be born a hundred years into the past—he was close to seventy in 1907 and was not known in literary circles except as a scholar of national history. Yet he had written, either in full or in part, his two masterpieces, which only his friends knew about: *Mont-Saint-Michel and Chartres: Study in the Unity of the Nineteenth Century* and *The Education of Henry Adams: Study in the Multiplicity of the Twentieth Century.* If I am ever forced to say which is the most important book written in the United States, I would point without hesitation to *The Education of Henry Adams.* It is a book about modern life in crisis, in perpetual crisis, a book that reflects the way in which any new trend of ideas brings forth, like a cyclone, dramatic changes in cities and the countryside; there is never enough time to plant new seeds because a new cyclone is always on the horizon. The permanent state of crisis pertains to thoughts and acts, science and politics, art and behavior, religion and business. Henry Adams, a child born into wealth and culture, tries to educate himself so as to find individual and collective improvement: according to the classic maxim, he wants "to serve his peers"; but each time he is sure to have given his education a sense of direction, the world changes and he is once again forced to start from scratch. At seventy, with as vast an erudition as Dr. Faust, Adams finally declares that he is quitting his education: he is abandoning it *in medias res* . . .

III

William James, George Santayana, Edith Wharton, Henry Adams: if these names represent an age in transition, and if transition must be followed by plenitude, then an age of incomparable plenitude would soon appear, not only in regard to talent but also to vision, discipline, and culture. It is sheer coincidence that links them all in 1907, as if each of them was nothing but an asteroid with an irregular orbit.

The new era begins around 1910, not with magisterial figures but with agitated, rebellious, destroying masses, which, although believing in discipline, have no respect for tradition, or at least no respect for the nation's brief intellectual tradition; and if these masses are hungry for culture, they want it to be functional and without luxury. Scope and tolerance are sacrificed so as to give room to intensity; narrow-mindedness will be preferred, since only with it can vigor be achieved.

The aesthetic revolution that came about followed three paths: one, the discussion and criticism of national objectives, military conquests, traditions, and mistakes; second, a change of themes and forms in the novel and theater; and third, the renewal of poetry.

The discussion of national life, fired with some hesitation in the midst of the optimistic bonanza, became honest and noisy when the European war forced the Americas to look inward. Since then, it has developed a great deal. It has its own organs of debate, where each viewpoint finds an intention: *The New Republic, The Nation, The American Mercury,* and *The Dial;* it penetrates magazines that were once conservative: *Harper's Magazine, The North American Review,* even *The Atlantic Monthly;* and it finds its climax in Socialist publications, among them some excellent ones, such as *The Liberator* (formerly *Masses*), *The New Masses,* and *The Survey.* The whole discussion is condensed in an organic work: *The Civilization of the United States* (1921), written by "thirty North-Americans": in it the U.S. Army's Chief of Staff reviews some thirty activities and, with few exceptions, finds problems in all of them. Everything is discussed in magazines and books with tremendous energy: from religion to the old Puritan code of ethics and the artistic taste of the "tired salesman," from the way North American imperialism loathes and offends Latin America to the mercantile tyranny that demoralizes the nation's institutions of higher learning.

It has long been a pattern in the United States to censor partial aspects of the nation's existence, hoping that time would eventually improve them. But this attitude changes with the aesthetic revolution that goes from 1907 to 1927: civilization is discussed as a whole, its meaning and values debated to exhaustion. The accusation against mercantilism is true, although superficial: American critics dig deep to find in it the root of all evils. Mercantilism, it is argued, the absorbing preoccupation with riches, is found in societies past and present: the question is why life in the United States is so meaningless to so many men and women, more than anywhere else, even though the country has a generalized sense of honesty and a commitment to kindness. About the Phoenicians, we don't know if they suffered from transcendental dissatisfaction. There are some that point to Venice during the Renaissance: if its mercantilism was similar to the one of today (I frankly doubt it), the compensations were enormous. Perhaps the analogy is with nineteenth-century England, with its imperialistic drive, its feline insensitivity to suffering when it affects other societies, its miserable salaries and its inhuman treatment of workers, which deprived the working class of health and strength. But England had an intense spiritual life, and generosity was ubiquitous; its social life was discreet, inclined to meditation and creation. Disraeli was capable of saying: "Life is worth living only in London and Paris; everything else is landscape." This Briton, a thinker and artist, was capable of living a life of rebellion, much like Carlyle, Matthew Arnold, and William Morris; but he was also able to live in harmony with his environment, like Thackeray and Tennyson. In the United States of the twentieth century, thinkers and artists, if at all genuine, are by definition rebels: instinct and reason tell them that acquiescence would sink them into mediocrity. The problem is not only one of economic obsession: it is the whole package of a narrow-minded legacy and an acquired set of values, a religion deprived of any Puritan light, an asphyxiating moral code that generates inhibitions and prohibitions, the fears and prejudices about race, the interpretation of democracy that is reverentially confused, the noble instinct that viciously assures that work brings forth prosperity, the intimate poverty of "life in the frontier," atrophied by a form of entertainment that emphasized only the body, the machine and enterprises that propagate the view that matter and spirit are the same. These limitations are not a concern to those who have satisfied their economic needs or to those who are on the road to upward social mobility. Financial splendor impedes the individual from contemplating the nakedness that results from this lack of tradition and manners. The acceptance by American thinkers and artists of these maladies would symbolize an endorsement of the mercantile optimism that oscillates between ingenuity and cynicism, one that results from having established a balance between Puritanism and hedonism.

It is to this army of rebels that the United States will owe its moral and intellectual salvation, that is, if the powerful army of Philistines, with metal boxes keeping vast quantities of gold, doesn't prevail first. The battle is still undecided.

IV

Of the battalion of American essayists, the one that intrigues his readers the most is Henry Louis Mencken. For the "good patriots," he is an indomitable nightmare, the genius of evil, the supreme corrupter. He challenges, with burlesque courage, the collective wrath and makes sure nobody escapes from listening to his blasphemies. Mencken has even written the following line, plagued by his hatred of absurd nationalism: "When the Japanese conquer the United States and the republic descends to hell . . ." He is a master of an epigrammatic style, scintillating, sonorous, seasoned with cultisms and tasty popular terms; and he is fecund while inventing humorous hyperboles, grotesque definitions, and categorical attacks. Restless in his hunt for the Philistine, Mencken will follow him to the temple where respect is a religion; and he will turn the Philistine's pride into opprobium: *homo americanus*. Rotary Clubs, loggias, congresses, alfalfa universities . . . Mencken has compiled, together with George Jean Nathan, another astute essayist and critic, a dictionary of national dogmas, from the common astrological and climatic mistakes to the most misconstrued of political formulas.

But Mencken accompanies every attack of his with laughter and song. The happiness of his hits announces a reconstruction: in order to rebuild, one needs first to destroy. Among the initiators in the era of demolition and rebuilding, Randolph Bourne hoped to create "a new spirit of fraternity in the youth of the United States, one that is the beginning of a revolutionary attitude in our whole life; a youth league, organized conscientiously in order to create, in the blind chaos of the American society, a cultural order, one that is free, harmonious, with a power of expression."

Among those devoted to this reconstruction, a tireless and visionary legion, is Waldo Frank, who awakens sympathy in us because he has felt himself profoundly attracted to the Hispanic world, seeking in it treasures whose secret will help him enrich his native land. In his book *Virgin Spain: Scenes from the Spiritual Drama of a Great People* (1926) Frank turns his prophetic furor into the chant of a mystical lover. The book has fervent indignation, an intense vision dictated to him by the book he dedicated to his native country: *Our America* (1919).

The discussion of national life in the United States prevails in literary criticism, turning it into social criticism. The most typical representative of this tendency is Van Wyck Brooks, with his studies on Emerson, Henry James, and Mark Twain. Many follow Van Wyck Brooks's example: for instance, Lloyd Morris, with his severe book on

Hawthorne, *The Rebellious Puritan* (1927). Against the censors, a group of apologists and defenders has emerged. Among the defenders is Stuart Pratt Sherman (d.1926), a lucid stylist, discreet thinker, and fine critic of literature. Sherman rehearses the justification of the North American spirit, summarizing its aspirations in the formula of "athletic asceticism." He attributes this formula to Greek virtues. Truth is, Greek virtues were richer.

In the back, a parade of irritated old men comes along: they believe that the country is on the road to moral and intellectual disaster; they don't blame the Philistine; they blame the rebel, the reformer. Irving Babbitt, the old academic from Harvard University, researched the modern malady and ascribed it to Rousseau: he predicated the rejection of all forms of romanticism and pushed for the return to academic rationalism.

Of all the critiques of national life, the most original, in my mind, is to be found in the autobiographical genre. The example started with Henry Adams, whose *Education* investigates all the antinomies of the Western Hemisphere. Three North American autobiographical books are by Ludwig Lewisohn, Alfred Kreymborg, and Sherwood Anderson.

Ludwig Lewisohn, in his *Up Stream: An American Chronicle* (1921), recalls his parents' suffering: German Jews of high culture, who, once they abandoned Europe, underwent the adaptation that is far easier to take by the rustic immigrant, the one that is a *tabula rasa,* on whom the character of the New World is easily imprinted. Lewisohn narrates his own suffering, the suffering of the Jews, victimized by silent and perpetual persecution. He narrates the bizarre prejudices of a society where apathy for the Jew prevails, forcing him to start his new life from scratch. In spite of its emphatic moments, of its moments of tectonic weight, the entire book is appealing and its pages are all moving.

Of a very different flavor, not tragic but lyrical, are the autobiographies of Alfred Kreymborg and Sherwood Anderson, two entirely admirable writers of the current generation. They don't complain, nor do they protest the mistakes, the harshness, even the disregard for spiritual forces in American life: they shake their shoulders, sing a song, and wander along solitary paths where birds still abound and the vociferous noise of cars is not heard. They renounce the mirage created by civilization: they are not attached to it by any given magnet, not by the iron-built palace, not by the solemn theory promulgated by universities. They escape in order to meditate, to observe, to listen, to imagine, to seek free thoughts and pure visions. Winds of freedom and purity color whatever they write: verses, novels, intimate stories— Sherwood Anderson opting to embrace energy. Alfred Kreymborg preferring subtlety instead.

V

The novel is saturated with national problems. It carries them along since the times of Howells and James, the latter one turning them into tales about people renouncing their social status and about Americans in Europe. And these problems become more dense in the Edith Wharton of the rough *The Custom of the Country.* Nowadays, the novelists dealing with such problems abound. Among those who set the pattern is Sinclair Lewis: in *Main Street,* he painted the closed horizon of the small city; in *Babbitt,* the conflict and defeat of the businessman, who is threatened by ruin and ostracism if he refuses to embrace the dogmas of society, and is finally bought out by the affection and help of strangers as he goes through difficult times; in *Arrowsmith,* the battle a man of science has to fight in order to defend his disinterested pursuits against the rapacious hunger for money of those around him, always ready to turn him into a slave; in *Elmer Gantry,* the picaresque story of religion turned enterprise. Diffuse in his narrative style, insecure in his critique, Sinclair Lewis is important because of the instinctive way in which he conceived situations and problems. Along with those who make a critique of American life in novels and short stories are those who turn it into a caricature, like Ring Lardner, whose bitter satire is hidden behind the picturesque use of slang.

It is a breakthrough among novelists to prefer the middle ground: a mid-size protagonist, a mid-size city. Prior to this trend, in Europe as well as in the United States, the preference was always for the extreme: either heroes or beasts, rich or poor, aristocrats and provincial people. There was little sympathy for the middle ground, the mediocre man as protagonist, the populace. When the French writers adopted this theme, it was to treat it with desolated dryness. But in the United States, the common man is Everyman: the arch-millionaire thinks just like the small businessman; and the proletariat is always of foreign extraction and its ascent in the social scale always coincides with the *Americanization* of its ideas. One cannot understand the United States without understanding the common man, without coming to terms with the middle ground. And the novel makes it its central concern.

But the themes that were once familiar have not been altogether abandoned, and the interpretation of life in the countryside allows for new developments, especially because this landscape is still unexplored. Finally, what is left, along with a study of everyday life, is the fantasy novel.

As in the case of plot, the novelistic technique also oscillates between conservation and innovation. Conservative writers endorse past models, inherited from the romantic movement as well as from realism; some of them lazily mistake the effort for the invention of new forms, as are the cases of Sinclair Lewis and Theodore Dreiser; others use a vigilant intelligence more actively, as is the case of Willa Cather, in whom we discover the intuition of the solitude of the North American soul that does not fall prey to the infatuation with materialism (*The Professor's House*) and the sense of itinerant agitation (*My Ántonia*).

At first sight, the constellation of innovators defies order. But no sooner do we study it carefully than we realize that it is divided into two halves: the intuitive writers and the imaginative ones. Among the intuitive bunch are Sherwood Anderson and John Dos Passos; among the imaginative, Joseph Hergesheimer and James Branch Cabell. On occasion, the two tendencies are combined, as is the case of Waldo Frank.

The intuitive writers take the thesis of metaphysical romanticism to its extreme. They proceed as if the ultimate reality were the reality of the spirit and of immediate intuition. Their novels evolve outside conventional time, disregarding physical space; they evolve in *real duration*, e.g., in the protagonist's mind. The natural form of such novels is the internal monologue: it was in gestation since it became a fashion to view historical events from a single viewpoint, contemplating them from the eyes of a single protagonist, something that in the old novels happened exceptionally, when letters or diaries were interspersed in the narrative. This is the river that is born in *The Red and the*

Black and culminates in James Joyce's *Ulysses*. The novel is thus built as a chain made of purely intuitive links—sensations, memories—in a spontaneous rhythm that finds its flow in internal monologues, without the artificial logic of classical narration. The archetype becomes a concrete reality, as in the case of the modulating *Dark Laughter,* by Sherwood Anderson.

The imaginative writers—I call them thus, lacking a less generic term—adorn the novel with complex images gathered from the outside world, weaned through strings that emerge from the plot. Instead of the simple sensation and introspection of the intuitive writers, who know only about themselves, the imaginative writers situate themselves at a distance from the spectacle they are about to evoke. They select unique perspectives and organize the whole universe at will. In Carl van Vechten or Ernest Hemingway, imagination becomes a pictorial adornment; or it allows for a reconstruction of remote and exotic environments in the case of Joseph Hergesheimer; or it allows for the creation of fabulous, delicious kingdoms, as happens in the work of James Branch Cabell.

Cabell and Hergesheimer are central figures. Cabell, whose style is driven by beauty but has some archaic twists much in the fashion of Valle-Inclán, has sharpened, with fine precision, his aesthetic ideas, just like Valle-Inclán. But the prevailing view is that the best novelist in the United States is Theodore Dreiser: he has admirers that exalt him as another Dostoievsky, another Conrad. Sherwood Anderson— whom I personally prefer—calls him "the most important man in the United States in our time," even though he deplores Dreiser's atrocities when it comes to form. But in spite of Dreiser's careless style, in spite of his enervating technique, he is a powerful novelist when it comes to passion and tenderness.

VI

At the beginning of the twentieth century, theater suffered in the United States the very same fate that destroyed it in England a hundred years ago: it refused to be considered literature. Producers forced this view, believing that it was the view of the audience, an eternally misunderstood element in the genre. Between the torrent of melodramas and *sainetes,* the mediocre realistic comedies of Augustus Thomas and Clyde Fitch tried hardly to come out from this mess by aspiring to some sort of cleanliness. Of Fitch only one or two scenes can be saved, like the ones at the beginning of *The Climbers,* in which a family returns from the father's burial declaring it was an absolute social success. Afterwards, there were attempts at poetic drama (Percy Mackaye) and some passing plays of vigorous breath, like *The Great Divide,* by the fine poet William Vaughan Moody, with its smell of desert landscapes in his opening scenes. Or plays of vivacious ingenuity, like *The New York Idea* (1907), by Langdon Mitchel. The renaissance finally came in regional theaters, ready to stage good dramas and apply Stanislavsky's method of acting, and ready, too, to innovate in set design. In 1914, in New York, the Washington Square Players emerge; its founders would later break apart to create new groups, such as the Greenwich Village Theater and the Theater Guild. They staged short plays, like *Trifles* by Susan Glaspell, *Overtones* by Alice Gerstenberg, *Helena's Husband* by Philip Moeller, which, in turn, gave room to bigger projects.

New independent troupes are constantly born in various cities: New York's Provincetown Players; Chicago's Little Theater of Maurice Browne; the itinerant Portmanteau Theater; and later on, New York's Playwright's Horizon, with revolutionary playwrights, the Repertory Theater, and many others, constantly dying out and being reborn. The audience sees Greek tragedies, dramas from India and Japan, farces from the European Middle Ages, novelties from Ireland, Russia, Australia, Germany, Spain. . . . Finally appears the magical impresario, Arthur Hopkins—whose example is followed by Winthrop Ames and Jed Harris. And then comes the playwright of light and shadow: Eugene O'Neill.

O'Neill is the first fully developed playwright of the United States. His origins are to be found in realism, but his realism is a sharp critique of the modern world, animated by the sympathy toward the poor, the oppressed, and the vanquished. But he also reaches the heights of poetic fantasy, always in a somber tone. There isn't really anyone comparable to O'Neill, either before or after him, although there are, of course, fine writers of dramatic literature, whose goal is not to fall prisoner to the easy applause of commercial hits. Among the best are Edna St. Vincent Millay, whose theatrical poems reach a clamorous success; George Kelly, sharp and vivacious in his comedies; Zoe Akins, whose irresistible play *Daddy's Gone Hunting* makes elegant life a paradox; and Booth Tarkington, whose sweetness as a bourgeois novelist is sometimes transformed on stage into delicate ingenuity.

VII

About prose, it is often debated whether the North American writer ever fulfills his duty of making it a well-tempered, secure instrument. Edith Wharton had an irreproachable style, and so do Willa Cather, Cabell, Mencken, all of today's generation. Still others, like Elinor Wylie in the novel, Stark Young in criticism. Much discussed, certainly not impeccable when it comes to style but with great expressive virtues, are Sherwood Anderson and John Dos Passos. And what about the long-breath journalistic prose of Sinclair Lewis? And about the pedantic mistakes of Hergesheimer, unequal in his aspirations to opulence? And the stylistic atrocities of Dreiser, comparable to those of Pío Baroja in Spanish? Prose needed a long, patient nurturing in order to reach the heights one is used to in France or England.

In poetry, the problem of form has been triumphantly solved: there is a good number of poets whose expression is efficient, even perfect for its own needs. Even more: in the last twenty years, it is in the United States, more than in England, where poetry in the English language has sought and found new forms. Since Harriet Monroe founded the magazine *Poetry*, in Chicago in 1912, thus opening a campaign in favor of all form of renovation, the United States has become, according to the paradox of Enrique Díez-Canedo, "the country where poetry flourishes." There are hundreds of poets, millions of readers. Anthologies, panoramic surveys, critical studies are published every year. There are *"The Best Poetry of 19 . . ."* released annually, as is the case of the one by Braithwaite. Among such abundance, there is a huge amount of dead leaves and much puerility; but little charlatanry. Poets are driven by high objectives. Two, in particular: one is form, achieved through well-crafted expression and free rhythm; and the other is content, the desire to give voice to the soul of Earth, to the country's spirit.

The formal renovation is the result, to a large extent, of the *Imagist* poets, an international school whose masters live in Europe and America. They are H.D. (the initials of Hilda Doolittle, wife of the British poet Richard Aldington); John Gould Fletcher, a poet of clear lines; Ezra Pound, active, revengeful, nourished by ten different literatures (he is a fine translator of Spanish verses); Amy Lowell, as rich in imagination as in culture, is a curious observer attracted equally to a flower's forms and colors as to the secret behind Keats's words (to the latter she devoted her latest and most formidable book). This group's affinity for free verse and variable rhythms has been extended to poets that have other interests and tendencies. This affinity is influenced by French symbolism and is supported by Whitman's poetic tradition. Its technique, the so-called *imagism,* tries to express sensation and feelings in quick yet firm images juxtaposed with subtle, at times remote elements. It reaches perfection in H.D.'s crystalline, diamondlike poems, which evidence her study of ancient arts, as well as Chinese and Greek poetry. One must situate T. S. Eliot close to the *Imagists;* his thick poetry aspires to be like the perfect classical poetry of the Mediterranean.

If the *Imagists* attracted attention and greatly influenced the literary life in the United States, the nationalist poets interested the nation as a whole. Two contrasting groups split the country's attention: one, on the Atlantic coast; the other, in the interior. The titles of their books reveal their geographical affiliations: *North of Boston* is one by Robert Frost; *Chicago Poems* is one by Carl Sandburg. Tête-à-tête: New England on one side, taciturn, dry, aged, with its rural towns possessed by taboos, loneliness, and snow; on the other, the country's center, the Midwest, with its sustaining plains, its ferociously industrial cities, blackened by steel and coal, dark in their moral harshness. New York, a complex *summa,* finds expression in its novelists (Waldo Frank, John Dos Passos) better than in its poets, in spite of their repeated attempts. The South, always asleep, not even murmurs. And the Southwest only begins to utter its tale in English, filled with landscapes of naked geology, gigantic forests, marvelous Indian survivors, a magnetic net of roads, and an architecture that still has traces from the age of Spanish and Mexican domination.

New England is personified by two poets: Edwin Arlington Robinson and Robert Frost. Traditionalist in their approach to form, severe in their style, both get close to the soul of the thinned grandchildren of the original Puritans, who served as the dogmatic teachers of the nation and carry in themselves the testament of its decline. In New England, Robinson says, human conscience always has the most comfortable chair and happiness sits down to make a quilt, always shrunk and shaking from the cold. In Frost's poems (he has returned to the brief, syllabic form), somber figures parade: the old man that lives alone and wanders around the house in a winter night, a house *he cannot fill;* the servant who returns almost dead to the house of his old patrons, adapting it intuitively into his own home, because a home is the place from where we will not be thrown out as death approaches us. . . .

The Chicago poets have a very different spirit: Edgar Lee Masters, Vachel Lindsay, and Carl Sandburg. The sepulchral note sounds like an organ note in Masters's famous *Spoon River Anthology;* in each verse he tells the life of one of the inhabitants of the town called Spoon River. He and all his peers are asleep in the cemetery. But in Spoon River life is not decrepit as in the towns of *North of Boston:* amidst its limits, it is full of activity and hope.

With Vachel Lindsay, poetry returns to song and dance, both with a popular breath. The poet writes so that his verses might be recited in the plenitude of rhythm, or might be turned into prayer, or song, or perhaps danced. He himself announces how they ought to be interpreted, telling us in public; for a while he even toured the country, reciting them to enthusiastic audiences, and, on the way, he wrote *The Handy Guide for Beggars, Especially Those of the Poetic Fraternity.* But he has not been spoiled by easy triumph and by the celebration of *The Congo and Other Poems* and *Going-to-the-Sun:* he has written sweet, severe poetry, with a lovable irony that is at the core of his soul.

In Carl Sandburg we listen to a torrential, profound voice, overwhelmed by the *élan* of the prairie, the fields thick with wheat and corn, the human torrent in cities swollen by labor. He is a poet capable of clamor: he clamors like Whitman, but he knows better how to put a break to his scream; his is a secure rhythm (when read aloud, his free verse is always convincing in its rhythmic balance); his word is precise, not only to say but also to suggest. If he makes a mistake, it is only when it comes to tone and when he confuses his levels of expression. His is never a forced emphasis, even when his throat, clean, enduring, lets everything out. And Sandburg knows all the different grades of modulation, even the whisper.

Aside from these essential centers, whose innovations bring about grave and resolute renunciations, there are many poets that prefer the variation of a theme or familiar rhythm, or those that divide their time between the warm insides of the sunny house and the excursions to its curious surroundings. And there are many other very fine poets, like Wallace Stevens, Ridgely Torrence, and Edna St. Vincent Millay.

But for the soul of the United States, spiritual salvation is incarnated in its best poets, such as Sandburg, Masters, Lindsay, Frost, Robinson, and even in its best novelists, such as Theodore Dreiser and Sherwood Anderson. They refuse to rest, they refuse to acquiesce. They go on with their life, a life filled with faith, effort. Theirs is a simple poverty that is surrounded by so much blind prosperity. By predicating their art, they build the structure that eventually becomes a house.

Translated by Melquíades Sánchez

José Martí on Walt Whitman

José Martí (1853–1895) first joined the cause of independence of his native Cuba in 1868 immediately after Cuba's first battle of independence against Spain. He was sentenced to hard labor for publishing revolutionary periodicals, an experience which resulted in his exposé on prison life, *El presidio político de Cuba* (*The Political Prison in Cuba,* 1871). His exile to Spain and travels landed him at last in the United States, where he wrote for the *New York Sun* under the pseudonym M. de S. (In New York, he met Walt Whitman, whom he thoroughly admired.) Martí politicked to garner support for the 1895 U.S. invasion of Cuba and involved himself in the careful planning of the Cuban Revolution, working with exiled generals and raising money for the island's cause. As one of the precursors of Latin America's *modernismo,* he was one of the leaders of a literary movement which sought to renovate the Spanish language. Martí's major works include three major books of poetry, *Ismaelillo* (1882), *Versos sencillos* (1891), and *Versos libres* (1913), a number of prose pieces about contemporary life in the United States, and a novel under the name Adelaida Ral. His return to Cuba in 1895 was rapidly followed by his death in combat. This essay was first published in *El Partido Liberal,* Mexico City, 18 April 1887, as well as in *La Nación,* Buenos Aires, 26 June 1887.

"Last night he looked like a god, sitting in his red plush chair, with his gray hair, his beard on his breast, his smokey eyebrows, his hand on a cane." This is what one of today's papers says about Walt Whitman, the seventy-year-old man to whom the sharpest critics, who are always a minority, assign an exceptional place in the literature of his country and his times. Only the sacred books of antiquity offer a doctrine comparable in language and vigorous poetry to that expounded in grandiose, priestly apothegms, like outbursts of light, by this old poet whose astounding book has now been banned.

Why, of course! Isn't it a natural work? Universities and Latin have made men ignore one another; instead of falling in each others' arms attracted by the essential and eternal, they separate, nagging each other like fishwives at the slightest disagreement; man is molded by a book or a teacher in contact with whom he has been placed by chance or fashion as a pudding is molded by its container; philosophic, religious, or literary schools disguise men as a livery does a lackey; men let themselves be branded like horses and bulls and go around in the world showing their brands. So, when they find themselves in front of a naked, virginal, loving, sincere, and potent man—in front of a man who walks, loves, fights, rows—who, not letting himself be blinded by misfortune, reads a promise of ultimate felicity in world equilibrium and grace; when they find themselves in front of the fatherly, sinewy, and angelic man, Walt Whitman, they flee as from their own conscience and refuse to recognize in this fragrant and superior humanity the prototype of their drab, becassocked, dollish species.

The daily paper tells us that yesterday, when that other adorable old man, Gladstone, had just set his opponents in Parliament right as to the justice of granting Ireland self-government, he seemed like a powerful mastiff standing unrivaled amid the mob of curs at his feet. Thus Whitman appears with his "natural person," his "unharnessed nature with original energy," his "myriad beautiful and gigantic youths," with his belief that "the smallest sprout shows there is really no death," with his formidable account of peoples and races in "Salut au Monde," his determination to "be silent while they discuss, and to go and bathe and admire himself, knowing the perfect fitness and harmony of things." Thus appears Whitman, "who doesn't say these things for a dollar"; who is "satisfied and sees, dances, sings and laughs"; who "has no chair, no church, no philosophy"; that is what Whitman is like compared to those rickety poets and philosophers, one-detail, one-aspect philosophers; honey and water, rhetorical poets; philosophical and literary mannequins.

He must be studied, because if he is not the poet of best taste, he is the most intrepid, comprehensive, and uninhibited poet of his time. In his little frame house, which verges on poverty, there hangs by the window a picture of Victor Hugo, bordered in black mourning; Emerson, whose books purify and exalt, used to put an arm around his shoulder and call him his friend; Tennyson, one of those who sees to the roots of things, sends from his oaken chair in England tender greetings to the "grand old man"; Robert Buchanan, that outspoken Englishman, thunders to the North Americans: "what can you possibly know about letters when you are letting your colossal Walt Whitman's old age pass without honoring him as he deserves?"

The truth is that on reading him, though at first astounded, our soul, tormented by universal pettiness, feels a delightful sensation of recovery. He creates his own grammar, his own logic. He reads in the ox's eye and the sap of the leaf! "That man who cleans the filth out of your house is my brother!" His apparent formlessness, which is at first disconcerting, turns out later, except for brief instants of portentous extravagance, to be like the sublime order and composition of mountain peaks on the horizon.

He does not live in New York, his "beloved Manhattan," his "superb-faced, million-footed Manhattan," which he visits when he wishes to intone "the song of what he beholds in Libertad"; he lives, since his books and lectures yield him barely enough to buy bread, with "loving friends" who care for him in a little out-of-the-way country house, from which he goes in his carriage, pulled by the horses he loves, to see the "athletic young men" in their virile pastimes, the "camerados" who are not afraid of rubbing elbows with this iconoclast who wishes to establish the institution of comradeship, to see the yielding fields, the friends who pass arm in arm singing, the loving couples gay and sprightly like quails. So he tells us in his "Calamus," the enormously strange book in which he sings of love between friends: "City of orgies . . . Not the pageants of you, not your shifting tableaux, your spectacles, repay me . . . Nor the processions in the streets, nor the bright windows with goods in them, nor to converse with learned persons . . . Not those, but as I pass O Manhattan, your frequent and swift flash of eyes offering me love . . . Lovers, continual lovers, only repay me." He is like the old man he announces at the end of his forbidden book, his "Leaves of Grass": "I announce myriads of youths, beautiful, gigantic, sweet-blooded, I announce a race of splendid and savage old men."

He lives in the country, where the man of nature can toil in the free earth, under the tanning sun, but not far from the city, amiable and warm, with its noises of life, its diversity of occupation, its variegated epic, the dust wagons raise, the smoke from panting factories, the all-seeing sun, "the loud laugh of work people at their meals," "the flap of the curtained litter, a sick man borne inside to the hospital," the "exclamations of women taken suddenly who hurry home and give birth to babes." But yesterday Whitman came from the country to recite for a gathering of loyal friends his oration on that other man of nature, that great and sweet soul, "that great star early droop'd in the western sky," Abraham Lincoln. All New York's intelligentsia attended in religious silence that brilliant lecture which, because of its sudden breaks, its vibrant tones, its hymn-like fugue, its olympic familiarity, seemed at times like the chatter of stars. Those sucklings fed on Latin, French, or academic milk will perhaps not understand this heroic graciousness. Man's free and secure life in a new continent has created a wholesome, robust philosophy which is emerging upon the world in Herculean epodes. Only a poetry of togetherness and faith becomes this largest conflux of freemen and workers the world has ever seen, a soothing and solemn poetry which rises like the sun from the sea, burning clouds, festooning the wave crests with fire, awakening in the prolific inland forests the drowsy flowers and nests. Pollen flies, mountain peaks exchange kisses, branches intermix, leaves seek the sun, everything exhales music. Such is the language of piercing light in which Whitman spoke of Lincoln.

Perhaps one of the most beautiful creations of contemporary poetry is Whitman's mystic dirge on Lincoln's death. All nature escorts the lamented deceased to his grave. The stars had prophesied, since a month before clouds had been turning black. There was a gray bird in the swamp singing a desperate song. Between thought and the certainty of death the poet wanders in the mournful fields as between two comrades. Like a musician he arranges, hides, restates these sad themes in a total twilight harmony. When the poem comes to a close it is as though the whole world were in mourning and possessed by the deceased from one ocean to another. We see the clouds, the heavy moon that forebodes the catastrophe, the gray bird's long wings. It is much more beautiful, strange, and profound than Poe's "The Raven." The poet has brought to the coffin a twig of lilac.

Such is his poetry.

Willows no longer wail over graves; death is "the harvest, the opener and usher into the heavenly mansion, the great revealer"; what is, was, and shall be again; the apparent oppositions and sorrows merge with each other in a calm, celestial spring; a bone is a flower. One hears, close by, the noise of suns moving majestically as they seek their definite places in space; life is a hymn; death is a hidden form of life; sweat is holy and the entozoan is holy; men should kiss each other on the cheek when they meet; those who live should embrace with ineffable love and love the grass, the animals, the air, the sea, pain, death; souls possessed by love suffer less; life holds no suffering for him who grasps its meaning in time; honey, light, and kisses are spawned together. In the resplendent peace, under the massive, starry vault, to the tune of a soft music there rises over the slumbering worlds stretched like hounds at its feet, a peaceful, gigantic lilac tree!

Every social condition contributes to literature its own expression, so much so that the history of nations can be told more truthfully through their literary movements than through their annals and chronicles. Nature cannot contradict itself; even the human aspiration to find in love, during this life or after death, a perfect type of grace and beauty, shows that the elements which in our present span of life seem disjointed and hostile will, in the totality of life, become happily adjusted. A literature which announces and promotes the ultimate and felicitous accord of apparent contradictions; a literature which promotes through nature's spontaneous advice and teaching, the identity, in a superior peace, of rival dogmas and passions which divide and bloody nations still in a primitive state; a literature which imparts to men's restive spirit so deep-rooted a conviction in definitive justice and beauty that life's distress and ugliness cease to dishearten and embitter them, will not only reveal a social condition nearer to perfection than any known so far, but will provide humanity, thirsty for wonders and poetry, by a fortunate combination of reason and grace, with the religion it has vaguely awaited since it discovered the emptiness and insufficiency of its ancient creeds.

Who is the dunce who maintains that poetry is not indispensable to nations? Some people are so short-sighted that they think a fruit is nothing but rind. Poetry, which unites souls or disbands them, fortifies or fills them with anguish, uplifts or defeats them, which gives to or takes from men hope and courage is more necessary to a people even than industry. Whereas industry provides the means for living, poetry affords the desire and the strength to live. What is to become of a nation of men who have lost the habit of thinking, with faith, of the significance and scope of their actions? The best, those whom nature has anointed with the sacred thirst for the future, will lose in a painful, muted undoing, all incentive to bear the ugly sides of life; and as for the masses, the vulgar, the children of lust, the common, they will breed empty offspring without sanctity, raise mere instruments to the category of essential faculties and will confuse the soul with the bustle of an ever incomplete prosperity, the soul whose incurable affliction only finds satisfaction in the beautiful and the great.

Liberty should be blessed, among other reasons, because its enjoyment affords modern man—previously deprived of the calm, the stimulus, and the poetry of existence—that supreme peace and religious well-being which an orderly world brings to those who live in it with the pride and serenity that free will brings. Look beyond the mountains, you poets who water deserted altars with childish tears!

You thought religion was lost because it was changing form over your heads. Arise, for you are the priests. The definitive religion is liberty. And the poetry of liberty is the new cult. It is poetry that soothes and embellishes the present, infers and illumines the future and explains the ineffable purpose and seductive goodness of the universe.

Let us hear what this hardworking, contented people sings; let us hear Walt Whitman. Self-assertion raises this people to majesty, tolerance to justice, order to happiness. He who lives according to an autocratic creed is like an oyster in its shell, which only sees the prison which holds it and in the darkness believes it to be the whole world. Liberty gives wings to oysters. And what, heard from inside the shell, seemed an uproarious battle, turns out in the open to be the natural flow of sap in the world's vigorous pulse.

To Walt Whitman the world was always as it is today. That a thing is, is sufficient reason for its having to be, and when it no longer should be, it will no longer be. What is no longer, what can no longer be seen, can be proved by what is and can be seen; because everything is in everything and one thing explains another; and when what now is is no longer, it will in turn be proven by what then will be. The infinitesimal collaborates with the infinite and everything is in its place, turtle, ox, birds, those "wing'd purposes." It is as fortunate to die as to be born, because the dead are alive: "no array of terms can say how much he is at peace about God and about death!" He laughs at what we call disillusionment and he knows the vastness of time, which he accepts absolutely. All is contained within him; all of him is contained in all; if another is debased, he is debased; he knows he is in the ebb and flow of every tide; no wonder he is proud, feeling himself to be a living and intelligent part of nature! What does he care if he returns to the womb that bore him, and the loving moist earth converts him into the useful vegetable or the lovely flower? He will nourish men after having loved them. His duty is to create; the atom that creates is of divine essence; the act of creation is exquisite and sacred. Convinced of the identity of the universe, he sings the "Song of Myself." This song of himself is woven out of everything: of creeds that quarrel and pass, of man who breeds and toils, of animals who help him, oh! those animals among which "not one kneels to another, not one is respectable or unhappy, nor sweats nor whines about his condition." He considers himself heir to the world.

Nothing is alien to him and he takes everything into account: the snail that drags itself along, the ox that gazes on him with its mysterious eyes, the priest who defends part of the truth as though it were the whole truth. Man should open his arms and then press everything against his heart, virtue as well as crime, filth as well as cleanliness, ignorance as well as wisdom; in his heart everything should fuse as in an oven; above all he should let his gray beard grow. But, to be sure, "we have had ducking and deprecating about enough." He scolds the unbelievers, the sophists, the chatterers: procreate instead of quarreling, add to the world! Create with the reverence with which a devout believer kisses the altar steps!

He belongs to all castes, creeds, and professions, and finds justice and poetry in all of them. He measures religions without wrath, but believes the perfect religion to be in nature. Religion and life are in nature. If there is a sick person in the house, he will tell both the doctor and the priest to go home: "I seize the descending man and raise him with resistless will . . . I will open windows, love him, speak to him in his ear; you will see him cured; you are words and grass, but I am stronger than you because I am love." The Creator is "the Lover divine and the comrade perfect"; men are *camerados* and the more they love and create the more they are worth, even though whatever occupies their place and time is as good as anything else; but let everyone see the world for himself, for Walt Whitman, who feels within himself the world since its beginning, knows, from what the sun and open air have taught him, that a sunrise reveals more than the best book. He thinks about the orbs above, desires women, feels himself possessed of a universal, frantic love. He hears rising from the scenes of creation and the toils of man a concert that fills him with joy, and when he looks toward the river at the hour factories are closing and the setting sun tints the water, he feels he has an appointment with the Creator, recognizes man is definitively good and from his head, reflected upon the surface, he sees rays of light emerging.

How can I convey an idea of this man's sweeping, flaming love? He loves the world with Sappho's fire. To him the world is like a gigantic bed and this bed an altar. "The words and ideas men have prostituted with secrecy and false modesty I shall make illustrious; I praise and consecrate what Egypt did." One of the sources of his originality is the Herculean strength with which he subdues ideas as though to rape them, when he means only to kiss them as would a saint. Another source is the material, brutal, corporal manner in which he expresses his most delicate ideals. Those who are incapable of understanding his greatness have found this language lewd; there even have been imbeciles, with a prudishness worthy of evil-minded school boys, who believed they found in "Calamus," when he praises the love between friends in the most ardent images possible, a return to Virgil's vile desire for Cebetes or Horace's for Gyges and Lyciscus. And when in "The Children of Adam" he sings of the divine sin in images beside which the most passionate images of "The Song of Songs" seem pale, he trembles, shrinks, surrenders, expands, goes mad with pride and satisfied virility, he recalls the god of the Amazon, who crossed over forests and rivers sowing the seeds of life: "my duty is creation!" "I sing the body electric!" he says in "The Children of Adam"; and to find anything comparable to the satanic strength with which he enumerates, like a hungry hero smacking his bloody lips, the parts of a woman's body, one must have read in Hebrew the genealogies of Genesis or followed through the forests primeval the naked, flesh-eating bands of primitive men.

You say this man is brutal? Listen to this poem, "Beautiful Women," a two-verse poem as are many of his poems: "Women sit and move to and fro, some old, some young, / the young are beautiful, but the old are more beautiful than the young." And this other, "Mother and Babe": "I see the sleeping babe nestling the breast of his mother, / the sleeping mother and babe hush'd, I study them long and long." He foresees that, even as in men of genius extreme virility and tenderness are joined, so in the delightful peace where life will come to rest, the two forces which have necessarily separated to continue the task of creation will reunite solemnly, jubilantly as becomes the Universe.

When he walks on the grass he says the grass caresses him, that he "feels his joints moving"; and the most restless youth would not find such fiery words to describe the joy of the body, which to Whitman is part of the soul, when he feels the sea's embrace. All living things love him: the earth, the night, the sea. "You sea . . . dash me with amorous wet." He relishes the air. He offers himself to the breeze like a trembling lover. He favors doors without locks, bodies in their natural beauty; he believes he sanctifies whatever he touches or touches him and finds virtue in all corporal things. He is "Walt Whitman, a kosmos, of Manhattan the son. / Turbulent, fleshy, sensual, eating, drinking and breeding / . . . no stander above men and women or apart from them." He describes truth as a frenzied lover who assaults his body and strips himself of his clothes in the anxiety of possession. But when the soul, free of drudgery and books, emerges whole, silent, as it looks back on the well-employed day, it meditates on the most pleasing subjects: night, sleep, death, the song of the universal for the benefit of the common man, the sweetness of dying, "advancing on," and falling at the foot of the primeval tree, ax in hand, bitten by the last serpent in the forest.

Imagine what new and strange effect is obtained by this language, filled with superb animality, when it praises the passion which should unite mankind. In one of the "Calamus" poems he enumerates the liveliest pleasures he owes to nature and fatherland; but he finds that only the ocean waves are worthy of accompanying his joy when by moonlight he sees the friend he loves sleeping by his side. He loves the humble, the fallen, the wounded, even the wicked. He has no disdain for the great, since for him only the useful are great. He throws an arm about the shoulder of teamsters, sailors, country laborers. He goes hunting and fishing with them and at harvest time climbs with them atop the hay wagons. The muscular Negro who, standing on the pole behind his horses, drives his wagon calmly through the turmoil of Broadway, seemed to him more beautiful than a victorious emperor. He understands all virtues, receives all prizes, works at all trades, shares all sorrows, feels a heroic pleasure when from the smithy threshold he sees the young blacksmiths, stripped to the waist, brandishing their sledges over their heads and striking alternately. He is the slave, the prisoner, the fighter, the fallen one, the beggar. When the slave knocks at his door, pursued and sweating, he fills the bath tub for him, sits him at his table; he has his loaded gun in the corner ready to defend him; should anyone try to attack his guest, he will kill the pursuer and sit again at the table as though he had only killed a viper!

Walt Whitman, therefore, is contented; why should pride prick him, since he knows one ends up being a blade of grass or a flower? Is a carnation, a sprig of sage, a branch of honey-suckle proud? How else can he look upon human tribulations but serenely, knowing that they will be followed by eternity for him who awaits his blissful merger with nature? Why should he hurry, since he believes everything is where it should be and that one man's will cannot change the course of the world? He suffers indeed; but the part of himself that suffers he considers a minor, perishable being, and he feels, over and above his trials and mysteries, that there is in him another being who cannot suffer because he knows universal greatness. It suffices him to be as he is and he witnesses, with impassivity or joy, the course of his life, be it unnoticed or praised. With a single stroke he puts aside romantic lamentation as a useless excrescence: "Not asking the sky to come down to my good will!" What majesty there is to that phrase in which he says he loves animals because "they do not sweat and whine about their condition!" The truth is there are too many scaremongers; it is urgent for us to see the world as it is, so as not to make mountains out of molehills; to make men strong instead of taking from them through lamentations whatever strength sorrow has left them; for lepers do not go around exhibiting their sores. Neither doubts nor science disturb him. "Gentlemen, to you the first honors always! / Your facts are useful, and yet they are not my dwelling, / I but enter by them to an area of my dwelling." "How beggarly appear arguments before a defiant deed!" "Lo! Keen-eyed towering science / . . . Yet again, lo! The soul, above all science; . . ." But where his philosophy has entirely conquered hatred, as wise men order, is in this phrase which partakes of the melancholy of defeat but uproots all reason for envy: Why should I be jealous, he says, of my brother for doing what I cannot do? "He that by me spreads a wider breast than my own, proves the width of my own. Let the Sun interpenetrate the Earth until it all be sweet and pure light, like my blood! Let the rejoicing be universal. I sing the eternity of existence, the happiness of our life and the beauty beyond change of the Universe. My signs are the calfskin shoe, the open collar and a staff cut from the woods."

All this he says in apocalyptic phrase. Rhymes or accents? Oh, no! His rhythm lies in the stanzas which he joins, amidst an apparent chaos of superimposed and convulsive phrases, according to a wise pattern that distributes ideas in great musical groups, a poetic form natural to a people who do not build stone by stone but in enormous blocks.

Walt Whitman's language, a complete departure from that used heretofore by poets, corresponds in its strangeness and power to his cyclic poetry and to a new humanity gathered on a fertile continent full of such portents that they cannot be expressed in affected, set, rhetorical forms. It is no longer a question of hidden loves, of ladies that break their troth, the sterile complaint of those who lack the necessary energy to conquer life nor the cunning that becomes cowards. It is no longer a question of jingles, of alcove complaints, but of the birth of a new era, the dawn of the definitive religion and man's renovation, of a faith which is to replace a dead one and arises radiantly clear from redeemed man's arrogant peace; of writing the sacred books of a people who, emerging out of the old world, absorbs at savage nature's udders all the virgin forces and cyclopean pomp of liberty; it is a question of painting with words the bustle of settling masses, working cities, conquered seas, and enslaved rivers. Will Walt Whitman seek rhymes with which to mold into soft couplets these mountains of merchandise, bristling forests, crowds of ships, battles where millions of men lay down their lives to uphold a right, the sun prevailing over everything and spilling its limpid fire across the vast panorama?

Oh, no! Walt Whitman speaks in biblical verses, with no apparent music, though soon we realize they sound like the crust of the earth being trodden upon by barefooted, glorious, victorious armies. At times Whitman's language is like a butcher's window where carcasses hang; again it is like the chant of patriarchs singing in a circle full of the world's sadness in the hour when smoke rises to the clouds; other times it sounds like a stolen kiss, like a rape, like the snapping of a dried-out parchment in the sun. But his phrase never loses the rhythmic movement of the wave. He himself tells us how he speaks in "prophetical screams," which are, he says, a few "indicative words for the future." That precisely is his poetry—an index. A sense of the universal pervades his book and gives it, despite the superficial confusion, a grandiose regularity; but his disjointed, lashing, incomplete, loose phrases emit, rather than express; "I send my imaginings over the hoary mountains," "Earth! . . . Say, old top-knot, what do you want?" "I sound my barbaric yawp over the roofs of the world."

He is not one to turn out a beggarly thought in regal garments to go stumbling, crawling along under the weight of its showy opulence. Nor does he blow up warblers to make them look like eagles; whenever he opens his fist he sows eagles as a farmer would grain. One verse will have five syllables, the next forty, the next ten. He does not press a comparison, in fact he does not compare, but tells what he saw or remembers, adding a graphic or incisive commentary and, with a masterful control of the general impression he is trying to create, without showing his hand, he uses his art in reproducing things in his picture with the same disorder in which he observed them in nature. Even when he raves there is no dissonance, because that is how the mind wanders unhampered from one subject to other analogous ones. But then, as though he had only slackened the reins, he suddenly pulls on them and regains full control over the runaway quadriga of his verses, as they gallop on devouring the land; at times they neigh eagerly like lustful stallions; at times, covered with lather, they trample clouds with their hoofs; at times they sink into the earth—daring and black—and are heard rumbling on for a long while. He sketches; but one would say he does so with fire. He can bring together in five lines, like a bundle of freshly gnawed bones, all the horrors of war. An adverb is all he needs to stretch out or shrink a phrase, an adjective to reinforce it. His must be a great method, since its effect is great. But it might seem that he proceeds with no method at all, especially in the use of words, which he combines with unheard of audacity, putting august and almost divine words next to others which seem the least appropriate and decent. Certain pictures he does not paint with epithets, which in him are always lively and profound, but by means of sounds, which he arranges and juggles with consummate skill. By thus alternating his procedures he sustains the reader's interest, which one monotonous mode might cause to lag. As savages do, he brings forth melancholy through repetition. His unexpected, impetuous caesura changes constantly and respects no rule, though one can perceive a wise order in its meanderings, stops, breaks. He prefers to describe by accumulation, and his reasoning never resorts to the vulgar form of argument nor the high-sounding form of oratory, but to the mystery of insinuation, the fervor of certitude and the fiery turn of prophecy. We find in his book at every step these words of ours: *viva, camarada, libertad, americanos.* And what could reveal his character better than the French words with which, with evident delight, he studs his verses, as though to expand their meaning; *ami, exalté, accoucheur, nonchalant, ensemble? Ensemble,* especially, seduces him because he sees the sky that embraces the life of peoples, the life of worlds. From the Italian he has taken one word: *bravura!*

Thus, praising muscles and boldness, inviting passers-by to put their hand on his shoulder without fear when he crosses, listening with open palms to the song of things, joyously catching and proclaiming gigantic fecundities, gathering in epic verses seeds, battles, and orbs, pointing out to these times filled with astonishment the radiant human hives that cover the American vales and mountains and graze with their bee's wings the garment of vigilant liberty, shepherding the friendly ages toward the tranquil waters of eternity, while his friends feast him rustically with champagne and the first fish caught this spring, Walt Whitman awaits the happy hour when his body will leave him, after having revealed to the world a real, resounding, loving man, and when, returned to the purifying airs, he will germinate and perfume them "disembodied, triumphant, dead."

Translated by Luis A. Baralt

Victoria Ocampo on John Steinbeck

In typical Argentine style, Victoria Ocampo (1891–1979), the grande dame of Argentine letters, was classically educated and heavily influenced by European thought and culture. She learned French, English, and Italian at an early age, and did much of her writing in French during the early part of her career. Although Ocampo faced a male-dominated literary world which was resistant to accepting women, she quickly earned the praise of the Spanish philosopher José Ortega y Gasset. In 1931 she founded the magazine *Sur*, which became one of Latin America's most important literary forums, achieving international renown and producing some of the region's greatest writers, including Borges and Bioy Casares. Later she became the director of the National Foundation of the Arts, and by the 1950s she had reached international recognition. When the government of Juan Perón arrested her in 1955, both Gabriela Mistral and Jawarhal Nehru interceded on her behalf and arranged for her release. A strong activist in the women's movements in Argentina, Ocampo was a cofounder of the Argentine Union of Women. Her translations, essays, and creative pieces reflect her interest in literature from beyond traditional Western sources, and her works have influenced two generations of Latin American literature and thought. Ocampo masterfully linked seemingly unrelated anecdotes and references in a smooth and fluid narrative which is free of pedantry and artificiality. The tone and outlook of most her work is optimistic. She published twenty-six volumes of essays, of which nine are entitled *Testimonios*. The two essays that follow, collapsed here into a single piece, were published in *Sur*, Buenos Aires, May and July 1940.

I

It is difficult to have read, imagined, lived a novel and be satisfied by the interpretation we see later on the screen. As we progress through a work, any work, we create the characters and places like a unique atmosphere, born from the meeting of our sensibility, our intelligence, our vision of the world (which varies with our states of mind), and those of the author, for all literature is collaboration. In fact, we are often shocked when we reread certain pages, not to return to find certain details, certain allusions (which we had made sprout from the text, yet were only its extension into us), and we marvel to discover new intentions and nuances that we had not, until that moment, perceived.

The cinematic translation of *Wuthering Heights* (and I deliberately use the word "translation" because it really deals with a shift into another language) must have been, for passionate and attentive readers of that singular novel, a deception. The distance between Emily Brontë's rough Heathcliff and the one portrayed by the docile Laurence Olivier is really a little too infinite. This actor, with the canine appearance of a friendly, excited puppy, does not even have the physical capacity to play the role of a great feline or bird of prey. Heathcliff is not a domesticated animal. Hollywood, faithful to its own inveterate custom, does not seem to have noticed.

Furthermore—if one can imagine something even more notable— the screen version of *Wuthering Heights* lacks that mysterious *interior atmospheric agitation*—very difficult to materialize, I know—that sticks in our throats from the novel's first pages and overwhelms and engulfs us until the last. Nonetheless, this "atmospheric agitation" is one of the elements that places Emily Brontë's book among those of great distinction. It inspires, symbolically, the very title of the work. Hollywood's translation has given us the letter of *Wuthering Heights*, but not the spirit. And in *Wuthering Heights,* spirit is everything.

On the other hand, American cinema has just offered us an almost perfect realization—letter and spirit—of *The Grapes of Wrath,* John Steinbeck's ferocious and generous novel. And I say *almost* because the work has pages so beautiful that cinematic translation is a daunting prospect. A few weeks ago I published an article in these columns about another exceptional film, inspired by the same author: *Of Mice and Men.* The film Steinbeck gives us today merits more than admiration for its director, John Ford, and his collaborators (photographers and interpreters magnificent at times, and continually good); it awakens a moving respect and a profound esteem toward the nation strong, free, and self-assured enough to allow this illustration, this divulgence, both at home and abroad, of such a painful and humiliating social document; humiliating for systems (or men?) that have not been able to remedy such injustices.*

The Grapes of Wrath does not flatter, does not praise people, nor things. It does not pretend to attract nor distract the public using the great cinematic industry's habitual means of seduction: Greta Garbo's fabulously fake, long eyelashes; Robert Taylor's fabulously real, uniform teeth; lousy heroicisms; cheap love; spectacular car chases between gunshots. Nor can it please those who still pretend that democracies function satisfactorily . . . (the ostriches of democracies). I believe it can only satisfy those willing to discuss salutary truths and those who defend democracy (believing it should purify and perfect itself) because it is the only system that, among absurd lies, allows the expression of necessary and saving truths. What nation, other than a great democratic nation, would allow the exhibition of a *mea culpa* like *The Grapes of Wrath*?

Let us not forget that the marvels we see in well-organized propaganda from countries that specialize in the genre, through image or word, are often a brilliant *tromp l'oeil*, a very peculiar farce from our era. How much worthier is *The Grapes of Wrath*'s sad and humble truth, and how well would it serve each nation to know its own miseries (and those it provokes in other peoples) so they could seek to correct such errors! What modifications, what reactions would similar cinematic documents produce by exposing infinitely more inhumane facts to the public eye: concentration camps, the *pogroms*? But these documents could never surface in the precise countries that would inspire them. Only authentic democracies allow these liberties, places that do not have such tremendous atrocities to denounce.

The cinematic *The Grapes of Wrath* is a disturbing, asphyxiating, but admirable social document. The novel upon which it is based is dark and lyrical; as painful to read as the film is to see. A painful but salutary film, like all truth, as bitter as it may be. Even more painful because we cannot interrupt the anguish as reading allows us to do,

---

*By his own admission, the president himself, Franklin Roosevelt, impressed by *The Grapes of Wrath*, asked Congress to take emergency measures to remedy the situation for the nomadic laborers. As a result, the "Columbia River Project" has been sanctioned, whose goal is to occupy the workers and organize public camps where they can provisionally install themselves, until the legislature makes laws to definitively resolve the problem.

closing the book to breathe every now and then. In the film the dose of anguish is overwhelming.

The Joad family, which Steinbeck describes to us, is one of many; a family of tenant farmers, forced to abandon the piece of land on which they were born and worked, to which they feel linked by the affection land stirs in those who cultivate it and live in direct contact with it. The Joad family lives in the region known as the *dust bowl,* where the earth has become desecated and impoverished. The property system is no longer productive enough there for either the landowners (large proprieters, banks, anonymous companies) or the tenant farmers. Tractors are taking man's place. One tractor, driven by one person, can replace fourteen families. The drama begins.

Like so many other farmers, the Joads become nomadic, defenseless workers we see filing along U.S. highways in old cars or dilapidated trucks, with the illusion of finding work in the California fruit harvest. Grandfathers, fathers, children young and old, a neighbor and the dog, crowded in next to the pigs, the indispensable clothing, buckets, pots, scarce provisions, and the no less scarce hopes, the rifle, the lantern, and the Bible . . . they travel. Under these conditions the Joad family travels, like so many others, along the roads from Oklahoma and California. The oldest son, Tom (Henry Fonda, perfect, with his silent sleepwalker's gait and the rebelliousness of a young animal that does not want to be caged), has reached the time to leave his family. He returns home after four years spent away in jail. He has killed a man in self-defense. An old friend he met on the way is with him, the Reverend Jim Casy, an old preacher, who had baptized him as a child. Jim Casy has become a vagabond; he agrees to join the Joad family on their trip to California. Paralyzed by a great disenchantment with himself and everyone else, he feels his existence has no purpose, that he no longer has anything to do anywhere, nothing to do in life other than to wander and watch people. Thus he hopes to learn something. He hardly preaches anymore, the man who once lived for preaching. "I ain't preachin no more much. The sperit ain't in the people much no more; and worse'n that, the sperit ain't in me no more . . . I ain't so sure of a lot of things." Reverend Jim Casy, the vagabond in overalls, blue shirt, grey canvas sneakers, leaning against a willow's trunk, confesses, "I got the sperit sometimes an' nothin' to preach about. I got the call to lead people, an' no place to lead 'em." This calling as a leader of souls and this not knowing where to lead them is the tragedy of Jim Casy. With the phrases of a sermon in which he no longer believes rattling around in his head, he comes upon a truth: a union of men forms one soul, of which each is but a part. That fraternity is Jim Casy's only faith.

More than that of the hungry children, "corn-headed children, with wide eyes, one bare foot on top of the other, bare foot, and the toes working"; more than that of the grandfather and grandmother who die on the way to the promised California; more than the mother, center, strength, and upon whose arms rest the entire weight of the family; more than Rosasharn with her abandoned woman's tremble, her youth in full bloom, her body malnourished and further suffering from feeding another body inside her; more than Tom, overwhelmed by injustices witnessed and withstood, the problem of Jim Casy, vagabond preacher, stands out, naked, blinding, and significant like a sword unsheathed in the sun . . . "I got the call to lead people an' no place to lead 'em." Jim Casy still prays, but no longer knows for what, or to whom. When he looks at the mountains, the fields, he feels he is a part of them, and that unity is, to him, "sacred." He thinks . . . he thinks . . . "on'y it wasn't thinkin, it was deeper down than thinkin."

He learns that men are also sacred when, together, they form a single thing; for example, when all men work *with* others, instead of working *for* others. Then, instead of feeling bound to them, he feels united with them.

All Jim Casy can say, when the Joad family asks for a prayer, is, "I'm glad there's love here."

The painful rediscovery of a faith almost lost, sickened by offering empty promises, mechanical and sterile plagiarisms; new faith in the strength and purity of fraternity and love among men.

Jim Casy believes that he has lost God's way. He cannot send him messages like before. But he knows plenty about fraternity, charity, and love. And to know that is to know God's way. I do not believe that there is a surer one. Jim Casy, sinner by instinct and preacher by trade, manages to point his people toward fraternity, charity, and love; he can die in peace. He has known God.

After returning to the United States, Maurois published a travel diary in which he, discussing *The Grapes of Wrath,* made commentaries on the perversity and sadism of the most talented North American writers. According to Maurois, this "perversity" consists of making us suffer by portraying, with malignant and evident predilection, monstrous creatures and distressing circumstances (examples: Faulkner and Steinbeck). Steinbeck's poor characters—Maurois affirms—are too poor; his vagabonds, too defenseless; his bosses, too ferocious; his assassins, too bestial; his children, too hungry. Why emphasize that—asks Maurois—in a country like the United States, in which the observer immediately discovers so much benevolence and generosity? Why will an entire generation write *Les Rougon-Macquart* and never *Les Misérables*? Maurois's criticism is accurate in a superficial sense. It is perfectly obvious that Steinbeck is content with his use and abuse of the most dismal colors. It is obvious that he emphasizes lugubrious events and never tires of describing miseries and horrors. But this tendency can very easily come as part of the generosity that Maurois observes and recognizes in the North American character. The preoccupation with confronting unknown miseries and horrors is, in effect, generosity. So many people—among those who have the ability to change things—ignore them! It is good, then, to put them on display, in a novel or film, where they cannot go unnoticed as in real life. This is terrifying, Maurois my friend: that we are moved in novels and films by what goes unnoticed in life; even more terrifying than the monsters and mad existences in Steinbeck's and Faulkner's works.

A man who loses his land feels alone and disconcerted, Steinbeck says in *The Grapes of Wrath*. But not two men. The "*I* have lost" becomes the "*We* have lost." Misery does not precisely love company, as the saying goes. Misery with company perhaps becomes liberation and justice for all. The step from "I" to "we" is an important step. "Here is the node, you who hate change and fear revolution."

Those two men, and later that multitude of men, who no longer say "*I* have lost . . .," but "*We* have lost" are united by that "*We,*" by that community and charity and fraternity of suffering that only the needy know well.

If you, those who have means and power to cure such plagues, could understand that—continues Steinbeck—you could protect yourselves. If you could understand that Paine, Marx, Jefferson, Lenin were effects and not causes (I would like to add more equally illustrious names to the list), you could survive. "But that you cannot know. For the quality of owning freezes you forever into 'I' and cuts you off forever from the 'We.' "

This has already been said with prettier words. The saying about the eye of the needle and the camel and the Kingdom of the Heavens.

Furthermore, one must be spiritually blind to see no more than poverty, ugliness, and hunger in *The Grapes of Wrath*.

The Joads' mother, who is known by no other name than "Ma," and who could have none other in our mind, the same way our mother has no name other than the one we gave her when we learned to love her and call to her; "Ma," of whom Jim Casy says, ". . . a woman so great with love—she scares me. Makes me afraid and mean," needs envy nothing in a *Les Misérables* character. If Maurois does not see the good in a character so alive, so strong and noble, it is not Steinbeck's fault.

When Tom returns to see "Ma" after four years' absence and prison, the emotion he feels does not appear in his expression. Steinbeck communicates it to us in one of his most inspired passages, describing "Ma" as her son sees her, with all the tenderness and understanding that Tom carries in his soul and his flesh.

"Ma," with her apron faded from use and washing, her body ample and resistant like those tree trunks that sit well with the earth, her feet naked and agile, her firm arms and her eyes that have faced so many pains, lacks bodily perfections and has passed the age of physical enchantment. However, Steinbeck, portraying "Ma" for us with a skillet in hand, shares something that is pure beauty. We see "Ma's" beauty like we saw it as children, with purer eyes, the beauty of those we loved and who loved us, because beauty was our tenderness and what we received.

"Ma" knows she cannot lose hope nor become weak without the entire family wavering and losing the energy they need to survive. Little by little she has learned not to lose hope, not to become weak, come what may.

Steinbeck, along with his crudeness and his cruelty, has the genius of carnal tenderness, that genius that has disappeared among contemporary European writers. It suffices to read a few choice pages in *The Grapes of Wrath* to be convinced. It is almost impossible for nuances so subtle and essential to pass from the novel to the film; they remain among the pages of the book along with so many other things.

Upon bidding farewell to his mother at the end of the film, maybe forever, Tom tells her that their separation should not distress her as if it were permanent. "How'm I gonna know 'bout you?" asks a tormented "Ma." And Tom answers "I'll be ever'where—wherever you look. Wherever they's a fight so hungry people can eat, I'll be there . . . I'll be in the way guys yell when they're mad an'—I'll be in the way kids laugh when they're hungry an' they know supper's ready . . ." To replace him, Tom wants his mother to adopt all the children she finds, that is to say, all of hurting humanity. And Tom realizes, upon pronouncing these words, that he is in the same state of mind as Jim Casy; Jim Casy, who died repeating to his killers, "You don' know what you're a-doin'."

Jim Casy can no longer preach, and "Ma" does not know how to talk, and Tom is a violent, desperate young man, but they all, in their own way, on distinct paths, with different imperfections, approach something that too closely resembles true Christian love to not be it: the love of one's fellow man.

All these things are difficult to carry to the screen and, it is difficult to express them in cinematic language. But those who bear them in their hearts cannot help but hazily sense them. Those who see them are not mistaken.

II

A story, about two unemployed men in search of work, George and Lennie. A deep friendship unites them, sullen in George, canine in Lennie, for it is precisely a dog's devotion that ties this giant to his friend. Lennie is an idiot. He hardly understands the spoken word, but nonetheless he can follow George's dreams of happiness. He likes to hear him describe the little farm they hope to have one day. Life will be sweet and peaceful; Lennie can raise rabbits. Because under his bestial infantilism hides a disturbed sensitivity that makes him seek silky contact. Since he is unaware of his strength, he usually kills anything in his hands. First small animals, mice which he stuffs in his pockets while he walks, so he can feel the smoothness of their fur; later a puppy; and finally Curley's wife, the daughter-in-law of the boss of the farm on which the two friends are working. So that the men don't lynch the killer, George tells him, for the last time, about the ideal farm and the coveted rabbits, and when he sees that Lennie is lost in his contented vision, he fells him with a shot in the back of the neck.

The cinematic version of *Of Mice and Men,* as everyone knows, is entitled "Brute Force," adapted from the novel's Spanish translation for commercial (that is, poor) reasons. This title, instead of helping one to understand the work, diverts the reader and the spectator from its profound, essential meaning.

The best-laid schemes o'mice and men gang aft a-gley.

The original title, *Of Mice and Men,* is a fragment from Robert Burns's poetry. Few people may recall this poem, if they have ever even read it. They will not have it in mind as they read the novel's title (as I did not at first) and perhaps will think what I thought: that *Of Mice and Men* is one of those titles that is deliberately bland and vague (how many different things could one write about mice and men!), but poetic, without knowing quite why. It is, above all, a modest title in that genre of modesty which characterizes our era's literary "elite." A title intended to dissimulate the kind of merchandise that it covers. But, like all modest gestures, it unconsciously signals and underscores what it tries to veil. By mentioning mice before men, placing men on the same level as mice, or even worse, on a lower tier, it reveals to us, willingly and frankly, that Steinbeck has seen, has proven such a humiliation of the human race and has been unable to digest it.

Of Mice and Men is, by any means, a title whose significance does not lie within the layman's reach; but it at least has the advantage and merit of not providing a false clue; it leaves its interpretation to one's own initiative. The opposite occurs with an explicit and limited title like "Brute Force," which would seem to say everything it needs to say, leaving room for little else. The innocent reader or viewer (I refer to the untutored) enters the book or theater thinking: "we're going to read a novel, or we're going to see a movie, about brute force." In reality, brute force is a secondary theme, as much in the book as in the film. It may appear to be the most important because it unleashes the catastrophe in the barn and prompts a few other episodes. But neither the catastrophe in the barn nor the episodes to which I refer (and which justify the cinematic title) are what truly concern the author. Steinbeck did not write *Of Mice and Men* to describe the extraordinary force of Lennie, the poor idiot (shameless romantics would have

elected a title like *Les Misérables*: Victor Hugo also wrote about sim-
pletons). Lennie's own force is only brute because he is big and blind.
Lennie and his unconscious force are not the main character. Neither
is George, despite the convergence of three unfortunate souls' hopes
upon him (a useless old man, a scorned and handicapped black man,
and a herculean idiot). The main character of this poem-turned-novel
is the *pain of solitude*. Pain which is felt, each in his own way, by
George, Lennie, Candy, Crooks, the nameless woman (she doesn't
have one in the novel), and even the hateful Curley. Solitude that men
will withstand only if they have a great dream, a great hope, a great
faith in their heart, that fortifies them or anaesthetizes them. Pain of
solitude that even Christ knew in Gethsemane: "What, could ye not
watch with me one hour?" (Matthew 26:40).

For these simple, instinctive men, hardened by manual labor, the
elements, and the urgency of earning their daily bread, the pain of
solitude is like a secret, open wound. "Guys like us," George says, "got
no fambly. They make a little stake an' then they blow it in. They ain't
got nobody in the worl' that gives a hoot in hell about 'em . . ." Pain
of intolerable solitude in creatures whose very roughness eternally
condemns them to it. Men without refinement, but through whose
veins flows what Shakespeare calls "the milk of human kindness."
That is how Steinbeck's workers are; that is how the ones Güiraldes
saw were. The struggle with America's land and immense, open
spaces unites them.

What are Lennie and George, in effect, but two species of drifters?
They search for work for a few days, in the country. The only thing
distinguishing them from other vagabonds is an insignificance, which,
however, changes the color of their lives: they are two, wandering
together, instead of being one. They are two solitudes who live
grudgingly with each other. The tie that binds them is similar to
Candy's with his only friend, an old dog. George protects Lennie, and
by protecting him he feels accompanied. Lennie follows and obeys
George, and doing so he, in turn, feels accompanied. Lennie does not
understand most of the things George says. George knows it. But it
does not matter. The feeling that unites them is beneath (or above)
understanding, as it is above sex and material interests.

When the boss asks George what he gets from the absolute idiot
Lennie's company and how George has devised to exploit him, the

boss knows little about his men. He knows little about them, like all those who try to live too hard and erase what is vulgarly called heart from their stingy calculations (always trying to provide an explanation that makes despicableness appear logical). The only thing that George gets from Lennie is his boundless happiness; happiness that he, George, provides by allowing him to accompany him. Lennie's infantile happiness intercedes between George and his solitude. George no longer feels isolated from the universe.

The death of Candy's dog and Lennie's in the brush are perhaps the culminations of the novel and the film. They have nothing to do with *brute force* but plenty, on the other hand, with "the milk of human kindness." What these workers feel sitting in their miserable room, while one of them takes Candy's dog to *put him out of his misery,* is restrained pity and tenderness. Pity and tenderness toward the poor, old, defenseless man who, upon losing his dog, loses everything in life that replaced human affection. And this *is not* what North Americans call, in cinematic jargon, "sob stuff," but something of a superior quality. What George feels when he kills Lennie is also pity and tenderness and fraternal love. But these words are not articulated, nor mentioned, nor do they confess these feelings.

I saw the theatrical adaptation of *Of Mice and Men* in London, ten months ago. It seemed a good play to me, admirably represented. But the movie United Artists offers us, under Lewis Milestone's direction, is incomparably superior. This is a rare film, as much for its quality as for its essentially and authentically American characteristics. American even in its most minuscule details: for the first time (and many are the films that pass before my eyes each year) I see some good corn served and eaten on screen like we do it all across America . . .

And speaking of meals, the silent scene in which Curley, his father, and his mother are gathered around the table savoring a pie (English heritage) strikes me as, in its genre, unsurpassed. I do not believe there is anything capable of provoking more irritation than to see and hear people eat who we fleetingly or perpetually detest. This explains why Curley's wife—whose manners are, let's say, not very refined, and who consequently should not have been bothered by the puffs, snorts, slurps, gargles, and resounding mastications of her husband and her father-in-law—becomes exasperated listening to them.

The scene is so well done, the French would say "emportée," and has such a masterly rhythm, that we can almost hear the words and curses that nobody is vocalizing.

I must reiterate that, in my opinion, *Of Mice and Men* has poetic beauties (I am, clearly, not referring to the comic and tragic scene to which I just alluded). It is difficult to express poetic terms in cinematic language. The director of *Of Mice and Men* unveils them with each minute. One cannot offer great praise to a film. Steinbeck, that "tremendous genius," as H. G. Wells calls him, has not been betrayed by Hollywood. Which should have been a concern . . .

The entire film develops with perfect rhythm. Perfect like Aaron Copland's music, which plays in the background with such skill, ease, and inspiration. Perfect like Curley's wife's silent gait, when she calmly, self-assuredly crosses the field precisely between two cars hurtling toward each other, seeming to converge on her, attracted by an irresistible centripetal force.

Translated by Jesse H. Lytle

Alejo Carpentier on Herman Melville

Born in Havana to an immigrant family, Alejo Carpentier (1904–1980) learned to speak French in his house and Spanish in school. His diverse cultural and linguistic background would be crucial in the development of his literary voice. Carpentier's writings sought to integrate and even harmonize the Spanish and African traditions of his native Cuba with his French background, and he shows a great concern for the theme of cultural and linguistic duality throughout his literary career. Carpentier studied music theory and wrote theatrical and musical critiques for Cuban newspapers and magazines in Paris, where he lived with his paternal grandparents. The publication of the now popular *Music in Cuba* (1946) attests to the writer's deep interest in music. Carpentier also studied architecture in Havana but abandoned his studies in 1922 due to economic need. From then on, he would devote himself to writing. He returned to his homeland and helped inspire a *Vanguardista* movement, before returning to Paris as a political refugee. Carpentier's departure was prompted when he was charged in a Cuban court with being a communist. Living in Venezuela from 1945 to 1959, Carpentier wrote a daily column which blossomed into his important novel *The Lost Steps* (1953), and he founded a radio station. After the Cuban Revolution in 1959, he again returned home and was later sent to France in a diplomatic role. While in Europe he wrote essays on cultural themes, such as *Tientos y diferencias* (1967), *Literatura y conciencia política en América Latina* (1969), and *Razón de ser* (1976). He received the Cervantes Prize in 1978. This brief comment on Melville's voyage to Peru was first published as "Herman Melville y la América Latina," in *El Nacional,* Caracas, 4 February 1955.

One of the most recent issues of *Panorama*, a superb magazine published by the Washington Pan American Union, included an intriguing essay written by the Peruvian essayist Eduardo Núñez. Núñez's essay examines Herman Melville's contact with Peru and other Latin American countries. After digging up and reading through old newspapers, the writer was able to determine that Melville docked on Peruvian soil on at least three occasions. In fact, Peru was apparently a regular stop on most of Melville's journeys. According to the author of *Benito Cereno,* those journeys aboard cargo clippers and whaling ships represented a sort of romantic and barbaric adventure for one of Plato's most faithful readers. This apprenticeship at sea transformed Melville. The author was surprisingly familiar with El Callao; he found Lima fascinating:

> What is it that makes Lima the strangest and most somber city you will ever find? The roots of this strange sadness do not lie with the memories of the earthquakes that demolished its cathedrals, the surf of its frenetic oceans, the scarcity of its rains, the spectacle of its vast spaces, or the suburban avenues in which immense walls rest on each other . . . No, the reasons behind this uncanny sadness rest with Lima's white veil and its resistance to the most extreme horrors through the whiteness that has come to define its tribulation. As ancient as Pizzas, this whiteness is never devoid of fresh branches, it always resists the jovial greenness of its decadence; Lima demonstrates the rigid courage of an apoplexy that fixes its own distortions over earthly gaps.

This short paragraph reveals Melville's understanding of the mystic qualities of everyday life. It is a testament to his uncanny ability at endowing his surroundings with mystical overtones. Through Eduardo Núñez's essay, we learn that the author of *Moby-Dick* was once in Chile, visited the Pacific coast, and traveled through Argentina as part of a journey that may have taken him through Venezuela and the Antilles. On one of his trips, he came across a dismantled ship which was apparently left to try its own fate in the Pacific. Upon being visited by the captain of another ship, the ship's crew examined the visitors with a strange reserve. He soon learned that the black slaves aboard the ship had rioted and were forcing the captain and his officials to return them to their native Africa. A skeleton was hung from the ship's bow: the ghastly remains of a Peruvian gentleman assassinated during the mutiny. Melville was therefore given all the necessary ingredients with which to write *Benito Cereno,* a tale named after the captain of that tragic vessel and one of his most hallucinatory and mystic works.

Núñez concludes his essay with the following phrase: "The remarkable enthusiasm of contemporary readers for the work of Herman

Melville is a fairly recent development. However, the mark left by Latin America in a few paragraphs of his distinguished literary career and the Peruvian inspiration of some of his pages have never been examined." Thus, we are lacking the difficult but illuminating study of Melville's wanderings through our lands.

Translated by José Matosantos

Carlos Fuentes on William Styron

Carlos Fuentes (b. 1928) has lived all over Europe and Latin America, but in his work he represents only his native Mexico. Many of his works are set in Distrito Federal, most notably his breakthrough novel *Where the Air Is Clear* (1958). As one of the original Boom writers, Fuentes helped renovate the literary language of Spanish America. His prose is fluid, but never devoid of word games or experimentations with time, space, and narrative perspectives. In addition, Fuentes, more than any other writer of the Boom, set up the theoretical origins and boundaries of the movement. Fuentes's essays and prose works often dismiss the validity of traditional historical analysis and have sparked a general interest in the boundaries which divide history and fiction. His oeuvre is primarily concerned with the search for a Mexican identity or, rather, the search for the culture's undefined origins. After the follow-up *Las buenas conciencias* (1959), he published the fantastic *Aura* (1962), which is a tribute to Henry James's *The Jolly Corner,* and *The Death of Artemio Cruz* (1962). *A Change of Skin* won him the Premio Bibioteca Breve in 1967, and was followed by *Christopher Unborn* (1987), *The Orange Tree* (1994), and *The Crystal Frontier* (1996). Fuentes has also produced a number of plays, short stories, and essay collections, where the reader may sense the influence of countryman Octavio Paz. His distinguished diplomatic career has allowed him to travel widely and to broaden his international appeal. He has been awarded the Premio Cervantes, among many other honors. He has been a close friend of American writers William Styron and Philip Roth. This essay is excerpted from *Casa con dos puertas* (Mexico City: Joaquín Mortiz, 1970).

To date, William Styron has published four novels: *Lie Down in Darkness* (1951), *The Long March* (1952), *Set This House on Fire* (1960), and *The Confessions of Nat Turner* (1967). This last novel won the Pulitzer Prize for Literature, and for twenty-two weeks headed the best-seller list in the United States. For many, Styron is the most important North American novelist of post-war years. For me, simply, *Lie Down in Darkness* is one of the great novels of our century: only Malcolm Lowry's *Under the Volcano* raised to a similar pitch the intensity and incandescence of the theme of the life of the individual: the difficulty of living, and the destruction in loving, of love. Styron uses as an epigraph to his work a quotation by Sir Thomas Browne: ". . . and therefore it cannot be long before we lie down in darkness and have our light in ashes: since the brother of death daily haunts us with dying momentos, and time that grows old in itself, bids us hope no long duration—divinity is a dream and folly of expectation." He might also have used these words of Saint Teresa of Avila: "Like Hell, love is hard and implacable."

The Hungarian critic and philosopher Georg Lukács has proposed Styron as the contemporary example of the historical, critical, and dialectical novelist. I would say that, more accurately, society and history are but one facet of Styron's work. True, his novels do situate us always in the opacity and density of a place and a time, and always imply a severe criticism of North American society. Slave-holding Virginia in 1830, and the underlying theme of oppressive history in *Nat Turner*. North American exile on the Amalfi coast, and the desolate perspective of the triumphant years of the Establishment in *Set This House on Fire*. A marine training camp in South Carolina, and the sadism of war in *The Long March*. The bourgeoisie and the contemporary South in *Lie Down in Darkness*. But Styron's South is not the idealized image of *Gone with the Wind*, nor the mythic image of *Absalom, Absalom*. The scent of Scarlett O'Hara's magnolia and the painful memories of William Faulkner have evaporated; this is the South of country clubs, dry martinis, and urbanity without *urbs:* the desolation of lonely crowds is transferred to the forsaken South, doubling its forlornness.

Because tragedy lies on the far shore of the verbal constructions of Styron: the knowledge of the unknown, the warning of insufficiency, voluntary destruction. And his novels are like bridges that unite history and tragedy across the abysses of the personal. Who crosses those bridges, who are those who meet halfway between the demands of society and the will of tragedy? Yes, it is these North Americans lost in the fogs of Puritanism and alcohol, uprootedness and exile, concupiscence and loneliness, which they both desire and reject: but Styron's greatness consists in making us feel that we too are those North Americans, that it is we who make love, drink, remember, and try to forget, the same as they. The specific epic of the founding of the North American dream disintegrates in the novels of Styron to re-emerge as tragic universality: that land of choice designated by God to trample, humble, and conquer in the name of "Manifest Destiny," that land of optimism and success, that land that had never known defeat, appears in the fictions of William Styron as a land devoured by its own secrets of loneliness, crime, corruption, and dissatisfaction; and in the act of recognizing its dark mask, it recognizes that the mask is the shared face of all men. One must not forget that Styron began to write during the beatified years of Truman and Eisenhower, years that seemed to assure the triumph of the "North American Dream" implacably, though sublimely, administered by what Wright Mills called the "Power Elite," years when from the pages of *Time* the Luce family proclaimed the splendor of "The American Century." If today the United States is captive to a violent sense of malaise and if the years between the first and last writings by Styron have witnessed the burning of Watts and Detroit, the assassinations of the Kennedy brothers and of Martin Luther King, the tragic buffoonery of Johnson, the youth rebellion, the encounters with the Chicago police, and the slaughters of My Lai, what is still true is that Styron, in *Lie Down in Darkness* and *The Long March,* was the novelist who touched the very bedrock of that malaise, who in the former novel convoked the spectre of the society the old were bequeathing to the young, demonstrating the personal impossibility, for some, of keeping it alive; and who, in *The Long March,* painted the diabolical picture of the mechanism of pointless, absurd war devouring itself as it is nourished by thousands of young that it degrades, marks, and mutilates forever.

"The wages of sin is not death, but isolation," says Styron in *Lie Down in Darkness,* and in his novels isolation appears as sin itself. The tragic tone of these works is born of the touching need of a few characters—Loftis, the father, and Peyton, his daughter, Lieutenant Culver, the ex-patriate Cass Kinssolving, the black insurgent Nat Turner—to break that isolation, to assume all sins, both their own and those of others, through love, compassion, exile, and when that is impossible, through revolution. They fulfill the acts of their lives knowing that they will fail. Their only vehicle for maintaining these tragic values is a novel: a verbal construction which at the moment it is written ceases to be reality and can only be the dual, fragile encounter between writing and reading.

Historic tone, tragic tone; but also a religious tone. The world is

struggle, and the world's struggle, in the novels of Styron, lies between simony and Pelagianism, between those who sell the secrets of
the spirit in exchange for money, and those who attempt the heretical
freedom of achieving grace without intermediaries. The simonist
world of capitalistic Anglo-Saxon Puritanism is perfectly and vividly
described in a few ordinary acts performed by Helen, the mother, in
Lie Down in Darkness: "She bore plates and dishes to the table like a
reluctant acolyte, votive, long-suffering, and there was menace in her
hurried tread, in those footsteps so quick and determined and cere-
monial. Like the trampling feet of some penitent no longer in love
with penitence . . ." Grace without intermediaries is achieved, in the
same novel, by a young girl who summer after summer awaits in the
fields of Virginia, a solitary meeting with a magician who wanders
through the fields only in the burning summer, and only for the child.
One summer, the magician does not appear. Grace will not return.
The child is no longer a child. She enters the simonist world of self-
compassion and self-hatred. And Styron shouts at his characters:
"What makes you believe you can allow yourself the luxury of this
compassion and this hatred?"

Styron is a militant citizen. He struggled on behalf of democratic
rights within the United States and against the criminal war of Vietnam. Even now [1969] he is arriving in Mexico from Chicago where he
was witness for the defense of the youths accused of conspiracy during
the demonstrations of the summer of 1968. I do not believe that
politics is the principal concern of the writer, but I do believe that in
our societies, characterized by an increasing concentration of power
and by a marked tendency toward fascist elitism—either technocratic
or underdeveloped—it is important that there exist an independent
intellectual class capable of criticizing power and of maintaining or
inventing the values that power, by its very nature, forgets, scorns, or
suppresses with force. Without an independent and courageous intellectual class to define its limits, power, all too easily, has but to extend
its empire of nothingness: an empire that leads always to death: sacri-
fices on the Aztec pyramid, the massacre of Saint Bartholomew, the
tortures of the Spanish Hapsburgs, Stalinist purges, Lidice and Auschwitz, Hiroshima and My Lai, Tlatelolco. To that Nothingness upon
which political power is supported in our time, the true writer responds with the All of real, multiple, and diverse experience. That is

why an attitude like that of Octavio Paz who renounced his post as Mexican Ambassador to India as a protest against the massacre of the Plaza de las Tres Culturas is so important to us. From this time forward it will be impossible to read Paz without taking into account the attitude that is the natural extension of his poetic expression. In the same way, Styron's response to the conflicts of his time is a natural extension of his narrative writing.

Because for a writer, in the beginning there will always be the word, and Styron is not a pamphleteer, but an artist. What he tells us about his country and its people he tells us with all the complexity, all the ambiguity, of language. That is why his last novel, *The Confessions of Nat Turner,* has often been so misunderstood. Those who expected from Styron a simple Manichaean declaration were frustrated. I said that the words of Styron extend between the shores of history and of tragedy; that bridge is the novel, and the novel is language. *Nat Turner,* a first-person narrative of the history of the first rebellious North American slave, of his birth, youth, love, rebellion, and execution, is founded in language as the first of all master-slave relationships. Nat is captured in the schizophrenia of language. As he is held by physical chains, the slave is constrained by the chains of two linguistic models which he alternately assumes: the openly servile pickaninny speech that the masters expect of their servant, and the secretly servile rhetoric, the language of the masters themselves imitated by the slave. The degradation of slavery presupposes a degradation of the language, and this is the truth which Styron has brought to life in the writing of *Nat Turner:* the Negro is a prisoner of the language of the elite, of the language of William Styron.

I speak of language, of course, as the heart of a culture. The rebellion of Nat Turner fails because he is incapable, still, of creating a new language and a new culture; but he will create them only if, in fact, he rebels again and again, adding failure upon failure: his success perhaps will be but the sum of his defeats. Styron instills power in paradox: he travels from the present to encounter a man of the past who is at the same time traveling toward him, but Styron does not carry with him the offering of an easy, reasonable, and finally philanthropic or condescending characterization of the rebellious Negro, rather the authentic tragedy of a culture and a language (Styron's own) as insufficient as those of the slave. Thanks to the masterly use of the first person (I emphasize this because the narrative technique has been one of the most criticized points of the book), Styron achieves the encounter between two alienations: the author's and that of the novel's protagonist, which is in this way converted into an encounter between excess and necessity.

Styron's imaginative feat in *Nat Turner* is not merely that of reproducing faithfully the past of slave-holding Virginia in 1830, but in creating a new and a true present, the present which only the novel (or poetry or myth) can create totally, deforming the false reality of the chronology of conventional reason to the end of forming and informing that total reality which, without literature, would never encounter its being: *jamais réel, toujours vrai.* This present is an encounter and a contamination: for that reason, *Nat Turner* is a thwarted, open-ended, incomplete book: it looks forward, not backward. Styron has taken the risk of creating a novel that is the point of encounter in the present of a future dreamed by Nat Turner and degraded by William Styron, of a past suffered by Nat Turner, and of a past suffered, also, by William Styron in the present. Perhaps without their book neither would have proof of his true existence, that is, of his shared existence.

It is in this tragic encounter between the denied man, who not being, was, and the man who denies himself, who discovers that being what others wished him to be—Christian, rational, and bourgeois—he ceases to be, that the extraordinary novel of Styron acquires its full significance. It is a novel of lost universality; it is a novel about the end of a language: the language of Reason, the Bible, Elegance, Puritanism, Pragmatism, and Optimism tempered by the suspicion of the Apocalypse. Styron kills his own language in order to provide an opportunity for language to be invented by free men. It is, finally, a novel about the ruin that history reserves as much for masters as for slaves. These words of Walter Benjamin might explain the novel of William Styron: "A Klee painting named 'Angelus Novus' shows an angel looking as though he is about to move away from something he is fixedly contemplating. His eyes are staring, his mouth is open, his wings are spread. This is how one pictures the angel of history. His face is turned toward the past. Where we perceive a chain of events, he sees one single catastrophe which keeps piling wreckage upon wreckage and hurls it in front of his feet."

From the center of this "historical meditation," as Styron himself has described *Nat Turner,* the novel speaks not only of a situation particular to the United States; it speaks also of the relations among open and closed forms of language, between inherited culture and unknown freedom; between suffered history and history still to be suffered; between the death of Man and the life of men in all the world; and certainly in our world, that of Latin America.

Translated by Margaret Sayers Peden

Jorge Luis Borges on Nathaniel Hawthorne

One of the greatest literary icons of all Argentine culture and perhaps Latin America's most influential writer, Jorge Luis Borges (1899–1986) was ironically Eurocentric in his intellectual pursuits. His early work includes many translations of English poetry and novels. Both English and Spanish were spoken in his household and most of his earliest readings were in English. A precocious child, Borges translated Oscar Wilde's *The Happy Prince* by the age of nine and published his first original story at thirteen. Although the early part of his career was devoted to poetry, he wrote mostly short stories and essays after the late 1930s. Borges reportedly wrote many of his stories while he worked as a librarian. He would finish the tasks assigned to him very quickly and then devote the rest of his workday to writing. His own fiction deviates from that of his Latin American colleagues in that, rather than reflecting reality, his works tend to create their own worlds, being purely metaphysical explorations completely divorced from politics or dogma. An endless labyrinth of obscure literary references and direct quotations from previously written works forces his readers to abandon their conventional visions of reality. His language is complex, precise, and perfect; his themes are cerebral and abstract. Among his more well known pieces are "Death and the Compass," "El Sur," and "Pierre Menard, Author of the *Quixote*." Borges was the director of the Argentine National Library under Juan Perón, and was omnipresent in Western academia, from the University of Buenos Aires to Harvard. He shared the Formentor International Publishers' Prize with Samuel Beckett in 1961. His passion for British and North American letters is well known, and among his favorite authors were Shakespeare, Poe, Hawthorne, and Melville. His complete fiction, essays, and poetry have been retranslated into English and published in three volumes by Viking. The lecture that follows was originally given at the Colegio Libre de Estudios Superiores, Buenos Aires, March 1949. It was collected in *Other Inquisitions: 1936–1952*.

I shall begin the history of American literature with the history of a metaphor; or rather, with some examples of that metaphor. I don't know who invented it; perhaps it is a mistake to suppose that metaphors can be invented. The real ones, those that formulate intimate connections between one image and another, have always existed; those we can still invent are the false ones, which are not worth inventing. The metaphor I am speaking of is the one that compares dreams to a theatrical performance. Quevedo used it in the seventeenth century at the beginning of the *Sueño de la muerte;* Luis de Góngora made it a part of the sonnet "Varia imaginación," where we read:

A dream is a playwright
Clothed in beautiful shadows
In a theatre fashioned on the wind.

In the eighteenth century Addison will say it more precisely. When the soul dreams (he writes) it is the theatre, the actors, and the audience. Long before, the Persian Omar Khayyām had written that the history of the world is a play that God—the multiform God of the pantheists—contrives, enacts, and beholds to entertain his eternity; long afterward, Jung the Swiss in charming and doubtless accurate volumes compares literary inventions to oneiric inventions, literature to dreams.

If literature is a dream (a controlled and deliberate dream, but fundamentally a dream) then Góngora's verses would be an appropriate epigraph to this story about American literature, and a look at Hawthorne, the dreamer, would be a good beginning. There are other American writers before him—Fenimore Cooper, a sort of Eduardo Gutiérrez infinitely inferior to Eduardo Gutiérrez; Washington Irving, a contriver of pleasant Spanish fantasies—but we can skip over them without any consequence.

Hawthorne was born in 1804 in the port of Salem, which suffered, even then, from two traits that were anomalous in America: it was a very old, but poor, city; it was a city in decadence. Hawthorne lived in that old and decaying city with the honest biblical name until 1836; he loved it with the sad love inspired by persons who do not love us, or by failures, illness, and manias; essentially it is not untrue to say that he never left his birthplace. Fifty years later, in London or Rome, he continued to live in his Puritan town of Salem; for example, when he denounced sculptors (remember that this was in the nineteenth century) for making nude statues.

His father, Captain Nathaniel Hawthorne, died in Surinam in 1808 of yellow fever; one of his ancestors, John Hawthorne, had been a judge in the witchcraft trials of 1692, in which nineteen women, among them the slave girl Tituba, were condemned to be executed by hanging. In those curious trials (fanaticism has assumed other forms in our time) Justice Hawthorne acted with severity and probably with sincerity. Nathaniel, our Nathaniel, wrote that his ancestor made himself so conspicuous in the martyrdom of the witches that possibly the blood of those unfortunate women had left a stain on him, a stain so deep as to be present still on his old bones in the Charter Street Cemetery if they had not yet turned to dust. After that picturesque note Hawthorne added that, not knowing whether his elders had repented and begged for divine mercy, he wished to do so in their name, begging that any curse that had fallen on their descendants would be pardoned from that day forward.

When Captain Hawthorne died, his widow, Nathaniel's mother, became a recluse in her bedroom on the second floor. The rooms of his sisters, Louise and Elizabeth, were on the same floor; Nathaniel's was on the top floor. The family did not eat together and they scarcely spoke to one another; their meals were left on trays in the hall. Nathaniel spent his days writing fantastic stories; at dusk he would go out for a walk. His furtive way of life lasted for twelve years. In 1837 he wrote to Longfellow: ". . . I have secluded myself from society; and yet I never meant any such thing, nor dreamed what sort of life I was going to lead. I have made a captive of myself, and put me into a dungeon, and now I cannot find the key to let myself out."

Hawthorne was tall, handsome, lean, dark. He walked with the rocking gait of a seaman. At that time children's literature did not exist (fortunately for boys and girls!). Hawthorne had read *Pilgrim's Progress* at the age of six; the first book he bought with his own money was *The Faërie Queene;* two allegories. Also, although his biographers may not say so, he read the Bible; perhaps the same Bible that the first Hawthorne, William Hawthorne, brought from England with a sword in 1630. I have used the word "allegories"; the word is important, perhaps imprudent or indiscreet, to use when speaking of the work of Hawthorne. It is common knowledge that Edgar Allan Poe accused Hawthorne of allegorizing and that Poe deemed both the activity and the genre indefensible. Two tasks confront us: first, to ascertain whether the allegorical genre is, in fact, illicit; second, to ascertain whether Nathaniel Hawthorne's works belong to that category.

The best refutation of allegories I know is Croce's; the best vindication, Chesterton's. Croce says that the allegory is a tiresome pleonasm, a collection of useless repetitions which shows us (for example) Dante led by Virgil and Beatrice and then explains to us, or gives us to understand, that Dante is the soul, Virgil is philosophy or reason or natural intelligence, and Beatrice is theology or grace. According to Croce's argument (the example is not his), Dante's first step was to think: "Reason and faith bring about the salvation of souls" or "Philosophy and theology lead us to heaven" and then, for *reason* or *philosophy* he substituted *Virgil* and for *faith* or *theology* he put *Beatrice,* all of which became a kind of masquerade. By that derogatory definition an allegory would be a puzzle, more extensive, boring, and unpleasant than other puzzles. It would be a barbaric or puerile genre, an aesthetic sport. Croce wrote that refutation in 1907; Chesterton had already refuted him in 1904 without Croce's knowing it. How vast and uncommunicative is the world of literature!

The page from Chesterton to which I refer is part of a monograph on the artist Watts, who was famous in England at the end of the nineteenth century and was accused, like Hawthorne, of allegorism. Chesterton admits that Watts has produced allegories, but he denies that the genre is censurable. He reasons that reality is interminably rich and that the language of men does not exhaust that vertiginous treasure. He writes:

> Man knows that there are in the soul tints more bewildering, more numberless, and more nameless than the colours of an autumn forest; . . . Yet he seriously believes that these things can every one of them, in all their tones and semi-tones, in all their blends and unions, be accurately represented by an arbitrary system of grunts and squeals. He believes that an ordinary civilized stockbroker can really produce out of his own inside noises which denote all the mysteries of memory and all the agonies of desire.

Later Chesterton infers that various languages can somehow correspond to the ungraspable reality, and among them are allegories and fables.

In other words, Beatrice is not an emblem of faith, a belabored and arbitrary synonym of the word *faith.* The truth is that something—a peculiar sentiment, an intimate process, a series of analogous states—

exists in the world that can be indicated by two symbols: one, quite insignificant, the sound of the word *faith;* the other, Beatrice, the glorious Beatrice who descended from Heaven and left her footprints in Hell to save Dante. I don't know whether Chesterton's thesis is valid; I do know that the less an allegory can be reduced to a plan, to a cold set of abstractions, the better it is. One writer thinks in images (Shakespeare or Donne or Victor Hugo, say), and another writer thinks in abstractions (Benda or Bertrand Russell); a priori, the former are just as estimable as the latter. However, when an abstract man, a reasoner, also wants to be imaginative, or to pass as such, then the allegory denounced by Croce occurs. We observe that a logical process has been embellished and disguised by the author to dishonor the reader's understanding, as Wordsworth said. A famous example of that ailment is the case of José Ortega y Gasset, whose good thought is obstructed by difficult and adventitious metaphors; many times this is true of Hawthorne. Outside of that, the two writers are antagonistic. Ortega can reason, well or badly, but he cannot imagine; Hawthorne was a man of continual and curious imagination; but he was refractory, so to speak, to reason. I am not saying he was stupid; I say that he thought in images, in intuitions, as women usually think, not with a dialectical mechanism.

One aesthetic error debased him: the Puritan desire to make a fable out of each imagining induced him to add morals and sometimes to falsify and to deform them. The notebooks in which he jotted down ideas for plots have been preserved; in one of them, dated 1836, he wrote: "A snake taken into a man's stomach and nourished there from fifteen years to thirty-five, tormenting him most horribly." That is enough, but Hawthorne considers himself obliged to add: "A type of envy or some other evil passion." Another example, this time from 1838: "A series of strange, mysterious, dreadful events to occur, wholly destructive of a person's happiness. He to impute them to various persons and causes, but ultimately finds that he is himself the sole agent. Moral, that our welfare depends on ourselves." Another, from the same year: "A person, while awake and in the business of life, to think highly of another, and place perfect confidence in him, but to be troubled with dreams in which this seeming friend appears to act the part of a most deadly enemy. Finally it is discovered that the dream-character is the true one. The explanation would be—the soul's instinctive perception." Better are those pure fantasies that do not look for a justification or moral and that seem to have no other substance than an obscure terror. Again, from 1838: "The situation of a man in the midst of a crowd, yet as completely in the power of another, life and all, as if they two were in the deepest solitude." The following, which Hawthorne noted five years later, is a variation of the above: "Some man of powerful character to command a person, morally subjected to him, to perform some act. The commanding person to suddenly die; and, for all the rest of his life, the subjected one continues to perform that act." (I don't know how Hawthorne would have written that story. I don't know if he would have decided that the act performed should be trivial or slightly horrible or fantastic or perhaps humiliating.) This one also has slavery—subjection to another—as its theme: "A rich man left by will his mansion and estate to a poor couple. They remove into it, and find there a darksome servant, whom they are forbidden by will to turn away. He becomes a torment to them; and, in the finale, he turns out to be the former master of the estate." I shall mention two more sketches, rather curious ones; their theme, not unknown to Pirandello or André Gide, is the coincidence or the confusion of the aesthetic plane and the common plane, of art and reality. The first one: "Two persons to be expecting some occurrence, and watching for the two principal actors in it, and to find that the occurrence is even then passing, and that they themselves are the two actors." The other is more complex: "A person to be writing a tale, and to find that it shapes itself against his intentions; that the characters act otherwise than he thought; that unforeseen events occur; and a catastrophe comes which he strives in vain to avert. It might shadow forth his own fate—he having made himself one of the personages." These games, these momentary confluences of the imaginative world and the real world—the world we pretend is real when we read—are, or seem to us, modern. Their origin, their ancient origin, is perhaps to be found in that part of the *Iliad* in which Helen of Troy weaves into her tapestry the battles and the disasters of the Trojan War even then in progress. Virgil must have been impressed by that passage, for the *Aeneid* relates that Aeneas, hero of the Trojan War, arrived at the port of Carthage and saw scenes from the war sculptured on the marble of a temple and, among the many images of warriors, he saw his own likeness. Hawthorne liked those contacts of the imaginary and the real, those reflections and duplications of art; and in the sketches I have mentioned we observe that he leaned toward the pantheistic notion that one man is the others, that one man is all men.

Something more serious than duplications and pantheism is seen in the sketches, something more serious for a man who aspires to be a novelist, I mean. It is that, in general, situations were Hawthorne's stimulus, Hawthorne's point of departure—situations, not characters. Hawthorne first imagined, perhaps unwittingly, a situation and then sought the characters to embody it. I am not a novelist, but I suspect that few novelists have proceeded in that fashion. "I believe that Schomberg is real," wrote Joseph Conrad about one of the most memorable characters in his novel *Victory,* and almost any novelist could honestly say that about any of his characters. The adventures of the *Quixote* are not so well planned, the slow and antithetical dialogues—reasonings, I believe the author calls them—offend us by their improbability, but there is no doubt that Cervantes knew Don Quixote well and could believe in him. Our belief in the novelist's belief makes up for any negligence or defect in the work. What does it matter if the episodes are unbelievable or awkward when we realize that the author planned them, not to challenge our credibility, but to define his characters? What do we care about the puerile scandals and the confused crimes of the hypothetical Court of Denmark if we believe in Prince Hamlet? But Hawthorne first conceived a situation, or a series of situations, and then elaborated the people his plan required. That method can produce, or tolerate, admirable stories because their brevity makes the plot more visible than the actors, but not admirable novels, where the general form (if there is one) is visible only at the end and a single badly invented character can contaminate the others with unreality. From the foregoing statement it will be inferred that Hawthorne's stories are better than Hawthorne's novels. I believe that is true. The twenty-four chapters of *The Scarlet Letter* abound in memorable passages, written in good and sensitive prose, but none of them has moved me like the singular story of "Wakefield" in the *Twice-Told Tales.*

Hawthorne had read in a newspaper, or pretended for literary reasons that he had read in a newspaper, the case of an Englishman who left his wife without cause, took lodgings in the next street and there, without anyone's suspecting it, remained hidden for twenty years. During that long period he spent all his days across from his house or watched it from the corner, and many times he caught a glimpse of his wife. When they had given him up for dead, when his wife had been resigned to widowhood for a long time, the man opened the door of his house one day and walked in—simply, as if he had been away only a few hours. (To the day of his death he was an exemplary husband.) Hawthorne read about the curious case uneasily and tried to understand it, to imagine it. He pondered on the subject; "Wakefield" is the conjectural story of that exile. The interpretations of the riddle can be infinite; let us look at Hawthorne's.

He imagines Wakefield to be a calm man, timidly vain, selfish, given to childish mysteries and the keeping of insignificant secrets; a dispassionate man of great imaginative and mental poverty, but capable of long, leisurely, inconclusive, and vague meditations; a constant husband, by virtue of his laziness. One October evening Wakefield bids farewell to his wife. He tells her—we must not forget we are at the beginning of the nineteenth century—that he is going to take the stagecoach and will return, at the latest, within a few days. His wife, who knows he is addicted to inoffensive mysteries, does not ask the reason for the trip. Wakefield is wearing boots, a rain hat, and an overcoat; he carries an umbrella and a valise. Wakefield—and this surprises me—does not yet know what will happen. He goes out, more or less firm in his decision to disturb or to surprise his wife by being away from home for a whole week. He goes out, closes the front door, then half opens it, and, for a moment, smiles. Years later his wife will remember that last smile. She will imagine him in a coffin with the smile frozen on his face, or in paradise, in glory, smiling with cunning and tranquility. Everyone will believe he has died but she will remember that smile and think that perhaps she is not a widow.

Going by a roundabout way, Wakefield reaches the lodging place where he has made arrangements to stay. He makes himself comfortable by the fireplace and smiles; he is one street away from his house and has arrived at the end of his journey. He doubts; he congratulates himself; he finds it incredible to be there already; he fears that he may have been observed and that someone may inform on him. Almost repentant, he goes to bed, stretches out his arms in the vast emptiness and says aloud: "I will not sleep alone another night." The next morning he awakens earlier than usual and asks himself, in amazement, what he is going to do. He knows that he has some purpose, but he has difficulty defining it. Finally he realizes that his purpose is to discover the effect that one week of widowhood will have on the virtuous Mrs. Wakefield. His curiosity forces him into the street. He murmurs, "I shall spy on my home from a distance." He walks, unaware of his direction; suddenly he realizes that force of habit has brought him, like a traitor, to his own door and that he is about to enter it. Terrified, he turns away. Have they seen him? Will they pursue him? At the corner he turns back and looks at his house; it seems different to him now, because he is already another man—a single night has caused a transformation in him, although he does not know it. The moral change that will condemn him to twenty years of exile has occurred in his soul. Here, then, is the beginning of the long adventure. Wakefield acquires a reddish wig. He changes his habits; soon he has established a new routine. He is troubled by the suspicion that his absence has not disturbed Mrs. Wakefield enough. He decides he will not return until he has given her a good scare. One day the druggist enters the house, another day the doctor. Wakefield is sad, but he fears that his sudden reappearance may aggravate the illness. Obsessed, he lets time pass; before he had thought, "I shall return in a few days," but now he thinks, "in a few weeks." And so ten years pass. For a long time he has not known that his conduct is strange. With all the lukewarm affection of which his heart is capable, Wakefield continues to love his wife, while she is forgetting him. One Sunday morning the two meet in the street amid the crowds of London. Wakefield has become thin; he walks obliquely, as though hiding or escaping; his low forehead is deeply wrinkled; his face, which was common before, is extraordinary, because of his extraordinary conduct. His small eyes wander or look inward. His wife has grown stout; she is carrying a prayer book and her whole person seems to symbolize a placid and resigned widowhood. She is accustomed to sadness and would not exchange it, perhaps, for joy. Face to face, the two look into each other's eyes. The crowd separates them, and soon they are lost within it. Wakefield hurries to his lodgings, bolts the door, and throws himself on the bed where he is seized by a fit of sobbing. For an instant he sees the miserable oddity of his life. "Wakefield, Wakefield! You are mad!" he says to himself.

Perhaps he is. In the center of London he has severed his ties with the world. Without having died, he has renounced his place and his privileges among living men. Mentally he continues to live with his wife in his home. He does not know, or almost never knows, that he is a different person. He keeps saying, "I shall soon go back," and he does not realize that he has been repeating these words for twenty years. In his memory the twenty years of solitude seem to be an interlude, a mere parenthesis. One afternoon, an afternoon like other afternoons, like the thousands of previous afternoons, Wakefield looks at his house. He sees that they have lighted the fire in the second-floor bedroom; grotesquely, the flames project Mrs. Wakefield's shadow on the ceiling. Rain begins to fall, and Wakefield feels a gust of cold air. Why should he get wet when his house, his home, is there. He walks heavily up the steps and opens the door. The crafty smile we already know is hovering, ghostlike, on his face. At last Wakefield has returned. Hawthorne does not tell us of his subsequent fate, but lets us guess that he was already dead, in a sense. I quote the final words: "Amid the seeming confusion of our mysterious world, individuals are so nicely adjusted to a system, and systems to one another, and to a whole, that by stepping aside for a moment a man exposes himself to a fearful risk of losing his place for ever. Like Wakefield, he may become, as it were, the Outcast of the Universe."

In that brief and ominous parable, which dates from 1835, we have already entered the world of Herman Melville, of Kafka—a world of enigmatic punishments and indecipherable sins. You may say that there is nothing strange about that, since Kafka's world is Judaism, and Hawthorne's, the wrath and punishments of the Old Testament. That is a just observation, but it applies only to ethics, and the horrible story of Wakefield and many stories by Kafka are united not only by a common ethic but also by a common rhetoric. For example, the protagonist's profound *triviality*, which contrasts with the magnitude of his perdition and delivers him, even more helpless, to the Furies. There is the murky background against which the nightmare is etched. Hawthorne invokes a romantic past in other stories, but the scene of this tale is middle-class London, whose crowds serve, moreover, to conceal the hero.

Here, without any discredit to Hawthorne, I should like to insert an observation. The circumstance, the strange circumstance, of perceiv-

ing in a story written by Hawthorne at the beginning of the nineteenth century the same quality that distinguishes the stories Kafka
wrote at the beginning of the twentieth must not cause us to forget
that Hawthorne's particular quality has been created, or determined,
by Kafka. "Wakefield" prefigures Franz Kafka, but Kafka modifies and
refines the reading of "Wakefield." The debt is mutual; a great writer
creates his precursors. He creates and somehow justifies them. What,
for example, would Marlowe be without Shakespeare?

The translator and critic Malcolm Cowley sees in "Wakefield" an
allegory of Nathaniel Hawthorne's curious life of reclusion. Schopenhauer has written the famous words to the effect that no act, no
thought, no illness is involuntary; if there is any truth in that opinion,
it would be valid to conjecture that Nathaniel Hawthorne left the
society of other human beings for many years so that the singular
story of Wakefield would exist in the universe, whose purpose may be
variety. If Kafka had written that story, Wakefield would never have
returned to his home; Hawthorne lets him return, but his return is no
less lamentable or less atrocious than is his long absence.

One of Hawthorne's parables which was almost masterly, but not
quite, because a preoccupation with ethics mars it, is "Earth's Holocaust." In that allegorical story Hawthorne foresees a moment when
men, satiated by useless accumulations, resolve to destroy the past.
They congregate at evening on one of the vast western plains of
America to accomplish the feat. Men come from all over the world.
They make a gigantic bonfire kindled with all the genealogies, all the
diplomas, all the medals, all the orders, all the judgments, all the coats
of arms, all the crowns, all the sceptres, all the tiaras, all the purple
robes of royalty, all the canopies, all the thrones, all the spirituous
liquors, all the bags of coffee, all the boxes of tea, all the cigars, all the
love letters, all the artillery, all the swords, all the flags, all the martial
drums, all the instruments of torture, all the guillotines, all the gallows
trees, all the precious metals, all the money, all the titles of property, all
the constitutions and codes of law, all the books, all the miters, all the
vestments, all the sacred writings that populate and fatigue the Earth.
Hawthorne views the conflagration with astonishment and even
shock. A man of serious mien tells him that he should be neither glad
nor sad, because the vast pyramid of fire has consumed only what was
consumable. Another spectator—the Devil—observes that the orga-

nizers of the holocaust have forgotten to throw away the essential element—the human heart—where the root of all sin resides, and that they have destroyed only a few forms. Hawthorne concludes as follows:

> The heart, the heart—there was the little yet boundless sphere wherein existed the original wrong of which the crime and misery of this outward world were merely types. Purify that inward sphere, and the many shapes of evil that haunt the outward, and which now seem almost our only realities, will turn to shadowy phantoms and vanish of their own accord; but if we go no deeper than the intellect, and strive, with merely that feeble instrument, to discern and rectify what is wrong, our whole accomplishment will be a dream, so unsubstantial that it matters little whether the bonfire, which I have so faithfully described, were what we choose to call a real event and a flame that would scorch the finger, or only a phosphoric radiance and a parable of my own brain.

Here Hawthorne has allowed himself to be influenced by the Christian, and specifically the Calvinist, doctrine of the inborn depravation of mankind and does not appear to have noticed that his parable of an illusory destruction of all things can have a philosophical as well as a moral interpretation. For if the world is the dream of Someone, if there is Someone who is dreaming us now and who dreams the history of the universe (that is the doctrine of the idealists), then the annihilation of religions and the arts, the general burning of libraries, does not matter much more than does the destruction of the trappings of a dream. The Mind that dreamed them once will dream them again; as long as the Mind continues to dream, nothing will be lost. The belief in this truth, which seems fantastic, caused Schopenhauer, in his book *Parerga und Paralipomena,* to compare history to a kaleidoscope, in which the figures, not the pieces of glass, change; and to an eternal and confused tragicomedy in which the roles and masks, but not the actors, change. The presentiment that the universe is a projection of our soul and that universal history lies within each man induced Emerson to write the poem entitled "History."

As for the fantasy of abolishing the past, perhaps it is worth remembering that this was attempted in China, with adverse fortune, three centuries before Christ. Herbert Allen Giles wrote that the prime minister Li Su proposed that history should begin with the new monarch, who took the title of First Emperor. To sever the vain pretensions of antiquity, all books (except those that taught agriculture, medicine, or astrology) were decreed confiscated and burned. Persons who concealed their books were branded with a hot iron and forced to work on the construction of the Great Wall. Many valuable works were destroyed; posterity owes the preservation of the Confucius canon to the abnegation and valor of obscure and unknown men of letters. It is said that so many intellectuals were executed for defying the imperial edict that melons grew in winter on the burial ground.

Around the middle of the seventeenth century that same plan appeared in England, this time among the Puritans, Hawthorne's ancestors. Samuel Johnson relates that in one of the popular parliaments convoked by Cromwell it was seriously proposed that the archives of the Tower of London be burned, that every memory of the past be erased, and that a whole new way of life should be started. In other words, the plan to abolish the past had already occurred to men and—paradoxically—is therefore one of the proofs that the past cannot be abolished. The past is indestructible; sooner or later all things will return, including the plan to abolish the past.

Like Stevenson, also the son of Puritans, Hawthorne never ceased to feel that the task of the writer was frivolous or, what is worse, even sinful. In the preface to *The Scarlet Letter* he imagines that the shadows of his forefathers are watching him write his novel. It is a curious passage. "What is he?" says one ancient shadow to the other. "A writer of story-books! What kind of a business in life—what mode of glorifying God, or being serviceable to mankind in his day and generation—may that be? Why, the degenerate fellow might as well have been a fiddler!" The passage is curious, because it is in the nature of a confidence and reveals intimate scruples. It harks back to the ancient dispute between ethics and aesthetics or, if you prefer, theology and aesthetics. One early example of this dispute was in the Holy Scriptures and forbade men to adore idols. Another example, by Plato, was in the *Republic*, Book X: "God creates the Archetype (the original idea) of the table; the carpenter makes an imitation of the Archetype; the painter, an imitation of the imitation." Another is by Mohammed, who declared that every representation of a living thing will appear before the Lord on the day of the Last Judgment. The angels will order the artisan to animate what he has made; he will fail to do so and they will cast him into Hell for a certain length of time. Some Moslem teachers maintain that only images that can project a shadow (sculptured images) are forbidden. Plotinus was said to be ashamed to dwell in a body, and he did not permit sculptors to perpetuate his features. Once, when a friend urged him to have his portrait painted, he replied, "It is enough to be obliged to drag around this image in which nature has imprisoned me. But why shall I consent to the perpetuation of the image of this image?"

Nathaniel Hawthorne solved that difficulty (which is not a mere illusion). His solution was to compose moralities and fables; he made or tried to make art a function of the conscience. So, to use only one example, the novel *The House of the Seven Gables* attempts to show that the evil committed by one generation endures and persists in its descendants, like a sort of inherited punishment. Andrew Lang has compared it to Émile Zola's novels, or to Émile Zola's theory of novels; to me the only advantage to be gained by the juxtaposition of those heterogeneous names is the momentary surprise it causes us to experience. The fact that Hawthorne pursued, or tolerated, a moral purpose does not invalidate, cannot invalidate his work. In the course of a lifetime dedicated less to living than to reading, I have been able to verify repeatedly that aims and literary theories are nothing but stimuli; the finished work frequently ignores and even contradicts them. If the writer has something of value within him, no aim, however trite or erroneous it may be, will succeed in affecting his work irreparably. An author may suffer from absurd prejudices, but it will be impossible for his work to be absurd if it is genuine, if it responds to a genuine vision. Around 1916 the novelists of England and France believed (or thought they believed) that all Germans were devils; but they presented them as human beings in their novels. In Hawthorne the germinal vision was always true; what is false, what is ultimately false, are the moralities he added in the last paragraph or the characters he conceived, or assembled, in order to represent that vision. The characters in *The Scarlet Letter*—especially Hester Prynne, the heroine—are more independent, more autonomous, than those in his other stories; they are more like the inhabitants of most novels and not mere projections of Hawthorne, thinly disguised. This objectivity, this relative and partial objectivity, is perhaps the reason why two such acute (and dissimilar) writers as Henry James and Ludwig Lewisohn called *The Scarlet Letter* Hawthorne's masterpiece, his definitive testimony. But I would venture to differ with those two authorities. If a person longs for objectivity, if he hungers and thirsts for objectivity, let him look for it in Joseph Conrad or Tolstoi; if a person looks for the peculiar flavor of Nathaniel Hawthorne, he will be less apt to find it in the laborious novels than on some random page or in the trifling and pathetic stories. I don't know exactly how to justify my difference of opinion; in the three American novels and *The Marble Faun* I see only a series of situations, planned with professional skill to affect the reader, not a spontaneous and lively activity of the imagination. The imagination (I repeat) has planned the general plot and the digressions, not the weaving together of the episodes and the psychology—we have to call it by some name—of the actors.

Johnson observes that no writer likes to owe something to his contemporaries; Hawthorne was as unaware of them as possible. Perhaps he did the right thing; perhaps our contemporaries—always—seem too much like us, and if we are looking for new things we shall find them more easily in the ancients. According to his biographers, Hawthorne did not read De Quincey, did not read Keats, did not read Victor Hugo—who did not read each other, either. Groussac would not admit that an American could be original; he denounced "the notable influence of Hoffmann" on Hawthorne, an opinion that appears to be based on an impartial ignorance of both writers. Hawthorne's imagination is romantic; in spite of certain excesses, his style belongs to the eighteenth century, to the feeble end of the admirable eighteenth century.

I have quoted several fragments from the journal Hawthorne kept to entertain his long hours of solitude; I have given brief résumés of two stories; now I shall quote a page from *The Marble Faun* so that you may read Hawthorne's own words. The subject is that abyss or well that opened up, according to Latin historians, in the center of the Forum; a Roman, armed and on horseback, threw himself into its blind depths to propitiate the gods. Hawthorne's text reads as follows:

> "Let us settle it," said Kenyon, "that this is precisely the spot where the chasm opened, into which Curtius precipitated his good steed and himself. Imagine the great, dusky gap, impenetrably deep, and with

half-shaped monsters and hideous faces looming upward out of it, to the vast affright of the good citizens who peeped over the brim! Within it, beyond a question, there were prophetic visions,—intimations of all the future calamities of Rome,—shades of Goths, and Gauls, and even of the French soldiers of today. It was a pity to close it up so soon! I would give much for a peep into such a chasm."

"I fancy," remarked Miriam, "that every person takes a peep into it in moments of gloom and despondency; that is to say, in his moments of deepest insight.

"The chasm was merely one of the orifices of that pit of blackness that lies beneath us, everywhere. The firmest substance of human happiness is but a thin crust spread over it, with just reality enough to bear up the illusive stage-scenery amid which we tread. It needs no earthquake to open the chasm. A footstep, a little heavier than ordinary, will serve; and we must step very daintily, not to break through the crust at any moment. By and by, we inevitably sink! It was a foolish piece of heroism in Curtius to precipitate himself there, in advance; for all Rome, you see, has been swallowed up in that gulf, in spite of him. The Palace of the Caesars has gone down thither, with a hollow, rumbling sound of its fragments! All the temples have tumbled into it; and thousands of statues have been thrown after! All the armies and the triumphs have marched into the great chasm, with their martial music playing, as they stepped over the brink . . ."

From the standpoint of reason, of mere reason—which should not interfere with art—the fervent passage I have quoted is indefensible. The fissure that opened in the middle of the Forum is too many things. In the course of a single paragraph it is the crevice mentioned by Latin historians and it is also the mouth of Hell "with half-shaped monsters and hideous faces"; it is the essential horror of human life; it is Time, which devours statues and armies, and Eternity, which embraces all time. It is a multiple symbol, a symbol that is capable of many, perhaps incompatible, values. Such values can be offensive to reason, to logical understanding, but not to dreams, which have their singular and secret algebra, and in whose ambiguous realm one thing may be many. Hawthorne's world is the world of dreams. Once he planned to write a dream, "which shall resemble the real course of a dream, with all its inconsistency, its eccentricities and aimlessness," and he was amazed that no one had ever done such a thing before. The same journal in which he wrote about that strange plan—which our "modern" literature tries vainly to achieve and which, perhaps, has only been achieved by Lewis Carroll—contains his notes on thousands of trivial impressions, small concrete details (the movement of a hen, the shadow of a branch on the wall); they fill six volumes and their inexplicable abundance is the consternation of all his biographers. "They read like a series of very pleasant, though rather dullish and decidedly formal, letters, addressed to himself by a man who, having suspicions that they might be opened in the post, should have determined to insert nothing compromising." Henry James wrote that, with obvious perplexity. I believe that Nathaniel Hawthorne recorded those trivialities over the years to show himself that he was real, to free himself, somehow, from the impression of unreality, of ghostliness, that usually visited him.

One day in 1840 he wrote:

Here I sit in my old accustomed chamber, where I used to sit in days gone by . . . Here I have written many tales—many that have been burned to ashes, many that have doubtless deserved the same fate. This claims to be called a haunted chamber, for thousands upon thousands of visions have appeared to me in it; and some few of them have become visible to the world . . . And sometimes it seems to me as if I were already in the grave, with only life enough to be chilled and benumbed. But oftener I was happy . . . And now I begin to understand why I was imprisoned so many years in this lonely chamber, and why I could never break through the viewless bolts and bars; for if I had sooner made my escape into the world, I should have grown hard and rough, and been covered with earthly dust, and my heart might have become callous . . . Indeed, we are but shadows . . ."

In the lines I have just quoted, Hawthorne mentions "thousands upon thousands of visions." Perhaps this is not an exaggeration; the twelve volumes of Hawthorne's complete works include more than a hundred stories, and those are only a few of the very many he outlined in his journal. (Among the stories he finished, one—"Mr. Higginbotham's Catastrophe"—prefigures the detective story that Poe was to invent.) Miss Margaret Fuller, who knew him in the utopian community of Brook Farm, wrote later, "Of that ocean we have had only a few drops," and Emerson, who was also a friend of his, thought Hawthorne had never given his full measure. Hawthorne married in 1842, when he was thirty-eight; until that time his life had been almost purely imaginative, mental. He worked in the Boston customhouse; he served as United States consul at Liverpool; he lived in Florence, Rome, and London. But his reality was always the filmy twilight, or lunar world, of the fantastic imagination.

At the beginning of this essay I mentioned the doctrine of the psychologist Jung, who compared literary inventions to oneiric inventions, or literature to dreams. That doctrine does not seem to be applicable to the literatures written in the Spanish language, which deal in dictionaries and rhetoric, not fantasy. On the other hand, it does pertain to the literature of North America, which (like the literatures of England or Germany) tends more toward invention than transcription, more toward creation than observation. Perhaps that is the reason for the curious veneration North Americans render to realistic works, which induces them to postulate, for example, that Maupassant is more important than Hugo. It is within the power of a North American writer to be Hugo, but not, without violence, Maupassant. In comparison with the literature of the United States, which has produced several men of genius and has had its influence felt in England and France, our Argentine literature may possibly seem somewhat provincial. Nevertheless, in the nineteenth century we produced some admirable works of realism—by Echeverría, Ascasubi, Hernández, and the forgotten Eduardo Gutiérrez—the North Americans have not surpassed (perhaps have not equaled) them to this day. Someone will object that Faulkner is no less brutal than our Gaucho writers. True, but his brutality is of the hallucinatory sort—the infernal, not the terrestrial sort of brutality. It is the kind that issues from dreams, the kind inaugurated by Hawthorne.

Hawthorne died on May 18, 1864, in the mountains of New Hampshire. His death was tranquil and it was mysterious, because it occurred in his sleep. Nothing keeps us from imagining that he died while dreaming and we can even invent the story that he dreamed—the last of an infinite series—and the manner in which death completed or erased it. Perhaps I shall write it some day; I shall try to redeem this deficient and too digressive essay with an acceptable story.

Van Wyck Brooks in *The Flowering of New England,* D. H. Lawrence in *Studies in Classic American Literature,* and Ludwig Lewisohn in *Story of American Literature* analyze and evaluate the work of Hawthorne. There are many biographies. I have used the one Henry James wrote in 1879 for the English Men of Letters Series.

When Hawthorne died, the other writers inherited his task of dreaming. At some future time we shall study, if your indulgence permits, the glory and the torment of Poe, in whom the dream was exalted to a nightmare.

Translated by Ruth L. C. Simms

Gabriel García Márquez on William Faulkner

Perhaps the greatest ambassador of Latin American letters to the international literary scene, Gabriel García Márquez (Colombia, b. 1928) authored what is considered one of the greatest books written in the Spanish language: *One Hundred Years of Solitude* (1967). This masterpiece inherited many of its themes and characters from earlier works, such as *Leaf Storm* (1955), *La mala hora* (1962), *No One Writes to the Colonel* (1962), and *Los funerales de Mamá Grande* (1962). His exquisite manipulation of magical realism and brilliant insight into Latin American society have made García Márquez both a favorite of scholars and a best-seller. In his works, he has been primarily concerned with the modern exploration of Greek myths, literary experimentation with both time and space, and psychoanalysis as it pertains to dreams. García Márquez is perhaps the most renowned of Latin America's so-called Boom writers, who brought the continent's literature international recognition, and he was awarded the Nobel Prize for Literature in 1982. He is also responsible for *Love in the Time of Cholera* (1985), *Strange Pilgrims* (1993), and *News of a Kidnapping* (1996), among other books. His primary literary influences, he has repeatedly stated, were Knut Hamsun and—as the following opinion piece makes clear—William Faulkner. The brief, enthusiastic comment, a reaction to the news from Stockholm that Faulkner had been awarded the Nobel Prize for Literature, was first published in *El Heraldo*, Barranquilla, Colombia, 13 November 1950. It appears in English in edited form.

Shockingly, the Nobel Prize for Literature for once has been awarded to a remarkable writer: William Faulkner. The globe's greatest living novelist and one of the most intriguing and impressive authors of all time is finally recognized. In his secluded house in Oxford, Mississippi, he must have received the news with the coldness with which one greets a late arrival. The Nobel Prize will not add anything to his long literary career; instead, it will turn him into a fashionable item, granting him an uncomfortable privilege he never sought.

The honor represents a surprising break with tradition. It shall undoubtedly compromise the judgment of Nobel committee members. Its importance and danger lie therein, for the choice demonstrates that judges adopted higher standards; a return to the question-able criteria of previous years is now difficult. If Faulkner received the award because of his merits rather than due to the short-sighted com-mittee judgment, then all dubious authors aspiring to this most pres-tigious prize are hereby automatically eliminated.

The prize is meant as a recognition of a life achievement. Hence, those of us who admire Faulkner face the difficulty of equating him with Pearl Buck, Herman Hesse, and Thomas Mann. Is anything more disturbing than for his legacy to be equated with that of the pygmies that make up the Nobel archives?

Unable to bear their humiliating ignorance, those unfamiliar with the master will now make every effort to know his fascinating and extraordinary characters on a personal basis: the Sartoris clan will surely be cited as a symbol of the wounded, decadent American South; and the Snopes shall be known as the angry fermentation of a future violently created through a direct confrontation with Nature. People will focus their attention on the small town of Oxford, a town full of tormented black people who know little about Nobel Prizes. Those people are probably the only ones who truly understand that the accomplishments of the man who discovered the neglected Yokna-patawpha continent within the splendor of modern America cannot be reduced to solemn award ceremonies.

Translated by José Matosantos

Hiber Conteris on Raymond Chandler

Born in Uruguay in 1941, Hiber Conteris lives in exile in the United States, where he came after he was imprisoned during Uruguay's dictatorship in the 1970s. He is a professor of Spanish at Alfred University. Among his works are his celebrated novel *Ten Percent of Life* (1987), a postmodern tribute to Raymond Chandler and the city of Los Angeles, and a collection of short stories entitled *Información sobre la ruta 9* (1984), for which Conteris was awarded the Letras de Oro Award. He is considered a crucial voice in Latin America's detective fiction, along with the Mexican writer Paco Ignacio Taibo II. He has published a vast quantity of essays pertaining to this genre, as well as many others on Latin American literature in general. This essay was written 18 April 1995. This is its first appearance in print.

I

How did I become acquainted with the writing of Raymond Chandler? I can't remember the exact date when I read one of his novels or short stories for the first time—which is probably a good reason to assume that what I read didn't leave a very deep impression on me. It was, undoubtedly, a time in my life in which my literary preferences were oriented toward another type of fiction, most likely that kind of narrative devoted to the service of any cause, whether political, philosophical, or simply aesthetic. A time in which my paradigms were Kafka's *The Trial* and Camus's *L'Etranger; Point Counter Point* by Aldous Huxley and *Homo Faber* by the Swiss Max Frisch; Faulkner's *Sound and the Fury* and Fitzgerald's *Tender Is the Night;* the *Ficciones* of Jorge Luis Borges, the Argentine Ernesto Sábato's *On Heroes and Tombs,* and *Pedro Páramo* by the Mexican author Juan Rulfo. Such a list could easily be extended yet further. The works by Chandler that I read at that time didn't enter into my personal canon. They were, most likely, chance readings, incidental, what one is mistakenly accustomed to calling "a simple pastime." Readings that served as distraction during hours of boredom, leisure, or rest, or provoked by one of those rare moments in which one casts a hand onto the nearest book in order to fend off assorted forms of nostalgia and melancholia.

No, I cannot retrieve my Chandler readings of that time, obscured by such an ensemble of writers and titles grouped together without any greater order in my personal Parnassus. On the other hand, I remember with utmost precision one Sunday in December in 1973, when without much in the way of alternative plan, two of my friends and I decided that the best thing that could be done on that wintry and rainy afternoon was to go to a movie theater in Leicester Square where they were showing *The Long Goodbye*, a film by Robert Altman based on the novel by Raymond Chandler, which critics—almost without exception—consider Chandler's masterpiece. The performance probably lasted something like two hours, but when we went out again, into the night rain, I experienced the sensation of having been transported to another place, a world that evoked the coasts of Pacific California and the neon lights of Los Angeles. That ambience had been injected into my retina by the film's images, and those same images had had the strange property of reanimating in an obscure zone of my memory names, places, and characters which without my realizing it had installed themselves there during my sporadic readings of some stories and perhaps one or two novels by Chandler. That was my almost virginal initiation to the work of Chandler, and the beginning of a long and inconclusive search that undertook to comprise the particulars of his turbulent biography, his professional activity, his passages through *Black Mask* and through Hollywood, his artistic and intellectual creation, his relationships with editors, literary agents, and other writers, and the almost sole love relationship of his life. And as a consequence of that diffuse exploration, I had my introduction into that strata of Californian society where crime and violence germinate, and which, according to virtually unanimous opinion, Chandler had succeeded in dissecting and exhibiting as no one had ever done before.

II

Since I mentioned Leicester Square, it should be obvious that when that rediscovery of the work and world of Raymond Chandler occurred, I was in London. I had traveled there in the company of two

Argentine friends who like myself were doing graduate studies at the Catholic University of Louvain. We had planned to stay a month in London in order to practice and perfect our English; find temporary jobs that might help us pay for expenses; explore the nightlife in Soho, the Pubs of Chelsea and Kensington Road, the Greek restaurants in Earl's Court; and if luck and money held out, to attend one of the concerts by Pink Floyd that was scheduled during those December days. Our intention was to return to Louvain before the end of the year. Having seen *The Long Goodbye* that Sunday didn't modify that project essentially; but instead, as I said before, it opened up a completely unexpected perspective on my literary tastes and preferences and also initiated an investigation whose results would not be concretized until years later, under circumstances that I could not, with even the most remote effort of the imagination, have predicted in the middle of that London winter.

Initially, neither the critical establishment nor the general public was particularly kind to Altman's film adaptation. The film opened in March 1973 and was closed down a few weeks later, due to what, according to Hollywood criteria, was considered a financial disaster. The critical reviews that followed immediately after the film's opening contributed to this relative failure. As Stephen Pendo recounts, *Variety* considered the film "an uneven mixture of insider satire of the gumshoe genre . . . [that] features a strong cast and an improbable plot." *Time* was even harsher, affirming that "Altman's lazy, haphazard putdown is without affection or understanding, a nose-thumb not only at the idea of Philip Marlowe but at the genre that his tough-guy–soft-heart character epitomized." And the *Los Angeles Times*'s critic Charles Champlin found the movie "distasteful" and ended his review sardonically: "You don't have to admire Chandler to regret the movie, but it helps."

In spite of this chilly critical and box-office reception, United Artists refused to abandon the film. The company had invested more than $1,700,000 in its production, and therefore resolved to attempt a reopening in the fall, without cuts or any other changes, although preceded this time by a new publicity campaign. The reopening took place in October, in New York City, and the reaction by the critics was totally different. The *New Yorker* celebrated its arrival in this way: "*The Long Goodbye* reaches a satirical dead end that kisses off the private-eye form . . . gracefully. . . . It's a knockout of a movie . . . probably the best American movie ever made that almost didn't open in New York. . . . It seems unbelievable that people who looked at this picture could have given it the reviews they did." The *New York Times* was no less enthusiastic: "In *The Long Goodbye* Robert Altman . . . attempts the impossible and pulls it off. . . . The film . . . is Altman's most entertaining, most richly complex film since *M.A.S.H.* and *McCabe and Mrs. Miller.* It's so good that I don't know where to begin describing it." One of the few voices that did not join in this chorus of praise was Andrew Sarris, in the *Village Voice,* who admitted that *"The Long Goodbye* contains some incidental virtues, but . . . rides off furiously in too many different directions with too many gratuitously Godardian camera movements to make even a good movie." Nevertheless, according to a comment that appeared in *Variety,* the magazine which before had so harshly criticized the film, "ten out of fifteen New York critics reviewed it favorably," and another article from the same magazine, published in January of 1974, confirmed it as one of the ten best of the year.

According to Stephen Pendo, whom I follow in this description, "production of the film involved three interesting aspects. First, the picture was shot entirely on location (no sound stages were used). Scenes in Los Angeles included Marlowe's house in back of the Hollywood Bowl; the Malibu Beach Colony (the new skyscraper at 9000 Sunset Boulevard); a $65,000 per client, per year Pasadena rest home, Westwood and Hollywood offices; the now-unused Lincoln Heights jail in East Los Angeles," and many other places, including the villages of Tepoztlan and Chinconcuac for the Mexican scenes. "Second, the entire film's negative was exposed to varying amounts of light after exposure and before developing, a technique called post-flashing. Perfected by director of photography Vilmos Zsigmond and Technicolor labs, this process had the effect of reducing color intensities to pastel levels"; according to Zsigmond's own words, "We did not want to recreate the fifties, but to remember them. . . . So what we decided to do was to put the picture into pastels. . . . Pastels are for memory. . . . The blue shading in night effects also will give a feeling of the fifties." And thirdly, Zsigmond used a constantly moving camera, explaining the procedure in this way: "Every shot was a moving shot. The camera was constantly in motion, slowly dollying back and forth along the track without apparent rhyme or reason during both the masters and the close-ups. . . . These slight moves, coupled with very slow zooms in and out, gave a feeling of improvisation and a three-dimensional quality as objects and people changed their relationships to one another.

Probably none of these technical aspects of the film influenced my reevaluation of Chandler's work in a conscious or decisive way, simply because at that time I didn't have the information I have at my disposal now, nor had my initiation into the resources of the cinematographic art reached the level of sophistication necessary for appreciating the technical subtleties of its achievement. The impact that the film had on me had another explanation. The best way of describing it is to say that it worked as a catalyst or another similar form of stimulus, revealing to me suddenly the most incisive, suggestive, and original components of Chandler's narrative. Certainly I had absorbed those elements subconsciously, or better said, they had been implanted there, in some section of the chromosomatic chain of my imagination or in my fantasies, but had remained there in a state of incubation or of lethargy, awaiting the magical instant of resurrection, until the contact with the Altman film succeeded finally in accelerating the process.

III

What are the elements of the Chandlerian narrative that have caused it to have such a powerful impact on the literature and society of its time? That impact is so much more significant if one takes into account how slim in volume that narrative is in comparison with the output of any of the great North American writers of that period (Hemingway and Faulkner, for example), and it comes as an even greater surprise if one thinks that the most important of Chandler's works (that is, the portion of his work that until today has been considered his most original contribution and that maintains its validity) was confined to what was considered by the "serious reader" to be second-class literature, *mystery stories,* or to use an expression that describes more specifically his manner of cultivating the genre, *hard-boiled* fiction.

There is no doubt that the originality of Chandler's contribution to fiction (and not only to the mystery or detective novel, the hard-boiled fiction, or the French *roman noir*) can be analyzed and broken down into three or four essential aspects, but the greatest impact that his work has on the reader stems not from the effect of isolated elements, but from something that could be described as an enveloping atmosphere that predominates in each of his stories. That atmosphere possesses an irresistible power of seduction, and if the reader is sensitive to its influence, he or she will feel immediately immersed in that ambience, installed there by an almost hypnotic process, until the point at which everything that occurs in that setting will seem plausible, logical, and even familiar. It is not necessary to have been born in or to have lived in Los Angeles for this to happen. A rare testimony of this hypnotic fascination that Chandler's writing is capable of producing can be found in the novel *Lancelot* (1977) by Walker Percy. In that novel, Lancelot Lamar, the protagonist-narrator, is confined in a New Orleans "Center for Aberrant Behavior." Seated in his *pigeonnier,* and after having surveyed the principal circumstances of his life, he admits that he feels "moderately happy." "The reason I was happy," he continues,

> was that I was reading for perhaps the fourth or fifth time a Raymond Chandler novel. It gave me pleasure (no, I'll put it more strongly: it didn't just give me pleasure, it was the only way I could stand my life) to sit there in old goldgreen Louisiana under the levee and read, not about General Beauregard, but about Philip Marlowe taking a bottle out of his desk drawer in his crummy office in seedy Los Angeles in 1933 and drinking alone and all those from-nowhere people living in stucco bungalows perched in Laurel Canyon. The only way I could stand my life in Louisiana, where I had everything, was to read about crummy lonesome Los Angeles in the 1930's. Maybe that should have told me something. If I was happy, it was an odd sort of happiness.

This no-less-than-magical re-creation of the atmosphere of a city is what has given the texts of Chandler their distinctive stamp, and it was precisely this which I must have experienced when I emerged into the nocturnal rain of Leicester Square after having been immersed for almost two hours in the carefully faded-out images and the pastel spectrum of *The Long Goodbye.* In a 1902 article, many years before Chandler would write his first stories, G. K. Chesterton had already written his famous defense of the detective novel, anticipating this essential characteristic of the Chandlerian narrative:

The first essential value of the detective story lies in this, that it is the earliest and only form of popular literature in which is expressed some sense of the poetry of the modern life. Men lived among mighty mountains and eternal forests for ages before they realized that they were poetical; it may reasonably be inferred that some of our descendants may see the chimney-pots as rich a purple as the mountain-peaks, and find the lamp-posts as old and natural as the trees. Of this realization of a great city itself as something wild and obvious, the detective story is certainly the "Iliad." No one can have failed to notice that in these stories the hero or the investigator crosses London with something of the loneliness and liberty of a prince in a tale of elfland, that in the course of that incalculable journey the casual omnibus assumes the primal colours of a fairy ship. The lights of the city begin to glow like innumerable goblin eyes, since they are the guardians of some secret, however crude, which the writer knows and the reader does not. Every twist of the road is like a finger pointing to it; every fantastic skyline of chimney-pots seems wildly and derisively signalling the meaning of the mystery.

I believe I can justify this extensive quotation because it alludes not only to that "realization of a great city itself as something wild and obvious," but also to other aspects of the detective novel that will reappear in a completely spontaneous manner in the work of Chandler. (I don't think that he had the Chesterton essay in mind when he arrived at the essential formula that is repeated in a more or less invariable manner in each of his novels.) There is a brief passage in *The Little Sister* (1949), Chandler's fifth novel, that condenses particularly well Chesterton's observation not only with regard to the poetry of the modern city but to the "hero or the investigator" who "crosses London [Los Angeles, in Chandler's case] with something of the loneliness and liberty of a prince in a tale of elfland." Driving across Los Angeles, Marlowe stops at a roadside restaurant, where he parodies the owner's mentality, and later drives as far north as Oxnard and returns along the sea: "On the right the great solid Pacific trudging into shore like a scrub-woman going home. No moon, no fuss, hardly a sound of the surf. No smell. None of the harsh wild smell of the sea. A California ocean." But suddenly, on this oceanic perspective, the city of Los Angeles emerges: "I smelled Los Angeles before I got to it. It smelled stale and old like a living room that had been closed too long.

Hiber Conteris on Raymond Chandler　**93**

But the colored lights fooled you. The lights were wonderful. There ought to be a monument to the man who invented neon lights. Fifteen stories high, solid marble. There's a boy who really made something out of nothing."

The creation of the character Philip Marlowe is another reason explaining the immediate success of Chandler's novels and their translation to cinema, radio, and later to television. Of course, the construction of a prototype, whether the private eye, inspector of police, or amateur investigator, who travels from one story to another within the author's oeuvre, and which grants it a certain unity, is not an invention of Chandler's, nor an exclusive characteristic of his narrative. Dashiell Hammett had already created his Sam Spade, and long before him Edgar Allan Poe his Auguste Dupin, Arthur Conan Doyle his Sherlock Holmes, and Agatha Christie her Hercule Poirot. Actually, this seems to be one of the unwritten rules of the detective novel, and almost all the great writers of the genre continued with that tradition. Georges Simenon conceived the Inspector Maigret; Robert B. Parker, Spenser; Ross McDonald, Lew Archer; Dorothy Sayers, Lord Peter Wimsey; and the list could be extended indefinitely. What gives Philip Marlowe his particular idiosyncrasy is the fact that Chandler—deliberately or not—avoided copying the prototype of the supertalented, hypercharismatic, no-less-than-indestructible investigator, endowing his character instead with a moderate set of virtues and weaknesses that are commonly found in all human beings. Even then, the invention of Marlowe came to be such a determining factor in Chandler's literary evolution that critics distinguish a "Chandler before Marlowe" and another after him, the latter being the author that continues to be read and republished even today.

In the cinema and on television the character of Philip Marlowe was interpreted successively by Dick Powell (*Murder, My Sweet*, 1945, a film based on the novel *Farewell, My Lovely*, 1940); Humphrey Bogart (*The Big Sleep*, 1946); Robert Montgomery (*Lady in the Lake*, 1947); George Montgomery (*The Brasher Doubloon*, 1947, a film based on *The High Window*, 1942); James Garner (*Marlowe*, 1969, based on *The Little Sister*, 1949), who also incarnated the character in a television series of the same name; Elliot Gould (*The Long Goodbye*, 1973); and finally Robert Mitchum (*Farewell, My Lovely*, 1975). No actor occupied the role in more than one film, which is certainly proof of the difficulty in converting the character into a simple stereotype. Stephen Pendo, who reviews each of these Marlowe interpretations in his book, has established his own preferences. Dick Powell and Humphrey Bogart seem to share first place. With respect to the former, says Pendo: "Powell is a superb Marlowe. He manages to blend his own slightly boyish charm and innocence perfectly into the character. His terse narration and dialogue composed of Chandler and Chandler-type lines effectively captures the spirit of Chandler's hero." The praise for Bogart's performance is similar: "Without a doubt, Bogart superbly personifies Marlowe, and several things contribute to his characterization. The rapid-fire delivery of his lines makes him the sharpest-tongued Marlowe. . . . Bogart so characterizes the role, in fact, that one is apt, as one critic suggested, to adjust the Marlowe character to fit Bogart and not the other way around." Pendo also seems to judge Robert Mitchum's interpretation favorably, reproducing four different critical opinions which affirm that "the part of Philip Marlowe has been waiting thirty years for Robert Mitchum to claim it" (Dick Richards), or else that "Mitchum gives strength, credence and sympathy to his Marlowe" (Rex Reed), or "we couldn't have a better choice" (Bob Salmmaggi), and finally, "Mitchum is altogether superb, possibly the best Marlowe of all" (Bernard Drew).

Stephen Pendo seems to have reservations with regard to the Marlowe re-creations of James Garner and Elliot Gould. Pendo admits that "Garner has some of Dick Powell's boyish charm," and "some of Humphrey Bogart's or Powell's flair for comedy," and also "physically, he more closely matches Chandler's detective than any other actor who has played the detective." However, "the chief criticism of the film was that Chandler's Marlowe and what he stood for were out of date when the film was made. There existed no possibility for such a romantic hero to survive the transition to modern day society." As for the Philip Marlowe that Elliot Gould composed for *The Long Goodbye*, the objections are even more serious, and are leveled as much at the actor as at the adaptation that Robert Altman and Leigh Brackett (screenwriter) proposed for the character. "Gould agreed with Brackett's and Altman's interpretation of Marlowe and played him perfectly in keeping with their ideas. Gould, then, becomes a new Marlowe: a loser whose outdated morals make him out of place in contemporary society. He shrugs off society's rebuffs with an 'I don't know' or 'That's okay.' He is totally asexual, going against the established 'Marlowe' film image." And finally, Pendo epitomizes his judgment of *The Long Goodbye*'s Marlowe in this way: "Gould's Marlowe is, of course, largely an ineffectual character out of place in society, but it doesn't bother him; he survives. He has physically, if not spiritually, made it from the fifties into the seventies. The sentimental, pessimistic Marlowe of the novel probably would never have survived the transition. Altman intended the film to 'put Marlowe to rest for good,' but he need not have bothered to try. Chandler did that better than anybody else, and a straight film version of the depressing novel would have laid our hero to rest far more effectively than the attempt made here."

My own opinion on the Altman film and the Philip Marlowe created by Elliot Gould differs in some fundamental respects from Stephen Pendo's opinion. As is known, Altman and Brackett's version of the Chandler novel is a very free adaptation. Leigh Brackett himself summed up the changes that were effected:

> The first script was a compromise. . . . We tried to keep the "flavour" of the original, the true Chandler touch, while streamlining and trying to inject a little excitement. But we got involved with a plot premise that simply did not work; the idea that Terry Lennox had plotted, planned, and premeditated Sylvia's murder, framed Roger for it, split for Mexico when something slipped up and simply waited to reappear, knowing exactly what everybody was going to do to clear him; Marlowe would do thus-and-such; Eileen would obligingly murder her husband, and etc. . . . Our only achievements were two: Terry Lennox had become a clear-cut villain, and it seemed that the only satisfactory ending was for the cruelly-diddled Marlowe to blow Terry's guts out. . . . The story line of the Roger Wade portion was greatly simplified. Much of it would have been unuseable in any case because of the WW II time-frame involved in the original relationship between Eileen and Terry. . . . We relieved Eileen of all the crimes except adultery, simplified the motives all round, made the murder of Roger a suicide, gave the gambler a satchelful of money to tie things together and stayed with the brutal ending.

Of course, I was neither familiar with Chandler's novel nor had a very clear image of Philip Marlowe when I saw *The Long Goodbye* in London. The character attracted me immediately, principally because of the ability of Elliot Gould to grant it a certain nonchalance, a distant attitude, casual and ironic with respect to everything happening in the world. That attitude appeared to be balanced, at the same time, by a human warmth, sympathy, and humor, and above all by a refined sensibility for perceiving injustice and aligning himself unfailingly on the side of justice, even when that might mean placing himself outside of the law. That is an essential trait of the Marlowe created by Raymond Chandler, and is the reason why the detective has been repeatedly compared with a modern knight errant, a rare survivor of an age in which adventure, the refusal to submit to all forms of established power and the unconditional defense of the weak constituted the chivalric code of honor. See, for example, these observations by J. O. Tate, that do no more than repeat what other critics had already signaled, and before them Chandler himself when he formulated his original conception of what the private detective should be, that is, what would later carry the name of Philip Marlowe:

> The code of chivalry, imported from England yet once again, finds a new incarnation in Philip Marlowe's sense of honor, loyalty and integrity. And we can add here that his first name — derived from the Greek for 'fond of horses' (*Philippos* derived from *philos* + *hippos*) — is also firmly connected to the chivalric ideal. *The Long Goodbye* is a novel about the meaning of loyalty and fidelity, a meditation on values that's Chandler's most ambitious attempt to make a novel out of the detective story and literature out of entertainment.

Precisely because Elliot Gould succeeds throughout the film in convincing the spectator that these "knightly" characteristics are intrinsic to the character, the final scene, when Marlowe shoots Terry Lenox in cold blood to take revenge for the way Lenox had deceived him (and for the death of his cat) is unacceptable and totally divergent from Chandler's original conception. Now is the time to quote the famous words with which Chandler described the detective in his no less famous essay *The Simple Art of Murder*:

> In everything that can be called art there is a quality of redemption. It may be pure tragedy, if it is high tragedy, and it may be pity and irony, and it may be the raucous laughter of the strong man. But down these mean streets a man must go who is not himself mean, who is neither

tarnished nor afraid. The detective in this kind of story must be such a man. He is the hero; he is everything. He must be a complete man and a common man and yet an unusual man. He must be, to use a rather weathered phrase, a man of honor—by instinct, by inevitability, without thought of it, and certainly without saying it. He must be the best man in the world and a good enough man for any world. . . . He is a relatively poor man, or he would not be a detective at all. He is a common man or he would not go among common people. He has a sense of character, or he would not know his job. He will take no man's money dishonestly and no man's insolence without a due and dispassionate revenge. He is a lonely man and his pride is that you will treat him as a proud man or be very sorry you ever saw him. He talks as the man of his age talks—that is, with rude wit, a lively sense of the grotesque, a disgust for sham, and a contempt for pettiness.

In defense of Altman's version of *The Long Goodbye* and Elliot Gould's interpretation of Marlowe, I should say that when years later (ten years to be exact) I carried out my only attempt at re-creating the world of Raymond Chandler, his persona, his ambience, his characters, and above all the figure of Philip Marlowe, the point of departure was the reconstruction in my retina, more than in my memory, of the film's images rather than any of Chandler's novels. The novel that I would write then began like this:

> In the middle of making breakfast Philip Marlowe abandons his half-cooked bacon and eggs and dashes out of his apartment and downstairs to pick up the mail in the box on the ground floor. It's the end of the summer, 1956. These days Marlowe's living in a small penthouse in the Bristol Apartments in Brentwood Heights, right outside Pacific Palisades. His new building is four stories tall and structurally somewhat baroque. Its honeycombed, arched windows and Mediterranean-style stuccoed walls recall the architecture of Gaudi. There isn't anything unusual about this, since Brentwood Heights is just a short distance from the Pacific and the building was designed to withstand the brutal California summer sun. A stiff wind of the distant, quivering mist-enshrouded ocean leaks into every seam.

These images of Philip Marlowe's habitat, of the pseudo-Mediterranean architecture of Brentwood Heights, of the resplendent sunlight of a mild September day on the California coast, and even the lanky figure of Marlowe interrupting the preparation of his breakfast in order to go down to get the mail on the ground floor of the building, were taken directly from Altman's film, at least as well as I could evoke them from ten years of distance in time and the many thousand of miles in space, in circumstances in which that purely visual effort of recuperation and the solitary reading of some text by Chandler were the only forms of approximation to his work and to the imaginary universe that I wanted in that moment to incorporate into my own work of fiction. I should permit myself here a brief autobiographical digression in order to explain this last statement.

IV

After that brief summer incursion in London in 1973, my two Argentine friends and I returned to Louvain. Our work at the university had practically been finalized, so that a short while later the three of us decided to make the trip back to South America together. We boarded the ship one freezing evening, on exactly the last day of the year, 1973, in the city of Barcelona. We reached the port of Buenos Aires around the 20th of January 1974. For my two friends, that was the final stop of their journey. I was undecided. I hesitated between returning to Montevideo, my own city, where my family and relatives resided, and where I had been living before moving to Europe for two years, or trying to establish residency in Argentina. The principal reason for this vacillation lay in the political circumstances in Uruguay. I had distanced myself from my country precisely as a result of the military repression that had been unleashed against political opposition groups and in particular against intellectuals and university students and faculty. In the two years that my absence lasted, the conditions had not improved, but had gotten worse. Parliament had been dissolved, political parties without exception had been outlawed, the university seized, and both the judicial power as well as the presidency of the government were under the control of the military. In light of this, I decided to remain for a time in Buenos Aires, and only after a lapse of several months, when I believed that the conditions had improved somewhat in terms of personal safety, did I return to live in my old apartment in Montevideo. It was a bad assessment of the situation. In October of 1976 I was detained for a month by the joint forces of the military and police and subjected to a lengthy interrogation. Two months later, when I was preparing to flee the country, having already boarded the plane, I was arrested for the second time. On this occasion I was taken away and sequestered for three months; I was interrogated and tortured, both physically and psychologically, summarily judged without having been able to secure my own lawyer or participate in the trial, and finally, condemned to fifteen years of prison plus five years for "preventive security." That sentence never neared completion. In 1985 the military resigned power in favor of a civilian and democratically elected government. One of the first acts of that government was to proclaim a law of amnesty for all political prisoners. The law went into effect on March 10 of that year. In total, my imprisonment had lasted eight years, three months, and eight days.

In that lapse of more than eight years, at least six had taken place in the maximum-security prison that the military regime had established exclusively for political prisoners. Even though the prison was officially called "Establecimiento Militar de Reclusión No. 1" (Military Institution for Confinement), the name by which it was ironically known was "Prisión de 'Libertad'" ("Liberty" Prison), owing to its incidental proximity to a small town on the Uruguayan seaboard with that name. The living conditions in this prison were contradictory. On the one hand, the place was hygienic, medical attention was adequate, food was decent; there was no forced labor regimen; family visits were carried out every two weeks; and the prisoners were allowed one hour of recreation and physical exercise a day. Nonetheless, in other ways the conditions could be unbearable. The hostility of the military guards submitted the prisoners to constant physical and psychological provocation; the disciplinary punishments imposed for faults that generally did not exist were extremely harsh; there was no information medium or contact with the outside world or, if there were, these were strictly controlled. Career studies and professional improvement were also forbidden. In addition, reading was submitted to severe censorship. The prisoners could receive books and some magazines from their family members, which after having been checked over by a censor and read by their intended recipient, entered into the presidium library for circulation among the prison population. Several disciplines were prohibited: politics, economics, sociology, philosophy, psychology, anthropology, law, linguistics, foreign languages, and others that escape me; history books could not extend beyond the eighteenth century, that is, up until immediately before the French Revolution. Censorship was also exercised according to author, so that even for works of literature and fiction, which constituted the bulk of the library, there existed considerable restrictions: no author who might be considered radical, revolutionary, marxist or materialist, was authorized; and naturally, the criteria employed by the military censorship for classifying an author within any of these categories was very arbitrary.

It was under these circumstances that my second or third encounter with Chandler's work took place. In general, no restrictions were placed on the reading of the detective genre, precisely because these novels were considered inoffensive entertainment, even though in some cases a book and an author were censored because of their apparent defense of violence or crime, or for their insufficient respect for the law and the established order. Chandler passed the censorship. The library ended up having all of his novels and two collections of short stories under the titles *Asesino en la lluvia* (*Killer in the Rain*) and *El simple arte del crimen* (*The Simple Art of Murder*). And even though I don't remember having read any of his articles in this period, there entered into the library *La vida de Raymond Chandler* (*The Life of Raymond Chandler*) by Frank MacShane, a biography that can still be considered even today the most thorough study on the life and work of the author. This book constituted for me, as it is easy to imagine, an indispensable resource for an in-depth knowledge of the details of Chandler's haphazard existence, and in particular, the torturous route that he had to follow in order to arrive at the creation of Philip Marlowe and the great novels that had won him a definitive place in contemporary literature.

V

This last approach to the work and life of Raymond Chandler resulted, therefore, in being the decisive encounter, and it marked a new orientation in the creation of my own narrative and my way of conceiving fiction. In the solitude of my cell, freed at least temporarily from work and from political and intellectual pressures, I managed to devote long and fruitful hours to the reading of Chandler's novels, as well as to the analysis of his narrative techniques and the original contributions that he made to the detective genre.

Chandler started off as a writer of mysteries or detective stories, in part because this genre was the only one that could supply him a quick source of income after he was fired from the oil company where he had served as an executive. Between 1933 and 1939 he published twenty-one stories principally in *Black Mask* and *Dime Detective Magazine,* for which he received payments that fluctuated between one and five cents per word, a rate that barely brought in enough money to survive on. In spite of this beginning to his career as a professional writer, Chandler resisted being classified exclusively as an author of detective or mystery stories from the start, if this classification meant establishing a qualitative distinction between a "serious literature" and a "literature of entertainment." In a letter of 1946 to his editor Alfred Knopf, he wrote: "From the beginning, from the very first pulp story, it was always with me a question (first of course how to write a story at all) of putting into the stuff something they [the readers] would not shy off from, perhaps even not know was there as a conscious realization, but which would somehow distill through their minds and leave an afterglow."

That preoccupation became obsessive at the same time as his fame was increasing and a number of important critics and writers, such as Edmund Wilson, W. H. Auden, Somerset Maugham, J. B. Priestley, and others began to pay attention to his work and to publish highly favorable commentaries about it. Around 1949, in a letter to Hardwick Moseley, Chandler tried to establish what his objectives were with regard to the reading public, and how he differed from other detective novel writers: "Our target is not the mystery addict; he knows nothing, remembers nothing. He buys books cheap or rents them. It all goes in one ear and crosses the vacuum to the other." And as for his colleagues at *Black Mask* and *Dime Detective Magazine,* he wrote: "Very likely, they write better mysteries than I do, but their words don't get up and walk. Mine do, although it is embarrassing to announce it." A few years later, this time in a letter to H. N. Swanson of 1954, that distinction came to be recorded in more definite terms: "I guess maybe there are two kinds of writers; writers who write stories and writers who write writing. . . . The thing is to squeeze the last drop out of the medium you have learned to use. The aim is not essentially different from the aim of Greek tragedy, but we are dealing with a public that is only semi-literate and we have to make an art of language they can understand."

In effect, the work of Raymond Chandler that has lasted until today could be classified in general within the detective genre, but he succeeded in making sure that the qualitative distinction which separated this genre from so-called serious literature for so long lost some of its meaning. Within the group of writers who transformed the traditional detective novel into what was called *hard-boiled fiction,* or more generically "poetry of violence," and that includes Dashiell Hammett, James M. Cain, W. R. Burnett, and Earle Stanley Gardner, among others, Chandler was, without a doubt, the one who made the most original and significant contribution. A variety of factors could explain this fact. Unlike other writers in the group, Chandler received an education that early on put him in contact with the classics of universal literature and that determined his taste and ideas with respect to what the literary work should be. This is noticeable in the management of dialogue and in the creation of characters, which according to Chandler himself constituted the greatest merits of his writing. Nevertheless, and perhaps attesting to his excessive modesty, he admitted on more than one occasion to having difficulties with plot construction: "When I started out to write fiction I had the great disadvantage of having absolutely no talent for it; I couldn't get characters in and out of rooms. They lost their hats and so did I. If more than two people were on the scene I couldn't keep one of them alive. This failing is still with me, of course to some extent. Give me two people snotting each other across a desk and I'm happy. A crowded canvas just bewilders me." This incapacity, real although perhaps exaggerated, led Chandler to develop a technique that constitutes one of the peculiarities of his method of work: the combining of two or more of his short stories in order to construct a plot for his novels. The habit, which he called "cannibalizing," resulted in the thematic and structural complexity of some of his best pieces of fiction, a fact that, rather than representing a disadvantage, enriched the narrative and demanded of the reader a greater engagement in the deciphering of the text.

This last feature could be considered perhaps the essential attribute of fiction, and in particular of the detective genre. All well-written mystery or detective novels oblige the reader to participate actively in the elucidation of the mystery, and that supposes an intellectual effort and an aesthetic pleasure that is not always found in other narrative genres. Raymond Chandler was especially strict about the norms that should rule the *hard-boiled fiction*, insisting that the honesty of the author lies in giving the reader all the necessary clues, so that the final solution to the case is not some gimmick by the detective or investigator turned *deus ex machina*, but the result of a rational deduction and a chain of logically demonstrable causes and effects. One can understand then why detective novels, and the work of Raymond Chandler in particular, might become "best-sellers" within the living conditions of the prison, where the possibility of totally losing oneself in the reading of a book and participating actively in the solving of an imaginary conflict would constitute one of the few forms of escape and intellectual activity within the narrow perimeter of the cell.

Much has also been said about the social criticism implicit in Chandler's novels, in particular the way in which they describe (or denounce) violence and crime, especially in Los Angeles, the city that constitutes the principal setting in his narrative. The poet and critic Edmund Wilson, for example, in an article that appeared in the *New Yorker* in 1945, in which he attacked the majority of mystery writers, had these words of praise for Chandler:

> His *Farewell, My Lovely* is the only one of these books that I have read all of and read with enjoyment. It is not simply a question here of a puzzle which has been put together but of a malaise conveyed to the reader, the horror of a hidden conspiracy which is continually turning up in the most varied and unlikely forms. To write such a novel successfully you must be able to invent character and incident and to generate atmosphere, and all this Mr. Chandler can do, although he is a long way below Graham Greene.

For his part, the English poet and playwright W. H. Auden issued a similar judgment: "Chandler is interested in writing, not detective stories, but serious studies of a criminal milieu, the Great Wrong Place, and his powerful but extremely depressing books should be read and judged, not as escape literature, but as works of art."

The social and moral criticism in Chandler's works stems precisely from that quality: the objective description of reality that is the genuine form of approaching it in aesthetic terms, and constitutes, definitively, the only valid commentary about its vices, crimes, and virtues. Chandler would have been incapable of carrying out this critical task and denunciation if he had not given absolute priority to the specifically literary values of his writing, which led him to conceive of and cultivate the detective genre as a part of literature per se, without restrictions, conditions, or hindrances of any kind. Such is the meaning of the declarations he would make in a letter to James Sandoe on 17 October 1948:

> Neither in this country nor in England has there been any critical recognition that far more art goes into these books at their best than into any number of fat volumes of goosed history or social-significance rubbish. The psychological foundation for the immense popularity with all sorts of people with the novel about murder or crime or mystery hasn't been scratched. A few superficial and a few frivolous attempts but nothing careful and cool and leisurely. There is a lot more to this subject than most people realize, even those who are interested in it. The subject has usually been treated lightly because it seems to have been taken for granted, quite wrongly, that because murder novels are easy reading they are also light reading. They are no easier reading than *Hamlet, Lear,* or *Macbeth.* They border on tragedy and never quite become tragic. Their form imposes a certain clarity of outline which is only found in the most accomplished "straight" novels. And incidentally—quite incidentally, of course—a very large proportion of the surviving literature of the world has been concerned with violent death in some form. And if you have to have significance (the demand for which is the inevitable mark of a half-baked culture), it is just possible that the tensions in a novel or murder are the simplest and yet most complete pattern of the tensions in which we live in this generation.

At some moment in the year 1983, while I was still in prison, and ten years after that Sunday in Leicester Square on which the film version of *The Long Goodbye* worked like a film developer or catalytic agent on my previous readings of Chandler, the rediscovery—and I would almost say the mimetic identification with his work, with the figure of Philip Marlowe, and perhaps also with the life of the writer—was the detonator that provoked the irresistible desire to conjure up the world that Chandler had created in his fiction. A world that in a few months had become incredibly real, familiar, and close. It was with this unique purpose that I began the writing of *Ten Percent of Life,* the novel in which Chandler and Marlowe meet face to face for the first time, converse about their common past and about their future plans, and even collaborate on solving the mysterious death of one of Chandler's literary agents. Up until this moment in which I now write, the novel has gone through two editions in its original language, Spanish, one in Spain and the other in South America, and has been the object of five translations, English, French, German, Italian, and Japanese. Within my modest literary production, it was the most successful book. But this has been more a triumph of Chandler and Marlowe than my own triumph.

It was, also, my way of bidding farewell with a long goodbye to Raymond Chandler.

Translated by Patricia L. Bornhofen

Ezequiel Martínez Estrada on Henry David Thoreau

Although he was born in rural Argentina, Ezequiel Martínez Estrada (1895–1964) moved to Buenos Aires as a young child, and both locations contributed to his fascination with the many facets of Argentine reality. Eternally frustrated with the pattern of corruption and misfortunes in his beloved Argentina, he grew especially bitter during the dictatorship of Juan Perón and remained a pessimistic observer until his death. He lived in Mexico and in Cuba, where he worked for the Casa de las Américas publishing house. Although his early efforts were in poetry, by 1929 he had shifted his energy toward analytical essays on Argentine culture. In spite of his solitary nature, he was a good friend of fellow writers Horacio Quiroga, Leopoldo Lugones, and Victoria Ocampo. In *X-Rays of the Pampa* (1933), Martínez Estrada was already dissecting the unhealthy historical, social, and psychological aspects of his homeland. Other books of his are *La cabeza de Goliath* (1940) and *Muerte y transfiguración de Martín Fierro* (1948). His writings were strongly influenced by Freud, Nietzsche, and other thinkers who shared a concern with the subconscious and the dark forces that drive mankind. A determinist, he viewed Argentina as a conflicted society which could not rid itself of its barbarism or restrain its desire to establish a "higher culture." Martínez Estrada continued to teach and publish from Buenos Aires, and by his death had produced twenty-eight essay collections and over three hundred journalistic pieces. This essay is excerpted from *En torno a Kafka* (Barcelona: Seix Barral, 1966); it appeared in English in *Review* (spring 1976).

In general, sensible people (I mean good people who easily become alarmed at the remote threat of imaginary dangers) have considered it a kindness to humanity to caution against true benefactors. Until the balance sheet is drawn up, quite a long time from now, no one will know with certainty who has worked for God and who for the Devil. A man of lucid intelligence and a free spirit, Henry David Thoreau quickly perceived in his youth, "that there is no uglier odor than that which is given off by corrupted goodness." From that moment he took sides, if not for evil, then for wild nature and for the wild life that he preserved in his heart.

I do not pretend to be able to condense his thought, which he condensed in a few pages, into a few words. But I think that I can assert that one of his axioms was that if progress in the moral and social order is so slow and difficult, compared to what has been realized in the material world, it must be due, among other things, to the intervention of those agents of good will who serve in the enemy ranks.

That is very often the case: the case of someone, like Orlando, who in the blindness of battle, attacks his companions, which is the same as fighting for the other side. Thoreau resolved to take sides for himself, for his conscience, at the risk of being denounced as a disturber of an order which is thought to be divine in the worldly order. Since he had more than enough ability to take care of his own defense, he left judgment up to Time, like Aeschylus. Time is proving him right, even though his case is lost. Mechanical civilization is a matter of money and not of conscience.

His adventure of living among friends who adhered to the strictest rules of philosophical and social orthodoxy proves to us, thank God, that foolish or paradoxical people, heretics or whatever one wants to call them, are the indispensable counterbalance. They fight, almost always risking their well-being and life, in order to clear away the primary world in which the inhabitant of large cosmopolitan centers lives contentedly. With only the precepts of the very ancient philosophers of the forest, without any political sociology, Thoreau not only thought paradoxes of this sort but also put them into practice, living according to them. Expressed in another way, he was one of those men who become rarer every day, one who decided to take upon himself the guilt of the inhabitants of the comfortable western world, persisting in enriching and embellishing the plot of land which he had the luck to inhabit.

He built his house, lived from what he produced and—in plain language—on departing, he left his land a little cleaner, more ordered and more prosperous than he had found it. He belonged to the most closed and exclusive environment of the United States: to the State of Massachusetts, to the area of Concord, to the municipality of Boston, to Harvard University and to the *petit bourgeoisie*, a stronghold of prejudices and conventionalism. He studied at and graduated from Harvard and was a private teacher by vocation as well as a pencil-maker by necessity. At a certain peak in his life while still quite young—he lived for forty-five years, from 1817 to 1862—he abandoned his family and scholarly attire and retired to the shores of Walden Pond. There he built a long and narrow cabin, with two windows and a door; he furnished it with a table, two chairs and a cot, all constructed by his own hands, using an adze which was loaned him and some rustic tool of his own. For two years he lived on what he produced in his garden: vegetables, a few fruits and many beans from whose abundance he carried on a business well accounted for in cents and fractions of a cent. After that experience and the surprise that man can live on a tenth of what he produces from almost any unspecialized labor, Thoreau formulated his own economic theory, which is still ignored by the specialists; namely, that man should only work a couple of weeks each year and dedicate the rest of his time to contemplation, meditation and study which—even though there is no exercise more noble or more necessary than manual labor—is what best suits humanity.

On some Sundays, friends and admirers, people who were curious and inclined toward extravagance, would come to visit him, and he received them with no other ceremony than to have them enter his cabin. In this he was more courteous than Diogenes. These were the years of his most valuable literary production, when he collected the most diverse knowledge: agronomy, zoology and botany, oriental philosophy, poetry and all those useless disciplines which defied the authentic Yankee spirit that abounded everywhere. In a way that no one had up until then, he observed nature in order to understand it and not in order to know it—with wisdom and passion. He loved nature with the heart of a satyr, of a forest animal, and he left behind some valuable suggestions for travelers who want to save their souls in this world without competing for the haunts of other creatures. To save his soul in life and also after death: "I become wilder every day," he wrote, "as if I ate raw meat. My domesticity is no more than the relaxation of my indomitability. I dream of contemplating summer and winter with a free gaze from somewhere else, from the side of some other mountain."

He was, I mean to say, a moralist and a philosopher who preached the conformity of man with nature, of the known with the unknown and the respect for conscience and its imperatives. A catechism as simple as Antigone's and at the same time as astute as Lao Tse's. In this passion for nature and what is natural he was a disciple of Rousseau and a teacher of Tolstoy, although we should look for Thoreau's teachers in China and in India, above all in the holy books—the *Bhagavad Gita,* most of all. To explain what his originality consists of and what his value is as a naturalist and a philosopher of the wild without any direct connections would take a lot of time. But it may be enough for me to say that something happened to Thoreau which is similar to what happened to our William Henry Hudson, who was a naturalist and a writer like many and like no one else. Would it make any sense if I said that he thought and felt—let's suppose—as a squirrel or a marmot might if it possessed human wisdom? His philosophy is that of a child of nature, much more profound, wilder and finer than Jean Jacques; that of a pantheist, if you want, that of a person who worships what is divine more than the divinity. Certainly not a rustic man; but, rather, an exquisite one in the manner of untouched nature: "In the wildest nature there exists not only the material of the most cultivated life and a type of anticipation of the final outcome, but also a refinement greater than man can ever reach."

Because he belonged to an exotic species he has been pinned down on many taxonomists' boards: anarchist, transcendentalist, theosophist, moralist, misogynist, atheist, mystic, panpsychist. Actually, there was a little of all of these in him and of the many other definitions from the botanical or zoological nomenclature of free thought—all of whose species are unclassifiable—definitions which would fit him well with some adjustment. What no one can accuse him of is trying to win by cheating in life, as many other forest-philosophers and sociologists of slavery did: of bending his head before the despot or preaching a creed in which he did not believe or of which he believed that one should not believe. It has never occurred to me to ask about his relatives, his ancestors or his offspring. We should content ourselves with him alone.

Thoreau is one of those men of whom we should not ask whether he was right or wrong, whether or not his doctrine is valuable for progress and civilization. There are questions that ought not to be asked not even of bus drivers who more or less know which way they are going and where they are taking us. In this journey, which we are taking and whose itinerary Thoreau knew very well, things other than the route and the destination are important. We have no yardstick to measure it, no scales to weigh it nor abacus to count it. My feeling is that only in a world that has sealed off the vigorous bright fountains of life, in a society that has put a price on all that man does and dreams, can Thoreau be prosecuted and brought before a court of appeals. And so he has been, by many segments of public opinion—but who will be the prosecutor?

His most dangerous thesis, which has caused a true revolution in the souls and in the tentacular empires—perhaps even the French Revolution has not had such consequence—is that of *On Civil Disobedience,* a pamphlet of thirty-five pages. There is nothing more placid and silent, more powerful and effective than persisting in the truth. Tolstoy received this apocalypse as a chrism and transmitted it to Gandhi, who dispersed it over the face of the earth, as an insurmountable, infinite power of gentleness and peace. It is the same path but dramatically opposed to that of violence to the point of death: docility to the death. Simply, one of the paradoxes of Lao Tse.

This simple and extraordinary idea or revelation was born in a jail—this is the danger of jails—Thoreau being a prisoner for having refused to pay the treasury a tax of one dollar for the war in Mexico. He established the legally and morally irrefutable principle that the State can collect taxes for public services, including free education, but not for the mass extermination of human beings. In such a case the citizen can resist the levy, and, if he is forced, can remain quiet, neither resisting nor paying. It is the "satyagraha," the song of the distaff of liberty, of Mahatma Gandhi. But this is the figure of Thoreau brought down to the political level of his philosophy of the sacred duties of man to himself and to his society, the principal article of the transcendentalist credo whose two eminent apostles were Thoreau and his close friend Emerson.

His love of the Creation at its height—of animals and plants—bordered on devotion and ecstasy. And because that devotion was pure and free from any religious intentions or imperative obligation of the creature to the Creator, it approached reverential wisdom. I do not know if I should excuse myself for presenting him as an example worthy of being understood and loved. My deep and sincere conviction is to do so: and since our younger generation already knows enough about politics and economics, what better advice is there than that of a purifying vacation at Walden Pond? A rest in that sanctuary where the daylight is so radiant that it illuminates even the most hidden recesses of the soul.

Translated by Gregory Kolovakos

Ilan Stavans on Julia Alvarez

Ilan Stavans was born in Mexico in 1961 into a Jewish household. Yiddish was the language of his early school education. In 1985, he moved to New York City, where he studied medieval philosophy at the Jewish Theological Seminary and literature at Columbia University. Among his works are the award-winning *The Hispanic Condition* (1995), *The One-Handed Pianist and Other Stories* and *Art and Anger: Essays on Politics and the Imagination* (both 1996), *The Oxford Book of Latin American Essays* (1997), *The Riddle of Cantinflas: Essays on Hispanic Popular Culture* and *The Oxford Book of Jewish Stories* (both 1998). His first literary experiments were in Yiddish. In his adult life, he writes equally in Spanish and English. His early collections of essays written in his mother tongue, *Prontuario* (1991) and *La pluma y la máscara* (1993), include essays on Whitman, Henry Roth, H. P. Lovecraft, Eudora Welty, Felipe Alfau, and John Updike, among other American writers. Stavans has been a National Book Critics Circle Award nominee and the recipient of the Latino Literature Prize and a Guggenheim Fellowship, among many honors. He teaches at Amherst College, Massachusetts. This essay was first published as "Las Mariposas," in *The Nation,* 13 April 1994.

Not long ago, I heard Julia Alvarez call attention to an intriguing linguistic tic in her native Dominican culture: When you ask somebody what's up and no easy reply can be found, people are likely to say, *Entre Lucas y Juan Mejía.* "Between the devil and the deep blue sea" isn't the right equivalent in English, Alvarez added, "because you aren't describing the sensation of being caught between a pair of bad alternatives."

"So-so" isn't the meaning either, because the Dominican expression isn't at all meant to suggest bland stasis, mediocrity. It's much more intriguing than that. "How are you doing?" "I'm between Lucas and Juan Mejía." And who are these guys? . . . The very story that inspired the saying is gone. So . . . you have to go on and tell the tale of why you feel the way you do. What are the forces you're caught between? How did you get there? And how does it feel to be there?

Alvarez's oeuvre is precisely about this type of crisis—the identity of the in-betweens—and about why she feels the way she does in somebody else's country and language (she immigrated to the United States with her family when she was ten). Although this subject is ubiquitous in ethnic literature in general, her pen lends it an authenticity and sense of urgency seldom found elsewhere. In fact, in the current wave of Latina novelists she strikes me as among the least theatrical and vociferous, the one listening most closely to the subtleties of her own artistic call. She stands apart stylistically, a psychological novelist who uses language skillfully to depict complex inner lives for her fictional creations.

Alvarez's journey from Spanish into English, from Santo Domingo to New York City, from Lucas to Juan Mejía, was the topic of *How the García Girls Lost Their Accents,* a set of loosely connected autobiographical stories published in book form in 1991, about well-off Dominican sisters exiled in *el norte.* The critical reception was mixed, though readers wholeheartedly embraced the book as charming and compassionate—a sort of minor echo of Laura Esquivel's *Like Water for Chocolate*—and it was welcomed with the type of jubilation often granted to works by suddenly emergent minorities. After all, Dominican literature, in Spanish or English, is hardly represented in bookstores and college courses in the United States. Indeed, not since the early-twentieth-century larger-than-life scholar and essayist Pedro Henríquez Ureña delivered the Charles Eliot Norton lectures at Harvard University in 1940–41, on the topic of literary currents in Hispanic America, had a writer from the Dominican Republic been the target of such admiration here.

In spite of Alvarez's fairly conservative, yet semi-experimental approach to literature, what makes her a peculiar, nontraditional Dominican writer is her divided identity. "I am a Dominican, hyphen, American," she once said. "As a fiction writer, I find that the most exciting things happen in the realm of that hyphen—the place where two worlds collide or blend together."

Alvarez's novelistic debut evidenced a writer whose control of her craft was sharp but less than complete. Some of the autonomous segments of *García Girls* were not knit together well, for example, leaving the reader holding several frustratingly loose ends. Now, three years later, such shortcomings have been largely erased, as her haunting second novel easily surpasses her earlier achievement. And while this vista of the political turmoil left behind by émigrés like the García girls still may not be proportional to her talents, it is extraordinary in that it exhibits quick, solid maturing as an artist. In spite of its title, *In the Time of the Butterflies* is not crowded with magic realist scenes à la Gabriel García Márquez and Isabel Allende. Instead, it's a fictional study of a tragic event in Dominican history, when, on November 25, 1960, three outspoken Mirabal sisters, active opponents of the dictatorship of Rafael Leónidas Trujillo, were found dead near their wrecked Jeep, at the bottom of a fifteen-foot cliff in the northern part of the country. Today the Mirabals are known throughout the Caribbean as The Butterflies—Las Mariposas. Alvarez uses her novel to explore their tragic odyssey and, metaphorically, to bring them back to life.

The novel's 300-plus pages are full of pathos and passion, with beautifully crafted anecdotes interstitched to create a patchwork quilt of memory and ideology. We see the sisters as teens, fighting with Papá, marrying, leading double lives, commenting on the Cuban revolution, becoming rebels themselves, going on to bury husbands and sons. The organization is symmetrical: The book's major parts are laid out in four sections, one devoted to each of the three murdered sisters and one to the fourth sister, who escaped their fate. We have thus a quatrain of novellas, only one of which doesn't end in tragedy. Here's how Alvarez has Dedé, the surviving Mirabal sister, remark on the assassination:

> It seems that at first the Jeep was following the truck up the mountain. Then as the truck slowed for the grade, the Jeep passed and sped away, around some curves, out of sight. Then it seems that the truck came upon the ambush. A blue-and-white Austin had blocked part of the road; the Jeep had been forced to a stop; the women were being led away peaceably, so the truck driver said, *peaceably* to the car.

While the Mirabal incident might seem a bit obscure to American readers (most of Dominican history, perhaps even the U.S. invasion, does), it offers an amazing array of creative opportunities to reflect on the labyrinthine paths of the Hispanic psyche. Others in the Dominican Republic have used this historical episode as a springboard to reflect on freedom and ideology, among them Pedro Mir in his poem "Amén de Mariposas" and Ramón Alberto Ferreras in his book *Las*

Mirabal. Alvarez takes a decidedly unique approach: She examines the martyrdom of these three Dominican women as a gender battlefield—three brave, subversive wives crushed by a phallocentric regime. In an openly misogynistic society, the Mirabals are initially dealt with by the government in a delicate, somewhat condescending fashion, which of course doesn't exclude the oppressive power from annihilating them in the end.

The official newspaper of the Trujillo regime, *El Caribe,* treated the deaths of Minerva, Patria, and María Teresa Mirabal and their driver, Rufino de la Cruz, all between twenty-five and thirty-seven years of age, as an accident. Not only did it report the incident without much explanation, it failed to mention the sisters' anti-Trujillo activities. Nor did it acknowledge that a fourth sister wasn't among the victims and had thus survived. Assuming her role as historian and marionetteer, Alvarez fills in the gaps. She didn't know the sisters personally, and she laments at the end of her volume that the reluctance of people in the Dominican Republic to speak out or open up to strangers, as well as the chaotic state of affairs in the nation's libraries and research centers, made it difficult for her to gather historical data. But her task was hardly biographical. "I wanted to immerse my readers in an epoch in the life of the Dominican Republic that I believe can only finally be understood by fiction, only finally be redeemed by the imagination," she writes. "A novel is not, after all, a historical document, but a way to travel through the human heart."

Alvarez writes, for instance, that Trujillo himself had a crush on Minerva, who responded publicly by slapping him in the face. She also analyzes the religious education María Teresa received and later metamorphosed into anti-authoritarian animosity. Much in the *Butterflies* novel resembles *How the García Girls Lost Their Accents:* Hispanic domesticity is at center stage, analyzed in light of the intricate partnerships and rivalries of the four sisters. The male chauvinism that dominates the Hispanic family is meant to mirror and complement Trujillo's own machismo, with home and country approached as micro- and macrocosms. The style is deliberately fragmentary and openly Faulknerian. Alvarez's pages made me think, time and again, of the Israeli writer A. B. Yehoshua: By intertwining disparate literary forms (journals, first-person accounts, correspondence, drawings, etc.) Alvarez allows each Mirabal to acquire her own voice. Pasted together, their voices provide a sense that Truth is a collective invention.

Unlike many Latino writers of her generation, Alvarez abandons the United States in theme and scenario to analyze the role of women under dictatorships in the Southern Hemisphere. Trujillo's presence is felt from afar, as an overwhelming shadow controlling and destroying human happiness—so overarching is the dictator, in fact, that it seems to me he becomes the central character. The Mirabal sisters fight *el líder* as both a real and a ghostlike figure. Their opposition is also an attack against phallocentrism as an accepted way of life in Hispanic societies. In this respect, *In the Time of the Butterflies* ought to be equated with a number of Latin American works about dictators (known in Spanish as *novelas del dictador*), including Miguel Angel Asturias's *El Señor Presidente* and Augusto Roa Bastos's *I, the Supreme*. And it is a first-rate addition to the shelf of works by Latina literary artists who write about chauvinism, from Delmira Agustini to Rosario Ferré. In her Postscript, Alvarez writes:

> During [Trujillo's] terrifying thirty-one-year regime, any hint of disagreement ultimately resulted in death for the dissenter and often for members of his or her family. Yet the Mirabals had risked their lives. I kept asking myself, What gave them that special courage? It was to understand that question that I began this story.

Fiction as an instrument to decodify a tyranny's hidden and manifest tentacles. Fiction as a tool of journalism and vice versa. Fiction as a device to reclaim a stolen aspect of history. Ironically, it is precisely at this level that Alvarez's volume is simultaneously invigorating and curiously disappointing. The author herself appears at the beginning of the plot: It is 1994 and, as an American woman with broken Spanish, she is eager to interview Dedé. Dedé offers much data about her sisters' journey, from their convent education to their first love affairs and subsequent marriages to high-profile activists in the fifties. Indeed, Dedé serves as the backbone to the entire story. But Alvarez leaves reaction to the Mirabals' assassination to a twenty-page epilogue, in which we find out about public outrage and the spectacular, media-oriented trial of their murderers, which took place a year after Trujillo was killed in 1961. Interleaving news clips, court testimony, interviews, and other paraphernalia throughout her narrative might have helped—anything, to insert the Mirabals more firmly in the flux of Dominican memory.

Notwithstanding this structural handicap, *In the Time of the Butterflies* is enchanting, a novel only a female, English-speaking Hispanic could have written. By inserting herself in the cast as *la gringa norte-americana,* Alvarez links the old and the new. At a time when many Latino writers seem so easily satisfied exploring the ghetto, in fictional terms of drugs, crime, and videotape, Alvarez, a writer on a different kind of edge, calls attention to the Latin American foundations of Hispanic fiction in English and dares once again to turn the novel into a political artifact. The inside covers of her book are illustrated with typography listing women and men assassinated by Trujillo. Recalling the Vietnam Memorial in Washington, D.C., the names seem endless, an homage to patriotic anonymity. Alvarez pays tribute to only three of these names, but the rest are also evoked in her lucid pages. Her novel is a wonderful examination of how it feels to be a survivor, how it feels to come from a society where justice and freedom are unwelcome and where the answer to the question "How are you?" often has to be, *Entre Lucas y Juan Mejía.*

Derek Walcott on V. S. Naipaul

Derek Walcott (b. St. Lucia, 1930), a unique Caribbean voice, was awarded the Nobel Prize for Literature in 1992. His oeuvre is crowned by the poetic master-piece *Omeros* (1990), the recipient of the W. H. Smith Literary Award. It is a retelling of the Homeric epic in a Caribbean landscape, using Greek names. In 1988 he received the Queen's Medal for Poetry in England. Walcott is also the author of many plays, such as *Dream on Monkey Mountain, The Joker of Seville, Beef, no Chicken,* and *The Odyssey.* Several of them have been staged in Europe and in regional theaters throughout the United States, as well as Off Broad-way. His poetry collections include *The Arkansas Testament* (1987), and *Collected Poems: 1948–1984* (1986). He is also the author of *What the Twilight Says: Essays* (1998). A friend of Joseph Brodsky and Octavio Paz, Walcott has written inspiredly on Robert Frost, Ernest Hemingway, Philip Larkin, C. L. R. James, Ted Hughes, and Patrick Chamoiseau's *Texaco.* He has taught at Harvard, Yale, Columbia, and Boston University, and lives in Boston and the Caribbean. This review was first published in the *New Republic,* 18 September 1987. It was reprinted in *What the Twilight Says: Essays.*

> The summer jobs were done. The fallen aspens
> about whose wide tangled spread of broken branches
> grass and weeds had grown tall and dark,
> a separate area of vegetation—
> the fallen aspens were cut up with a chain-saw
> and the cut-logs piled up in the back garden.

Press one foot on the soil of England and the phantoms spring. Poets, naturalists, novelists have harrowed and hallowed it for centuries with their furrowing pens as steadily as its yeomen once did with the plough. No other literature is so botanical as English, so seeded with delight and melancholy in the seasons, from "The Shepherd's Calendar" to Edward Thomas to those wistful prose poems that still appear on the editorial pages of English newspapers. Boundless as its empire became, England remained an island, a manageable garden to its poets, every one of whom is a pastoralist; and if now it has succumbed to the despair of Hamlet, "an unweeded garden that grows to seed /

things rank and gross in nature" possessing it, or the malicious midden that is in Ted Hughes, still the provinciality of English poetry through Langland, Shakespeare, Spenser, Milton, Marvell, Pope, Keats, Wordsworth, Hardy, the Georgians, Thomas, is its pride.

Culture and agriculture are synonyms over there. The sense of England is not so much of setting out to see the world as of turning one's back on it, of privacy, not adventure. The lines used as an epigraph above could have been written by the phantom of Edward Thomas, or by others: by Clare, Cobbett, Hardy, even a meticulous Georgian. They are from V. S. Naipaul's novel *The Enigma of Arrival*, and they celebrate Wiltshire. They are his homecoming, his devotions. But to those of us for whom his direction has always been clear, this arrival is neither enigmatic nor ironic but predictable. The final essay examination has been submitted, and the marks are in. Gentlemen, we now have among us another elegiac pastoralist, an islander himself, the peer of Clare and Cobbett, not only in style, but in spirit. And if the cost to that spirit has meant virulent contempt towards the island of his origin, then rook, shaw, and hedgerow, tillage and tradition, will soothe him, because although he may reject his own soil, his own phantoms, the earth everywhere is forgiving, even in Trinidad, and rejects no one.

When two long sections of Naipaul's book appeared in *The New Yorker*, I cherished them as the tenderest writing Naipaul had ever done. Tempered and delicate, the mood of these pieces had the subdued subtleties of the weather their pliant sentences celebrated. They were pious in their tribute, and close to glory, to that glory that in Edward Thomas's poems brings us to tears in their natural affections; and they had a bracing, springing rhythm, as cool, as fresh, as pneumatic as moss underfoot. If there was any enigma at all, it was that of astonishment, because Naipaul was celebrating. There was no acidity in his pleasures, no ascetic tartness in this mellowing. Then the book began to disfigure itself. The old distemper set in. The elation and gratitude shrivelled and puckered and once again left the teeth on edge, the scour on the tongue.

The Enigma of Arrival calls itself a novel. But unless we are meant to take the novel to be the enigma of all autobiography—that everything recorded by the act of memory is inevitably a fiction, that in life there is no such thing as a hero because a hero presumes a plot—the book is negligible as a novel and crucial as autobiography. Or vice versa, if you like transparent puzzles. The chronology of events, the family names, the geography, all coincide with Naipaul's own; but as we read, mischievous uncertainty irritates us because of the suppression of those things that advance fiction: whether the narrator lived in total solitude in the Wiltshire countryside, and, if the narrator did, whether he avoided, for the sake of art, the temporary solaces of sex or marriage, whether he cooked for himself—because all this happens over years.

If the narrator's only companion was work, the hermitage is made admirable, but only in the way legends are—by a concentrated selfishness, by that self-canonization of the dedicated writer in a hostile world, the misunderstood, the displaced, the exiled, all of whom are becoming as corny as Dickensian orphans, because either every writer is an exile (not only this narrator-Naipaul) or no writer is. What keeps plot and excitement alive in *Robinson Crusoe* is not the myth of isolation but the challenge of endurance through ordinary objects, and through the vibrations of such objects the increase of loneliness, the growing scream inside the heart for companionship or, in another word, for love.

Here is where Naipaul's book sours, because the narrator is not interested in love. He falls neither in nor out of it, and this is a defeat he must accept if he is both narrator and Naipaul. The same lovers of gardens enslaved and finally ignored their empire once they had exhausted the soil that produced sugar for afternoon tea; and so, wondrously broad as the novel begins, it shallows into a fretful murmur, a melodious whine. Trinidad injured him. England saves him.

The book takes its title from a painting by de Chirico. A wharf. An empty city. A wanderer. A dangerous model already, and one that Naipaul has never used before: the art of someone else. More dangerous because surrealism, or metaphorical painting, is the imagination at its most second-rate. It is illustrated cliché: every arrival is a journey, etc. The surrealist tries to disturb us by upsetting formulas, then rigidifies his own. For time he gives us melting clocks, for phantasma, elephants on spiderish legs, hats floating without heads beneath them, infinite perspectives. The worst aspect of surrealism is that it requires so much labour to preserve the evanescent.

Naipaul does not go down that cul-de-sac; he is too much the rationalist, too deliberately commonsensical, too devoted to the parallel lines of history and reason to go after ambiguity, hallucination, and magic. But for the first time in his work we are thrilled by the temptation offered him, a temptation the narrator rejects, avoiding the seduction of writing a novel about that arrival in a hallucinatory port in the Roman Empire. Replace British for Roman, Naipaul for the traveller, the autobiography for the unwritten novel, and we have a neat trick, a prosaic irony. An aside, not a hymn. And this aside on the idea of history says simply that a man whose background was that of the degradation of indenture, of displacement, has used that background to master his craft, to move from servitude to certainty, and has found that certainty on the imperial soil of England.

The concept of English literature once belonged, naturally, to England. And, synonymously, to its power and its morality. It produced its books and exported them to the provinces. In those provinces the native writer absorbed the best of the language, but also the stuff that came with it, the power and the morals. It was this that magnetized Joseph Conrad, a provincial from the Third World of Poland under the peaks of the French, German, and British Empires. Naipaul has avoided this absorption with the suspicion of the servant. What is the cost to his Indianness of loving England (because that is what love of the English countryside means)? To whom does he owe any fealty? Ancestors? The surroundings that history placed them in, the cane fields of Trinidad, were contemptible, as they themselves would have to be, having lost both shame and pride. Therefore, the only dignity is to be neither master nor servant, to choose a nobler servitude: writing. The punishment for the choice is the astonishment of gratitude, to be grateful to the vegetation of an English shire. Not to India or the West Indies, but to the sweet itch of an old wound.

To detail the plot of this non-autobiography / non-novel would be to consider it by the very terms it avoids. If nothing happens in it, or rather, if what happens takes place across a fence, or on the far side of a field, that is in fact how life itself is: people betray each other as they do in this book, murder for jealousy, wither into old age, lose their jobs, while our own egocentricity absorbs other people's tragedies as interruptions or irritations. *The Enigma of Arrival* is mercilessly honest in its self-centredness, in its seasonal or eruptive sadnesses. It is as true as life, in the terrible sense that nothing really concerns us.

So what is observed by the narrator is oblique experience, seen and registered from the side of the eye, the parallel that is another's sorrow, until the end of the book, when the narrator's young sister dies and his grief blocks any sense of purpose. What is looked at—stream, hedge, deer—can be seen clearly, registered, and praised. But it can also be trusted to be itself, its variations not treacheries, its changes vitalizing. The early wonder of the book lies in the vigour of its stride, in its health. Year after healing year passes in the calendar that Naipaul calls his Book of Hours. His delight is treated with exactness, and the growth of pleasure draws the reader in without fancy. There isn't a better English around, and for me this is wonderful without bewilderment, since our finest writer of the English sentence, by praising the beauty of England, however threatened with industrial encroachment, preserves it from itself.

The best leaves of this book are touched by grace, and the wonder would have remained if the anonymity of the narrator had remained one with the landscape he cherishes. But the "I," the novelist in the autobiographer, moves from the present tense of lyric verse rhythms to the past tense of fiction, and the phantoms of the old Naipauline trauma—the genteel abhorrence of Negroes, the hatred of Trinidad, the idealization of History and Order—appear at the end of Naipaul's garden path. The self-assurance of the author's direction has to be fortified, dramatized, exaggerated, and so the author's lie begins. Here is Naipaul as an eighteen-year-old writer en route to England on his island scholarship. He is in New York, and this is how he remembers seeing the light:

> Without the paper [a newspaper] I would not have known that the weather was unseasonable. But I did not need the paper to make me see the enchantment of the light. The light indoors in the hotel was like the light outdoors. The outdoor light was magical. I thought it was created by the tall buildings, which, with some shame, I stopped to look up at, to get their size. Light indoors flowed into light outdoors: the light here was one. In Trinidad, from seven or eight in the morning to five in the afternoon, the heat was great; to be out of doors was to be stung, to feel the heat and discomfort . . . The colors of the New York streets would have appeared to me, in Trinidad, as "dead" colors, the

colors of dead things, dried grass, dead vegetation, earth, sand, a dead world—hardly colors at all.

To whom? Not to a painter. What happens in the summer in New York? Why is the sticky, insufferable humidity of any city summer preferable or more magical than the dry fierce heat of the Caribbean, which always has the startling benediction of breeze and shade? Why is this heat magical in Greece or in the desert, and just heat in Trinidad? We move easily from the climate to its people:

People had no news; they revealed themselves quickly. Their racial obsessions, which once could tug at my heart, made them simple people. Part of the fear of extinction which I had developed as a child had partly to do with this: the fear of being swallowed up or extinguished by the simplicity of one side or the other, my side or the side that wasn't mine.

It was odd: the place itself, the little island and its people, could no longer hold me. But the island—with the curiosity it had awakened in me for the larger world, the idea of civilization, and the idea of antiquity; and all the anxieties it had quickened in me—the island had given me the world as a writer.

Or, more honestly, "had given the world me as a writer." Nothing wrong with that. Despite his horror of being claimed, we West Indians are proud of Naipaul, and that is his enigmatic fate as well, that he should be so cherished by those he despises. But the estimate of his lonely journey towards becoming a writer is conservative. The statistics aren't fixed; they're ignored. His own island, a generation before, gave the world C. L. R. James (a Negro) and Samuel Selvon, and other islands offered the world George Lamming, Wilson Harris, Roger Mais, Jean Rhys, Edgar Mittelholzer, John Hearne, Shiva Naipaul, Jamaica Kincaid, scores of excellent short stories, the poets Eric Roach, Cecil Herbert, George Campbell, Edward Braithwaite, a few hundred calypsonians, Bob Marley, Sparrow, Kitchener. But how weak Naipaul's struggle would seem if it were communal; if his dedication was seen to be shared; if what he felt in his youth was held to be felt in common by thousands of young Asian, African, Canadian, Australian writers from all the former provinces of the empire: if more people knew *Beyond a Boundary* and *The Black Jacobins* (by James), and *The Lonely Londoners* and *Ways of Sunlight* (by Selvon), *In the Castle of My Skin* (by Lamming), *The Palace of the Peacock* (by Wilson Harris), and so on. Naipaul moans about the fact that in our youth the bookshelves of English literature were lined with Penguins and Everymans, when in fact the islands had small but excellent libraries (since they could only afford the classics). Still, he must perpetuate this oblique deceit to appear as a marvel. For who would want to attend a convention of Crusoes, a conference of hermits?

The myth of Naipaul as a phenomenon, as a singular, contradictory genius who survived the cane fields and the bush at great cost, has long been a farce. It is a myth he chooses to encourage—though he alone knows why, since the existence of other writers in no way diminishes his gift. If he doesn't want to play, like the peevish sixth-grader still contained in an almost great writer, he can go and play by himself; but that is not going to stop the game. Nobody draws more attention to himself than a conspicuous hermit; nobody is going to get more applause, more solemn nods of respect. There is something alarmingly venal in all this dislocation and despair. Besides, it is not true. There is, instead, another truth. It is Naipaul's prejudice.

Frankness doesn't absolve him of it. Of course prejudice comes from history, from the hoarded genealogy of the tribe; yet if Naipaul's attitude towards Negroes, with its nasty little sneers (injurer and injured can seek them out for themselves in this book), was turned on Jews, for example, how many people would praise him for his frankness? Who would have exalted that "honesty" for which he is praised as our only incorruptible writer from the Third World?

Victims are now as articulate as their oppressors, and this is not merely a matter of polemics. Prejudice taints the imaginations of Conrad, of Hemingway, of Greene, as much as it does the adventure novel; and it deserves to be judged with all the japes and apologies of gangs. Joyce, Shakespeare, Dante, for all their clear hatreds, are beyond this self-disfigurement. Naipaul's book, which began as a healing, is not an advance. *That* is its sadness, *that* is its disenchantment. There is the absence of all enigma, for once again those abstract nouns History and Empire acquire a serenity equal to their alleged synonyms, Culture and Art. Over there in the lanes of England, these words survive and refresh.

If the world that Naipaul has left behind for others to care about has, for the descendants of slave and indentured worker, neither Art nor Culture, neither flower gardens nor venerable elms, it is because none of that was given to the slave or the indentured worker. To write about this lack as if it were the fault of the African and the Indian is not only to betray them but to lie. Naipaul is unfair. He is unjust. And he is unfair and unjust at an obscene cost, at the cost of those who do not have his eloquence, his style. Slavery and indenture were technological concepts, not aesthetic ones. They were part of the daily accountancy of a basically banal empire. But things have their price. The enigma or, more simply, the revenge, exacted by a belief in history is that the descendants of the enslaved will revere their servitude if it will lead them to those peaks of Art and Culture, to the heart of that empire, to its pastoral villas, manors, temples, and streets. This makes History and Empire worth all their suffering, if the suffering will produce Art. But the servant's present tense is not Naipaul's pluperfect. That tense has been refined, rewritten, judged, given an epic sweep, compressed into the precise yet still elegiac simplicity of this kind of epiphany:

> I could see, in the documents of this later period, the lineaments of the world I had grown up in. Asian-Indian immigrants had come in the period of nineteenth-century torpor. As a schoolboy I had assumed that torpor to be a constant, something connected with the geographical location of the island, the climate, the quality of the light. It had never occurred to me that the drabness I knew had been man-made, that it had causes, that there had been other visions, and indeed other landscapes there.

What is this but style without truth? What sort of torpor? And for a hundred years? One had imagined that the nineteenth century was a bit more energetic—if not in industry, at least in art. And how much torpor were slave and indentured worker allowed? Yet in the pluperfect tense of the twentieth century, the descendant of the indentured can elegize the torpor of the nineteenth. Naipaul is talking about the torpor of the intellect, not about anything as ordinary as work.

One sighs and proceeds to:

This empire explained my birth in the New World, the language I used, the vocation and ambition I had; this empire in the end explained my presence there in the valley, in the cottage, in the grounds of the manor.

This is modest enough to be messianic. But the empire also explained the birth of hundreds of thousands of immigrants, of the language they use, of their vocations and their ambitions, of their presence in valley and cottage on a manor ground, in Brixton and elsewhere.

Naipaul tires of racism in Trinidad and returns home to Britain. Not to the Britain of Paki-bashing, or of the race riots of Brixton, but to the comforts of its countryside. This may strike the average mind as the equivalent of a Soviet dissident going home to Gorky, of a thirties Jew finding rest in Berlin, of a Bantu celebrating the delights of Johannesburg. Perhaps the Pakis and the black Brits brought hatred on themselves, as so many Third World countries in Naipaul's travel books have brought about their own psychic collapse by attempting to compete with their former empires. The horror in these books, from *The Middle Passage* through *Eva Perón and the Killings in Trinidad* to *Finding the Center*, is the horror encountered in bush frontiers, in the pseudo-cities of Latin America, India, and the Middle East, but never in the central horrors of our century: the concentration camps, the forced-labour camps of Soviet Russia, their scale so much larger than many Caribbean islands, those archipelagoes of calculated, refined social science.

There is the real enigma: that the provincial, the colonial, can never civilize himself beyond his province, no matter how deeply he immures himself in the woods of a villa outside Rome or in the leafy lanes of Edwardian England. And that is not pathetic; it is glorious. It is the other thing that is the final mimicry: to achieve absorption into what is envied not because that absorption is the dissolution of individuality, the sort of blessed anonymity that Hinduism teaches, but because it is only the vain mutter of "I have survived."

As beautiful as the prose becomes in the first chapters of this novel, it is scarred by scrofula, by passages from which one would like to avert one's eye; and these reveal, remorselessly, Naipaul's repulsion towards Negroes. It is a physical and historical abhorrence that, like every prejudice, disfigures the observer, not his object. To cite examples would reduce the critic to the role of defender or of supplicant, would expose him to more of Naipaul's scorn. That self-disfiguring sneer that is praised for its probity is only that: a wrinkling of the nostrils, a bemused crinkling of the eyes at the antics of mimicking primates, at their hair, at their voices, at their hands extended in the presumption of intimacy.

In the twentieth century, the languages of all the tribes can sound like a Babel, and that sound can terrify the secondary genius. Therefore, that genius hoards itself and its tribal language, convincing itself that amid the echolalia of screaming victims and confessional apologists it must immure itself in the sacred, priestly dedication of being "a writer," but cautiously keeping both callings distinct: writer and priest. Thus the writer becomes his own confessor. He blesses or curses or absolves himself by the rites of his writing, preserving his secularity, his public, his profitable mask.

Shantih to his pen, though, and a benediction on the peace that has come to him after the exhaustions of a world whose features he has still described more honestly than most. In a small hillside hotel whose back verandah looks out on a serenity of pasture, saddle ridge, grazing cattle, and a view of the Caribbean between its bushy hills, I found an appropriate blessing under the photograph of a sadhu in an old *National Geographic*: "Renouncing possessions, sadhus are life-long pilgrims. For such a holy man, said the god Indra, patron of travelers: 'All his sins are destroyed by his fatigues in wandering.' " That is how I prefer to end—to cherish the narrator of *The Enigma of Arrival,* not as an enigmatic English squire who has finally arrived, but as the sadhu that he might have become. Peace to the traveller, and calm to the mind growing nearer to that radiance, to the vision that sees all earth as sacred, including his birthplace, and all people as valuable, including Trinidadians.

José Bianco on Ambrose Bierce

Known for his innovations and a deep human vision, Buenos Aires native José Bianco (1908–1986) had already published two books of short stories by age eighteen and had begun to write for several magazines. He published a collection of short stories, *La pequeña Gyaros* (1932) when he was twenty-four, and went on to edit the most important magazine in Latin American literature, *Sur,* from 1938 to 1961, as well as directing the University Press in Buenos Aires. He received a Guggenheim grant in 1975 and was awarded the Odre des Palmes Academiques by the French government. Bianco was also a superb translator of English and French works. The two novellas *Shadow Play* (1941) and *The Rats* (1972) are among his most acclaimed pieces, as well as the collection of essays, *Ficción y realidad* (1976). This is Bianco's prologue to Ambrose Bierce's *Cuentos de soldados y civiles* (Buenos Aires: Jorge Alvarez, 1968).

Ambrose Bierce's characters, as tends to be the case in life, are the handcrafters of their fate. And theirs is not an enviable fate. Bierce usually makes them victims of horrible circumstances that they themselves provoke in one way or another. They collaborate with adversity. Character is destiny, but in Bierce's protagonists we don't find character flaws. They kill or die miserably for dignified causes and nobel sentiments: patriotism, the cult of courage, of friendship, of the promise kept.

This dirty trick of fate repeats itself again and again in his soldiers' stories. Invariably Bierce's characters succumb to their virtues. They succumb—that is the word—because their virtues supply praiseworthy motives to obscure, repressed impulses, because maybe in them these impulses find an escape valve. They no longer need to repress them. These impulses, common to all men, are very characteristic of the man that Bierce presents to us. We will outline his principle features further on; for the moment let's limit ourselves to pointing out that Bierce hints at or proclaims these impulses, and that at the end of his stories—that end that seems so cruel—the law of just punishment is exacted. Occasionally, when the resolution of the story does not thwart the designs of its actor, Bierce hastens the moral inferno that he has prepared for himself.

We know very little of Bierce's characters. It is for this reason, without a doubt, that we perceive no greater defects in them. Bierce confines himself to the standards of the traditional story: he imagines a situation and doesn't delay, or barely delays, in developing his characters. Let us add that he imagines situations heavy with violence and horror. For example: a soldier takes aim at a horseman from the other side, or a captain orders the firing of the canons at another canon set in front of a house. At the end of the story we have found out that the mounted soldier was the other's father, the house, the captain's own house, and that he has killed his wife and daughter. The protagonists of each story measure exactly the reach of their actions: they violate unwritten law and they are condemned to a terrible suffering beyond any material punishment that could be imposed by other men. Nevertheless, there is an ambiguous tone to the sacrifice they are subjected to. Around 1900, a theory capable of establishing other motives for the heroic behavior of Bierce's characters would be elaborated. Today, a psychoanalyst could suspect that the young Oedipus—at the beginning, the soldier was unaware of the identity of the horseman—wanted to replace his father, a supreme figure who inspires in him a thoroughly ambiguous mixture of admiration and emulation. A psychiatrist could suspect that the captain of the second story destroys a home already morally destroyed. (Although an angry southerner, the captain's wife is faithful. Jealousy, if not resentment on the part of the husband, would be improbable. But is there anything more improbable, more furiously improbable than the conduct of Othello?)

These conjectures might be less risky than they seem. When he reveals the nature of his characters' hidden tendencies, Bierce has no qualms about lifting the deceiving veils from their eyes as well. This is clear in one of his stories about civilians, "The Death of Halpin Frayser," in which he directly takes up the theme of incest. And in another of his most famous stories of civilians, "The Man and the Snake," the snake "reared its head . . . and looked at [the man] with his dead mother's eyes." Nevertheless, in his soldier stories Bierce discerns up close only a single common sentiment: the fulfillment of duty. Duty justifies the vicissitudes of the action and apparently legitimizes the conduct of the characters. But fate punishes them because it allows them—or doesn't—to carry out their aim, as if, when they put their heroism to the service of the state, they have betrayed the solidarity they owe to human kind. "Patriot: One to whom the interests of a part seem superior to those of the whole." This is how Bierce defines it in his *Devil's Dictionary.*

In the stories of civilians to which I referred earlier, the protagonists are two sane men, in the prime of life. As doubts might have been cast upon the health of the man and the snake because of the perverse charm the snake has over him, Bierce doesn't fail to mention his physical and moral strength in his summary description of the character. But when dealing with soldiers, Bierce stays away from any mention of health. The soldier is almost always a boy with a wife and a few children waiting for him. He is kind, daring, open, without greater powers except when calling upon all means of shrewdness to enable the multiple and precise resources of his athlete's body. Yes, heroism is necessarily united with youth, with strength, with health. Where better to follow the progress of suffering than in these semi-gods with muscles bulging, shining with sweat, faces smooth and slightly stupid, wrinkle-free except for when clenched in the useless effort to avoid death? Where better to prove the inherent weakness in the human condition than in these warriors of tempered nerves and six feet of height, straining, sure in their boldness and who suddenly crumble, invaded by an anguish which fascinates them by reason of the very stupor it brings. In the feeling of the jacket tightening around their thorax, or in the accelerated rhythm of their blood, they discover the symptoms of a rare emotion; they speak or laugh without realizing it, and in the sound of their voice or in the echo of their laughter they are startled by the accent of death. And Bierce, till the end of his story, describes the detailed torture they are submitted to—in the double sense, materially and spiritually, of the word—leaning over them like a minister of death.

They are guilty because they are soldiers, and "the duty of the soldier is to kill." Beyond this, Bierce points to the direct, untransferable part each one plays in that shame that unites everyone. An assistant dies of terror, immobilized in the middle of a field of rubble before a rifle without bullets, because the rifle has discharged at the exact moment that he took aim at a distant column of gray uniforms, calculating his best chance at making a widow, an orphan, or a mother without a son, or maybe all three at the same time, even though the shot could have not the slightest influence on the duration nor the outcome of the war; a second lieutenant, thrilled by the glory of battle yet disgusted at the spectacle of corpses, dies as a consequence of that paradoxical repugnance as he struggles body to body with a corpse. The worst punishment is saved for a captain who deals the coup de grâce to his friend in agony and about to be devoured by a herd of swine: upon his head will rest the death of a friend who enlisted in the army, with no affinity for arms nor disposition for a military career, only to keep from leaving his side.

It is unnecessary to continue enumerating. The world of the soldier is a "world of assassins." There, men show themselves in the full truth of their nature; there they give free rein to the instincts of their past in Central Asia, joined by the new barbarisms of modern civilization. Evil is inevitable, ineluctable. For Bierce, no one saves himself: in combat after combat, when justice is done, he passes out punishment with paternal concern.

The true purpose of the war of secession wasn't to abolish slavery. Bierce knows this. In June of 1864 he wrote to his girlfriend's sister: "Oh how pleasant death would be if it were for you and Tima, instead of for my country—for a cause which may be right and may be wrong. Do you think I lack patriotism for talking this way? Perhaps so. Soldiers are not much troubled by that sort of stuff."

He was twenty-three years old. Since the age of nineteen he'd fought as a volunteer in the Yankee lines. He'd risen from the rank of soldier to sergeant, then official topographer, then Union official. He participated in many battles, was gravely wounded at Kenesaw Mountain. When the war ended and they awaited an era of reconstruction and peace, Bierce decided definitively to join the military. The number of troops had been reduced to a minimum; they could only offer him the rank of second lieutenant. Bierce refused. With this we have to ask ourselves why he wanted to enter the army when he judged the role of the soldier to be so mean. Bierce answers us (*Devil's Dictionary*): "The soil of peace is sown with the seeds of war and singularly suited to their germination and growth. . . . War loves to come like a thief in the night." From this paraphrase from his writings, we can see that peace is a transitory state, ephemeral. Bierce continues longing for the day of the great tribulation. And that day comes again and again for him, when, at the age of twenty-five, he writes his soldiers' stories. Then he avenges himself through these soldiers for the torments he suffered, but at the same time he suffers alongside them, in the same way that Sade—as Paulhan, in the prologue to *The Misfortunes of Virtue,* makes note of—finds the most effective of his accomplices in the wretched Justine. Bierce is the tormentor and the victim, the double subject, active and passive, of the tortures that he inflicts on his characters.

The soldiers' stories show us the obverse and the inverse of war. On one hand, its honorable, glamorous aspect, which Bierce was so aware of: the strategies of the generals in charge, the spectacle of the arms, the display of the battalions, the horses spurred forward through a torrent of bullets, the columns moving ahead amid explosions, their towers of smoke rising. On the other hand, the wounded in agony and the corpses swarming with larva, disintegrating into the indifferent, ceaseless life of the forest. We pass from slightly ingenuous scenes of neat colors in the style of Horace Vernet to portraits in greenish tones, hues of corruption, that make one think of Delacroix, or to unsparing black and whites like the *Désastres* of Goya; and, finally, to the accounting of the dead, a half million deaths, left by the war of secession. To Bierce the sacrifice of human life seems equally monstrous on both sides, Union and Confederate, but it is curious that among the latter, his enemies, he often admired that mixture of simplicity and refined manners that accentuated, if that is possible, their courage.

We ought to point out a characteristic that in some way links the technique that Bierce pursues in his stories with one of the theories proclaimed by the *nouveau roman:* I refer to the primacy assigned to the visual, to the importance of a precise, detailed focus on setting and the movements of the characters. There is no danger in one detail or another slipping from memory, as long as we retain the landscape, grounding ourselves in the supposed emotions awakened in the actor of the fable, who is "austere" or "calm," as Robbe-Grillet* says, without being able to remember any of his principal elements. Neither is description merely informative, circumstantial, a catalog of superimposed images, which many years ago André Breton—citing a passage from *Crime and Punishment*—derided with so much grace in his *First*

*Alain Robbe-Grillet, *Pour un nouveau roman* (Paris: Gallimard, 1962).

Manifesto of Surrealism. Bierce's descriptions don't provide "atmosphere" or the "frame" within which the action takes place. Bierce, who was the official topographer in the war, shows us the setting for the action with a rhythm which will later be popularized by the cinematographer, a morose, guarded rhythm, and suddenly the setting comes to conflict with the character, and the conflict becomes a tragedy that only can happen there, in that place explored foot by foot, rigorously. The already mentioned relationship with the fable has now disappeared. *Things* exist with the same authority as the man. As Robbe-Grillet would want, between the two there is no harmony nor flawed coexistence. There is, though—and in this Bierce's stories part company with the *nouveau roman*—an extravagant indifference to latent antagonisms, poised to play themselves out. We see a solid beam and cables, but beam and cable bind the arm of the soldier; we see the trunk of a tree where an official is seated among the moon beams filtering through the branches, but a corpse comes out of the darkness and advances in the direction of the tree; we see a crag against the sky, at an immense height, but along the crag a horseman gallops straight over our heads. The setting is a trick, and the trick is no less consistent than the actor about to stumble or fight his way into it. Sometimes Bierce loads his dungeons with dusk, in the depths of a forest. Sometimes he strings the lightest of threads between two distant pinnacles, and the rising sun makes this web gleam with the shades of a rainbow. In this landscape, airy, movingly beautiful, something is about to happen, something ill-fated.

And it happens, unerringly, because destiny intervenes, one of those strange coincidences, small or large, so frequent in daily life, but before which the story writers or novelists of today, fearful, back away. Bierce's actors provoke them. In one way or another, they have chosen their misfortunes and they participate in the inexorable justice that punishes them. Before Schopenhauer established the voluntary element within all the acts that happen to a man, before psychoanalysis incorporated this idea into its method to bring to light the deepest motives of human behavior and to cure neurosis, Balzac had already said it: "Most accidents are premeditated."

Translated by Jennifer Radtke

Antonio Benítez Rojo on Lafcadio Hearn

Born in Havana in 1931, Antonio Benítez Rojo was educated at the University of Havana and American University in Washington, D.C. He was an important Cuban cultural figure from the 1960s through 1980, when he defected while serving on a Cuban delegation in Paris. While in Cuba, he published *Tute de Reyes* (1967), *El escudo de hojas secas* (1969), *Heroica* (1976), *Los inquilinos* (1976), *La tierra y el cielo* (1978), *Sea of Lentils* (1979), *El enigma de los esterlines* (1980), and voluminous critical work. Once in the United States, Benítez Rojo has produced the theoretical study *The Repeating Island* (1989), as well as the fiction collections *The Magic Dog and Other Stories* (1990) and *A View from the Mangrove* (1998). He and his wife both currently teach at Amherst College in Massachusetts. The following autobiographical essay was written in May 1996. This is its first appearance in print.

Many years ago, when summers were still long and I chased down birds in my backyard in a Sherwood Forest hat, my aunt Gloria gave me a book entitled *Japanese Fairy Tales*. I accepted the book with a condescending silence and, without opening it, threw it into the old toy chest, where there lay, in an undifferentiated pile, ten or twelve books filled with castles, giants, fairies, witches, and dwarves, which had drawn my attention until not long before. The months passed, and with them there passed as well the rousing pages of *The Three Musketeers, Captain Blood,* and *The Last of the Mohicans.* I had just discovered Jules Verne when something terrible happened at Pearl Harbor. Suddenly we were at war and everyone was speaking ill of the Japanese. Hirohito, Zero, Tokyo, Tojo, and Banzai entered our ordinary speech. I remember that the word *hara-kiri* became very popular in my school when a fifth grader, upon flunking mathematics, sank to his knees before Father García and stuck a pencil in his belly. On our block we played ball less and less; now we preferred to walk for half a mile in the direction of the wilderness of Monte Barreto—quickly converted into the Bataan Peninsula—where the roles of Robert Taylor, Thomas Mitchell, and the Filipino Anthony Quinn, along with a half-dozen anonymous Japanese, were handed out at random before staging bloody battles with hand grenades of mud. Then we found out about the Death March, and we rejoiced when someone brought the news that the Japanese were none of them Christians and would all go to Hell.

Yes, I must confess, for that group of boys in 1940s Havana the last thing in life that one could be was Japanese; nothing in the world could be more evil, cruel, and treacherous, not even a Nazi in the Gestapo. What made me seek out *Japanese Fairy Tales*, then, and why did I read it? I don't know. I can't remember. Probably the conjunction of a rainy day and the natural curiosity one has toward an enemy. The fact is that I read those tales again and again; I read them at night, in secret, when everyone in the house was sleeping; I read them and reread them feeling the strange mixture of attraction and repulsion that the poetry of fear evokes. I was a long way from thinking that this new and frightening thing that was entering my life was an entire literary form. To me it was entirely a matter of Japanese fairy tales, stories where there were no fairies, just dead people; stories that after I had turned off the light would make me peer, with my soul suspended, into the corners of the room to look for phantasmagoric samurai and women whose faces were frighteningly pale; stories that were repeated in my nightmares or would wake me up with a start, believing absolutely that some person from the other world had been calling out my name. Many times, perhaps tormented by some guilt for my addiction—it was after all a thing come from Japan—I had tried to read some Verne or Salgari or the funny adventures of William Brown. But if those books indeed would entertain me during the day, nothing could compare with the terrifying pleasure of reading "In a Cup of Tea" or "The Black Hair" while the grandfather clock in the dining room struck midnight. It consoled me to think that those stories had not been written by a Japanese; they had been signed by a certain Lafcadio Hearn, an American writer, according to Aunt Gloria.

I suppose that my relations with Aunt Gloria would have become closer over the years. But the epidemic of typhus that hit Havana in the spring of 1943 got to my grandfather's house, and Aunt Gloria died after two weeks of illness. I never found out much about her. Shuffled in among six others of my mother's sisters, she had been until then just another aunt, a kiss on the cheek, a few pats on the shoulder, and a gratifying "How this boy has grown since I last saw him!" After she died I found out that she had worked in a milliner's and was about to marry a policeman. All that was left of her was a hand-colored photograph—color film would get to Cuba along with air conditioning and penicillin—that did not flatter her. Nonetheless, in spite of these commonplaces, my Aunt Gloria must have had something special: she was the only one of my aunts who ever gave me a book.

One day we found out that the war had ended and the world had entered the atomic age. By then I'd learned to dance, was getting lessons on the guitar, would kiss girls in the movie theater, and played second base on the high school baseball team. But, apart from doing more or less what was expected of me, I would read until almost dawn and take long, solitary walks wearing winged shoes to places where my imagination would break loose and fly daringly away. Little by little my addiction to nocturnal terrors was weakening, perhaps because I'd conjured so many ghosts in my room that I'd begun to see them regularly, among them my Aunt Gloria's, which was always pensive and dressed in a milky, loose-fitting gown; her feet, by some rule of the spirit world, were the part of her body least apt to materialize. In any case, I was taking the supernatural as something perfectly natural to my life; something that occurred by night and by day; something whose existence, if uncontrollable, should be taken for granted, without my worrying much about making distinctions between whether some presence that vanished before my eyes had been real or imagined. Lafcadio Hearn had left his mark on me, and it was to be permanent, for it had opened the window on the other world, on the exciting and mysterious landscape of the inexplicable.

My adolescence—and a good number of my adult years—went by as do most people's, that is, in a struggle to earn a living and carve out a future that would let me raise a family—I mean by this that I was (and still am) a practical man. But it also went by among books that tried to explain, through metaphysics, the complexity of the universe and the role of the human spirit on earth. I read tons of mystical and esoteric books; no important spiritual doctrine was completely foreign to me, nor any means of divination, from astrology to tarot. A day came, however, on which my search took another course, and that course was not outside of myself. Thus, the moment came when I understood that everything real, from what is natural to us to what we deem supernatural, from the most elemental particles of matter to the immeasurable presence of God, was contained in my own being. Furthermore, I understood that my life until then, far from having two windows as I had supposed—one that looked out upon practical things and the other that looked toward the supernatural—had always been one single life, one single large window. In saying this I'm not trying to impose my opinion on anyone else. I'm only saying that this is my own modest experience, and that this experience or truth, as minuscule as it is, began forming during the nights when, trembling with pleasure and with fear, I read Hearn's *kwaidan* stories.

In the summer of 1964 I decided to be a writer. It was an easy decision to make. Until then I had earned my living as an economist, but my post-Keynesian training did not fit within the rigid system of central planning that socialist Cuba had adopted. What course was I to take? The answer to this question entered my life in the abrupt and efficacious way that fateful things often do. I fractured two vertebrae in an accident and it was now a matter of nothing else but staying in bed for three months, of getting tired of reading and listening to music, and of asking my wife Hilda, before she left for work, to put up the portable table where they served my food, and to get me a pencil, an eraser, and a pad of paper.

My first story was deplorable—the main character boarded a bus filled with people who didn't know that they had died. It's better not to speak of my subsequent attempts. "I think you have a talent for the fantastic," a friend of mine who visited on Sundays said, "but there's something in your stories that doesn't work." The next time he came to see me he held out a book he'd borrowed from the National Library. "Read the article I've marked for you," he said to me, leaving the book on the bed. To my surprise, it turned out to be an essay by Lafcadio Hearn on literature and the supernatural. I read it with the avidity of one bewitched, or rather, of one predestined, since on read- ing the first lines I found out that my true vocation was literature. Hearn soon made me see what my mistake had been. Nothing having to do with fantastic literature—ghosts, the protagonist's fear, the un- canny effect, the suspense—should be copied from another writer's work. To write successfully about the supernatural, Hearn affirmed, one had to be authentic; one had to depend not on another's ghosts, but one's own; not on the fear suffered by another, but the super- natural terror that one experienced oneself. And if nothing of the sort had happened in one's life, one could always resort to dreams, and take one's own nightmares as models.

In 1965 I finished my first book of stories. I sent the manuscript to a fancy literary competition. If I didn't earn any distinction, I would keep on working as an economist; if I figured among the finalists, I would live for literature. I won first prize.

Translated by James E. Maraniss

Juan Carlos Onetti on Vladimir Nabokov

Juan Carlos Onetti (Uruguay, 1909–1994) wrote in relative obscurity for most of his literary career, while working as a magazine editor and director of Montevideo's municipal library system. As the literary editor of *Marcha* from 1939 to 1974, he helped voice the discontent of the most progressive elements of Uruguay's intellectual community. When Latin American literature reached international recognition in the 1960s, Onetti began to experience critical and popular success, which was heightened by the support he received from human rights groups and Latin American intellectuals after his 1974 arrest. Uruguay's military dictatorship arrested and imprisoned Onetti for his participation in a jury that awarded a prize to a short story which the regime considered subversive and pornographic. The international uproar that followed the arrest led to his release and involuntary exile in Madrid after 1975. After this incident, Onetti finally reached the recognition he deserved. Onetti, considered one of the great novelists of Latin America, was Faulknerian in his complex, self-reflexive brand of fiction, as seen in *La vida breve* (1950) and *El astillero* (1961). Among his other important works are *El pozo* (1939), *Alizado y otros cuentos* (1951), *El infierno tan temido* (1962), *Juntacadáveres* (1964), *Tiempo de abrazar* (1974), *Cuentos Completos* (1974), and *Tierra de nadie* (1980). He was awarded the Cervantes Prize in 1980. This review first appeared as "Otras vez *Lolita*," in *Marcha*, Montevideo, 29 May 1959.

Lolita is apparently aimed at a reduced elite audience and women are the first group to be excluded from it. After serious research, this reviewer has discovered that a nymphet is for most men as alien to love as a sewing machine or an umbrella. Thus, Vladimir Nabokov, the Russian émigré active in English, is only addressing readers capable of grasping his book's tragic undertones. He shares secret symbols, melancholy, and handshakes with them. I must insist on the smallness of this brotherhood: Simone de Beauvoir says somewhere that women are not born but made; on the contrary, men obsessed with nymphets are born that way and it is an utter mistake to associate this obsession with senile perversions.

And yet, *Lolita*, I predict, shall enjoy a similar success in the Spanish-speaking world to the one it encountered in the United States and France. Nabokov is undoubtedly very talented; proof of it is his cynicism and vigorous humor. His only regrettable aspect is his relentless desire to write a best-seller; and he has accomplished just that. He employs remarkable skills in writing the volume: he fills it with pornography, grotesque details, and tedious social critiques. *Lolita,* I'm convinced, will be widely read among us and might even become the source of a few scandals; the snobbish Argentine monthly *Sur,* under whose aegis it is published in Latin America, might even make up for the losses it incurs while publishing one Argentine and Uruguayan writer too many.

The last chapter of Nabokov's book ought to be cited as an example of his perversions. Although these pages reveal the disturbing influence of Mickey Spillane, Spillane wouldn't have signed his name to them. The following paragraph, part of that chapter, is a fine example of the aforementioned melancholy:

Sometimes . . . Come on, how often exactly, Bert? Can you recall four, five, more such occasions? Or would no human heart have survived two or three? Sometimes (I have nothing to say in reply to your question), while Lolita would be haphazardly preparing her homework, sucking a pencil, lolling sideways in an easy chair with both legs over its arms, I would shed all my pedagogic restraint, dismiss all our quarrels, forget all my masculine pride—and literally crawl on my knees to your chair, my Lolita! You would give me one look—a gray furry question mark of a look: "Oh no, not again" (incredulity, exasperation); for you never deigned to believe that I could, without any specific designs, ever crave to bury my face in your plaid skirt, my darling! The fragility of those bare arms of yours—how I longed to enfold them, all your four limpid lovely limbs, a folded colt, and take your head between my unworthy hands, and pull the temple-skin back on both sides, and kiss your chinesed eyes, and—"Please, leave me alone, will you," you would say, "for Christ's sake leave me alone." And I would get up from the floor while you looked on, your face deliberately twitching in imitation of my *tic nerveux.* But never mind, never mind, I am only a brute, never mind, let us go on with my miserable story.

On the back cover of *Lolita,* Graham Greene is quoted as saying this is a brilliant book; he is guilty of an astounding overstatement. John

Hollander, on the other hand, may very well be right in saying this is the most enjoyable book he has ever read, for it entertains, intrigues, and may be read in a single sitting. But its qualities conspire against its artistic success. With the exception of the book's most desperate moments, Nabokov is able to unveil his obsession with nymphets. His parody of a cheap brand of sexuality betrays an eagerness to apologize; he unsuccessfully tries to convince the reader that his is really not a serious theme.

Let me finish with a warning: *Lolita* contains a monumental disappointment. Its protagonist (Lola, Dolores, Dolly, Lolita . . .) is twelve years old in the first pages of the book; at the end, however, she is a repugnant—albeit respectable—fifteen-year-old woman bearing an advanced pregnancy.

Translated by José Matosantos

Mario Vargas Llosa on Ernest Hemingway

Born in Peru in 1936 and educated in Bolivia, Mario Vargas Llosa burst onto the literary scene with his second work, *The Time of the Hero* (1963). He followed this success with other notable novels, *The Green House* (1966), *Los cachorros* (1968), and *Conversation in the Cathedral* (1969). His extensive bibliography also includes *Captain Pantoja and the Secret Service* (1973), *Aunt Julie and the Script Writer* (1977), *The War of the End of the World* (1981), *Mayta* (1984), *In Praise of the Stepmother* (1988), and *The Notebooks of Don Rigoberto* (1997). He has also written theatrical pieces, excellent critical works, especially on Gabriel García Márquez, and essays, which have been collected in various volumes, including *Making Waves*. Vargas Llosa is considered one of the greatest living writers in the Spanish language. His prose demonstrates the writer's vast culture and the meticulousness with which he constructs his works. He has been inducted into the Spanish Royal Academy, was made an honorary citizen of Spain, and was awarded the Premio Cervantes in 1992. He has lectured at Harvard, Princeton, and Georgetown universities, among other institutions in the United States. This prologue was written in London, 23 June 1987. It introduced the Spanish translation of Hemingway's *A Movable Feast* (Barcelona: Seix Barral, 1987).

I read *A Movable Feast* for the first time in the middle of 1964, in the English edition that had just appeared. I identified immediately with the protagonist of this tender evocation. I was then also, like the Hemingway of the book, a young man serving his literary apprenticeship in Paris. I wrote the following review of the book at the time.

I

The newspapers have made us accustomed to confusing him with one of his characters. What is his biography? That of a man of action: journeys, violence, adventures and, at times, between a bout of drunkenness and a safari, literature. He had dedicated himself to literature as he had to boxing or hunting, brilliantly, sporadically: for him the most important thing was to live. Almost as by-products of his eventful life, his short stories and novels owed their realism and authenticity to his life. None of this was true; if anything it was the other way round, and Hemingway himself clears up this confusion and puts things straight in the last book he wrote, *A Movable Feast*. Who would have believed it? This genial, good-natured globetrotter takes stock of his past at the end of his life, and among the thousand adventures—wars, women, exploits—that he experienced, he chose, with a certain nostalgic melancholy, the image of a young man fired by an inner passion to write. Everything else, sports, pleasures, even the smallest joys and the daily disappointments and, of course, love and friendship, revolve around this secret fire, stoking it and finding there either condemnation or justification. It is a beautiful book in which he shows simply and casually how a vocation is both privileged and enslaving.

The passion to write is essential, but it is only a starting point. It is useless without that "good and severe discipline" that Hemingway mastered in his youth in Paris, between 1921 and 1926, those years evoked in the book when he "was very poor and very happy." Apparently these were the years of his bohemian existence; he spent the day in the cafés, he went to the races, he drank. In reality, a secret order governed this "movable feast" and the disorder was really a form of freedom, of being always open. All his actions converged on one point: his work. The bohemian life can, of course, be a useful experience (but no more or less than any other) as long as one is an experienced horseman who will not be thrown by his horse. Through stories, meetings, conversations, Hemingway reveals the rigid laws that he had imposed on himself to avoid shipwreck in the troubled waters through which he was sailing. "My training was never to drink after dinner, nor before I wrote nor while I was writing. I would write one story about each thing that I knew about." However, at the end of a good day, he treats himself to a glass of kirsch. He cannot always work with the same enthusiasm; at times he feels emptiness, depression, in front of the blank page. Then he would recite in a low voice: "Don't worry. You have always written before and you will write now. All you have to do is to write a good sentence. Write the truest sentence you know." To stimulate himself, he sets out fabulous goals. "I will write a story about each thing that I know about." And when he finishes a story he always feels empty, sad, and happy at the same time, as if he had just made love.

He went to cafés, that's true, but he used them as his study. On those tables of fake marble on the terraces that overlook the Luxembourg Gardens, he did not go woolgathering or pontificate like the South American bohemians of the rue Cujas: he wrote his first books of stories and corrected the chapters of *The Sun Also Rises*. And if someone interrupted him, he was thrown out with a volley of insults: the pages where he narrates how he treats an intruder, in La Closerie des Lilas, are a thesaurus of curses. (Years later Lisandro Otero spotted Hemingway one night in a bar in Old Havana. Timidly and respectfully, he went up to greet the author whom he admired and Hemingway, who was writing standing at the counter, despatched him with a punch.) After writing, he says, he needs to read, so as not to stay obsessed by what he is telling. These are difficult times, there is no money to buy books, but Sylvia Beach, the director of Shakespeare and Company, gives him books. As do friends like Gertrude Stein in whose house he also finds beautiful pictures, a friendly atmosphere, and delicious cakes.

His desire to *learn* in order to write is behind all his actions: it determines his tastes, his relationships. And whatever could be seen as an obstacle, like that intruder, is rejected without a second thought. His vocation is a whirlwind. Let us take the example of horse racing. He befriended jockeys and trainers who gave him tips for the races: one lucky day the horses allow him to dine at Chez Michaux, where he spots Joyce talking in Italian to his wife and children. The world of the races, furthermore (and he gives this as his main reason for going racing), provides him with material for his work. But one evening, he discovers that this passion is wasting his time, has become almost an end in itself. He immediately suppresses it. The same occurs with journalism from which he earns a living; he gives it up, despite the fact that the North American magazines are still turning down his stories. Although literature is a constant, essential preoccupation of the young Hemingway, it is scarcely mentioned in *A Movable Feast*. But it is there, all the time, hidden in a thousand forms, and the reader can feel it, invisible, sleepless, voracious. When Hemingway goes out to the quays and studies like an entomologist the customs and art of the fishermen of the Seine, during his conversations with Ford Madox Ford, while he is teaching Ezra Pound how to box, when he travels, speaks, eats, and even sleeps, there is a spy hidden within him looking at him with cold and practical eyes, selecting and rejecting experiences, storing them. "Did you learn something today, Tatie?," Hemingway's wife asks him every night when he returns to their apartment in the rue de Cardinal Lemoine.

In the final chapters of *A Movable Feast*, Hemingway remembers a colleague of his generation: F. Scott Fitzgerald. Famous and a millionaire thanks to his first book, written when he was a very young man, Fitzgerald in Paris is the writer who cannot control the reins. The bohemian steed drags him and Zelda down to the depths of alcohol, masochism, and neurosis. These are pages similar to the last episode in *A Farewell to Arms*, in which an icy current flows beneath the clear surface of the prose. Hemingway seems to hold Zelda responsible for the precocious decadence of Fitzgerald; jealous of literature, it was she who pushed him to excess and to this frenetic lifestyle. But others accuse Fitzgerald himself of the madness which led Zelda to an asylum and to death. Whatever the reason, one thing is evident: the bohemian life can only help literature when it is a pretext for writing: if the reverse occurs (as it does frequently), then the bohemian life can kill a writer.

Because literature is a passion and passion is exclusive. It cannot be shared, it demands every sacrifice and gives in to nothing. Hemingway is in a café and by his side there is a young woman. He thinks "You belong to me and Paris belongs to me, but I belong to this notebook and pencil." That is exactly what slavery means. The condition of the writer is strange and paradoxical. His privilege is freedom, the right to see, hear, and investigate everything. He is authorized to dive into the depths, to climb the peaks: the whole of reality is his. What is the purpose of this privilege? To feed the beast within which enslaves him, which feeds off all his acts, tortures him mercilessly, and is only appeased, momentarily, in the act of creation. When the words flow forth. If one has chosen the beast and carries it in one's guts, there is no alternative, one has to give it everything. When Hemingway went to the bullfights, visited the Republican trenches in Spain, killed elephants, or fell over drunk, he was not indulging in adventure or pleasure, but he was a man satisfying the whims of this insatiable, solitary beast. Because for him, as for any other writer, the most important thing was not to live but to write.

II

Rereading it today, with all that we now know about the Hemingway who wrote it and about his relationships with the figures explored in its pages, *A Movable Feast* takes on a somewhat different meaning. In fact, the health and optimism that it displays are literary constructs which do not correspond with the dramatic reality of physical and intellectual decline that its author was suffering. He is right at the end of his literary career and he suspects it. He also knows that he would not now recover from the rapid diminution of his physical faculties that he was suffering at the time. None of this is mentioned in the book. But for today's reader, informed by the biographies of Hemingway that have appeared in recent years, this knowledge offers one of the keys through which, by reading between the lines of this testimony of the literary origins of a great writer that seems at first sight so clear and direct, he can discover the unhappy trauma that underlies it.

Rather than a nostalgic evocation of youth, the book is a magical spell, an unconscious attempt to return, through memory and the word, to the apogee of his life, the moment of his greatest energy and creative force, so as to recuperate that energy and lucidity which was now rapidly draining away. And the book is also a posthumous revenge, a settling of accounts with former companions in literature and in the bohemian world. A book of pathos, a swan-song—because it was the last book that he wrote—it conceals beneath the deceptive patina of his youthful memories a confession of defeat. The man who began in this way, in the Paris of the mad 1920s, so talented and so happy, so creative and so vital, who in a few months was capable of writing a masterpiece—*The Sun Also Rises*—at the same time as he drank in all the succulent juices of life—trout fishing and going to the bullfights in Spain, skiing in Austria, betting on the horses in Saint-Cloud, drinking the wines and spirits of La Closerie—is already dead; he is a ghost who is trying to cling on to life through that age-old conjuring trick invented by men to gain an illusory triumph over death: literature.

We now know that the book is full of pettinesses and spite against old friends and ex-friends and that, for example, some of his stories, perhaps the best—about Gertrude Stein and Scott Fitzgerald—are false. But these pettinesses do not cheapen what is admirable in the text: the fact that Hemingway was able to turn defects into virtues, to create a beautiful literary work out of loss and the limitations which, from that time on, prevented him from producing any memorable story or novel.

According to Mary, his widow, Hemingway wrote *A Movable Feast* between autumn 1957 and autumn 1960, with long interruptions in between. This was a moment of continual crisis for him, of nervous depression, of deep bitterness which rarely showed in his public appearances where he kept up the impression of being the happy and adventurous giant that he had always been, full of appetites and light. (That's how he seemed to me, in the summer of 1959 in the Plaza de Toros in Madrid, the one time that I saw him, at a distance, on the arm of another living myth of the age: Ava Gardner.)

In reality he was a wounded colossus, semi-impotent, incapable of the mental concentration of undertaking an important work, terrified by his loss of memory, a deficiency which for a man who plays at being a deicide—the novelist, who reinvents reality—is quite simply fatal. Yes, how can one invent a coherent fictional world in which the whole and the parts are vigorously linked in order to simulate the real world, the whole of life, if the memory of the creator is fading and the spell of the fiction is broken at every moment by incongruities and mistakes in the tale? Hemingway's answer to the question was this book: writing a fiction under the guise of memory, whose disconnected and fragmentary nature is concealed by the unity imposed on it by a narrator who remembers and writes the work.

Memory in *A Movable Feast* is a literary device to justify the vagaries of a memory which can no longer concentrate on the concrete or undertake the rigorous structure of a fiction, but which jumps, disorganized and free, from image to image, without any harmony or continuity. In a novel, this atomization would have been chaotic; in a book of memories it offers, instead, an impressionistic meandering through certain faces and places afloat in the river of time, unlike the innumerable other people who have been swallowed up by forgetfulness. Each chapter is a short story in disguise, a snapshot organized with the virtues of his best fictions: the terse prose, the taut dialogues which always suggest more than (and sometimes the opposite of) what they are saying, and the descriptions whose stubborn objectivity seems to beg us to forgive them their perfection.

But alongside the real history, in each of these elegant snapshots there are more distortions than reliable testimonies. But what does that matter? It does not make them any the less persuasive or exciting for a lover of literature, that is, someone who expects a novelist to write books which are capable of telling him not necessarily the Truth, in capital letters, but rather his own particular truth, and in a way that is so convincing and clever that there is no alternative but to believe him. And in this final autobiographical fiction, Hemingway achieved this magnificently.

Furthermore, although he was not identical to the figure that he sketches in this portrait of his youth, some essential characteristics of his personality do appear in his book. His anti-intellectualism, for example. It is a pose that he always cultivated and which, above all in the final years, he took to extreme lengths. In this book also, authentic—not bookish—literature is presented as a physical skill, something that the consummate sportsman, the writer, perfects and controls through discipline and steadfastness, a healthy life, and healthy body. The very idea that art or literature might in some way imply a retreat into the purely mental, a withdrawal from everyday life, a bathing in the wellsprings of the unknown or a challenge to the rational order of existence is energetically rejected and ridiculed. For that reason the sketch that the book offers of Ezra Pound, although lively and generous, does not even skim the surface of Pound's contradictory nature. And yet it is clear that Hemingway was not completely incapable of perceiving below or between the interstices of these permissible rituals of life, which sufficed for him, that other life, the life of the depths, of prohibition, of misconduct. It was a world that he feared and that he always refused to explore except in its most superficial manifestations (such as the cruel and fascinating ceremony of the bullfight). But he knew that it existed and could identify those damned souls who inhabited it, like Wyndham Lewis, who is badly treated in these pages. He inspired the best and the most disconcerting sentence in the book. "Some people show evil as a great racehorse shows breeding. They have the dignity of a hard *chancre*."

Mario Vargas Llosa on Ernest Hemingway **149**

Another of his prejudices is also to be found in abundant measure: the *machismo* which, together with his passion for killing animals and the spell that violent sports held over him, constitute a morality and a code of life which is very different from our own, which is concerned with feminism and its truths, the conservation of nature and the struggle for freedom of sexual minorities. The conversation with Gertrude Stein, in which she tries to gain Hemingway's sympathy for lesbianism, with arguments that would today make a schoolgirl smile, and his reticence and replies are instructive in this respect. They show how far customs have evolved and how old-fashioned are many of the values that Hemingway extolled in his novels.

But, despite these anachronisms, this short book gives immense pleasure. The magic of his style, its Flaubertian insidious simplicity and precision, the passion for the elements and for physical prowess, the vivid recreation of the Paris of expatriate Americans in the period between the two world wars and an affirmation of the writer that the book symbolizes—a resolute affirmation of a vocation at a time when he could scarcely still write—blend to give a unique status to what would become his literary testimony. Although it contains as many additions and modifications to life as a novel, it remains an important autobiographical document and, with all the liberties that it takes with objective facts, it offers an incomparable picture of the times and the happy insouciance with which France stimulated art and excess, while, inside and outside its frontiers, its subsequent ruin was being brought about. But, above all, its pages, which are as clear and sonorous as a mountain stream, enable us to draw close, with the immediacy of successful fiction, to the secrets of art which allowed Hemingway to transmute the life he lived and the life that he only dreamed of, into this shared feast that is literature.

Translated by John King

Nicolás Guillén on Langston Hughes

The oeuvre of Nicolás Guillén (1906–1989), widely acclaimed as one of the great Cuban poets of late, spans *Modernismo,* folklorism, social protest, and, most notably, *poesía negrista.* In what was a radical rupture from the manner in which blacks had been previously treated in Cuban literature, Guillén's works portray blacks or blackness not as an exotic element but as an integral element of Cuban culture and a necessary component of the search for a Cuban identity. Guillén's works immediately caught the attention of those who were unwilling to accept Cuba's racial reality. He was the editor of the newspaper *Información* and the weekly humor journal *El loco.* After being dismissed from his job as a typist in the Department of Culture, Guillén increased his involvement in politics. He was a member of the National Committee of Revolutionary Communist Union and of the Cuban Communist Party. He would later collaborate actively with the Revolution and was to become an ambassador-at-large and plenipotentiary minister of the country's foreign service for Fidel Castro's regime. Guillén published *Cantos para soldados y sones para turistas* in 1937, the same year he joined the Communist Party. His most famous works came later: *El gran zoo* (1967), *El diario que a diario* (1972), and *Poesías completas* (1973). His poetry has also been widely translated; 1972 saw the publication of both *Patria o muerte: The Great Zoo and Other Poems by Nicolás Guillén* and *Man-Making Words: Selected Poems of Nicolás Guillén* in the United States. Guillén was president of the Cuban Writer's Union and an active cultural and political figure his entire life. This light piece of reportage first appeared as "Conversación con Langston Hughes," in *Diario de la Marina,* Havana, 9 March 1930.

Those of us who only knew Langston Hughes, the great Black poet of the United States, from a strictly intellectual viewpoint after reading *The Weary Blues* and *Fine Clothes to the Jew,* his two early books of verse, attributed to him a physical maturity he hadn't quite reached, one he has taken time to fully grasp.

I heard José Antonio Fernández de Castro—known lately as "patient No. 20," because of the illness that has afflicted him for more than two weeks—announce loudly that Mr. Hughes was about to arrive. Soon after, someone told me: "I will recognize him, I know how he looks: he's about forty or forty-five years of age; is tall, very stout, and almost white-skinned; and has a tiny English mustache adorning his thin, embittered lips." On the contrary, when Mr. Hughes himself appeared, we were totally surprised, for what we saw was a youngster of twenty-seven, slight and slim, with skin the color of wheat, and without an English mustache; in fact, without any mustache whatever.

Mr. Hughes looks just like a Cuban *mulatico* studying at a national university who spends his time organizing small family parties at two pesos a ticket. Behind this nondescript appearance, nonetheless, breathes a burning spirit permanently bound to the issues of the Black race, an intensely personal poet observing his people closely so as to make them accessible, known, and loved by others.

More than any other poet in the English language, Mr. Hughes has incorporated into the literature of the U.S. the most distilled manifestations of popular music, so influenced by Blacks: his jazz and blues poems, as well as his spirituals, are proof of it.

Apart from this, Mr. Hughes, a warm and generous man, seldom attracts the interest of journalists. So rather than do a flashy reportage, one prefers to slow-dance with him in order to see the contours of his personality emerge from the haze.

This *norteamericano* is always interested in African civilization. "Now it's a trend, *sabe usted?*," he explains. "But these things have always interested me. Six years ago, in my country, only Russian literature was read—a fever! Today, though, nothing interests the public more than Blacks. So in the future, when our own story is exhausted, the frenzy, I assume, will be turned onto native Americans—a symbol of the continent's aboriginal past . . . Everything about *los indios, las razas autóctonas del Contiente.*"

Mr. Hughes's Spanish isn't very rich; but he uses it marvelously, always managing to say exactly what he wants. And, above all, he always has something to say.

He talks about his personal life: "I should have had a more conventional career. My folks wanted me to be a lawyer, a doctor, an engineer. The truth is, since I was fourteen years old, I didn't do anything but write poems. I wrote, wrote, wrote . . . , which, as you know, is a commodity worth very little. Poetry is my reaction against the misery of the humble classes and against the terrible situation in which Blacks in the U.S. live today."

"After studying for a year at Columbia University, I set out to travel the world, free of all ties and social conventions. My first job was as a ploughman, ¿sabe usted? Later I worked as a waiter on a ship and as a sailor too. I traveled to Africa."

"Africa?"

"Sí, señor. I visited Dakar, Nigeria, Rwanda . . . These lands strengthened my love for Blacks, which shall never abandon me. In touch with mi gente, whose arms were cut off by Belgium and whose bodies were brutally decimated by France in the jungle, as journalist Alberto Londres has shown, I understood the necessity of being their friend— their voice, their consolation: in short, their poet. I don't have any other ambition but to be a Black poet and a poet for Blacks, ¿comprende usted?

Yes, I understood.

(Actually, one of Mr. Hughes's famous poems about Africa enchants me: "I am a Negro: Black like the night is black, Black like the depths of my Africa.")

"From Africa," Mr. Hughes continues, "I went to Europe. I visited Paris, Milan, Venice, Verona. I suffered a great deal working the most humble jobs. But I got to know human suffering intimately. I then returned to the U.S. but without a nickel, paying the price of the voyage with my arms."

"I docked in New York, poor and ragged, on a winter afternoon. By night, I stayed in Harlem. Happily, my verses found an audience. Some friends helped me out. . . . In late 1926, I published my first book, The Weary Blues, where my first Black poems appear, as do my jazz poems, written to the rhythm of Black music. The volume also includes poems about the sea, written while I walked barefooted over the decks of ships in Africa and Europe. And it has some love poems, for in my journey there was time for love too . . ."

"And after that?"

"Fine Clothes to the Jew, my second volume, came out. It is about race and work, made of blues and spirituals. In all my poems, I always had my people in mind, you know? . . . In August, my next book will be out, a novel called Not Without Laughter, about the life of a Black family in the Midwest. In it I show how, in spite of the formidable struggle against White prejudice, tragedy is always muted by a note of joy. . . . The manuscript is in my editor's hands."

I ask: "How do you see the race problem in the United States with regard to women? Is there a solution?"

The poet smiles. He plays with his graduation ring, its traditional golden seal flashing in our eyes. Finally he answers: "Look, I'm no sociologist. I'm simply a poet. I live amongst my people: I love them—the blows they get hurt me to the core. I sing their pain, I translate their sorrow, I let their longings soar. And I do all this as spontaneously as the people do it themselves. Did you know that I've never taken the time to study classic verse? I'm lucky enough never to have been forced to write a poem, *¿sabe usted*? I write spontaneously. I write what comes to me from inside. . . . I don't 'study' Blacks, I 'feel' them."

He says afterwards: "I only strive to maintain the Black man's spontaneity. White civilization will eradicate *lo primitivo* in Black people, dressing them up in clothes not truly theirs. Of course, some Blacks ignore me; they think my poems are only about the lower classes. They prefer to spend their time playing aristocratic games, living the 'high life,' imitating their old owners! . . . But what's one to do?"

Black Cuba attracts Mr. Hughes. Wherever he goes, he investigates the condition of Blacks, and our homeland is no exception. "Do Blacks come to this cafe?," he asks. "Does this or that orchestra admit them? Are there Black artists in Cuba? I'd love to go to a Black cabaret in Havana! . . ."

I take him to a dance club attended only by Blacks. The moment he sets foot in it, he seems possessed by the spirit of the *suezos*—of what is mine. "My people!" he exclaims.

And for a long time he remains near the raucous band where a *son* spreads its echoes. His breathing broken by emotion, Mr. Hughes feels rejuvenated. Later, as he watches the bongo players—*negros como la noche,* black like the night—he exclaims, with a sigh of unsatisfied longing: "*¡Yo quisiera ser negro! Bien negro. ¡Negro de verda!*"

Translated by Laura Santiago

Octavio Paz on William Carlos Williams

The poetic gift of Octavio Paz (1914–1998), considered a poet unmatched in production and versatility by almost any other Latin American writer, clearly shines through to his prose as well. Studying in the United States, he gained remarkable insight into his native Mexico and its relationship to her nations and societies, which laid the foundation for his great analysis of Mexican culture, *The Labyrinth of Solitude* (1950, rev. 1959). Diplomatic duties in France led to his interest in Surrealism. He also served as ambassador to India, which led to *The Monkey Grammarian* (1974). Other important nonfiction works include *Conjunctions and Disjunctions* (1969), *Children of Mire: Poetry from Romanticism to the Avant-Garde* (1974), *The Philantropic Ogre* (1979), *Of Poets and Others* (1986), and *The Other Voice: Essays on Modern Poetry* (1991). Paz is also responsible for an outstanding biography, *Sor Juana: The Traps of Faith* (1982), a study of gender, politics, and culture in colonial Mexico. His complete works in Spanish, spanning fourteen volumes, are published in Mexico by Fondo de Cultura Económica. This essay was written in Zihuatanejo, Mexico, 10 January 1973. It served as prologue to Williams's *XX Poemas* (Mexico City, 1973).

for James Laughlin

In the first third of our century, a change occurred in the literatures of the English language which affected verse and prose, syntax and sensibility, imagination and prosody alike. The change—similar to those which occurred about the same time in other parts of Europe and in Latin America—was originally the work of a handful of poets, almost all of them Americans. In that group of founders, William Carlos Williams occupies a place at once central and unique: unlike Pound and Eliot, he preferred to bury himself in a little city outside New York rather than uproot himself and go to London or Paris; unlike Wallace Stevens and e. e. cummings, who also decided to stay in the United States but who were cosmopolitan spirits, Williams from the outset sought a poetic Americanism. In effect, as he explains in the beautiful essays of *In the American Grain* (1925), America is not a given reality but something we all make together with our hands, our eyes, our brains, and our lips. The American reality is material, mental, visual, and above all, verbal: whether he speaks Spanish, English, Portuguese, or French, American man speaks a language different from the European original. More than just a reality we discover or make, America is a reality we speak.

William Carlos Williams was born in Rutherford, New Jersey, in 1883. His father was English, his mother Puerto Rican. He studied medicine at the University of Pennsylvania. There he met Pound—a friendship that was to last throughout his life—and the poet H.D. (Hilda Doolittle), who fascinated the two young poets. After taking his doctorate and a short period of pediatric study in Leipzig, in 1910 he settled definitively in Rutherford. Two years later he married Florence Herman: a marriage that lasted a lifetime. Also for a lifetime he practiced a double vocation: medicine and poetry. Though he lived in the provinces, he was not a provincial: he was immersed in the artistic and intellectual currents of our century, traveled on various occasions to Europe, and befriended English, French, and Latin American writers. His literary friendships and enmities were varied and intense: Pound, Marianne Moore, Wallace Stevens, Eliot (whom he admired and condemned), e. e. cummings, and others, younger, like James Laughlin and Louis Zukofsky. His influence and friendship were decisive on Allen Ginsberg and also on the poetry of Robert Creeley, Robert Duncan, and the English poet Charles Tomlinson. (Poetic justice: a young English poet—and very English—praised by one who practiced almost his whole life a kind of poetic anti-Anglicism and who never tired of saying that the American language wasn't really English.) In 1951 he suffered his first attack of paralysis but survived a dozen years, dedicated to a literary program of rare fecundity: books of poetry, a translation of Quevedo, memoirs, lectures, and readings of his poems across the whole country. He died on 4 March 1963, where he was born and spent his life: in Rutherford.

His work is vast and varied: poetry, fiction, essays, theater, autobiography. The poetry has been collected in four volumes: *Collected Earlier Poems* (1906–1939), *Collected Later Poems* (1940–1946), *Pictures from Breughel* (1950–1962), and *Paterson* (1946–1958), a long poem in five books. Also there is a slim book of prose-poems which sometimes make one think of the automatic writing Breton and Soupault were engaged in around this time: *Kora in Hell* (1920). But in taking over a poetic form invented by French poetry, Williams changes it and converts it into a method of exploring language and the varied strata of the collective unconscious. *Kora in Hell* is a book which could only have been written by an American poet and ought to be read from the perspective of a later book which is the axis of Williams's Americanism, his *ars poetica: In the American Grain*. I will not consider his novels, stories, or theater pieces. Suffice it to say that they are extensions and irradiations of his poetry. The boundary between prose and verse, always hard to draw, becomes very tenuous in this poet: his free verse is very close to prose, not as written but as spoken, the everyday language; and his prose is always rhythmic, like a coast bathed by poetic surf—not verse but the verbal flux and reflux that gives rise to verse.

From the time he started writing, Williams evinced a distrust of ideas. It was a reaction against the symbolist aesthetic shared by the majority of poets at that time (remember López Velarde) and in which, in his case, American pragmatism was combined with his medical profession. In a famous poem he defines his search: "To compose: no ideas but in things." But things are always beyond, on the other side: the "thing itself" is untouchable. Thus Williams's point of departure is not things but sensation. And yet sensation in turn is formless and instantaneous; one cannot build or do anything with pure sensations: that would result in chaos. Sensation is amphibious: at the same time it joins us to and divides us from things. It is the door through which we enter into things but also through which we come out of them and realize that we are not things. In order for sensation to accede to the objectivity of things it must itself be changed into a thing. The agent of change is language: the sensations are turned into verbal objects. A poem is a verbal object in which two contradictory properties are fused: the liveliness of the sensation and the objectivity of things.

Sensations are turned into verbal objects by the operation of a force which for Williams is not essentially distinct from electricity, steam, or gas: imagination. In some reflections written down in 1923 (included among the poems in the late edition of *Spring and All* as "dislocated prose"), Williams says that the imagination is "a creative force which makes objects." The poem is not a double of the sensation or of the thing. Imagination does not represent: it produces. Its products are poems, objects which were not real before. The poetic imagination produces poems, pictures, and cathedrals as nature produces pines, clouds, and crocodiles. Williams wrings the neck of traditional aesthetics: art does not imitate nature: it imitates its creative processes. It does not copy its products but its modes of production. "Art is not a mirror to reflect nature but imagination competes with the compositions of nature. The poet becomes a nature and works like her." It is incredible that Spanish-language critics have not paused over the extraordinary similarity between these ideas and those that Vicente Huidobro proclaimed in statements and manifestos. True, it's a matter of ideas that appear in the work of many poets and artists of that time (for example, in Reverdy, who initiated Huidobro into modern poetry), but the similarity between the North American and Latin American are impressive. Both *invert* in almost the same terms the Aristotelian aesthetic and *convert* it for the modern era: imagination is, like electricity, a form of energy, and the poet is the transmitter.

The poetic theories of Williams and the "Creationism" of Huidobro are twins, but hostile twins. Huidobro sees in poetry something homologous with magic and, like a primitive shaman who *makes* rain, wants to make poetry; Williams conceives of poetic imagination as an activity that completes and rivals science. Nothing is further from magic than Williams. In a moment of childish egotism, Huidobro said: "The poet is a little God," an expression that the American poet would have rejected. Another difference: Huidobro tried to produce verbal objects which were not imitations of real objects and which even negated them. Art as a means of escaping reality. The title of one of his books is also a definition of his purpose: *Horizonte cuadrado* (*Square Horizon*). Attempting the impossible: one need only compare the pictures of abstract painters with the images which microscopes and telescopes provide us to realize that we cannot get away from nature. For Williams the artist—it is significant that he was supported and inspired by the example of Juan Gris—*separates* the things of the imagination from the things of reality: cubist reality is not the table, the cup, the pipe, and the newspaper as they are but *another* reality, no less real. This *other* reality does not deny the reality of real things: it is *another* thing which is *the same thing* at the same time. "The mountain and the sea in a picture by Juan Gris," Williams says, "are not the mountain and the sea but a painting of the mountain and the sea." The poem-thing isn't the thing: it is something else which exchanges signs of intelligence with the thing.

The non-imitative realism of Williams brings him close to two other poets: Jorge Guillén and Francis Ponge. (Again, I am pointing out coincidences, not influences.) A line of Guillén's defines their common repugnance for symbols: "the little birds chirp without design of grace." Do design and grace disappear? No: they enter the poem surreptitiously, without the poet's noticing. The "design of grace" is no longer in the real birds but in the text. The poem-thing is as unattainable as the poem-idea of symbolist poetry. Words are things, but things which mean. We cannot do away with meaning without doing away with the signs, that is, with language itself. Moreover: we would have to do away with the universe. All the things man touches are impregnated with meaning. Perceived by man, things exchange being for meaning: they are not, they mean. Even "having no meaning" is a way of meaning. The absurd is one of the extremes that meaning reaches when it examines its conscience and asks itself, What is the meaning of meaning? Ambivalence of meaning: it is the fissure through which we enter things and the fissure through which being escapes from them.

Meaning ceaselessly undermines the poem; it seeks to reduce its reality as an object of the senses and as a unique thing to an idea, a definition, or a "message." To protect the poem from the ravages of meaning, poets stress the material aspect of language. In poetry, the physical properties of the sign, audible and visible, are not less but more important than the semantic properties. Or rather: meaning returns to sound and becomes its servant. The poet works on the nostalgia which the signified feels for the signifier. In Ponge this process is achieved by the constant play between prose and poetry, fantastic humor and common sense. The result is a new being: the *objeu*. All the same, we can make fun of meaning, disperse and pulverize it, but we cannot annihilate it: whole or in living fragments and wriggling, like the slices of a serpent, meaning reappears. The creative description of the world turns, on the one hand, into a criticism of the world (Ponge as moralist); on the other, into *proeme* (the *précieux* Ponge, a sort of Gracián of objects). In Guillén the celebration of the world and of things results in history, satire, elegy: again, meaning. Williams's solution to the amphibious nature of language—words are things and are meanings—is different. He is not a European with a history behind him ready made but one ahead and to be made. He does not correct poetry with the morality of prose or convert humor into a teacher of resignation in song. On the contrary: prose is a ground where poetry grows, and humor is the spur of the imagination. Williams is a sower of poetic seeds. The American language is a buried seed which can only come to fruition if irrigated and shone upon by poetic imagination.

Partial reconciliation, always partial and provisional, between meaning and thing. Meaning—criticism of the world in Guillén, of language in Ponge—becomes in Williams an active power at the service of things. Meaning *makes,* is the midwife of objects. His art seeks "to reconcile people and stones through metaphor," American man and his landscape, speaking being with mute object. The poem is a metaphor in which objects speak and words cease to be ideas to become sensible objects. Eye and ear: the object heard and the word drawn. In connection with the first, Williams was the master and friend of the so-called Objectivists: Zukofsky, Oppen; in connection with the second, of the Black Mountain school: Olson, Duncan, Creeley. Imagination not only sees: it hears; not only hears: it says. In his search for the American language, Williams finds (hears) the basic measure, a meter of variable foot but with a triadic accentual base. "We know nothing," he says, "but the dance: the measure is all we know." The poem-thing is a verbal object, rhythmical. Its rhythm is a transmutation of the language of a people. By means of language Williams makes the leap from thing and sensation to the world of history.

Paterson is the result of these concerns. Williams goes from the poem-thing to the poem-as-system-of-things. Single and multiple system: single as a city were it one man only, multiple as a woman were she many flowers. *Paterson* is the biography of a city of the industrial East of the United States and the history of one man. City and man are fused in the image of a waterfall that cascades down, with a deafening roar, from the stone mouth of the mountain. Paterson has been founded at the foot of that mountain. The cataract is language itself, the people who never know what they say and who wander always in search of the meaning of what they say. Cataract and mountain, man and woman, poet and people, preindustrial and industrial age, the incoherent noise of the cascade and the search for a measure, a meaning. *Paterson* belongs to the poetic *genre* invented by modern American poetry which oscillates between the *Aeneid* and a treatise on political economy, the *Divine Comedy* and journalism: huge collections of fragments, the most imposing example of which is Pound's *Cantos*.

All these poems, obsessed as much by a desire to *speak* the American reality as to *make* it, are the contemporary descendants of Whitman, and all of them, one way or another, set out to fulfill the prophecy of *Leaves of Grass*. And in a sense they do fulfill it, but negatively. Whitman's theme is the embodiment of the future in America. Marriage of the concrete and the universal, present and future: American democracy is the universalizing of national-bound European man and his rerooting in a particular land and society. The particularity consists in the fact that that society and that place are not a tradition but a present fired toward the future. Pound, Williams, and even Hart Crane are the other side of this promise: their poems demonstrate to us the ruins of that project. Ruins no less grand and impressive than the others. Cathedrals are the ruins of Christian eternity, *stupas* are the ruins of Buddhist vacuity, the Greek temples of the *polis* and of geometry, but the big American cities and their suburbs are the living ruins of the future. In those huge industrial waste-bins the philosophy and morality of progress have come to a standstill. With the modern world ends the titanism of the future, compared with which the titanisms of the past—Incas, Romans, Chinese, Egyptians—seem childish sand castles.

Williams's poem is complex and uneven. Beside magical or realistic fragments of great intensity, there are long disjointed chunks. Written in the face of and sometimes against *The Waste Land* and the *Cantos*, it gets out of hand in its polemic with these two works. This is its principal limitation: reading it depends on other readings, so that the reader's judgment turns fatally to comparison. The vision Pound and Eliot had of the modern world was somber. Their pessimism was instinct with feudal nostalgias and precapitalist concepts; thus their just condemnation of money and modernity turned immediately into conservative and, in Pound's case, Fascist attitudes. Though Williams's vision is not optimistic either—how could it be?—there are in it no reminiscences of other ages. This could be an advantage, but it is not: Williams has no philosophic or religious system, no coherent collection of ideas and beliefs. What his immediate tradition (Whitman) offered him was unusable. There is a kind of void at the center of Williams's conception (though not in his short poems) which is the very void of contemporary American culture. The Christianity of *The Waste Land* is a truth that has been burned, calcined, and which, in my view, will not put out leaves again, but it was a central truth which, like light from a dead star, still *touches* us. I find nothing like that in *Paterson*. Comparison with the *Cantos* is not to Williams's advantage either. The United States is an imperial power, and if Pound could not be its Virgil he was at least its Milton: his theme is the fall of a great power. The United States gained a world but lost its soul, its future — that universal future in which Whitman believed. Perhaps on account of his very integrity and morality, Williams did not see the imperial aspect of his country, its demonic dimension.

Paterson has neither the unity nor the religious authenticity of *The Waste Land* — even if Eliot's religious feeling is negative. The *Cantos*, for their part, are an incomparably vaster and richer poem than Williams's, one of the few contemporary texts that stand up to our terrible age. So what? The greatness of a poet is not measured by the extent but by the intensity and perfection of his works. Also by their liveliness. Williams is the author of the *liveliest* modern American poems. Yvor Winters rightly says, "Herrick is less great than Shakespeare but probably he is no less fine and will last as long as he. . . . Williams will be almost as indestructible as Herrick; at the end of this century we will see him recognized, along with Wallace Stevens, as one of the two best poets of his generation." The prophecy came true before Winters expected it to. As to his ideas about New World poetry — is he really the most American of the poets of his age? I neither know nor care. On the other hand, I know he is the freshest, the most limpid. Fresh like a flow of drinking water, limpid as that same water in a glass jug on an unpolished wooden table in a white-washed room in Nantucket. Wallace Stevens once called him "a sort of Diogenes of contemporary poetry." His lantern, burning in full daylight, is a little sun of his own light. The sun's double and its refutation: that lantern illuminates areas forbidden to natural light.

In the summer of 1970, at Churchill College, Cambridge, I translated six Williams poems. Later, on two escapades, one to Veracruz and another to Zihuatanejo, I translated others. Mine are not literal translations: literalness is not only impossible but reprehensible. Nor are they (I wish they were!) re-creations: they are approximations and, at times, transpositions. What I most regret is that I was unable to find in Spanish a rhythm equivalent to Williams's. But rather than embroil myself in the endless subject of poetry translation, I prefer to tell how I met him. Donald Allen sent me an English version of a poem of mine ("Hymn Among Ruins"). The translation impressed me for two reasons: it was magnificent, and its author was William Carlos Williams. I vowed that I would meet him, and on one of my trips to New York I asked Donald Allen to take me with him, as he had taken me before to meet cummings. One afternoon we visited him at his house in Rutherford. He was already half-paralyzed. The house was built of wood, as is common in the United States, and it was more a doctor's than a writer's house. I have never met a less affected man—the opposite of an oracle. He was possessed by poetry, not by his role as a poet. Wit, calmness, that not taking yourself seriously which Latin American writers so lack. In each French, Italian, Spanish, and Latin American writer—especially if he is an atheist and revolutionary—a clergyman is concealed; among the Americans plainness, sympathy, and *democratic* humanity—in the true sense of this word—break the professional shell. It has always surprised me that in a world of relations as hard as that of the United States, cordiality constantly springs out like water from an unstanchable fountain. Maybe this has something to do with the religious origins of American democracy, which was a transposition of the religious community to the political sphere and of the closed space of the Church to the open space of the public square. Protestant religious democracy preceded political democracy. Among us democracy was anti-religious in origin and from the outset tended not to strengthen society in the face of government, but government in the face of the Church.

Williams was less talkative than cummings, and his conversation induced you to love him rather than admire him. We talked of Mexico and of the United States. As is natural we fell into talking about roots. For us, I told him, the profusion of roots and pasts smothers us, but you are oppressed by the huge weight of the future which is crumbling away. He agreed and gave me a pamphlet which a young poet had just published with a preface written by him: it was *Howl* by Allen Ginsberg. I saw him again years later, shortly before his death. Though ill health had battered him hard, his temper and his brain were intact. We spoke again of the three or four or seven Americas: the red, the white, the black, the green, the purple. . . . Flossie, his wife, was with us. As we talked I thought of "Asphodel," his great love poem in age. Now, when I recall that conversation and write this, in my mind I pick the colorless flower and breathe its fragrance. "A strange scent," the poet says, "a *moral* scent." It is not really a scent at all, "except for the imagination." Isn't that the best definition of poetry: a language which does not say anything except to the imagination? In another poem too he says: "Saxifrage is my flower that splits open rocks." Imaginary flowers which work on reality, instant bridges between men and things. Thus the poet makes the world habitable.

Translated by Michael Schmidt

Pablo Neruda on Robert Frost

Chilean Pablo Neruda (née Neftali Reyes, 1904–1973), one of the great poets of the twentieth century, spent the early portion of his career publishing his poetry in magazines and newspapers, and later released *Twenty Love Songs* (1924) and co-authored a book of essays, *Anillos* (1926). Neruda's poetic style was popular in its appeal and he became not only the poet of a nation but the poet of a continent. Although he sometimes used complex structures, the language and metaphors of Neruda's works remained relatively accessible. The next two decades saw Neruda travel all over the world in a diplomatic capacity, from whence he produced *Residence on Earth* (1925–35), followed by his masterpiece, *Canto General* (1950). Through the 1940s, Neruda became increasingly active politically as a Communist. His posthumous volume *Memoirs* (1974) is important as a record of his ideological and aesthetic commitments. Neruda was awarded the Nobel Prize for Literature in 1971. This essay, drafted during the Vietnam era, was published as "Robert Frost and the Prose of Poets," in *Passions and Impressions,* edited by Matilde Neruda and Miguel Otero Silva (New York: Farrar, Straus and Giroux, 1983).

Someone has sent me a well-translated book, the prose of Robert Frost, an admirable poet.

As I read through it, it renewed in some manner a private dialogue or discussion I've been having with myself for some time.

What always attracted me to the poetry of Frost was its personal truth, the naturalness of its structure. He was the poet of conversation. He told and he sang ballads about people who were never entirely real, never entirely imaginary.

I remember that poem about a man who'd lived a long life, an old man sitting close to his fireplace and close to death, now very near:

A light he was to no one but himself
Where now he sat, concerned with he knew what,
A quiet light, and then not even that.

The lines of "A Leaf Treader," and those of "The Cow in Apple Time," have always stayed in my mind. In short, a poet of country scenes, of "north of Boston," of Vermont, of muddy roads covered with fallen leaves, a poet with the shoes of a wanderer and a translucent gift of song—one of the poets I like best.

But Robert Frost's prose surprised me. It is the book of a rationalist with a perfect library, a humanist. But also of a virtuoso of ideas, those ideas about poetry and metaphor that lead nowhere. I have always believed that a study of poetry by poets is pure ashes. That ashen foam may well be beautiful, but it will be carried away on the wind.

Maybe what I like—maybe—is for a critic to meddle and tinker in what interests him but isn't vital to him. For me the critical spirit, when too refined, becomes intellectual obscenity, bloody insolence. The analytical dagger doesn't reveal the guts of the poet but the insides of the one who wielded the dagger.

The prose of Robert Frost leads one down roads of metaphor, and though to me Frost is a great man, I continue to believe that the revelation that kills what it reveals is indecent, however luminous the words and irreproachable the conduct.

In any case, I want to make clear my loyalty to Frost the poet both in his natural poetry and in his intellectual prose.

As for my own writing, I am a fanatic enemy of my own prose. But what can you do? If we speak in prose, we also have to write it. Juan Ramón Jiménez, that pitiful great poet consumed by envy, said once that I didn't even know how to write a letter. In that I believe he was not mistaken.

I was also surprised by Robert Frost's lukewarm, bourgeois liberalism. In New York, at conventions for social progress, I met his daughter, an anti-war, anti-imperialist young woman. I thought her principles must have come from her illustrious father. But in his book I find that when he speaks of *protest* in poetry, he does it from the point of view of the *establishment*.

> But for me, I don't like grievances. I find I gently let them alone wherever published. What I like is griefs and I like them Robinsonianly profound. I suppose there is no use in asking, but I should think we might be indulged to the extent of having grievances restricted to prose if prose will accept the imposition, and leaving poetry free to go its way in tears.

Frost's words are beautiful, but more appropriate for a Victorian romantic. They wouldn't be bad in Lord Tennyson, the bard of *In Memoriam,* pure poetry and pure tears.

I ask the great poet: "But, Frost, whom shall we honor with our tears? Those who are dying or those who are being born? Isn't that wrapping life and death in the same shroud?"

I am a man of tears and of protest. I can't confine prose to struggle and poetry to suffering. It seems to me they can have the same cataclysmic destiny. At times I believe that the "Marseillaise" is choral poetry, unequaled in beauty. I also think at times that Keats's "Ode to a Nightingale" and his "Ode on a Grecian Urn" belong at the taxidermist's or in the British Museum.

Fortunately, Frost is a bigger man than his prose, broader than his analysis. And in spite of this, or perhaps thanks to it, a venerable nation circulates through his poetry, spacious and free, the United States of long ago, with its beautiful mountains, its inexhaustible rivers, and, what it seems to have lost, its capacity to be sufficient unto itself, without bathing the world in blood.

Translated by Margaret Sayers Peden

Julio Cortázar on Edgar Allan Poe

One of the master storytellers in Latin America, Julio Cortázar (1914–1984) was raised in Argentina but moved to France in 1951 as a result of Perónism. His most famous book, *Hopscotch* (1963), was written to be read in multiple sequences of chapters. His stories also display this creativity, as they intermingle fantasy and reality, with aid from his own poetry, photos, and sketches. A voracious reader with a remarkable curiosity, Cortázar demonstrates in his works his interest in romantic poetry, jazz, oriental philosophy, the supernatural, and puzzles. Although his career as an essayist has brought him less attention, his essays have earned him critical praise. Cortázar's essays often mingle fiction and traditional essay writing in a style which has transformed the essay as a genre. His intellectual agenda can be more clearly seen in his essays, as in *Last Round* (1969), *Viaje alrededor de una mesa* (1970), and *Literatura en la revolución y revolución en la literatura* (1970), where he discusses everything from politics to society to art. Cortázar also wrote texts for graphical and photographical books, like *Buenos Aires, Buenos Aires* (1968), *Prosa del observatorio* (1972), and *Territorios* (1978). Among his influences were Edgar Allan Poe and the French experimentalist Boris Vian. This essay is an excerpt from Cortázar's introduction to his translation of Poe's *Obra Completa* (Rio Piedras: Editorial de la Universidad de Puerto Rico, 1956).

The Poet

In his brief preface to the edition of *The Raven and Other Poems,* Poe says: "I think nothing in this volume of much value to the public, or very creditable to myself. Events not to be controlled have prevented me from making, at any time, any serious effort in what, under happier circumstances, would have been the field of my choice. With me poetry has not been a purpose, but a passion." Does this last statement coincide with his explicit poetics? Taking for granted that he is a poet, we believe that the man who tells us how he composed "The Raven" [in "The Philosophy of Composition"] began with the *inten-*

tion of composing it, that is to say, with the purpose of writing a poem which would achieve certain effects. However, the prologue to the book in which the very poem appears tells us that poetry has not been his purpose, but his passion. Are we to distinguish between poetry, which is a passion, and the poem, which is a proposition? Such a distinction seems neither possible nor sensible. Furthermore, those words indirectly illuminate a paragraph in "The Philosophy of Composition" which may otherwise pass unnoticed. "Let us dismiss, as irrelevant to the poem, *per se,* the circumstance—or say the necessity—which, in the first place, gave rise to the intention of composing a poem, etc." *Passion* and the *necessity* of poetry—faced with these terms the guiding intention reverts to a mere principle of technique. Poetry is a need which is satisfied by fulfilling certain formal requirements, adopting certain procedures. But the notion of "looking at the poem coldly," which seems to have been born in the text of "The Philosophy of Composition," is noticeably diminished. "The Raven" ought to be re-evaluated in light of this admission of a poetic impetus having all the violence for which the Romantics were noted. There is no doubt that in this poem there is excessive fabrication, tending to achieve a profound overall effect by means of an intelligent gradation of partial effects of psychological preparation and of musical enchantment. In this sense, Poe's recounting of how he wrote the poem seems to be corroborated by the result. Nonetheless, one knows that the truth lies elsewhere, "The Raven" was not born of an infallible, preconceived plan, but of a series of successive and obsessive stages. For years Poe was a hostage of the theme, born of his reading of Dickens's *Barnaby Rudge.* Gradually approaching the final version, Poe tested that theme in different stages, rejecting them or perfecting them until a text was achieved where the task of adding and subtracting words, weighing each rhythm carefully and balancing the weights, reached a more mechanical than architectonic perfection. This raven is a little like the Chinese emperor's mechanical nightingale; it is, literally, a "rhythmical creation of beauty"; but it is a cold beauty, a magic elaborated by the flawless conjurings of the great magician, a supernatural tremor like the wobbling of a table with only three legs. There is no question of denying this evidence. But, in the light of a global analysis of impulses and intentions, it is correct to suspect that the machinery of "The Raven" is born more from passion than from reason, and that, as in all poets, intelligence is therefore auxiliary to that other force, to that which "is agitated in the depths," as Rimbaud sensed.

If this is true for "The Raven," what does one then say about the other great poems which Poe has left us? Read "To Helen," "The Sleeper," "Israfel," "Dreamland," "The City in the Sea," "For Annie," "The Conqueror Worm," and "The Haunted Palace." The driving force in them is so clearly analogous to the driving force of his most autobiographical and obsessive stories that one can only suspect that they have the same *inevitability* and that only the polishing, the last touches were dispassionate. Do not all poets do the same? The hand that corrects the first draft is not the one that writes it; other forces guide the correcting hand, other *reasons* make it erase words and lines, substituting, polishing, adding on. . . .

I have left aside two of the most beautiful of Poe's poems that offer complementary proof for what I am suggesting. In "Annabel Lee," Poe mourned the death of his wife, and he did so with flourishes that never could have come from a "careful, patient and comprehensive combination." His admirable technique informed an urgent passion, an anguish too intimate to be hidden, with music. And in "Ulalume"—for me, along with "To Helen," his most beautiful poem— Poe delivered his defenseless self over to poetic material which came to life and took form before his very eyes, but which, because it was so profoundly his own, was incomprehensible to him at the conscious level. However much he ordered the stanzas, however much he created or perfected the obsessive music of that necrophilic evocation, that final confession of defeat, *Poe did not know what he had written*, just as a surrealist could assert that he was writing automatically. There is evidence of his perplexity when he was asked for an explication of "Ulalume." An explication! Those were still the times when a poem had to be understandable to one's intelligence, had to pass through the custom house of reason. But the poet who had proudly affirmed his absolute control over the poetic material of "The Raven," the poet enamoured of verse technique and verbal music, more than once confessed that the ending of "Ulalume" was as much an enigma to him as it was to his readers.

The Story-writer

. . . Poe's best stories demonstrate his perfect understanding of the guiding principles of that genre. To his theoretical observations, we can add those that we can deduce from his work, which are, of course, the truly important ones. Poe was the first to realize the rigor demanded by the genre of the short story, to realize that its distinction from the novel was not merely a question of length. It has been said that the period between 1829 and 1832 saw the birth of the short story as an autonomous genre. France saw the rise of Mérimée and Balzac; the United States, of Hawthorne and Poe. But only Poe would write a series of stories so extraordinary as to give the new genre a definitive push forward, not only in his own country but in the world as well, and only Poe would invent or perfect forms that would have great importance for the future. Poe immediately discovered how to construct a story, how to differentiate it from a chapter in a novel, from autobiographical tales, and from contemporary chronicles. He understood that the effectiveness of a story depends on *its intensity as pure event;* that is to say, all commentary on the event itself (which, in the form of preparatory description, marginal dialogue, *a posteriori* considerations, fill out the body of a novel and a bad story) should be radically suppressed. Each word ought to be in confluence and actually coincide with the event, *the thing that occurs,* and this thing that occurs should be only an event and not an allegory or a pretext for psychological, ethical, or didactic generalizations—as in many of Hawthorne's stories, for example. A story is a literary mechanism for creating interest. It is absolutely literary; if it ceases to be so, as, for example, in thematic literature, it becomes the literary vehicle of an extra-literary effect; that is, it ceases to be a story in the oldest sense of the word.*

Poe has been greatly eulogized for his creation of "atmosphere." One has to think of the other masters of the genre—Chekhov, Villiers de

---

*The three accepted meanings of the word *story,* according to Julio Casares, are "The relating of an event. The narrating, spoken or written, of an untrue event. A fable told to children for entertainment." Poe encompasses all three meanings in his work: the event to be related is what is important; the event is not true; the story's purpose is entertainment.

l'Isle Adam, Henry James, Kipling, Kafka—to find his equals in the creation of that magnetic-like property of great short stories. Poe's ability to thrust us into a story in a manner similar to the way we enter a room—immediately sensing the multiple influences of its forms, colors, furniture, windows, objects, sounds and smells—is born from his notion of the intensity of the event, which I have just described. In this case, economy is not merely a question of theme, of reducing the episode to its essence; but, rather, of making it coincide with its verbal expression, at the same time adjusting it so as not to exceed its limits. Poe expects his words to evoke the presence of the thing spoken about, not to be a discussion *of* that thing. In Poe's best stories the method is frankly poetic: form and content lose their meaning as such. In "The Cask of Amontillado," "The Tell-tale Heart," "Berenice," "Hop-Frog" and many others, the atmosphere results from the nearly total elimination of transitions as well as of the presentation and the drawing of character sketches. Poe places us in the drama; he makes us read the story as if we were on the inside. Poe is never a chronicler; his best stories are windows, holes of words. For him, an atmosphere does not idealize what happens; rather, it takes shape alongside the event and at times is the event itself.

Perhaps with these observations I can end my discussion of the doctrine which Poe conceives and applies in his stories. But, a much more extensive and complex terrain immediately opens before us, a *terra incognita* where we must move between intuition and conjecture, where we encounter profound elements which, much more than what has already been seen, give some of Poe's stories their unmistakable tonality, their resonance and their prestige.

Leaving aside the second-rate stories (many were written to fill magazine columns, to earn a few dollars in moments of terrible misery) and turning our attention to the more masterful stories, which otherwise are in a clear majority, it is easy to see that Poe's *themes* are born of the peculiar tendencies of his own nature, and that in all of them creative imagination and fantasy work from primordial material, an unconscious product. This material, which imposes itself irresistibly on Poe and gives him the story—providing him at the same time with both the need to write and the core of the theme—may present itself in the form of a dream, an hallucination or an obsessive idea. The influence of alcohol and especially of opium may facilitate the material's irruption into his consciousness as well as its appearance as a discovery of his imagination, a product of the ideal or of the creative faculty—at least to Poe, in whom we find the desperate desire for self-deception.

It is true that even in his analytic stories Poe is not saved from his worst obsessions. But I want to limit myself to asking whether neurosis—present, according to the critics, in both the form and the content of the stories, in both their themes and techniques—is enough to explain the stories' effect on the reader, their existence as valid literature. The neurotics capable of reasoning with regard to their neuroses are legion, but they do not write "The Man of the Crowd" or "The Imp of the Perverse." Of course they can provide us with fragments of pure poetry, with unconscious overflow which momentarily brings us closer to the nucleus, to the primordial prattle of that which we call spirit, heart, or whatever. Thus Gérard Nerval's *Aurelia,* thus so many poems by Antonin Artaud, thus the autobiography of Leonora Carrington. But the neurotics, the monomaniacs, the madmen, are not story-writers, they do not know how to be story-writers since a story is a work of art and not a poem; it is literature, not poetry. It seems to say, with a certain deference to Poe's clinical analysts, that even though he may not be able to avoid his obsessions, which are manifest *at all levels* of his stories (even the ones he believes to be the most independent, purely conscious), it is nonetheless true that he possesses the most extraordinary freedom a man can have: that of channeling, directing, and consciously shaping the unbridled powers of his unconscious. Instead of surrendering to his obsessions at the level of expression, he situates them, plots them out, orders them; he takes advantage of them, converts them into literature, distinguishes them from the psychiatric document. And this saves the story, it creates the work as a story, and it proves that Poe's genius in the last instance has nothing to do with neurosis (it is not a "sick genius," as it has been called), but rather that his genius enjoys splendid health, to the point of being doctor, guardian, and psychopomp to his sick soul.

Poe's "realism" as such does not exist. In his stories, the most concrete details are always subject to the pressure and the domination of the central theme, which is not realistic. Not even *Gordon Pym,* begun as a mere adventure novel, escapes subjection to the profound forces which govern Poe's narrative; the sea adventure ends with a terrifying glimpse of a hostile and mysterious world for which there are no longer any possible words. It is not surprising, then, that the publication of the first series of his stories disconcerted contemporary critics, who sought an explanation for the stories' "morbidity" in the supposed influence of German literature of the fantastic genre as headed by Hoffman. Defending himself against this (in effect, unfounded) charge, Poe wrote, in the prologue to *Tales of the Grotesque and Arabesque:* "With a single exception, there is no one of these stories in which the scholar should recognize the distinctive features of that species of pseudo-horror which we are taught to call Germanic, for no better reason than some of the secondary names of German literature have become identified with its folly. If in many of my productions terror has been the thesis, I maintain that terror is not of Germany, but of the soul—that I have deduced this terror only from its legitimate sources, and urged it only to its legitimate results."

After what we have just been saying, the admission is eloquent. Instead of "the terror of the soul," one should read "the terror of my soul." Poe frequently incurs this type of generalization, due to his absolute inability to penetrate other minds. His own laws seem to him the laws of the species. And, in a subtle way, he is not mistaken, because his stories involve us by means of their analogical bridges, their capacity to awaken echoes and to satisfy obscure needs. Nevertheless, that schizophrenia illuminates the astonishing lack of communication of his work with the outside world. It is not a question of his substituting a fantasy world for the real world, as in the case of Kafka or Lord Dunsany. Rather, in a setting which is excessive and suffocating ("Usher," "The Masque of the Red Death"), or meager and schematic (*Gordon Pym*), or in a setting which is always or almost always a *deformation* of the human setting, Poe situates and manipulates completely dehumanized characters, beings that obey laws which are not man's usual laws, but rather man's most infrequent, peculiar, exceptional mechanisms. By lacking a knowledge of his fellow human beings, whom he invariably divided into camps of angels and devils, he is ignorant of all normal conduct and psychology. He only knows, however clearly or obscurely, what happens within himself. This is how the terror of *his* soul becomes the terror of *the* soul.

Poe does not manage to hold any of his characters to a normal, average path, even when he tries, as sometimes seems to be the case. Even in the lightest and most unapprehensive of his tales, shadow of horror, grotesqueness, or ridicule of the worst kind soon appears. Off the hero goes to the common gallery of Poe's other characters, and that gallery is very similar to a wax museum.

But beyond this tacit acceptance of what his own mode of being imposes upon him, Poe will try explicitly to justify it, to rationalize it. Thus the recurrence, in his stories and his short critical pieces, of a sentence by Bacon which had profoundly and understandably influenced him: "There is no exquisite beauty without some strangeness in the proportion." The sentence, which is used in "Ligeia" with regard to the heroine's physical features, takes on a more general meaning in that story, as it does in so many others. Poe consciously leans toward events whose truth imposes itself on him from other dimensions. Nothing is important to him if it does not have that "strangeness" in its proportions, that distance from any canon, from any common denominator.

But this very lack of communication with the outside world becomes an instrument of power in Poe. His stories hold the same fascination for us that aquariums or crystal balls do, presenting a transparent, immobilized scene at their unreachable center. Perfect mechanisms for producing sudden effects, the stories do not try to be a mirror moving along a road, as Stendahl saw the novel, but rather a mirror to those fairy-tales which only reflects the strange, the unusual, the fateful. In his stories, Poe can dispense with the world, disregard the human dimension, ignore laughter, the passion of hearts, the conflict of characters and action. His own world has variety and intensity, it adapts itself so surprisingly well to the structure of the short story as literary genre, that it is worth mentioning paradoxically that had he *feigned* all his inabilities, he would have done so in the legitimate defense of his work, satisfactorily achieved within its own dimensions and with only its own resources. In the end, his enemies of yesterday and today are the enemies of prose fiction (how well that term applies to Poe's stories!), those eager for the *tranche de vie,* Poe understood creative prose in another way because he valued life differently. And never did he, by means of his literature, give any illusions of life's perfectability.

Translated by John Incledon

II

North Reading South

Prologue: John Barth

John Barth was born in Cambridge, Maryland, in 1930, and educated at the Juilliard School of Music and Johns Hopkins University. A realist in the earlier stages of his literary career, he has devoted most of his later works to the exploration of myths, fables, and the process of literary creation, often blurring the distinctions between the genres of history, fiction, legend, and parody. As a whole his literary career demonstrates the author's concern with the metaphysical and the trials of self-consciousness, in a style which is ambitious, humorous, and highly cerebral. He has written *The Floating Opera* (1956), *The End of the Road* (1958), *The Sot-Weed Factor* (1960), *Giles Goat-Boy, The Revised New Syllabus* (1966), *Chimera* (1972), *The Friday Book* (1984), *Further Fridays* (1995), and *On with the Story: Stories* (1996). Barth has received the National Book Award, a Rockefeller grant, and the Brandeis University Creative Arts Award and has taught at Johns Hopkins University and Pennsylvania State University. Among his acknowledged influences are the works of Borges, Gabriel García Márquez, and Machado de Assis. This essay originally appeared as "The Literature of Exhaustion," in the *Atlantic Monthly*, April 1967.

I want to discuss three things more or less together: first, some old questions raised by the new "intermedia" arts; second, some aspects of the Argentine writer Jorge Luis Borges, whose fiction I greatly admire; third, some professional concerns of my own, related to these other matters and having to do with what I'm calling "the literature of exhausted possibility"—or, more chicly, "the literature of exhaustion."

By "exhaustion" I don't mean anything so tired as the subject of physical, moral, or intellectual decadence, only the used-upness of certain forms or the felt exhaustion of certain possibilities—by no means necessarily a cause for despair. That a great many Western artists for a great many years have quarreled with received definitions of artistic media, genres, and forms goes without saying: Pop Art, dramatic and musical "happenings," the whole range of "intermedia" or "mixed-means" art, the kind that requires expertise and artistry as well as bright aesthetic ideas and / or inspiration. I enjoy the Pop Art in the famous Albright-Knox collection, a few blocks from my house in Buffalo, like a lively conversation; but I was on the whole more impressed by the jugglers and acrobats at Baltimore's old Hippodrome, where I used to go every time they changed shows: not artists, perhaps, but genuine *virtuosi*, doing things that anyone can dream up and discuss but almost no one can do.

I suppose the distinction is between things worth remarking and things worth doing. "Somebody ought to make a novel with scenes that pop up, like the old children's books," one says, with the implication that one isn't going to bother doing it oneself.

However, art and its forms and techniques live in history and certainly do change. I sympathize with a remark attributed to Saul Bellow, that to be technically up-to-date is the least important attribute of a writer—though I would add that this least important attribute may be nevertheless essential. In any case, to be technically *out* of date is likely to be a genuine defect: Beethoven's Sixth Symphony or the Chartres cathedral, if executed today, might be simply embarrassing (in fact, they *couldn't* be executed today, unless in the Borgesian spirit discussed below). A good many current novelists write turn-of-the-century-type novels, only in more or less mid-twentieth-century language and about contemporary people and topics; this makes them less interesting (to me) than excellent writers who are also technically contemporary: Joyce and Kafka, for instance, in their time, and in ours, Samuel Beckett and Jorge Luis Borges. The intermedia arts, I'd say, tend to be intermediary, too, between the traditional realms of aesthetics on the one hand and artistic creation on the other. I think the wise artist and civilian will regard them with quite the kind and degree of seriousness with which he regards good shoptalk: He'll listen carefully, if noncommittally, and keep an eye on his intermedia colleagues, if only the corner of his eye. Whether or not they themselves produce memorable and lasting works of contemporary art, they may very possibly suggest something usable in the making or understanding of such works.

Jorge Luis Borges will serve to illustrate the difference between a technically old-fashioned artist, a technically up-to-date non-artist, and a technically up-to-date artist. In the first category I'd locate all those novelists who for better or worse write not as if the twentieth century didn't exist, but as if the great writers of the last sixty years or so hadn't existed. Our century is more than two-thirds done; it is dismaying to see so many of our writers following Dostoevsky or Tolstoy or Balzac, when the question seems to me to be how to succeed not even Joyce and Kafka, but those who *succeeded* Joyce and Kafka and are now in the evenings of their own careers. In the second category—technically up-to-date non-artists—are such folk as a neighbor of mine in Buffalo who fashions dead Winnies-the-Pooh in sometimes monumental scale out of oilcloth stuffed with sand and impales them on stakes or hangs them by the neck. In the third category belong the few people whose artistic thinking is as *au courant* as any French New Novelist's, but who manage nonetheless to speak eloquently and memorably to our human hearts and conditions, as the great artists have always done. Of these, two of the finest living specimens that I know of are Samuel Beckett and Jorge Luis Borges—with Vladimir Nabokov, just about the only contemporaries of my reading acquaintance mentionable with the "old masters" of twentieth-century fiction. In the unexciting history of literary awards, the 1961 International Publishers' Prize, shared by Beckett and Borges, is a happy exception indeed.

One of the modern things about these two writers is that in an age of ultimacies and "final solutions"—at least *felt* ultimacies, in everything from weaponry to theology, the celebrated dehumanization of society, and the history of the novel—their work in separate ways reflects and deals with ultimacy, both technically and thematically, as for example *Finnegans Wake* does in its different manner. One notices, for whatever its symptomatic worth, that Joyce was virtually blind at the end, Borges is literally so, and Beckett has become virtually mute, musewise, having progressed from marvelously constructed English sentences through terser and terser French ones to the unsyntactical, unpunctuated prose of *Comment C'est* and "ultimately" to wordless mimes. One might extrapolate a theoretical course for Beckett: Language after all consists of silence as well as sound, and mime is still communication ("that nineteenth-century idea," a Yale student once snarled at me), but by the language of action. But the language of action consists of rest as well as movement, and so in the context of Beckett's progress, immobile, silent figures still aren't altogether ultimate. How about an empty, silent stage, then, or blank pages—a "happening" where nothing happens, like Cage's *4'33"* performed in an empty hall? But dramatic communication consists of the absence as well as the presence of the actors: "we have our exits and our entrances"; and so even that would be imperfectly ultimate in Beckett's case. Nothing at all, then, I suppose; but Nothingness is necessarily and inextricably the background against which Being, et cetera. For Beckett, at this point in his career, to cease to create altogether would be fairly meaningful: his crowning work; his "last word." What a convenient corner to paint yourself into! "And now I shall finish," the valet Arsene says in *Watt*, "and you will hear my voice no more." Only the silence *Molloy* speaks of, "of which the universe is made."

After which, I add on behalf of the rest of us, it might be conceivable to rediscover validly the artifices of language and literature—such far-out notions as grammar, punctuation . . . even characterization! Even *plot!*—if one goes about it the right way, aware of what one's predecessors have been up to.

Now, J. L. Borges is perfectly aware of all these things. Back in the great decades of literary experimentalism he was associated with *Prisma,* a "muralist" magazine that published its pages on walls and billboards; his later *Labyrinths* and *Ficciones* not only anticipate the farthest-out ideas of The Something Else Press crowd—not a difficult thing to do—but, being excellent works of art as well, they illustrate in a simple way the difference between the *fact* of aesthetic ultimacies and their artistic *use.* What it comes to is that an artist doesn't merely exemplify an ultimacy; he employs it.

Consider Borges's story "Pierre Menard, Author of the *Quixote*": The hero, an utterly sophisticated turn-of-the-century French Symbolist, by an astounding effort of imagination, produces—not *copies* or *imitates,* but *composes*—several chapters of Cervantes's novel.

> It is a revelation [Borges's narrator tells us] to compare Menard's *Don Quixote* with Cervantes's. The latter, for example, wrote (part one, chapter nine):
>
> > . . . truth, whose mother is history, rival of time, depository of deeds, witness of the past, exemplar and adviser to the present, the future's counselor.
>
> Written in the seventeenth century, written by the "lay genius" Cervantes, this enumeration is a mere rhetorical praise of history. Menard, on the other hand, writes:

> ... truth, whose mother is history, rival of time, depository of deeds, witness of the past, exemplar and adviser to the present, the future's counselor.
>
> History, the *mother* of truth: the idea is astounding. Menard, a contemporary of William James, does not define history as an inquiry into reality but as its origin.

Et cetera. Borges's story is of course a satire, but the idea has considerable intellectual validity. I declared earlier that if Beethoven's Sixth were composed today, it might be an embarrassment; but clearly it wouldn't be, necessarily, if done with ironic intent by a composer quite aware of where we've been and where we are. It would have then potentially, for better or worse, the kind of significance of Warhol's Campbell's Soup cans, the difference being that in the former case a work of art is being reproduced instead of a work of non-art, and the ironic comment would therefore be more directly on the genre and history of the art than on the state of the culture. In fact, of course, to make the valid intellectual point one needn't even recompose the Sixth Symphony, any more than Menard really needed to recreate the *Quixote.* It would have been sufficient for Menard to attribute the novel to himself in order to have a new work of art, from the intellectual point of view. Indeed, in several stories Borges plays with this very idea, and I can readily imagine Beckett's next novel, for example, as *Tom Jones,* just as Nabokov's recentest was his multivolume annotated translation of Pushkin. I myself have always aspired to write Burton's version of *The 1001 Nights,* complete with appendices and the like, in ten volumes, and for intellectual purposes I needn't even write it. What evenings we might spend discussing Saarinen's Parthenon, D. H. Lawrence's *Wuthering Heights,* or the Johnson Administration by Robert Rauschenberg!

The idea, I say, is intellectually serious, as are Borges's other characteristic ideas, most of a metaphysical rather than an aesthetic nature. But the important thing to observe is that Borges *doesn't* attribute the *Quixote* to himself, much less recompose it like Pierre Menard; instead, he writes a remarkable and original work of literature, the implicit theme of which is the difficulty, perhaps the unnecessity, of writing original works of literature. His artistic victory, if you like, is that he confronts an intellectual dead end and employs it against itself to accomplish new human work. If this corresponds to what mystics do—"every moment leaping into the infinite," Kierkegaard says, "and every moment falling surely back into the finite"—it's only one more aspect of that old analogy. In homelier terms, it's a matter of every moment throwing out the bath water without for a moment losing the baby.

Another way of describing Borges's accomplishment is with a pair of his own terms, *algebra* and *fire*. In one of his most often anthologized stories, *Tlön, Uqbar, Orbis Tertius,* he imagines an entirely hypothetical world, the invention of a secret society of scholars who elaborate its every aspect in a surreptitious encyclopedia. This *First Encyclopedia of Tlön* (what fictionist would not wish to have dreamed up the *Britannica?*) describes a coherent alternative to this world complete in every respect from its algebra to its fire, Borges tells us, and of such imaginative power that, once conceived, it begins to obtrude itself into and eventually to supplant our prior reality. My point is that neither the algebra nor the fire, metaphorically speaking, could achieve this result without the other. Borges's algebra is what I'm considering here—algebra is easier to talk about than fire—but any smart cookie could equal it. The imaginary authors of the *First Encyclopedia of Tlön* itself are not artists, though their work is in a manner of speaking fictional and would find a ready publisher in The Something Else Press. The author of the story *Tlön, Uqbar, Orbis Tertius,* who merely *alludes* to the fascinating *Encyclopedia, is* an artist; what makes him one, of the first rank, like Kafka, is the combination of that intellectually serious vision with great human insight, poetic power, and consummate mastery of his means—a definition which would have gone without saying, I suppose, in any century but ours.

Not long ago, incidentally, in a footnote to a scholarly edition of Sir Thomas Browne, I came upon a perfect Borges datum, reminiscent of Tlön's self-realization: the actual case of a book called *The Three Impostors,* alluded to in Browne's *Religio Medici* among other places. *The Three Impostors* is a nonexistent blasphemous treatise against Moses, Christ, and Mohammed, which in the seventeenth century was widely held to exist, or to have once existed. Commentators attributed it variously to Boccaccio, Pietro Aretino, Giordano Bruno, and Tommaso Campanella, and though no one, Browne included, had ever seen a copy of it, it was frequently cited, refuted, railed against, and generally discussed as if everyone had read it—until, sure enough, in the *eighteenth* century a spurious work appeared with a forged date of 1598 and the title *De Tribus Impostoribus*. It's a wonder that Borges doesn't mention this work, as he seems to have read absolutely everything, including all the books that don't exist, and Browne is a particular favorite of his. In fact, the narrator of *Tlön, Uqbar, Orbis Tertius* declares at the end:

> . . . English and French and mere Spanish with disappear from the globe. The world will be Tlön. I pay no attention to all this and go on revising, in the still days at the Adrogue Hotel, an uncertain Quevedian translation (which I do not intend to publish) of Browne's *Urn-Burial.*

This "contamination of reality by dream," as Borges calls it, is one of his pet themes, and commenting upon such contaminations is one of his favorite fictional devices. Like many of the best such devices, it turns the artist's mode or form into a metaphor for his concerns, as does the diary-ending of *Portrait of the Artist as a Young Man* or the cyclical construction of *Finnegans Wake*. In Borges's case, the story *Tlön*, etc., for example, is a real piece of imagined reality in our world, analogous to those Tlönian artifacts called *hrönir*, which imagine themselves into existence. In short, it's a paradigm of or metaphor for itself; not just the *form* of the story but the *fact* of the story is symbolic; the medium is (part of) the message.

Moreover, like all of Borges's work, it illustrates in other of its aspects my subject: how an artist may paradoxically turn the felt ultimacies of our time into material and means for his work—*paradoxically,* because by doing so he transcends what had appeared to be his refutation, in the same way that the mystic who transcends finitude is said to be enabled to live, spiritually and physically, in the finite world. Suppose you're a writer by vocation—a "print-oriented bastard," as the McLuhanites call us—and you feel, for example, that the novel, if not narrative literature generally, if not the printed word altogether, has by this hour of the world just about shot its bolt, as Leslie Fiedler and others maintain. (I'm inclined to agree, with reservations and hedges. Literary forms certainly have histories and historical contingencies, and it may well be that the novel's time as a major art form is up, as the "times" of classical tragedy, Italian and German grand opera, or the sonnet-sequence came to be. No necessary cause for alarm in this at all, except perhaps to certain novelists, and one way to handle such a feeling might be to write a novel about it. Whether historically the novel expires or persists as a major art form seems immaterial to me; if enough writers and critics *feel* apocalyptical about it, their feeling becomes a considerable cultural fact, like the *feeling* that Western civilization, or the world, is going to end rather soon. If you took a bunch of people out into the desert and the world didn't end, you'd come home shamefaced, I imagine; but the persistence of an art form doesn't invalidate work created in the comparable apocalyptic ambience. That is one of the fringe benefits of being an artist instead of a prophet. There are others.) If you happened to be Vladimir Nabokov, you might address that felt ultimacy by writing *Pale Fire:* a fine novel by a learned pedant, in the form of a pedantic commentary on a poem invented for the purpose. If you were Borges you might write *Labyrinths:* fictions by a learned librarian in the form of footnotes, as he describes them, to imaginary or hypothetical books. And I'll add that if you were the author of this paper, you'd have written something like *The Sot-Weed Factor* or *Giles Goat-Boy:* novels which imitate the form of the Novel, by an author who imitates the role of Author.

If this sort of thing sounds unpleasantly decadent, nevertheless it's about where the genre began, with *Quixote* imitating *Amadis of Gaul,* Cervantes pretending to be the Cid Hamete Benengeli (and Alonso Quijano pretending to be Don Quixote), or Fielding parodying Richardson. "History repeats itself as farce"—meaning, of course, in the form or mode of farce, not that history is farcical. The imitation, like the Dadaist echoes in the work of the "intermedia" types, is something new and *may be* quite serious and passionate despite its farcical aspect.

This is the difference between a proper, "naïve" novel and a deliberate imitation of a novel, or a novel imitative of other kinds of documents. The first sort attempts (has been historically inclined to attempt) to imitate actions more or less directly, and its conventional devices—cause and effect, linear anecdote, characterization, authorial selection, arrangement, and interpretation—have been objected to as obsolete notions, or metaphors for obsolete notions: Alain Robbe-Grillet's essays *For a New Novel* come to mind. There are replies to these objections, not to the point here, but one can see that in any case they're obviated by imitations-of-novels, for instance, which attempt to represent not life directly but a representation of life. In fact such works are no more removed from "life" than Richardson's or Goethe's epistolary novels are; both imitate "real" documents, and the subject of both, ultimately, is life, not the documents. A novel is as much a piece of the real world as a letter, and the letters in *The Sorrows of Young Werther* are, after all, fictitious.

One might imaginably compound this imitation, and though Borges doesn't, he's fascinated with the idea. One of his more frequent literary allusions is to the 602nd night in a certain edition of *The 1001 Nights,* when, owing to a copyist's error, Scheherazade begins to tell the King the story of the 1001 nights, from the beginning. Happily, the King interrupts; if he didn't, there'd be no 603rd night ever, and while this would solve Scheherazade's problem, it would put the "outside" author in a bind. (I suspect that Borges dreamed this whole thing up; the business he mentions isn't in any edition of *The 1001 Nights* I've been able to consult. Not *yet*, anyhow: After reading *Tlön, Uqbar, Orbis Tertius,* one is inclined to recheck every semester or so.)

Borges is interested in the 602nd night because it's an instance of the story-within-the-story turned back upon itself, and his interest in such instances is threefold. First, as he himself declares, they disturb us metaphysically: When the characters in a work of fiction become readers or authors of the fiction they're in, we're reminded of the fictitious aspect of our own existence—one of Borges's cardinal themes, as it was of Shakespeare, Calderón, Unamuno, and other folk. Second, the 602nd night is a literary illustration of the *regressus in infinitum,* as are many other of Borges's principal images and motifs. Third, Scheherazade's accidental gambit, like Borges's other versions of the *regressus in infinitum,* is an image of the exhaustion, or attempted exhaustion, of possibilities—in this case literary possibilities—and so we return to our main subject.

What makes Borges's stance, if you like, more interesting to me even than, say, Nabokov's or Beckett's, is the premise with which he approaches literature. In the words of one of his editors: "For [Borges] no one has claim to originality in literature; all writers are more or less faithful amanuenses of the spirit, translators and annotators of preexisting archetypes." Thus his inclination to write brief comments on imaginary books: For one to attempt to add overtly to the sum of "original" literature by even so much as a conventional short story, not to mention a novel, would be too presumptuous, too naïve; literature has been done long since. A librarian's point of view! And it would itself be too presumptuous if it weren't part of a lively, relevant metaphysical vision, slyly employed against itself precisely to make new and original literature. Borges defines the Baroque as "that style which deliberately exhausts (or tries to exhaust) its possibilities and borders upon its own caricature." While his own work is *not* Baroque, except intellectually (the Baroque was never so terse, laconic, economical), it suggests the view that intellectual and literary history has been Baroque, and has pretty well exhausted the possibilities of novelty. His *ficciones* are not only footnotes to imaginary texts, but postscripts to the real corpus of literature.

This premise gives resonance and relation to all his principal images. The facing mirrors that recur in his stories are a dual *regressus.* The doubles that his characters, like Nabokov's, run afoul of suggest dizzying multiples and remind one of Browne's remark that "every man is not only himself . . . men are lived over again." (It would please Borges, and illustrate Browne's point, to call Browne a precursor of Borges. "Every writer," Borges says in his essay on Kafka, "creates his own precursors.") Borges's favorite third-century heretical sect is the Histriones—I think and hope he invented them—who believe that repetition is impossible in history and who therefore live viciously in order to purge the future of the vices they commit; to exhaust the possibilities of the world in order to bring its end nearer. The writer he most often mentions, after Cervantes, is Shakespeare; in one piece he imagines the playwright on his deathbed asking God to permit him to be one and himself, having been everyone and no one; God replies from the whirlwind that He is no one either: He has dreamed the world like Shakespeare, and including Shakespeare. Homer's story in Book IV of the *Odyssey,* of Menelaus on the beach at Pharos, tackling Proteus, appeals profoundly to Borges: Proteus is he who "exhausts the guises of reality" while Menelaus—who, one recalls, disguised his own identity in order to ambush him—holds fast. Zeno's paradox of Achilles and the Tortoise embodies a *regressus in infinitum* which Borges carries through philosophical history, pointing out that Aristotle uses it to refute Plato's theory of forms, Hume to refute the possibility of cause and effect, Lewis Carroll to refute syllogistic deduction, William James to refute the notion of temporal passage, and Bradley to refute the general possibility of logical relations. Borges himself uses it, citing Schopenhauer, as evidence that the world is our dream, our idea, in which "tenuous and eternal crevices of unreason" can be found to remind us that our creation is false, or at least fictive. The infinite library of one of his most popular stories is an image particularly pertinent to the literature of exhaustion: The "Library of Babel" houses every possible combination of alphabetical characters and spaces, and thus every possible book and statement, including your and my refutations and vindications, the history of the actual future, the history of every possible future, and, though he doesn't mention it, the encyclopedia not only of Tlön but of every imaginable other world—since, as in Lucretius's universe, the number of elements and so of combinations is finite (though very large), and the number of instances of each element and combination of elements is infinite, like the library itself.

That brings us to his favorite image of all, the labyrinth, and to my point. *Labyrinths* is the name of his most substantial translated volume, and the only current full-length study of Borges in English, by Ana María Barrenechea, is called *Borges the Labyrinth-Maker.* A labyrinth, after all, is a place in which, ideally, all the possibilities of choice (of direction, in this case) are embodied, and—barring special dispensation like Theseus's—must be exhausted before one reaches the heart. Where, mind, the Minotaur waits with two final possibilities: defeat and death or victory and freedom. The legendary Theseus is non-Baroque; thanks to Ariadne's thread he can take a shortcut through the labyrinth at Knossos. But Menelaus on the beach at Pharos, for example, is genuinely Baroque in the Borgesian spirit, and illustrates a positive artistic morality in the literature of exhaustion. He is not there, after all, for kicks; Menelaus is *lost,* in the larger labyrinth of the world, and has got to hold fast while the Old Man of the Sea exhausts reality's frightening guises so that he may extort direction from him when Proteus returns to his "true" self. It is a heroic enterprise, with salvation as its object—one recalls that the aim of the Histriones is to get history done with so that Jesus may come again the sooner, and that Shakespeare's heroic metamorphoses culminate not merely in a theophany but in an apotheosis.

Now, not just any old body is equipped for this labor; Theseus in the

Cretan labyrinth becomes in the end the aptest image for Borges after all. Distressing as the fact is to us liberal democrats, the commonalty, alas, will *always* lose their way and their soul; it is the chosen remnant, the virtuoso, the Thesean *hero,* who, confronted with Baroque reality, Baroque history, the Baroque state of his art, need *not* rehearse its possibilities to exhaustion, any more than Borges needs actually to *write* the *Encyclopedia of Tlön* or the books in the Library of Babel. He need only be aware of their existence or possibility, acknowledge them, and with the aid of very special gifts—as extraordinary as saint- or herohood and not likely to be found in The New York Correspondence School of Literature—go straight through the maze to the accomplishment of his work.

John Updike on Augusto Roa Bastos

Born in Shillington, Pennsylvania, in 1932, John Updike was educated at Harvard University. A former staff member and frequent contributor with the *New Yorker,* Updike is a prolific essayist, novelist, playwright, poet, and short-story writer. His novels reveal a moralist who remains skeptical about human sensibility and is concerned with the tenuous and fragmented continuity of meaning and a higher moral order. Most of his characters find themselves struggling to both enjoy their lives and understand their place in the modern chaos which they inhabit. However, despite the meaninglessness that seems to pervade modern existence in his works, Updike's narrative voice seems to insist on the persistence of meaning. His career as an essayist, particularly in his work for the *New Yorker,* demonstrates his deep artistic sensibility and his broad array of interests. Much of his nonfiction prose engages the work of fellow artists and transcends geographical and cultural barriers. Among his voluminous oeuvre—spanning more than 150 titles—are the novels *The Music School* (1966), *The Centaur* (1972), *A Month of Sundays* (1975), *Marry Me: A Romance* (1976), the tetralogy beginning with *Rabbit Run* (1960), for which he received two Pulitzer Prizes, *Brazil* (1994), and *In the Beauty of the Lilies* (1996), as well as his essay collection *Hugging the Shore* (1984). Updike has received a Guggenheim Fellowship and a National Book Award and is a member of the National Institute of Arts and Letters. This portion of a book review appeared as "The Great Paraguayan Novel and Other Hardships," in the *New Yorker,* 23 September 1987.

I, the Supreme, by Augusto Roa Bastos, is a deliberately prodigious book, an elaborate and erudite opus saturated in the verbal bravura of classic modernism. Its Paraguayan author, a professor at the University of Toulouse until his retirement last year, has lived in exile since 1947; he found haven in Buenos Aires until 1976, when—to quote an interview he gave the Madrid journal *Leviatán*—"the military dictatorship was beginning to deploy the hecatomb" and "it was necessary to escape the rather sinister climate which was incubating." A journalist and poet in Paraguay, he began to write fiction in Argentina, most notably a long novel centered upon the Guariní Indians, *Hijo de hombre* (*Son of Man*), and *Yo el supremo*, published in 1974.

"El Supremo" was the popular nickname for the founder of independent Paraguay, José Gaspar Rodríguez de Francia, who, after the bloodless coup against Spanish colonial rule in 1811, went from being secretary of the ruling junta to being Supreme Dictator; he ruled the country possessively and absolutely from 1814 until his death in 1840. A lawyer and one-time postulate for the priesthood, he held the degrees of master of philosophy and doctor of theology; he never married, and lived austerely, in an isolation akin to that which he imposed on the country he had founded. He forbade immigration and emigration and maintained neither diplomatic nor commercial ties with foreign countries. Within the embattled, landlocked country, his policies were aimed at developing a sense of independence and solidarity; a follower of the French Enlightenment, he curbed the power of the church and the aristocracy, introduced modern methods of agriculture, defended the rights of the Guaraní Indians, and maintained a formidable army. He wore a black suit and red cape and was rumored to be something of a sorceror. Paraguay, known to Americans mostly as the remote domain of the long-lived dictatorship of Alfredo Stroessner, has had an interesting history. From its capital of Asunción the Spanish ruled a vast area and founded Buenos Aires. Its southeastern region was the site of communistic Jesuit missions—the eighteenth-century *reducciones*, which one writer on Latin America, Carlos Rangel, has described as "the best possible materialization of a *City of God* on earth." And in the War of the Triple Alliance (1865–70) Paraguay defended itself against its two mighty neighbors, Brazil and Argentina, at the staggering cost of over half its population, including three-quarters of its men.

The founder of this stubborn country, a George Washington with elements of Huey Long, Enver Hoxha, and Merlin, lies dying and raving, aloud and within his skull, through the over four hundred large pages of *I, the Supreme*, whose texture is varied with double-column excerpts from historical works, some of which are imaginary.* The

*". . . I didn't want to write an historical work. That's why I took it upon myself to completely distort all historical references, because I don't believe one can mix the two genres. History as the basic material of a work of fiction is a special matter. What in Latin America we call history, that is, the history of the

valor and labor and intelligence exerted in this novel and in its faithful translation (including bits from the Guaraní, Portuguese, and Latin) intimidate criticism; suffice it to say that, if a masterpiece, it is the sort one should read for academic credit, and that much of its charm and interest presumably lie bound up in its virtuoso use of the original language. Many books have gone into the making of this book: contemporary and historical accounts of Francia's Paraguay, government documents and the eighteenth-century sources of the dictator's own extensive erudition, and the crabbed modern works of Joyce, Borges, and García Márquez, among others—there is even a sharp whiff of contemporary French interest in the elusiveness of texts and the multiplicity of signs.

In books as in dinosaurs, however, largeness asks a strong spine, and *I, the Supreme* holds no action as boldly intelligible as Leopold Bloom's peregrination or the hunt for the Great White Whale. The looming, and virtually only, human relationship exists between the dying Francia and his obsequious secretary, Policarpo Patiño; their dialogues are given not only without quotation marks but without dashes or indentation, so that the secretary and dictator (himself once a secretary) tend to merge, while allusions to Don Quixote and Sancho Panza thicken around them. The central issue of suspense—the authorship of an anti-Francia pasquinade nailed to the door of the cathedral—is never, that this reader noticed, resolved. Nor does the author's attitude toward his polymorphous, logorrheic hero come into clear view. Repulsion and fascination, clearly, but to what end? A kind of long curse concludes the novel—an enthusiastic descriptive catalogue of the insects and worms that will devour El Supremo's corpse, and some condemnatory sentences in the author's (or Patiño's) voice:

> You fooled yourself and fooled others by pretending that your power was absolute. You lost your oil, you old ex theologian passing yourself off as a statesman. . . . You ceased to believe in God, but neither did you believe in the people with the true mystique of Revolution; the only

---

official historians, has no value whatsoever. On the contrary, it is precisely this false reality which we who write fiction feel obliged to contradict in every possible way" (Roa Bastos, in the *Leviatán* interview, translated from the Spanish by Peggy Boyers in *Salmagundi*).

one that leads a true locomotive-engineer of history to identify himself with its cause, not use it as a hiding place from his absolute vertical Person, in which worms are now feeding horizontally.

One is led, by this learned book bristling with quaint particulars and amiable puns and verbal tumbles ("Yet the genes of gens engender tenacious traitorous taints"; "the filigreed fleuron in the vergered-perjured paper, the flagellated letters"), into a spiritual dungeon, a miasmal atmosphere of hate and bitter recalcitrance. The fictional Francia is most eloquent in his inveighing against the others—the devilish ecclesiastics, the "Porteños" of Buenos Aires—who threaten his power. He knows no positive connections; all is betrayal and potential assault. The inanimate objects that inspire and console and fortify him—a polished skull, a fallen meteorite, his ivory pen—supplant human faces and voices and whatever humane motives inspired, at the forging of a nation, his polity. The static, circling quality of many modernist masterworks is here overlaid with a political rigidity, an immobilizing rage that seizes both the tyrant and the exiled writer. *I, the Supreme* differs from García Márquez's *Autumn of the Patriarch* in that the dictator-hero of the latter is a coarse ignoramus, whereas Francia, in Roa Bastos's reconstruction, suffers, amid the trappings of omnipotence, the well-known impotence and isolation of the modern intellectual.

Grace Paley on Clarice Lispector

An eminent activist and poet, Grace Paley (b. 1922) is a storyteller of astonishing and moving simplicity. Her Yiddish-speaking parents emigrated from Eastern Europe to the United States in 1906 and settled in New York. Her father's "first language" was actually not Yiddish but Italian, for as a photographer he worked in a studio among Italian Americans. And he taught himself English by reading Charles Dickens. Eventually, he went to medical school and became a doctor. Paley's fiction deals with this cultural experience. She is also known for outspokenness against the Vietnam War and the U.S. involvement in Latin America. Her stories, similar in style and spirit to those of her compatriot Raymond Carver, read like snapshots of life, like porcelain reproductions of human moments. Paley's books include *The Little Disturbances of Man* (1959), *Enormous Changes at the Last Minute* (1974), *Later the Same Day* (1985), and *Just as I Thought* (1998). In 1994 her *Collected Stories* were published in a single volume. Paley was raised in the Bronx, attended Hunter College in New York, and has taught at Sarah Lawrence College, Columbia University, and Syracuse University. This is Paley's introduction to Clarice Lispector's *Soulstorm: Stories* (New York: New Directions, 1987).

Clarice Lispector spent the first two months of her life in the town of Chechelnik in the Ukraine. This is a small short fact. The interesting question, unanswered in the places I've looked for it, is—at what age did she enter the Portuguese language? And how much Russian did she bring with her? Any Yiddish? Sometimes I think this is what her work is about . . . one language trying to make itself at home in another. Sometimes there's hospitality, sometimes a quarrel.

Why did they go to Brazil anyway?, an American immigrant Jew provincially asks. Well, a South African cousin answers, since Jews are often not wanted in their old homes, they travel to distant, newer, more innocent places. My mother's best friend emigrated to Argentina. There was a letter from Buenos Aires once. But not again.

Unless Clarice Lispector's parents were linguists with an early knowledge of Portuguese, they must have spoken Russian, as my parents did most of my childhood. It must have been that meeting of

Russian and Portuguese that produced the tone, the rhythms that even in translation (probably difficult) are so surprising and right.

It's not unusual for writers to be the children of foreigners. There's something about the two languages engaging one another in the child's ears that makes her want to write things down. She will want to say sentences over and over again, probably in the host or dominant tongue. There will also be a certain amount of syntactical confusion which, if not driven out of her head by heavy schooling, will free the writer to stand a sentence on its chauvinistic national head when necessary. She will then smile.

There are not many smiles in Lispector's work, but they happen in the successful illumination of a risky sentence. You feel that even the characters are glad.

Once you have stood a sentence on its head or elbow, the people who live in those sentences seem to become states of literary mind—they seem almost absurd, but not in a cold or mean way. (There isn't a mean bone in the body of Lispector's work.) But there is sadness, aloneness (which is a little different than loneliness). Some of the characters try desperately to get out of the stories. Others retreat into their own fictions—seem to be waiting for and relieved by Lispector's last embracing sentence.

Lispector was lucky enough to have begun to think about all these lives, men's lives as well as women's, in the early years of the women's movement—that is, at a time when she found herself working among the scrabbly low tides of that movement in the ignorance which is often essential to later understanding. That historical fact is what has kept her language crooked and clean.

In this collection there are many solitary middle-class Brazilian women, urban, heavily European. There are a couple of black cooks, nannies. I thought at one point in my reading that there was some longing for Europe, the Old World; but decided I was wrong. It was simply longing.

It seems important to say something about geography. First Lispector's. She lived for an infant's moment in Russia. Then in Brazil in Recife, then in Rio de Janeiro; then with her diplomat husband in Europe and the United States; then her last eighteen years in Brazil.

Brazil is a huge country. Its population is African black, Indian brown and golden, European white. There are landless peasants.

There are the Indian people, whole villages and tribes driven out of their forest homes by development. There is the vast ancient forest which, breathing, we absolutely require. There is the destruction of that forest continuing at such a rate that a sensible breathing world might be terrified. Imagine living in, being a citizen of a country in which the world's air is made. Imagine the woman, the urban woman writing not about that world but in it. She had to find a new way to tell. Luckily it was at the tip of her foreign tongue.

Katherine Anne Porter on
José Joaquín Fernández de Lizardi

Born in India Creek, Texas, Katherine Anne Porter (1890–1980) was never completely dependent on her fiction in order to earn a living. During a life which was often shaped by extensive traveling, and a stay in both Europe and Mexico, Porter worked as a reporter, screenplay writer, translator, lecturer, and guest speaker. Her financial security may very well be at the root of her unwillingness to publish anything with which she was unsatisfied. Porter, who placed severe limits on the number of her stories which she would allow to be published, is revered by many for her meticulous and perceptive prose. Her works often explore the deterioration of the most basic human relationships, such as marriages and parent-offspring relationships, and the disappointments and moral crises of human existence. Porter's narrative voice is concerned with the gestures and personality of her characters, most of whom are introspective. She often juxtaposes these predominantly cerebral characters with children whom she portrays as passionate and spontaneous. For Porter the path to adulthood entails the abandonment of spontaneity and the adoption of a traumatic and self-deluding self-consciousness. Among her best-known works are *Flowering Judas, and Other Stories* (1930), *Pale Horse, Pale Rider: Three Short Novels* (1939), and *Ship of Fools* (1962). The recipient of numerous literary awards and honorary degrees, Porter was awarded two Guggenheim fellowships in the 1930s, Fulbright and Ford Foundation grants in the 1950s, and the Pulitzer Prize in 1966. This is Porter's introduction to *The Itching Parrot*, by José Joaquín Fernández de Lizardi, published by Doubleday in 1942.

The author of *The Itching Parrot* was born November 15, 1776, in Mexico City, baptized the same day, in the parish church of Santa Cruz y Soledad, and christened José Joaquín Fernández de Lizardi.

His parents were Creoles (Mexican-born Spaniards), vaguely of the upper middle class, claiming relationship with several great families. They were poor, she the daughter of a bookseller in Puebla, he a rather unsuccessful physician, a profession but lately separated from the trade of barber. They made an attempt to give their son the education proper to his birth, hoping to prepare him for the practice of law.

The child, who seems to have been precocious, willful, and somewhat unteachable, spent his childhood and early youth in an immensely Catholic, reactionary, socially timid, tight-minded atmosphere of genteel poverty and desperately contriving middle-class ambitions. Though his parents' heads were among the aristocracy, their feet threatened daily to slip into the dark wallow of the lower classes, and their son witnessed and recorded their gloomy struggle to gain enough wealth to make the worldly show that would prove their claim to good breeding. There was no other way of doing it. In Spain, as in Europe, scholarship might be made to serve as a second choice, but in Mexico there was no place for scholarship. The higher churchly honors were reserved for the rich and nobly born; as for the army, it offered for a young Mexican only the most ignoble end: a father could wield as the last resort of authority the threat to send his son to be a soldier.

The outlook was pretty thin for such as our hero. But he was to prove extraordinarily a child of his time, and his subsequent career was not the result of any personal or family plan, but was quite literally created by a movement of history, a true world movement, in which he was caught up and spun about and flung down again. His life story cannot be separated in any particular from the history of the Mexican Revolutionary period. He was born at the peak of the Age of Reason, in the year that the thirteen states of North America declared themselves independent of England. When he was a year old, the United States government decreed religious freedom. In Mexico the Inquisition was still in power, and the Spanish clergy in that country had fallen into a state of corruption perhaps beyond anything known before or since. The viceregal court was composed entirely of Spanish nobles who lived in perpetual luxurious exile; the Indian people were their natural serfs, the mixed Indian and Spanish were slowly forming a new intractable, unpredictable race, and all were ruled extravagantly and unscrupulously by a long succession of viceroys so similar and so unremarkable it is not worthwhile to recall their names.

The French Revolution occurred when Lizardi was about fourteen years old. At twenty, he was a student in the University of Mexico, College of San Ildefonso. It is not likely that any newfangledness in social or political theory had yet managed to creep in there. There was very little thinking of any kind going on in Mexico at that time, but there were small, scattered, rapidly increasing groups of restless, inquiring minds, and whoever thought at all followed eagerly the path of new doctrines that ran straight from France. The air was full of mottoes, phrases, name-words for abstractions: Democracy, the Ideal Republic, the Rights of Man, Human Perfectibility, Liberty, Equality, Fraternity, Progress, Justice, and Humanity; and the new beliefs were based firmly on the premise that the first duty of man was to exercise freedom of conscience and his faculty of reason.

In Mexico as in many other parts of the world, it was dangerous to mention these ideas openly. All over the country there sprang up secret political societies, disguised as clubs for literary discussion; these throve for a good many years before discussion became planning, and planning led to action and so to revolution.

In 1798, his twenty-second year, Lizardi left the university without taking his bachelor's degree, perhaps because of poverty, for his father died about this time, and there seems to have been nothing much by way of inheritance. Or maybe he was such a wild and careless student as he describes in *El Periquillo*. It is also possible that he was beginning to pick up an education from forbidden sources, such as Diderot, d'Alembert, Voltaire, Rousseau. At any rate, he never ceased to deplore the time he had spent at acquiring ornamental learning, a thing as useless to him, he said, as a gilded coach he could not afford to keep up. The fact seems to be, his failure was a hard blow to his pride and his hopes, and he never ceased either to bewail his ignorance. "To spout Latin is for a Spaniard the surest way to show off his learning," he commented bitterly, and himself spouted Latin all his life by way of example. In later days he professed to regret that his parents had not apprenticed him in an honest trade. However, there was no help for it, he must live by his wits or not at all.

After he left the university without the indispensable academic laurel that would have admitted him to the society of the respectably learned, he disappeared, probably penniless, for seven long years. These years of the locust afterwards were filled in suitably with legends of his personal exploits as a revolutionary. He was supposed to have known Morelos, and to have been in active service with the early insurgents. He says nothing of this in his own account of his life, written a great while afterwards: it is probable that he was a public scrivener in Acapulco. In 1805 he returned to Mexico City and married Doña Dolores Orendain, who brought him a small dowry. As late as 1811 he appears to have been a Justice of the Peace in Taxco, when Morelos took that town from the Viceroy's troops, and was said to have delivered secretly a store of royalist arms and ammunition to Morelos. For this act he was supposed to have been arrested, taken to Mexico, tried and freed, on the plea that he had acted not of his own will but under threat of death from Morelos' insurgents.

The particularly unlikely part of this story is that the royalist officers would never have taken the trouble to escort Lizardi, an obscure young traitor to the Spanish throne, all the way from Taxco to Mexico City for trial. It is still a long road, and was then a terrible journey of several days. They would have shot him then and there, without further ceremony. A more unlikely candidate than Lizardi for gun-toting was never born. He shared with all other humanist reformers from Erasmus onward a hatred of war, above all, civil war, and his words on this subject read like paraphrases from Erasmus' own writings, as indeed many of them were. Lizardi's services to his country were of quite another kind, and his recompense was meager to the last degree.

Just when those agile wits of his, which he meant to live by, first revealed themselves to him as intransigent and not for sale, it is difficult to discover. As late as 1811 he wrote a poem in praise of the Virgin of Guadalupe, who had protected the capital city and defeated by miracle the insurgent army led by Hidalgo. He wrote another entirely loyal and conventional poem to celebrate the accession of Philip VII to the Spanish throne. He belonged with the Liberal faction, that is, he opposed alike the excesses of the extreme insurgents and the depravities of the viceroys, he began by believing himself to be a citizen of the world, wrote against narrow patriotism, and refused to put himself at the service of any lesser cause than that of absolute morality, in every department of state and church. His literary career began so obscurely that it is difficult to trace its beginnings, but by 1811 he was writing and publishing, on various presses in Mexico City, a copious series of pamphlets, poems, fables, dialogues, all in the nature of moral lectures with rather abstract political overtones, designed to teach broadly social sanity, political purity, and Christian ethics. These were sold in the streets, along with a swarm of broadside, loose-leaf literature by every kind of pamphleteer from the most incendiary Mexican nationalist to the most draggle-tailed anonymous purveyors of slander and pornography.

A series of rapid events occurred which brought Lizardi out into the open, decided the course of his beliefs and therefore of his acts, and started him once for all on his uncomfortable career as perpetual dissenter. In 1810 the Council of Cádiz decreed the freedom of the press, for Spain and her colonials. The Viceroy of Mexico, Xavier Vanegas, believed, with his overworked board of censors, that the Mexican press had already taken entirely too much freedom for itself. He suppressed the decree, by the simple means of refraining from publishing it.

By July, 1811, the insurgent army under Hidalgo had been defeated, and late in that month the heads of Hidalgo and his fellow heroes, Aldama, Jiménez, and Allende, were hanging as public examples in iron cages at Guanajuato. The Empire was re-established, with Vanegas still Viceroy, and during that year and into the next, the censorship of the press became extremely severe. Every printer in Mexico was required to show a copy of every title he published, and among the items that showed up regularly were quite hundreds of flimsy little folders with such names as "The Truthful Parrot," in which a loquacious bird uttered the most subversive remarks in the popular argot of the lower classes, mixed freely with snatches of rhyme, puns in Mexican slang, and extremely daring double meanings. There were such titles as "The Dead Make No Complaints"; "The Cat's Testimony," a fable imitating La Fontaine; "It Is All Right to Cut the Hair But Don't Take the Hide Too," which in Spanish contains a sly play on words impossible to translate; "There Are Many Shepherds Who Shall Dance in Bethlehem," another punning title, meaning that many priests shall go to Belén (Bethlehem), the great prison which exists still in Mexico City; "Make Things So Clear That Even the Blind May See Them"; "Even Though Robed in Silk, a Monkey Is Still a Monkey"; "All Wool Is Hair," which has a most salty double meaning; "The Nun's Bolero," concerning scandals in convents; "The Dog in a Strange Neighborhood"; "The Devil's Penitents"—these were only a few of the provocations Lizardi showered upon the censors, the royalist party, the church, venal politicians of all parties, social and political abuses of every kind.

The censors could hardly find a line that did not contain willful but oblique offense, yet nothing concrete enough to pin the author down on a criminal charge, so the Council of Safety contented itself with harrying him about somewhat, suppressing his pamphlets from time to time, forbidding various presses to publish for him, and threatening him occasionally with worse things.

But it is plain that Lizardi had discovered that he was, in particular, a Mexican, and a patriotic one, though still in general a citizen of the world. It would seem that those truly heroic heads of Father Hidalgo and the others in Guanajuato had brought him down from the airy heights of abstract morality to a solid and immediate field of battle. For, in June, 1812, three months before the new constitution took effect, Viceroy Vanegas, who seems to have been a rather weak, short-sighted man, alarmed by the continued rebelliousness of a people he had believed he had conquered, took a fateful step. He issued an edict condemning to death all churchmen of regular or secular state who might take part in the revolution. This clause dealt with those many priests who rose to take the place of Father Hidalgo. All officers from the rank of sublieutenant upwards were condemned to death. There were all over the country an immense number of captainless men who went independently into battle. These were to be decimated on the spot wherever captured. This last clause might seem to have covered the business; but the Viceroy added a final generous provision for wholesale slaughter. After such decimation, those who by chance had escaped death were, if convenient, to be sent to the Viceroy for suit-able punishment. If this was not convenient, it was left to the discretion of each commandant to do with them as he saw fit.

So far, the edict was in its nature a fairly routine measure in times of emergency. But there was a further clause condemning to death all authors of incendiary gazettes, pamphlets, or other printed matter. This was sensational, considering that unpublished decree granting freedom of the press. The liberal wing of the Constitutionalist (or royalist) party, together with all the forces that aimed for a peaceable settlement and some sort of compromise with the revolutionists, pro-tested against this edict and advised the Viceroy seriously against such drastic means. The Viceroy did not cancel the edict, but as a sop to public opinion, he did publish the Cádiz decree on October 5, 1812, and the Mexican press, theoretically at least, was free.

Lizardi was ready to take advantage of this freedom. He leaped into print just four days later with the first number of his first periodical, which had for title his own pen name, *The Mexican Thinker*. For two numbers he praised the glories of a free press and the wonders of liberty, but in the third he broke out in high style against the whole Spanish nation, its pride, its despotism; against the corruptions of the viceregal court, the infamies of officials in every station. Seeing that no revenge overtook him, he dared further in a later number: "There is no civilized nation which has a worse government than ours, and the worst in America, nor any other vassal country that has suffered more harshly in its arbitrary enslavement." He turned upon the Spanish governors the very words they had used against Hidalgo. "Cursed monsters," he wrote, and printed, and sold in the streets to be read by all, "you despots and the old evil government are responsible for the present insurrection, not as you say the Cura Hidalgo. It is you together who have stripped our fields, burned our villages, sacrificed our children and made a shambles of this continent."

It is worth noticing here that among his fellow pamphleteers, Lizardi was famous for his moderate language and his courtesy in debate.

No consequences followed this wrathful page. Lizardi went on safely enough until the ninth number, published on December 2, 1812. He devoted this number to an appeal to the Viceroy Vanegas to revoke at least that clause of the edict against revolutionaries which called for the trial of insurgent priests before a military court. He also wrote a personal letter to the Viceroy, timed the publication date to coincide with the Viceroy's Saint's Day, and appeared at court with a specially printed copy. With his own hands he delivered this little bombshell into the very hands of Vanegas, and received the viceregal thanks.

It is hardly probable that Vanegas troubled to examine the papers given him, but the Council of Safety, alarmed, informed him of its contents. The following day the Viceroy and his council suspended the freedom of the press, "for reason of the unsettled conditions of the country." They sent for Lizardi's printer, manager of the Jáurigui press, who admitted that Lizardi had written the offending article.

On the fifth of December they ordered Lizardi to appear before the Court. He disappeared into ineffectual hiding in the house of a friend, Gabriel Gil, where, at three o'clock in the morning, December 7, he was seized and taken to prison. He wrote the story ten years later at great length, and he was still as indignant as he was the day it occurred, but he was proud, also, of the number of men who came to help with the arrest. There were more than seventy of the "dirty birds."

It must be remembered that, under the edict, Lizardi was in danger of death. It would appear his jailers set out methodically to terrorize him, and they succeeded. It does not appear that his judges had any intention of sentencing him to death, but the whole proceedings had the air of making a stern example of troublesome scribblers. They put him in the death cell, where he passed a hideous night, expecting a priest to come to administer the last rites, expecting to be tortured, mistaking the rattle of the jailor's keys for chains. In the morning they took him before a judge he knew, and suspected of having headed the plot to imprison him, where he had to listen patiently to a great deal of foul insult and injury.

Lizardi, in the speeches of his celebrated hero, El Periquillo, declared repeatedly that he feared physical violence more than anything else. The Periquillo is merry and shameless about it, for cowardice is possibly the most disgraceful trait known to man in Mexico, but his author did not find it amusing in himself. Later in his defense to the Viceroy he admitted quite simply that he had refused to obey the first summons to appear because he feared violence and not because he had a sense of guilt. His fears were reasonable. Worse had happened to other men for less cause, or at any rate for no more.

Still, when he gathered that harsh language was probably going to be the worst of it, and he was not going to be tortured and hanged, or at any rate, not that day, he recovered his spirits somewhat and took a rather bantering tone with his infuriated questioners. He was a tall, slender man of a naturally elegant manner, of the longheaded, well-featured Hidalgo kind; his portrait shows a mouth sensitive almost to weakness, and a fine alert picaresque eye. His judges, being also Spanish, and prone to judge a man's importance by his dress—a reflection of his financial state, which was in turn proof of his caste—were inclined to doubt he was so dangerous as they had thought, since Lizardi at that moment was "emaciated, pallid, of shabby appearance," with his "black cloak smeared and crumpled from using it as a bed" in his cell; ten years after he remembered with regret that he had no time to clean it properly before having to show himself. Lizardi told them that indeed they were right, not he but two ladies, one respectable, the other plebeian, had written the articles. They insisted humorlessly that he explain himself. He sobered down and confessed himself as the author. "The respectable lady was the constitution of Cádiz, which allowed him to write on political questions; the plebeian was his own ignorance which had misled him into believing the Viceroy would not be angered by a request to revoke an edict distasteful to the people."

Their ferocity rose at this, they demanded an account of his whole life, and pursued him with questions meant to trap him until, seeing the affair still threatened to be serious, he grew frightened again and implicated his friend Gabriel Gil as well as Carlos María Bustamante, an active insurgent, and writer, who had "warned him his life was in danger and advised him to leave the city."

Probably because of these interesting bits of evidence and not, as Lizardi boasted years afterwards, on account of his own astuteness, for he certainly does not seem to have shown any, the sentence of solitary confinement was lifted, he was remanded to the common jail among a number of his comrade insurgent prisoners, and Gil was arrested.

Feeling himself betrayed by the man whom he had befriended at so much danger to himself, Gil said that Lizardi had come to him in distress, and that he, Gil, had done his best to persuade him to obey the summons. Gil then went on to make a bad matter worse by saying that Lizardi had confided that a certain friend had told him he could escape safely with five hundred insurgents who were about to leave the city.

In panic, Lizardi denied this and involved another friend, Juan Olaeta, who had, Lizardi said, offered to allow him to escape with the insurgents. Olaeta, brought before the judges, passed on the responsibility to an unnamed priest from Toluca, who had overheard a conversation between two persons unknown to him, concerning the plans of five hundred insurgents who were about to leave the city. Olaeta's part had been merely an offer to Lizardi to take him to the priest. Lizardi insisted to Olaeta's face that Olaeta had "told him the Tolucan priest would arrange for his escape with the insurgents. Olaeta insisted that Lizardi had misunderstood him, and the two, together with Gabriel Gil, were sent back to jail." If they were in the same cell, it must have been a frightfully embarrassing situation for Lizardi. And he was not done yet.

After nine days in prison, exhausted by repeated questioning and anxieties, he wrote a personal appeal to the Viceroy saying in effect and in short that he had acted innocently in handing him the protest against the edict and that before giving it he had shown it to a priest who approved of it, and by way of justifying himself further, he added with appalling lack of ethical sense that Carlos María Bustamante, and a Doctor Peredo had "written with more hostility than he against the same edict." He continued to drag names into the business, adding that of a Señor Torres, and even blaming his error on them.

The first Judge advised the Viceroy to turn Lizardi's case over to the Captain General and the Military Court. Lizardi asked for bail which was his constitutional right, but it was refused. He was handed about from court to court, military and civil, for months, gradually modifying his statements, or retracting, or insisting that he had been misunderstood. Gil and Olaeta were freed, Bustamante, Torres, and Peredo were never arrested at all, and Bustamante, an admirable and heroic spirit, never held any grudge against him, but wrote well of him afterwards. But Lizardi lingered on in jail, writing to the Viceroy, asking for an attorney, asking that his case be turned over to the war department, being mysteriously blocked here and there by hostile agencies, and there he might have stayed on to the end if Vanegas had not been succeeded as Viceroy on March 4, 1813, by Calleja.

Lizardi began a fresh barrage of importunities and explanations to this new, possibly more benign power. He praised him for the good he hoped for from him, and published this praise as a proclamation of the Thinker to the People of Mexico. This got him no new friends anywhere and did not get him his liberty either. He was allowed now and then to visit his family, which consisted of his wife, a newly born daughter, and four unnamed members which, dependent upon him, were almost starving. He had supported them somewhat while in prison by getting out number 10 and number 11 of *The Mexican Thinker*, in December, and number 12 and number 13 in January, but in a considerably chastened and cautious style.

One of its periodic plagues came upon Mexico City and raged as usual, and the churches were crowded with people kissing the statues and handing on the disease to each other. In one number of *The Thinker,* Lizardi advised them to clean up the streets, to burn all refuse, to wash the clothes of the sick not in the public fountains but in a separate place, not to bury the dead in the churches, and as a final absurdity, considering the time and place, he counseled them to use the large country houses of the rich as hospitals for the poor. None of these things was done, the plague raged on and raged itself out.

Lizardi also wrote a statement of his quarrel with the existing state of politics, but a very discreet one, and he could think of no better remedy, his own situation being still perilous as it was, than that both sides in the struggle should obey the counsels of Christ and love one another.

Naturally this sloppy thinking brought upon him the contempt of all sides. The royalists thought no better of him than before, and the liberals, who favored the new constitution, now distrusted him, as they had no intention of loving either an out-and-out royalist or any insurgent, and as for the insurgents themselves, they damned Lizardi freely.

All this was going on, remember, while our hero was still in prison.

In Mexico there was the celebrated "Society of Guadalupe," the most effective of such societies which, under cover of more polite interests, were at the service of Morelos and kept him well informed of events in the capital. The new Viceroy, Calleja, proved to be an even more bitter enemy of the insurgents than Vanegas had been, and Lizardi's unfortunate eulogy of Calleja had been sent to Morelos with a note by a member of the Society of Guadalupe. "This person," said the note, "is not worth your attention, because when they imprisoned him, he showed his weakness, and has written several pamphlets praising this damnable government, and has most basely harmed several men."

At last the Viceroy, finding no new things against Lizardi, wearied of the case; the last judge who took it over recommended that Lizardi be set free, and so he was, on July 1, 1813, after nearly seven months in prison. "Enough to ruin me, as I was ruined, with my family," he wrote.

This is the least handsome episode of Lizardi's life, and he behaved like a green recruit stampeded under his first fire, who may yet become as good a soldier as any man. Lizardi became a better soldier than most, and if he had been once afraid to die, he was not afraid to suffer a long, miserable existence for the sake of his beliefs. He was by no means ruined. He had scarcely been scotched. He returned to his dependents, his six-month-old daughter and the wife who had almost died at her birth, to a brazier without coals and a cupboard without food; and sat down at once to write indignantly against all the causes of misery and the effects of injustice in this maddening world.

The Holy Office of the Inquisition had recently been abolished by decree. Lizardi, with that unbelievable speed of his, wrote a history of that institution, a very bitter history, and he rejoiced over its downfall. He published it on September 30, 1813, as a number of *The Thinker*, and went on with his many projects for local reforms, not attacking the government except by indirection. He wrote against ignorant doctors; against the speculators in food who hoarded for higher prices; he wrote rebuking the Creoles, telling them they had the vices of both the Indians and the Spaniards. If he had poured boiling oil upon them he could not have offended them more bitterly. He wrote against the depravity of the lower classes, and the plague of thieves, beggars, and drunkards in the streets. In November he enjoyed a small popular triumph. A crowd gathered at sight of him and cheered him in the street, shouting that he told them the naked truth. ("La Verdad Pelada" was one of his most lively efforts.) But no royalist or liberal or insurgent or priest or anyone that mattered then was in this cheering rabble; these were the shirtless ones, the born losers no matter which side might win. They shouted his name, and worsened his reputation, but they did not follow his advice and could not if they would. They liked him because he was sharp and angry, full of their own kind of humor, and talked to them in their own language. It was the first time they had ever seen their own kind of talk in print. The flattery was great and they responded to it; for a few centavos they could buy this highly flavored reading matter which expressed all their secret wrongs and grudges and avenged them vicariously; and his words worked afterwards in their thoughts; they trusted him and believed him.

In December, 1813, three months after Lizardi's attack, the Inquisition was reestablished. The absolutist monarch Ferdinand VII after his eclipse was back on the throne of Spain, and all grudgingly granted liberties were at an end again for Spain and her colonies.

Lizardi was by then a man without a party indeed. For in that month someone of the Society of Guadalupe sent Morelos a marked copy of Lizardi's attack on the native-born Mexicans, commenting: "Merely to show you how this author abuses us. We know his weakness since the time of his imprisonment, and we wish that in the press of Oaxaca you shall give him a good shaking up [literal translation] as a mere sycophant."

And one month later, January 14, 1814, a priest called the attention of the head Inquisitor, Flores, to *The Mexican Thinker*'s denunciation of the Inquisition. More than a year later Flores sent the article to two priests for examination, and in June, 1815, they denounced it as "a mass of lies, impostures, iniquitous comparisons, scandals, seductions, offensive to pious ears, injurious to the sanctity of the sovereign Popes, and the piety of our monarch."

Once more the harassed manager of the Jáuregui press was tracked down, this time by an officer of the Inquisition. The printer said that Lizardi lived in Arco Street, number 3, tenement A, then reconsidered and said Lizardi had lived there when he wrote the article but was now living in Prieto Nuevo Street. Lizardi was always moving about from one poverty-stricken tenement in a shabby back street to another. Nothing more came of this affair just then.

The only sign Lizardi gave that he knew he had been denounced to the Inquisition was a softening in the tone of his indignation, a generally lowered quality of resistance, a methodical search for themes on which he might express himself freely without touching too dangerous topics. That year he wrote some rather sensible plans for relieving the sufferings of lepers; against gambling and gambling houses; and criticisms of the prevailing systems of public education. He began a campaign for modern education, based on the ideas of Blanchard, a Jesuit priest who had modified Rousseau's theories as expressed in *Emile* "to suit the needs of Christian education."

Sometime during 1815 Lizardi tried a new series of pamphlets under a single title, "Alacena de Frioleras," meaning a cupboard of cold food, scraps, leftovers. He fell into disgrace with the censors at the second number, and was refused license to print it. He was bitterly discouraged but not without some resources still. He decided to try his hand at a novel; what censor would look for political ideas in a paltry fiction?

Lizardi's friend Dr. Beristain, a man of letters, who was writing and compiling a Library of Northern Spanish Americana, did not agree with the censors, but declared Lizardi to be "an original genius, native of New Spain." Dr. Beristain also believed that Lizardi, for his knowledge of the world and of men, and for his taste in literature, merited to be called "if not the American Quevedo, at least the Mexican Torres Villaroel . . . he has now in hand a life of Periquito Sarmiento, which judging by what I have seen of it, much resembles Guzman de Alfarache."

The censor's report for February, 1816, mentions the appearance of *El Periquillo* from the prologue to chapter 6; in July, another series of chapters; the third series was suppressed on November 29, 1816, because it contained an attack on the system of human slavery.

This is the first mention of that book, undertaken as Lizardi's last hope of outwitting the censorship, as well as of making a living by its sales as it was being written. He finished it, but it was not published in full until after his death.

There followed a long dreary period of pamphlet writing, against bullfighting, against dandyism—his Don Catrín remains a stock character in that line until today—calendars, almanacs, stainless essays on morals and manners, hymns, and little songs for children. In the meantime the insurgents, who had been growing in strength, were weakened and the Liberal-Constitutionalist party got into power. At once they suppressed both the Inquisition and the Board of Press Censorship, and at once Lizardi was ready for them. He founded a small periodical called *The Lightning Conductor* and began to tell again the naked truth.

There were to be several changes of government yet during Lizardi's lifetime, but there was never to be one he could get along with, or accept altogether. After twenty-four numbers of *The Lightning Conductor*, he could not find a printer who would risk printing his periodical for him. Lizardi by no means defended the entire Constitutionalist idea, he only defended those tendencies which led to such reforms as he had just witnessed in regard to the Inquisition and the censorship. But in doing this he offended again the rockbound royalist clergy, who used the whip of spiritual authority to force their parishioners to oppose the constitution, as it curtailed the Spanish power and automatically their own. These and all other die-hard royalists hated Lizardi; the insurgents distrusted him. He was a gadfly to the Viceroy, always addressing complaints directly to him: he was opposed to war still, civil war above all, and considered the insurgents to be almost as obnoxious to the good of the country as the royalists themselves. He considered himself "as Catholic as the Pope," but the clergy hated and attacked him bitterly. A priest named Soto wrote such a vicious pamphlet against him that the censors suppressed it.

During that period, almost frantic in his hornets' nest of personal and public enemies, Lizardi found time and a little money to open a reading room, where for a small fee the public might read the current books, newspapers, pamphlets. Almost nobody came to read; he lost his money and closed the place after a few months.

The struggle between Mexico and Spain was approaching the grand climax, and with peculiar timeliness Lizardi did precisely the thing calculated to get him into trouble. In February, 1821, Augustín Iturbide and Canon Monteagudo, at the head of the Anti-constitutionalist party, boldly declared themselves ready to separate Mexico from Spain, without any further compromises. The Liberal party had held out for an independence to be granted by Spain, peacefully. The new constitution granted when Vanegas was Viceroy had been a makeshift affair, with no real concessions in it. Iturbide's party appeared to be only the acting head of the insurgents, for this seizing of independence for Mexico was exactly what the insurgents had been fighting for all along. Iturbide, with an ambition of his own, decided to use the strength of the insurgents and the growing nationalist spirit to his own ends. He and Monteagudo published their program as the Plan of Iguala.

In the meantime, Lizardi had been writing on this topic, too. Just four days after the Plan of Iguala was published, Lizardi printed a pamphlet which was described as a serio-comic dialogue between two popular and sharp-tongued characters called Chamorro and Dominiquín. They discussed the possibilities of independence for Mexico, and looked forward to the day of freedom, believed it would be a good thing for both countries, but still hoped it might be granted legally by the Spanish government.

The liberal constitutionalist but still very royalist government, with its free press, saw nothing to laugh at in this work, suppressed it at once, arrested Lizardi, and kept him in jail for several days. On this occasion he flattered no one, implicated no one, and retracted nothing. He was released, and wrote a halfhearted pamphlet on the beauties of reconciliation between factions. And in his next pamphlet he stated boldly a change of mind. "It is true that if we do not take our independence by force of arms, they will never concede us our liberty by force of reason and justice."

When he had been imprisoned, he was accused of being a follower of Iturbide, and a supporter of the Plan of Iguala. Lizardi replied merely that he had not known about the plan when he wrote his own suggestions; in effect no answer at all, and perhaps true in itself. But immediately after this last pamphlet boldly counseling the violent way to freedom, the next thing we know, Lizardi is showing a letter from Iturbide to a certain Spaniard, and this Spaniard is supplying him with money and equipment and a horse, and Lizardi, by urgent request of Iturbide, is riding toward Tepotzotlan to take charge of the insurgent press there. This press was devoted entirely to the doctrine of Mexican independence and the necessity of gaining it by force.

Iturbide's troops fought their way steadily through the country toward Mexico City, and Lizardi was close on their heels with his press turning out patriotic broadsides. Iturbide entered the capital in triumph on September 21, 1821. The great deed was accomplished, the eleven years of revolutionary war came to a close, and Mexico was declared an independent government. Lizardi naturally entered the city in triumph also, with his press still going at top speed. Let the censors fume. He had a whole victorious army with him.

There was still no thought in anyone's mind of establishing a Republic. Lizardi expressed the hopes of the victors clearly: that Iturbide should be made Emperor by acclamation, at the first session of Congress. "Oh," cried our misguided hero, who had waited so long to espouse any faction, and now had taken to heart so utterly the wrong one, "may I have the joy of kissing once the hand of the Emperor of America, and then close my eyes forever in death."

How little becoming to Lizardi was this new garment of acquiescence. It was never made for him and he could not carry it off. Two months later his eyes, closed in enthusiasm, were opened violently, he gazed clearly upon the object of his infatuation, and rejected it. He saw that Iturbide had done as other ambitious men do. He had used the force of a great popular movement to seize power for himself, and meant to set himself up as head of a government more oppressive if possible than the old.

Lizardi wrote a pamphlet called "Fifty Questions to Whoever Cares to Answer Them," and the questions were very embarrassing to the new Emperor, to the church authorities leagued with him, and to all who had promised reforms in government. Iturbide had at least gone through the formality of having himself elected Emperor, and Lizardi accused the priests of controlling the election. They called Lizardi unpatriotic, hostile to religion, accused him of political ambitions. Iturbide was disconcerted by the sudden defection of a man to whom he had given money and a press and a horse to boot, and finding that Lizardi was abusing the freedom of the press, urged that a new censorship be established.

Finding himself the chief obstacle to that freedom of the press which had now become his main object in life, Lizardi proceeded to multiply his offenses. Freemasonry had been creeping in quietly from France by way of Spain. It was the nightmare of the Church everywhere and two Popes had issued bulls against it: Clement XII in 1738, Benedict XIV in 1751. The alarmed clergy in Mexico republished these bulls in 1821, and by way of response Lizardi wrote a pamphlet called plainly "A Defense of the Freemasons." He used arguments that were in the main those of a good Christian, an informed Catholic, and a fairly good student of the Bible. It was also a heated, tactless, and illogical performance, and the Church simply came down on him like a hammer. Nine days after the pamphlet was published, Lizardi was publicly and formally excommunicated by the board of ecclesiastical censorship, and the notice was posted in all the churches.

So it was done at last, and The Thinker passed a little season in hell which made all his former difficulties seem, as he would say, "like fruit and frosted cake." He was kept more or less a prisoner in his own house, where by the rules no member of his own household was supposed to speak to him, or touch him, or help or serve him in any way.

It is improbable that this state of affairs ever existed in that family, but the neighbors would not speak to his wife or daughter, they had great hardships procuring food, and no servant would stay in the house. When he ventured out certain persons drew aside from him; at least once a small mob gathered and threatened to stone him; a group of friars also threatened to come and beat him in his own house, and he advised them defiantly to come well prepared. They did not come, however. He had no defenders for no one would defend an excommunicated man. His wife went to appeal to the Vicar-General, who would not allow her to approach or speak, but waved her away, shouting, "In writing, in writing," since it was forbidden to speak to any member of his family.

Lizardi, announcing that he was "as Catholic as the Pope," which in fact he does not seem to have been, began to defend himself. It was a sign of the times that he could still find presses to print his pamphlets. He appealed to Congress to have the censure of the Church lifted within the prescribed legal period, and asked that body to appoint a lawyer to defend him in the secular courts, but nothing was done in either case. He continued to harry the government, giving sarcastic advice to Iturbide, and recorded with pride that after he had been cut off from humankind by his excommunication his friends were more faithful than ever. It is true he did enjoy some rather furtive moral support from radical sources, but he was bold as if he had all society on his side. He wrote a second defense of the Freemasons, wrote a bitter defense of his entire career and beliefs in the famous "Letter to a Papist," and dragged on his miserable life somehow until 1823, when Iturbide was overthrown by General Antonio López de Santa Ana, head of a "Federalist" party which pretended to found a Republic based on the best elements of the American and French models. It turned out to be another dictatorship which lasted for about thirty years, with Santa Ana at its head. The Catholic Church was still the only recognized religion, a blow to Lizardi, but he took hope again. The appearance of the written Constitution deceived him momentarily, and as unofficial, uninvited member of the Federalist party he began again agitating for all those reforms so dear to his heart: Freedom of the press, first, last, and forever, compulsory free education, religious liberty, liberty of speech and universal franchise, and naturally, almost as a result of these things, justice, sweet justice, for everybody, regardless of race, class, creed, or color.

Almost at once he found himself in jail again.

He gives his account of it as follows, tongue in cheek: "In the month of June (1823), I was imprisoned for writing an innocent little paper called 'If Congress Sits Much Longer We Shall Lose Our Shirts.' I described a dream I had in which a set of petty thieves were debating the best way of robbing us . . . they denounced me . . . on the strength of the title alone, arrested me and I was forced to labor again in my own defense." ("Letter to a Papist.")

This must have blown over, for on the 20th of that same June he was again prisoner in St. Andrés' hospital, but this was probably one of those dreary mischances which befall poor people unable to keep up with the rent: at any rate he insulted the landlady and she threw him out of the house, lock, stock, and barrel, accusing him of defamation of her character. He got out of this, too, and in revenge wrote a poem called "Epithalamium" in which he seems to have married off the judge and the landlady with appropriate ribaldry; but they could do nothing as he mentioned no names.

By then no printer would publish for him: he appears to have got hold of a press of his own, but the authorities forbade newsboys to sell his papers in the streets. At last he left the city for a while, but there was no fate for him in such a case except death in exile. He returned and late in December, 1823, he wrote a letter to the ecclesiastical board of censorship, saying he would no longer attempt to defend himself by civil law, and asked for absolution. This was granted and the documents were published in a periodical in January, 1824.

"Time will mend all things," he wrote at about this time, "in effect, today this abuse will be remedied, tomorrow, another . . . in eight or ten years everything will go as it should." He lived by, and for, this illusion, but these are the words of a mortally weary man. He had never been strong and he was already suffering from the tuberculosis of which he was to die. He had at this time an intimation of approaching death.

He began a small bi-weekly sheet called *The Yokel and the Sacristan,* and in June, 1825, a number of this was pronounced heretical. He was given eight days in which to make a reply, and asked for three months, which was not granted. He allowed himself even a little more time than he had asked for, then made an evasive and unsatisfactory reply. He was not pursued any further about this.

The reason may have been that Lizardi had quarreled successfully, even triumphantly, just five months before, with the Bishop of Sonora. This Bishop had issued a manifesto pronouncing the new Federalist Constitution of Mexico Anti-Catholic (in spite of that clause legalizing the Church alone which had so nearly broken Lizardi's spirit). The Bishop argued for the divine right of Kings, and said that God had been deprived of his rights. Lizardi replied with a defense of the republican form of government, in his usual animated style. The public response to him was so great a governmental commission waited upon the Bishop, escorted him to Acapulco, and put him on board a ship which returned him to Spain for good. And Santa Ana's government suddenly gave Lizardi a pension of sixty-five pesos a month "to reward him for his services to the revolution, until something better could be found." The something better was the editorship of the official organ of the new government, called *The Gazette*, at a salary of 100 pesos a month. For the times, this was not a bad income for a man who had never had one and this short period was the only one of his life in which Lizardi was free from financial misery. He was at once pestered by his enemies who coveted no doubt the fortune he had fallen into, and though he went on with the job for a year or two, in the end he quarreled with everybody and was out of favor again. . . .

So it went, to the end. The rest of the history has to do with suits for defamation, plays about to be produced and failing, troubles with the censors, suppressions rather monotonously more of the same. "Let the judges answer whether they are fools or bought men," he wrote, when they found for his enemy in a slander trial. He maintained this spirit until the end. He wrote publicly denying that he had ever yielded to the ecclesiastical censors, or asked for absolution. The fact is clear that if he had not done so, the sentence of excommunication would never have been lifted. He boasted of his prudence in the business, and hinted at secret, important diplomatic strategy. Let it go. In the end, it was a matter of yielding, or of starving his family and himself to death.

In 1825, General Guadalupe Victoria, then President, proclaimed the end of slavery. One might have thought this would please Lizardi, and perhaps it did in a measure. But at once he discovered that the proclamation referred only to Negro slaves, and to the outright buying and selling of human flesh. It did not refer to the slavery of the Indian, which he found as bitter and hopeless under the Creole Republic as it had been under the Spanish Viceroys. . . . He pointed out this discrepancy, and insisted that it should be remedied. By that time, he had such a reputation for this kind of unreasonableness, the new government decided to ignore him as far as they were able. He was dismissed from consideration as a crackbrained enthusiast.

By the end of April, 1827, Lizardi knew that death was near. Someone reported on his state of health: he was "a mere skeleton." Lying in bed, he wrote and had printed his "Testament and Farewell of The Mexican Thinker." At some length, and with immense bitterness, he repeated for the last time his stubborn faiths, his unalterable beliefs, his endless opposition to every form of social, political, and human wrong, to every abuse of power and to every shade of dishonesty, particularly the dishonesty of those in power. He still considered himself as Catholic as the Pope, but he could not admit the infallibility of His Holiness. He still did not believe in the apparitions of saints, calling them "mere goblins." He was as good a patriot as ever, but he was still no party man, and he could not condone in the republican government those same abuses he had fought in the days of the Empire. With sad irony he willed to his country "A Republic whose constitution denies religious freedom; a Cathedral on which the canons would at the first opportunity replace the Spanish coat of arms; an ecclesiastical chapter which ignores the civil law altogether; streets full of stray dogs, beggars, idle police; thieves and assassins who flourish in criminal collusion with corrupt civil employees," and so on as ever, in minute detail, no evil too petty or too great for attack, as if they were all of one size and one importance. I think this does not argue at all a lack of the sense of proportion, but is proof of his extraordinary perception of the implicit relationship between all manifestations of evil, the greater breeding and nourishing the lesser, the lesser swarming to support and confirm the greater.

He advised the President of the Republic to get acquainted with the common people and the workers, to study his army and observe the actions of his ministers; and he desired that his wife and friends should not make any loud mourning over him; they were not to light candles around him, and they were to bury him not in the customary friar's robe, but in the uniform of a soldier. Further, he wished that his wife would pay only the regular burial fees of seven pesos, and not haggle with the priest, who would try to charge her more for a select spot in the cemetery. He wished that his epitaph might be: "Here lies the ashes of The Mexican Thinker, who did what he could for his country."

For long days and nights he strangled to death slowly in the wretched little house, number 27, Fuente Quebrado (The Broken Fountain), with his wife and young daughter watching him die, unable to relieve his sufferings with even the most rudimentary comforts, without medical attendance, without money, almost without food. He called two priests to hear his final confession, wishing them to be witnesses for each other that he had not died without the last rites; but he put off receiving Extreme Unction because he hoped the ritual might be attended by a number of former friends who believed him to be a heretic. The friends for some reason failed to arrive for this occasion. Lizardi lingered on, hoping, but no one came; and on June 27, still hoping, but refusing the ceremony until his witnesses should arrive, he died. Almost at once it was rumored abroad that he died possessed of the devil. The friends came then, to see for themselves, and his pitiable corpse was exposed to public view in the hovel where he died, as proof that the devil had not carried him off.

The next day a few former acquaintances, his family, and a small mob of curious busybodies followed the body of Fernández de Lizardi to the cemetery of San Lázaro, and buried him with the honors of a retired Captain. Neither the epitaph that he composed for himself, nor any other, was inscribed on his gravestone, for no stone was ever raised. His wife died within four months and was buried beside him. His fifteen-year-old daughter was given in charge of a certain Doña Juliana Guevara de Ceballos, probably her godmother, or a female relation, who seems to have handed her over to the care of another family whose name is not known. This family removed to Vera Cruz shortly, and there Lizardi's daughter died of yellow fever.

So the grave closed over them all, and Mexico almost forgot its stubborn and devoted Thinker. The San Lázaro cemetery disappeared, and with it his unmarked grave. His numberless pamphlets disappeared, a few into private collections and storerooms of bookshops; a great many more into moldering heaps of wastepaper. In effect, Lizardi was forgotten.

His novel, his one novel that he had never meant to write, which had got itself suppressed in its eleventh chapter, is without dispute The Novel of the past century, not only for Mexico but for all Spanish-speaking countries. It was published in full in 1830, three years after

Lizardi's death, and there were eight editions by 1884. In spite of this, in 1885 there appeared an edition, "corrected, explained with notes, and adorned with thirty fine illustrations," and announced as the second edition, though it was really the ninth.

After that, no one troubled any more to number editions correctly or not. Until the recent disaster in Spain, a big popular press in Barcelona reprinted it endlessly at the rate of more than a million copies a year, on pulp paper, in rotten type, with a gaudy paper cover illustrating some wild scene, usually that of the corpse-robbing in the crypt. In Mexico I used to see it at every smallest sidewalk book stall; in the larger shops there were always a good number of copies on hand, selling steadily. It was given to the young to read as an aid to manners and morals, and for a great while it must have been the one source of a liberal education for the great mass of people, the only ethical and moral instruction they could have, for Lizardi's ideas of modern education got no foothold in Mexico for nearly a century after him.

It is not to be supposed that anybody ever read a picaresque tale for the sake of the sugar plums of polite instruction concealed in it, but Lizardi had the knack of scattering little jokes and curious phrases all through his sermons, and he managed to smuggle all his pamphlets into the final version of El Periquillo. They were all there, at great length; the dog in the strange neighborhood, the dead who make no noise, the monkey dressed in silk; with all his attacks on slavery, on bullfighting, on dishonest apothecaries and incompetent doctors; his program for enlightened education, his proposals for cleaning the city in time of plague; against the vicious and mercenary clergy, the unscrupulous politicians; against gambling, against—ah well, they are all there, and the trouble for the translator is getting them out again without leaving too many gaps. For try as he might, by no art could the good Thinker make his dreary fanatic world of organized virtue anything but terrifying to the reader, it was so deadly dull. But once these wrappings are stripped from the story, there is exposed a fine, traditional Rogue's Progress, the history of a true pícaro, a younger brother of Guzman de Alfarache, as Dr. Beristain said, or of Gil Blas. He has English relations too—Peregrine Pickle, Roderick Random, Tom Jones, all of that family of lucky sinners who end well. In the best style, more things happen to El Periquillo than might reasonably happen to one man, events move at top speed, disasters pile up; but he comes through one way or another, shedding his last misadventure with a shake of his shoulders, plunging straightway into the next. Like all his kind, he is hard and casual and thickskinned and sentimental, and he shares their expedient, opportunist morality, which always serves to recall to his mind the good maxims of his early upbringing when his luck is bad, but never once when it is good.

The typical pícaro also is always the incomplete hero of his own story, for he is also a buffoon. Periquillo is afflicted with the itch, he loses his trousers during a bullfight in the presence of ladies, he is trapped into the wrong bed by the malice of his best friend, he is led again and again into humiliating situations by wits quicker than his own.

Living by his wits, such as they are, he is a true parasite, attaching himself first to one then another organism to feed upon. He is hardly ever without a "master" or "mentor" or "patron" and this person is always doing something for him, which El Periquillo accepts as his right and gives nothing, or as little as possible, in return.

Only once does he feel real gratitude. After leaving the house of the Chinese Mandarin, improbable visitor from the Island Utopia, whom Periquillo has succeeded in gulling for a while, he has been beaten and called a pimp by three girls. None of his other disgraces could equal this, so he gets drunk and goes to hang himself. He fails of course, goes to sleep instead, and wakes to find himself robbed and stripped to the shirt by wayside thieves. He is rescued by a poor old Indian woman who clothes and feeds him. In an untypical rush of tenderness, he embraces and kisses the unsightly creature. This is almost the only truly and honestly tender episode in the book, uncorrupted by any attempts to point a moral, for Lizardi's disillusionment with human nature was real, and based on experience, and most of his attempts to play upon the reader's sentiments ring false.

As El Periquillo's adventures follow the old picaresque pattern, so do those of the other characters, for they are all pretty much fairly familiar wares from the old storehouse. But the real heroes of this novel, by picaresque standards, are some of El Periquillo's comrades, such as Juan Largo, and the Eaglet. One is hanged and one dies leading a bandit raid, neither of them repents or ponders for a moment, but goes to his destined end in good form and style. Juan Largo says, "A good bullfighter dies on the horns of the bull," and El Periquillo answers that he has no wish to die a bullfighter's death. Indeed, he wants no heroics, either in living or dying. He wants to eat his cake and have it too and to die at last respectably in a comfortable bed surrounded by loving mourners. He does it, too. A thoroughly bad lot.

As in all picaresque literature, the reader has uneasy moments of wondering whether it is the hero or the author who is deficient in moral sensibility; or whether the proposed satire has not staggered and collapsed under its weight of moral connotation. When Januario is about to become a common thief, there is a long and solemn dialogue between him and Periquillo, Januario holding out firmly against Periquillo's rather cut-and-dried exhortations to honesty, or at any rate, as a last resort, plain prudence. Januario there repeats word for word the whole Catechism. Having done this, he goes out on his first escapade, and is half successful—that is he escapes from the police, but leaves his swag. On this occasion, Lizardi, by the demands of the plot, is hard beset to have Periquillo present, a witness, yet innocent. The best he can manage is to have him act as lookout, by distracting the watchman's attention and engaging him in conversation. Periquillo then believes that this act does not involve him in the least, and is most virtuously outraged when he is arrested and accused as confederate.

Again, Periquillo, in prison, and watching for a chance to cheat at cards, reflects at length and piously on the illicit, crafty methods of the trusty for turning a dishonest penny by cheating the prisoners. Thinking these thoughts, Periquillo refrains from cheating only because he realizes that he is in very fast company and will undoubtedly be caught at it. Don Antonio, a jail mate, formerly a dealer in contraband, in telling his story of how he lost his ill-gained fortune, innocently assumes and receives the complete sympathy of his hearers, not all of them mere thugs either. This Don Antonio, by the way, who is meant to shine as an example of all that is honorable, upright, and unfortunate in human nature, is certainly one of the most abject and nitwitted characters in all fiction. He is smug, pious, dishonest, he feels dreadfully sorry for himself, and his ineptitude and bad management of his affairs cause much suffering to innocent persons. In fact, Lizardi was singularly uninspired in his attempts to portray virtue in action. In his hands it becomes a horrid device of boredom, a pall falls over his mind, he retreats to the dryest kind of moral saws and proverbs. He seemed to realize this, seemed to know that this kind of goodness, the only kind he dared recommend or advertise, was deadly dull. He tried to make it interesting but could not, and turned again with relief to his tough thieves and merry catchalls and horners and unrepentant bandits. Their talk is loose and lively, their behavior natural; he cheers up at once and so does his reader.

A contemporary critic complained that the book was "an uneven and extravagant work in very bad taste . . . written in an ugly style, with a badly invented plot . . . made worse by the author's treatment." He then confessed that what really annoyed him was the author's choice of characters, who were all from the lowest walks of life. They talked and behaved exactly like the vulgar people one saw in the streets, and their language was the sort heard in taverns. This left-handed praise must have pleased Lizardi, who had aimed at precisely this effect. The critic went on to say that the vices of polite society were perhaps no less shocking, but they seemed less gross because it was possible to gloss them over, decorate them, polish them up a bit, and make them less ridiculous. "When a rich man and a poor man drink together," answered Lizardi, in a little jingle, "the poor man gets drunk, but the rich man only gets merry."

Lizardi's infrequent flights into a more rarefied social atmosphere are malicious, comic, and a conventional caricature, designed to confirm in his lower-class readers all their worst suspicions regarding the rich and titled. Now and again he drags in by the ears a set speech on the obligations of nobility to be truly noble and of the poor to be truly virtuous, in the most Lizardian sense of those words, but he makes it clear that he has no real hopes that this will come to pass.

For him, the very rich and the very poor are the delinquent classes, to use a current sociological phrase. He called aloud for the pure mediocrity of morals and manners, the exact center of the road in all things. The middling well off, he insisted, were always good, because they practiced moderation, they were without exorbitant desires, ambitions, or vices. (That this was what made them middling was what Lizardi could never see, and that only those born to the middling temperament, rather than middling fortune, could practice the tepid virtues.) Every time El Periquillo falls into poverty, he falls also into the vices of the poor. When by his standards he is rich, he practices at once the classical vices of the rich. His feelings, thoughts, and conduct contract and expand automatically to the measure of his finances. He was always astounded to meet with morality in the poor, though he did meet it now and then, but never once did he find any good among the rich. His favorite virtue was generosity, and particularly that generosity practiced toward himself, though he almost never practiced it toward others. Even during a period of relative respectability, financially speaking, when El Periquillo is planning to marry, he discusses with Roque, one of his fly-by-night friends, the possibility of Periquillo's Uncle Maceta standing as security for the bridegroom's finery at the tailor's and the silversmith's, along with a plot to rid himself of his mistress, a girl whom he had seduced from a former employer. All goes smoothly for a time: the Uncle is complacent, the mistress is thrown out of the house in good time, the marriage takes place, with bad faith on both sides, El Periquillo's transitory small fortune is thrown away on fast living, and the Uncle is rooked out of his money. El Periquillo comments that it served him right for being such a stingy, unnatural relative.

So much for the Parrot as the faulty medium of Lizardi's social and moral ideas: some of his other characters were hardly less successful in this role . . . for example, his army officer, a colonel, in Manila.

This man is a brilliant example of what a military man is not, never was, could not in the nature of things be, yet Lizardi introduces him quite naturally as if he believed him to be entirely probable. The Colonel is full of the most broadly socialistic ideas, democratic manners, with agrarian notions on nationalism. He believes that rich deposits of gold and silver are a curse to a country instead of the blessings they are supposed to be, and that the lucky country was one which must depend upon its fruits, wool, meats, grain, in plenty but not enough to tempt invaders. He notes that Mexico and the Americas in general are deplorable examples of that false wealth which caused them to neglect agriculture and industry and fall prey to rapacious foreigners. . . . The Colonel, in his fantasy, is no more strange than the entire Manila episode. El Periquillo is deported there as a convict. It is hardly probable that Lizardi ever saw Manila, though there was a legend that he had visited there during the vague "lost years." It is more probable that while he lived in Acapulco he listened to stories of storm and shipwreck and life in strange ports. That he loved the sea is quite plain, with a real love, not romantic or sentimental; he expresses in simple phrases a profound feeling for the deep waters and the sweet majesty of ships. But otherwise, the Manila episode has the vague and far-fetched air of secondhand reporting.

It is not his moral disquisitions, then, nor his portrayal of character, nor his manner of telling his story, that keeps El Periquillo alive after more than a hundred years: it is simply and broadly the good show he managed to get up out of the sights and sounds and smells of his native town. His wakes, funerals, weddings, roaring drunken parties, beggars in their flophouses, the village inns where families rumbled up in coaches, bringing servants, beds, food, exactly as they did in medieval Europe: they all exist with extraordinary vividness, and yet there is very little actual description. There are dozens of scenes which stick in the memory: Luisa standing in the door, greeting with cool scorn her former lover; the wake with the watchers playing cards through the night, and as their own candles give out, borrowing one by one the blessed candles from the dead; the robbing of the corpse, with its exaggerated piling of horror upon horror; the hospital scenes, the life in prisons; all this is eyewitness, first-hand narrative, and a worm's-eye view beside. It is a true picture of the sprawling, teeming, swarming people of Mexico, ragged, eternally cheated, crowding about the food stalls which smoke along the market side, sniffing the good smells through the dirt and confusion, insatiably and hopelessly hungry, but indestructible. Lizardi himself was hungry nearly all his life, and his Periquillo has also an enormous, unfailing preoccupation with food. He remembers every meal, good or bad, he ever ate, he refers punctually three times a day to the fact that he was hungry, or it was now time to eat: "And my anxious stomach," says Periquillo, in one of the more painful moments of his perpetual famine, "was cheeping like a bird to gobble up a couple of plates of chile sauce and a platter of toasted tortillas." Even in exile, in Manila, when he had almost forgotten persons he had known, could hardly remember the lovely face of his native city, he still remembered with longing the savory Mexican food. . . .

Lizardi was once insulted by a picayune critic, who wrote that his work was worthless and he himself a worthless character who wrote only in order to eat. This was not altogether true, for if it had been, Lizardi might easily have been much better fed than he was: but he did, having written, do what he could to sell his work to gain his bread, and though he did not choose the easy way, still he was bitterly stung by this taunt, poor man, and to save his pride, mentioned that at least he had lived by what he made, and not squandered his wife's dowry.

The Thinker's style has been admired as a model of clarity in Mexican literature by some of his later friends, but I think that must be the bias of loyalty. By the loosest standard, that style was almost intolerably wordy, cloudy, vague, the sentences of an intricate slovenliness, the paragraphs of inordinate length; indeed it was no style at all, but merely the visible shape of his harassed mind which came of his harassed life. He nearly always began his pamphlets, as he began his novel, with great dignity, deliberation, and clearness, with a consciously affected pedantry, with echoes of the grand manner, a pastiche of Cervantes or Góngora, but he knew it could not last; he knew also his readers' tastes; he could do no more than promise a patchwork, and patchwork it was. There are times too when it is apparent he wrote at top speed in order to get the number finished and handed to the printer, needing desperately the few pesos the sale would bring him, padding and repeating, partly because his mind was too tired to remember what he had written, and partly because he must give his readers good weight for the money, or they would not buy.

The censors complained constantly of his obscenity and use of double meanings, and indeed he was a master in this mode. All of his writings I have seen are full of sly hints and some not so sly, curious associations of ideas one would need to be very innocent indeed to miss. The Mexicans love them with a special affection, the language is a honeycomb of them, no doubt Lizardi enjoyed writing them, and it was a certain device for catching his readers' undivided attention. He did not need to invent anything, he had only to listen to the popular talk, which was and is ripe and odorous. Some of it is very comic and witty, some of it simply nasty, humorless, and out of place in a translation where the meaning could be conveyed only by substituting a similar phrase in English, since they are often untranslatable in the technical sense. And was he—to imitate one of his own rhetorical questions—so simple as to believe that his readers would take the trouble to wade through his moral dissertations if he did not spice them with the little obscenities they loved? He was not, and he did his best by them in the matter of seasoning. At least a hundred million readers have found his novel savory, and perhaps a few of them repaid his hopes by absorbing here and there in it a little taste of manners and morals, with some liberal political theory besides. Certainly the causes for which he fought have been never altogether defeated, but they have won no victory, either: a lukewarm, halfway sort of process, the kind of thing that exasperated him most, that might well end by disheartening the best and bravest of men. Lizardi was not the best of men, nor the bravest, he was only a very good man and a very faithful one. If he did not have perfect courage or judgment, let him who has require these things of him.

William H. Gass on Jorge Luis Borges

William H. Gass (b. 1924), who received a Ph.D. from Cornell University, is a writer and professor of philosophy. Although much of his fiction is devoted to the lives of ordinary characters and life in the Midwest, many of these characters serve as stepping stones to Gass's philosophical and aesthetic meditations. For example, in *Willie Master's Lonesome Wife* (1970) Gass uses the recollections and activities of a stripteaser to make a comment about art in general. His other works include *Omensetter's Luck* (1966) and *In the Heart of the Country* (1968), both of which are set in the Midwest; Gass's essays are collected in *Fiction and the Figures of Life* (1970), *The World within the Word* (1978), *Habitations of the Word* (1985), and *Finding a Form: Essays* (1996). His most important novel is the encyclopedic *The Tunnel* (1995). This piece first appeared in the *New York Review of Books,* 20 November 1969.

Among Paul Valéry's jottings, André Maurois observes the following: "Idea for a frightening story: it is discovered that the only remedy for cancer is living human flesh. Consequences."

One humid Sunday afternoon during the summer of 1969, in a slither of magazines on a library table, I light like a weary fly upon this, reported by Pierre Schneider: "One of Jean-Paul Riopelle's stories is about a village librarian who was too poor to buy new books; to complete his library he would, whenever he came across a favorable review in a learned journal, write the book himself, on the basis of its title."

Both of these stories are by Borges; we recognize the author at once; and their conjunction here is by Borges, too: a diverse collection of names and sources, crossing like ignorant roads: Valéry, Maurois, Riopelle, Schneider—who could have foreseen this meeting of names in *The New York Review*?

Shaken out of sleep on a swift train at night we may unblind our compartment window to discover a dim sign making some strange allegation; and you, reader, may unfist this paper any moment and pick up a book on raising herbs instead, a travel folder, letter from a lover, novel by Colette; the eye, mind, memory which encounters them as vague about the distance traversed as any passenger, and hardly startled anymore by the abrupt change in climate or terrain you've undergone.* How calm we are about it; we pass from a kiss to a verb and never tremble; and having performed that bound, we frolic or we moon among our symbols, those we've assigned to Henry Adams or those we say are by Heraclitus, as if there were nothing to it. Like the hours we spent mastering speech, we forget everything; nor do our logicians, our philosophers of language, though they may coax us like cats do their fish, very often restore what we once might have had—a sense of wonder at the mental country we inhabit, lost till we wander lost into Borges, a man born as if between syllables in Argentina where even he for many years believed he had been raised in a suburb of Buenos Aires, a suburb of adventurous streets and visible sunsets, when what was certain was that he was raised in a garden, behind a wrought-iron gate, and in a limitless library of English books.**

Just as Carriego, from the moment he recognized himself as a poet, became the author of verses which only later he was permitted to invent, Borges thought of himself as a writer before he ever composed a volume. A nearsighted child, he lived where he could see—in books and illustrations (Borges says "shortsighted," which will not do); he read English authors, read and read; in clumsy English wrote about the Golden Fleece and Hercules (and inevitably, the Labyrinth), publishing, by nine, a translation of *The Happy Prince* which a local teacher

---

*Unless the changes are forcibly called to our attention. See "The Leading Edge of the Trash Phenomenon."

**Or so he asserts in the prologue to *Evaristo Carriego,* according to Ronald J. Christ (*The Narrow Act: Borges' Art of Allusion* [New York: New York University Press, 1969]), although errors are constantly creeping in—his, Christ's, mine— errors, modifications, corruptions, which, nevertheless, may take us nearer the truth. In his little note on Carriego, does he not warn us that Carriego is a creation of Carriego? and in the parable "Borges and I" does he not say, "I am quite aware of his perverse custom of falsifying and magnifying things"? does he not award all the mischievous translations of *A Thousand and One Nights* higher marks than the pure and exact one of Enna Littmann? and in his conversations with Richard Burgin (*Conversations with Jorge Luis Borges* [New York: Holt, Rinehart & Winston, 1969]) does he not represent memory as a stack of coins, each coin a recollection of the one below it, and in each repetition a tiny distortion? Still we can imagine, over time, the distortions correcting themselves, and returning to the truth through a circle like a stroller and his dog.

adopted as a text under the impression it was the father's doing, not the son's. In Switzerland, where his family settled for a time, he completed his secondary education, becoming more and more multi-tongued (acquiring German), yet seeing no better, reading on. He then traveled extensively in Spain, as if to meet other authors, further books, to enlarge the literary landscape he was already living in—deepening, one imagines daily, his acquaintance with the conceptual country he would eventually devote his life to. Back in Argentina, he issued his first book of poems. He was twenty. They sang of Buenos Aires and its streets, but the few lines Christ quotes give the future away:

> Perhaps that unique hour
> increased the prestige of the street,
> giving it privileges of tenderness,
> making it as real as legend or verse.

Thus he was very soon to pass, as he says himself, from "the mythologies of the suburbs to the games with time and infinity" which finally made him famous—made him that imaginary being, the Borges of his books.

Becoming Borges, Borges becomes a librarian, first a minor municipal one like our poor French village author, and then later, with the fall of Perón, after having been removed for political reasons from that lesser post, the director of the National Library itself.

Idea for a frightening story: the books written by the unknown provincial librarian ultimately replace their originals, which are declared to be frauds. Consequences.

Inside the library, inside the books, within their words: the world. Even if we feel it no longer, we can remember from our childhood the intenser reality which opened toward us when like a casket lid a cover rose and we were kings on clipper ships, cabin boys on camel back, Columbuses crossing swimming holes to sack the Alps and set free Lilliput, her golden hair climbing like a knight up the wall of some crimson battle tent . . . things, men, and moments more than merely lived but added to ourselves like the flesh of a fruit. In Borges' case, for instance, these included the lamp of Aladdin, the traitor invented by H. G. Wells who abandoned his friend to the moonmen, and a scene which I shall never forget either, Blind Pew tapping toward the horses which will run him down. Señor Borges confides to Burgin's tape that

> I think of reading a book as no less an experience than traveling or falling in love. I think that reading Berkeley or Shaw or Emerson, those are quite as real experiences to me as seeing London. . . . Many people are apt to think of real life on the one side, that means toothache, headache, traveling and so on, and then on the other side, you have imaginary life and fancy and that means the arts. But I don't think that distinction holds water. I think that everything is a part of life.

Emerson? Many of Borges' other enthusiasms are equally dismaying, like the Russians' for Jack London, or the symbolist poets' for Poe; on the whole they tend to be directed toward obscure or marginal figures, to stand for somewhat cranky, wayward, even decadent choices: works at once immature or exotic, thin though mannered, clever rather than profound, neat instead of daring, too often the products of learning, fancy, and contrivance to make us comfortable; they exhibit a taste that is still in its teens, one becalmed in backwater, and a mind that is seriously intrigued by certain dubious or jejune forms, forms which have to be overcome, not simply exploited: fantastic tales and wild romances, science fiction, detective stories, and other similar modes which, with a terrible theological energy and zeal, impose upon implausible premises a rigorous gamelike reasoning; thus for this minutely careful essayist and poet it's not Aristotle, but Zeno, it's not Kant, but Schopenhauer; it's not even Hobbes, but Berkeley, not Mill or Bradley, but—may philosophy forgive him—Spencer; it's Dunne, Beckford, Bloy, the Cabbalists; it's Stevenson, Chesterton, Kipling, Wells and William Morris, Browne and De Quincey Borges turns and returns to, while admitting no such similar debt to James, Melville, Joyce, and so on, about whom, indeed, in these *Conversations,* he passes a few mildly unflattering remarks.*

*I am of course not suggesting that Borges regards Wells, say, as a better writer than Joyce, or that he pays no heed or tribute to major figures. Christ's treatment of this problem is fair and thorough. He tells us, incidentally, that in an introductory course on English literature, Borges' own interests led him to stress the importance of William Morris. Though Borges himself appears in most ways a modest man, such preferences are nevertheless personal and some-

Yet in the country of the word, Borges is well traveled, and has some of the habits of a seasoned, if not jaded, journeyer. What? see Mont Saint Michel again? that tourist trap? far better to sip a local wine in a small café, watch a vineyard comb its hillside. There are a thousand overlooked delights in every language, similarities and parallels to be remarked, and even the mightiest monuments have their neglected beauties, their unexplored crannies; then, too, it has been frequently observed that our childhood haunts, though possibly less spectacular, less perfect, than other, better advertised, places, can be the source of a fuller pleasure for us because our familiarity with them is deep and early and complete, because the place is ours; while for other regions we simply have a strange affinity—they do not threaten, like Dante or the Alps, to overwhelm us—and we somehow find our interests, our designs, reflected in them. Or is it we who function as the silvered glass? Idea for a frightening story.

Thus, reading Borges, we must think of literature as a landscape, present all at once like space, and we must remember that literary events, unlike ordinary ones—drinking our coffee or shooting our chancellor—repeat themselves, although with variations, in every mind the text fills. Books don't plop into time like stones in a pond, rippling the surface for a while with steadily diminishing waves. There is only one Paris, we suppose, and one Flaubert, one *Madame Bovary*, but the novel has more than a million occurrences, often in different languages, too. Flaubert may have ridden a whore with his hat on, as has been reported, but such high jinks soon spend their effects (so, comparatively, does the murder of any Caesar, although its initial capital is greater), whereas one sentence, divinely composed, goes on and on like the biblical proverbs, the couplets of Pope, or the witticisms of Wilde.

We may indeed suspect that the real power of historical events lies in their descriptions; only by virtue of their passage into language can

---

what vain. Just as Borges becomes important by becoming Borges, Morris becomes important by becoming Borges, too. "An author may suffer from absurd prejudices," he tells us in his fine and suggestive lecture on Hawthorne, "but it will be impossible for his work to be absurd if it is genuine, if it responds to a genuine vision." As for Spencer, it might be worth noting that this philosopher tended to think of art as a form of *play*.

they continue to occur, and once recorded (even if no more than as gossip), they become peculiarly atemporal, residing in that shelved-up present which passes for time in a library, and subject to a special kind of choice, since I can choose now to read about the war on the Peloponnesus or the invasion of Normandy; change my climate more easily than my clothes; rearrange the map; while on one day I may have traveled through Jonson to reach Goldsmith, they are not villages, and can be easily switched, so that on the next I may arrive directly from De Quincey, Goethe, or Thomas Aquinas. New locations are constantly being created, like new islands rising from the sea, yet when I land, I find them never so new as all that, and having appeared, it is as if they had always been.*

It is a suggestion, I think, of Schopenhauer** (to whom Borges turns as often as he does to Berkeley), that what we remember of our own past depends very largely on what of it we've put our tongue to telling and retelling. It's our words, roughly, we remember; oblivion claims the rest—forgetfulness. Historians make more history than the men they write about, and because we render our experience in universals, experience becomes repetitious (for if events do not repeat, accounts do), and time doubles back in confusion like a hound which has lost the scent.

Troy, many times, was buried in its own body, one city standing on the shoulders of another, and students of linguistic geography have observed a similar phenomenon. Not only are there many accounts, both factual and fictional, of Napoleon's invasion of Russia (so that the event becomes multiplied in the libraries), there are, of course, commentaries and critiques of these, and then again examinations of those, which lead, in turn, to reflections upon them, and so on, until it

*That all our messages are in the present tense, as I have tried to suggest, is fundamental to Barthelme's method of composition. See "The Leading Edge of the Trash Phenomenon."

**Borges's good friend and collaborator, Bioy Casares, once attributed to a heresiarch of Uqbar the remark that both mirrors and copulation were abominable because they increased the number of men. Borges momentarily wondered, then, whether this undocumented country and its anonymous heresiarch weren't a fiction devised by Bioy's modesty to justify a statement, and perhaps it's the same here. It should be perfectly clear, in any case, that Schopenhauer has read Borges and reflects him, just as Borges reflects both Bioy and Borges, since the remark about mirrors and copulation appears more than once.

sometimes happens that the originals are quite buried, overcome (idea for a frightening story), and though there may be a definite logical distance between each level, there is no other; they sit side by side on our shelves. We may read the critics first, or exclusively; and is it not, in fact, true that our knowledge of most books is at least second hand, as our knowledge of nearly everything else is?

Borges knows of the treacheries of our histories (treachery is one of his principal subjects)*—they are filled with toothache—and in his little essay called "The Modesty of History" suggests that most of its really vital dates are secret—for instance, the introduction, by Aeschylus, of the second actor.** Still, this is but one more example of how, by practicing a resolute forgetfulness, we select, we construct, we compose our pasts, and hence make fictional characters of ourselves, as it seems we must to remain sane (Funes the Memorious remembers everything, while the Borges who receives a zahir in his drink change following a funeral one day finds the scarred coin literally unforgettable; both suffer).

It isn't always easy to distinguish *ficciones* from *inquisiciones,* even for Borges (of the famous Pierre Menard, he says: ". . . it's not wholly a story . . . it's a kind of essay . . .") though the latter are perhaps more unfeignedly interrogations. It is his habit to infect these brief, playful, devious, solemn, *outré* notes, which, like his fictions, are often accounts of treacheries of one sort or other, with small treacheries of his own, treasons against language and its logic, betrayals of all those distinctions between fact and fancy, real life and dreaming, memory and imagination, myth and history, word and thing, fiction and essay, which we're so fond of, and find so necessary, even though keeping them straight is a perpetual difficulty.

If, as Wittgenstein thought, "philosophy is a battle against the bewitchment of our intelligence by means of language," then Borges' prose, at least, performs a precisely similar function, for there is

*He published his *Universal History of Infamy* in 1935, a work which is very carefully not a universal history of infamy. See Paul de Man, "A Modern Master," *New York Review,* Nov. 19, 1964.

**Professor Celerent has complained bitterly that there is scarcely a history of Western Europe which troubles itself to mention Aristotle's invention of the syllogism—one of that continent's most formative events. "Suppose," he says, "that small matter had been put off, as it was in India, to the 16th century?"

scarcely a story which is not built upon a sophistry, a sophistry so fanatically embraced, so pedantically developed, so soberly defended, it becomes the principal truth in the world his parables create (puzzles, paradoxes, equivocations, and obscure and idle symmetries which appear as menacing laws); and we are compelled to wonder again whether we are awake or asleep, whether we are a dreamer or ourselves a dream, whether art imitates nature or nature mirrors art instead; once more we are required to consider whether things exist only while they are being perceived, whether change can occur, whether time is linear and straight or manifold and curved, whether history repeats, whether space is a place of simple locations, whether words aren't more real than their referents—whether letters and syllables aren't magical and full of cabbalistic contents—whether it is universals or particulars which fundamentally exist, whether destiny isn't in the driver's seat, what the determinate, orderly consequences of pure chance come to, whether we are the serious playthings of the gods or the amusing commercial enterprises of the devil.

It is not the subject of these compulsions, however, but the manner in which they are produced that matters, and makes Borges an ally of Wittgenstein. It is not hard to feel that Borges' creatures are mostly mad. This is, in many ways, a comforting conclusion. The causes, on the other hand, remain disturbing; they resemble far too literally those worlds theologians and metaphysicians have already made for us and in which we have so often found ourselves netted and wriggling. When Schopenhauer argues that the body in all its aspects is a manifestation of the will, he is composing poetry; he is giving us an idea for a frightening story, one which derives its plausibility from facts we are quite unpoetically aware of (teeth are for biting), but the suggestion that the will grew its body as a man might make some tool to do his bidding is a fiction which, if we responded to the cry for consequences implicit in it, would advertise its absurdity with the mad metaphysical fantasy which would grow from its trunk like a second head.

Thus the effect of Borges' work is suspicion and skepticism. Clarity, scholarship, and reason: they are all here, yet each is employed to enlarge upon a muddle without disturbing it, to canonize a confusion. Ideas become plots (how beautifully ambiguous, for Borges, that word is), whereupon those knotty tangles the philosopher has been so patiently picking at can be happily reseen as triumphs of esthetic design.* In the right sun suspicion can fall far enough to shadow every ideology; the political schemes of men can seem no more than myths through which they move like imaginary creatures, like fabulous animals in landscapes of pure wish; the metaphors upon which they ride toward utopia now are seldom seen (such is the price one pays for an ignorance of history) to be the same overfat or scrawny nags the old political romancers, puffing, rode at windmills in their time, and always futilely. "The illusions of patriotism are limitless." Hitler tries to turn the world into a book; he suffered from unreality, Borges claims, and collaborated in his own destruction. Under the right sun one may observe little that is novel. The world of words spins merrily around, the same painted horses rising and falling to the same tunes, and our guide delights in pointing out each reappearance. We have seen this before: in Persepolis, and also in Peking . . . in Pascal, in Plato, in Parmenides. The tone, throughout, is that of a skeptical conservative (this shows up very clearly, too, in his conversations with Burgin). Least government is best, and all are bad. They rest on myth. "Perhaps universal history is the history of a few metaphors." And we have had them all already, had them all.

As a young poet Borges pledged himself to Ultraism, a Spanish literary movement resembling Imagism in many ways, whose principles he carried back to Argentina in his luggage. It demanded condensation, the suppression of ornament, modifiers, all terms of transition; it opposed exhortation and vagueness—flourish; it praised impersonality, and regarded poetry as made of metaphors in close, suggestive combinations. It was primarily a poetry of *mention*, as Borges' prose is

*Borges has made this point repeatedly himself (in the Epilogue to *Other Inquisitions*, for example); yet his commentators persist in trying to pin on him beliefs which, for Borges, are merely materials. They want him more imaginary than he already is. Perhaps this accounts for the statement, written we can imagine with a smile, which Borges includes in each of the little prefaces he has written to imprimatur the books about him: in Barrenechea, in Burgin (he "has helped me to know myself"), in Christ ("Some unsuspected things, many secret links and affinities, have been revealed to me by this book"), though he does not refrain, in the latter instance, from adding: ". . . I have no message. I am neither a thinker nor a moralist, but simply a man of letters who turns his own perplexities and that respected system of perplexities we call philosophy into the forms of literature."

now, and Christ has no difficulty in showing how these early slogans, like the literary enthusiasms of his childhood, continue to affect the later work. Any metaphor which is taken with literal seriousness requires us to imagine a world in which it can be true; it contains or suggests a metaphorical principle that in turn gives form to a fable. And when the *whole* is an image, local images can be removed.

Borges makes much of the independence of the new worlds implied by his fiction; they are "contiguous realities"; the poet annexes new provinces to Being; but they remain mirror worlds for all that; it is our own world, *misthought,* reflected there. And soon we find in Wittgenstein, himself, this ancient idea for a frightening story: "Logic is not a body of doctrine, but a mirror-image of the world."

Mirrors are abominable. A photographer points her camera at Borges like a revolver. In his childhood he feared mirrors—mahogany—being repeated . . . and thus becoming increasingly imaginary? In the beautiful bestiary (*The Book of Imaginary Beings*) which has just been translated for us,* it is suggested that one day the imprisoned creatures in our looking glasses will cease to imitate us; fish will stir in the panes as though in clear water; and "we will hear from the depths of mirrors the clatter of weapons." How many times, already, have we been overcome by imaginary beings?

This bouquet which Borges has gathered in his travels for us consists largely of rather harmless animals from stories, myths, and legends, alphabetically arranged here in the texts which first reported them or in descriptions charmingly rebuilt by Borges. Most of these beasts are mechanically made—insufficiently imaginary to be real, insufficiently original to be wonderful or menacing. There are the jumbles, created by collage: centaurs, griffins, hydras, and so on; the mathematicals, fashioned by multiplication or division: one-eyed, half-mouthed monsters or those who are many-headed, sixteen-toed, and triple-tongued; there are those of inflated or deflated size: elves, dwarfs, brownies, leviathans, and fastitocalon; and finally those who have no special shape of their own—the proteans—and who counterfeit the forms of others. A few, more interesting, are made of metal, and one, my favorite, the A Bao A Qu, is almost wholly metaphysical, and very Borges.

The Book of Imaginary Beings by Jorge Luis Borges with Margarita Guerrero, trans. by Norman Thomas di Giovanni in collaboration with the author (New York: Dutton, 1969).

There's no longer a world left for these creatures to inhabit—even our own world has expelled them—so that they seem like pieces from a game we've forgotten how to play. They are objects now of curiosity or amusement, and even the prospect of one's being alive and abroad, like the Loch Ness serpent or abominable snowman (neither of whom is registered here), does not deeply stir us. Borges' invented library of Babel is a far more compelling monster, with its mirrored hallways and hexagonal galleries, its closets where one may sleep standing up, its soaring and spiral stairways. Even those lady-faced vultures the harpies cannot frighten us, and hippogriffs are tame. It is that library we live in; it is that library we dream; our confusions alter not the parts of animals anymore, they lead on our understanding toward a culmination in illusion like a slut.

And which is Borges, which his double? which is the photograph? the face perverted by a mirror? image in the polish of a writing table? There is the Borges who compiles *A Personal Anthology*,* and says he wishes to be remembered by it, and there is the Borges who admits to Burgin that he did not put all of his best things in it; there is the Borges who plays with the notion that all our works are products of the same universal Will so that one author impersonally authors everything (thus the labors of that provincial librarian are not vain), and the Borges whose particular mark is both idiosyncratic and indelible. The political skeptic and the fierce opponent of Perón: are they one man? Can the author of *The Aleph* admire Chesterton? Wells? Croce? Kipling? And what about those stories which snap together at the end like a cheap lock? with a gun shot? Is this impish dilettante the same man who leaves us so often uneasily amazed? Perhaps he is, as Borges wrote so wonderfully of Valéry,

> A man whose admirable texts do not exhaust, or even define, his all-embracing possibilities. A man who, in a century that adores the chaotic idols of blood, earth, and passion, always preferred the lucid pleasures of thought and the secret adventures of order.

Yet can this be a figure that same age salutes? Consequences.

A Personal Anthology, ed. Anthony Kerrigan (New York: Grove, 1967).

Mark Strand on Nicanor Parra

Mark Strand was born in Summerside, Prince Edward Island, Canada, in 1934, and raised and educated in the United States and Latin America. He has been the recipient of MacArthur, Guggenheim, and Ingram Merrill fellowships, the Bobbitt National Prize, the Bollingen Prize, and the Pulitzer Prize. He has taught at Johns Hopkins University and Columbia University. Strand has published children's books and has edited *New Poetry of Mexico* (1970), with Octavio Paz, and *Another Republic* (1976), with Charles Simic. He is also the author of a number of stories in magazines like the *New Yorker,* later collected in *Mr. and Mrs. Baby and Other Stories* (1985). But it is as a poet that he is widely known. His books include *Sleeping with One Eye Open* (1963), *The Story of Our Lives* (1973), *The Late Hour* (1978), *The Continuous Life* (1990), *Dark Harbor* (1993), and *Blizzard of One* (1998). He has translated the work of Brazilian poet Carlos Drummond the Andrade and the Spaniard Rafael Alberti. His interest in American painting has produced first-rate essays on Neil Welliver, William Bailey, and others and a book-length work on Edward Hopper (1994). This piece is a book review of Nicanor Parra's *Antipoems* (New York: New Directions, 1967). It was first published in the *New York Times Book Review,* 10 December 1967.

In providing a fine selection from the Chilean poet Nicanor Parra's four books of poems, Miller Williams has done American readers a great service. Parra, a professor of theoretical physics at the University of Chile, is one of South America's leading—and most controversial—poets. He writes skillful narratives in which he is able to integrate unconscious and fantastic imagery with the literal and realistically observed.

Parra's poems are hallucinatory and violent, and at the same time factual. The well-timed disclosure of events—personal or political—gives his poems a cumulative, mounting energy and power that we have come to expect from only the best fiction. His imagery is often bizarre, but never ornamental. The style succeeds always in being plain.

His method is amply demonstrated in the book's opening poem, "Nineteen-Thirty," where factual data, syntactical simplicity, and emotional reticence combine to release a great deal of tension. The poet tells us that he is a "camera," "a recorder of dates," even "a machine producing a certain number of buttons per minute":

> I give the same attention to a crime as to an act of mercy
> I vibrate the same to an idyllic landscape
> And the spastic flashes of an electrical storm.
> I diminish and exalt nothing
> I confine myself to telling what I see.

What begins as a dispassionate account of the year 1930 becomes, among other things, a nerve-wracking insistence on the objective posture. In the end, the poem is a moving statement of man's failure to transcend history, his mortality mirrored in the events of any given time.

Only occasionally does the unity of Parra's monologues break down. In "Funeral Address" an uneasiness about death alternates with a tone of high indignation at the falsity, vanity, and pointlessness of funeral proceedings. And though it is an address, as many of his poems are, one is not sure in this case where the variant and often vagrant intensity of emotion is directed—to the speaker in the forms of mild self-pity or near hysteria, or at the event in tones of disgust or confused questioning.

The translations, by ten poets, are almost all very good, and those of W. S. Merwin exceptional. Of course, the problems in translating Parra are not so difficult as they are in translating such poets as Jorge Guillén. Guillén's poems are elaborately verbal and their content is philosophical and elusive; the translator's major job in dealing with Parra's poems is preserving their anecdotal elegance.

If the reader has a problem deciding what an "antipoem" is, Parra provides him with an opportunity to find out. His poem "Test" is in the form of a multiple-choice exam in which the reader is to underline the definitions he believes are correct in identifying an antipoem. Of course, an antipoem is any and all of the choices, but more than that it is, in this case, a poem with the effrontery to thrust the responsibility for its existence upon the reader.

In the broader sense, an antipoem—Parra's or anybody else's—is a "modern" poem. And Parra, though some of his poems date from 1938, is a comparative newcomer to modernism's battle against the old, the conventional, and the "poetic." In his own language, he was preceded by Rafael Alberti and Gerardo Diego, and by his famous countrymen Pablo Neruda and Vincente Huidobro. It is the difference between Parra's antipoems and anybody else's that is significant. He sounds like nobody else and yet he sounds contemporary. To many readers Parra will be a new poet, but a poet with all the authority of a master.

Paul West on Alejo Carpentier

Born in Derbyshire, England, in 1930, Paul West is an American poet, essayist, and novelist. He is a regular contributor to the *Nation,* the *New York Times Book Review, Paris Review,* and the *Times Literary Supplement.* Among his nonfiction works are *The Growth of the Novel* (1959) and *The Wine of Absurdity: Essays on Literature and Consolation* (1966). His fiction includes *I, Said the Sparrow* (1963), *Bela Lugosi's White Christmas* (1972), *Lord Byron's Doctor* (1989), and *The Women of Whitechapel and Jack the Ripper* (1991). West's fiction reveals the author's quest for new ways of looking at the world. He was awarded the Aga Khan Prize for fiction in 1974. This piece first appeared in *Review* (fall 1976).

Not quite deadpan, he stares from the jacket with forbearing suavity. His cleft chin droops like a wattle and his left hand, advanced along his thigh to span its girth between thumb and forefinger, looks draped, vegetal, and, because so near the camera, oversized. Thus Jean-Pierre Couderc's photograph of Alejo Carpentier, as of a haughtier or exasperated Herbert Marshall: but what comes through most subtly of all in this extraordinary portrait is the fastidious, high-level canniness of a mind as much attuned to ephemera as to cyclical time, as much aware of time that is seasonal as of time that is mere chronicity. This is Cuba's UNESCO man in Paris (the very concept gives one pause), but also, and perhaps more than any novelist since Proust, Our Man in Continuum, whose chosen emblems—Haitian history; a voyage up the Orinoco; the Machado dictatorship; conquered Guadaloupe; time reversed seen as an exercise in optional thinking—have always more than a topical resonance and pluck at the mind's underside with irresistible energy, scotching roles and eras and taxonomies in the interests of a profuse contingency, a flux we never quite see whole or get accustomed to but temporarily endure while trying to relish it as the only thing that consciousness is offered. In a word, Carpentier implies an All. *Imply* means to infold, and that he does non-stop, with tough finesse.

What a spacious, noble view of fiction he has, proposing not chemisms, the darkling plain, the long arm of coincidence, the involuntary memory, the absurd, an E. M. Forsterian small platoon, or an "analogical consciousness" out of "Morelli" by Cortázar, but a vision of the horn of plenty forever exploding, forever settling in bits that belong together more than they don't because there is nothing else for them to do. In Carpentier the All and the One remain unknown, and suspect even, but the aggregate of the Many, gorgeous and higgledy-piggledy, does duty for them, never construable but always lapped up.

This is unusual, a far *cri de coeur* from the doting, philatelical, *chosisme* of Robbe-Grillet, say, or the infuriated listing (in both senses) of Goytisolo's *Count Julian,* or the voluptuous tactilities of Yukio Mishima. It's akin to the optical illusions Claude Simon practices in *Conducting Bodies,* but altogether more voluminous, zestful, and more fun. A wild and whirling head has developed a flair for appetizing specificities, and Carpentier is a master of both detail and mass, of both fixity and flux. With none of Beckett's reductive extremism, little of Joyce's word-smelting multiplicity, he sometimes seems the only senior novelist today possessed of the view from a long way off: as if, during a sojourn on some noetic planet circling Barnard's star, he had seen mankind plain, and all our thinking, our births and deaths, our myths and structures and dreams, all our bittersweet velleities, rammed up against the anonymous doings of nature. Unlike Robert Graves, who once claimed that by holding a Roman coin in his hand he could transport himself back to Roman times, Carpentier uses astute vicariousness to guess what the coin would be like. He is one of the few writers of whom you can say: If we didn't exist, he would be able to imagine us (assuming he was the only human). In other words, he can not only describe; he can describe what no-one has seen; and, best, he seems to have the hypothetical gift of suggesting, as he describes, that his description—a text woven from words—is experience newly reified, made more available, more dependable, and more reassuring, than daily bread or daily trash.

How odd, then, to find critical notices of *Reasons of State* which chide Carpentier for anachronism or inaccuracy, or which regard the book simply as an exercise in quasi-historical portraiture, or politicist cops and robbers; yet no odder than the complaint, made against his previous novels, that he engages in heavy pondering and actually dares to hold up "the action" in order to think. The truth is that his fiction is ostensible, and his characters—Juan the Pilgrim and Noah in *War of Time,* the downhearted musicologist in *The Lost Steps,* Hugues the revolutionary in *Explosion in a Cathedral*—are pretexts. He has something more than narrative, or storytelling, in mind, and he uses it as bait (much as Eliot envisioned a poem's meaning as the poet-burglar's lump of meat provided for the reader's watchdog while the poem goes about its real business). What keeps on coming is the deluge of phenomena, against and amidst whose Niagara not only sentences and paragraphs, but mind and will themselves, are virtually helpless. And this is not only a theme in Carpentier's work: it is also a procedural mannerism evinced in thousands of exquisitely crafted sentences which, lovely in distension, threaten to distend further just because everything evokes everything else, and therefore all sentences are unsatisfactory surrogates for The Sentence, absolute and final, which unlinearly would render them unnecessary. Read in series, these sentences thrive on their own failure, an obbligato of also-rans: not so much near-misses as distant misses; and the drama, the action, in one sense, is less in the events than in this linear prometheanism which never gives up yet never succeeds, which exhausts itself in trying to exhaust the world (until the next time, the next sentence), and evokes a complementary opposite to the Eskimo fad of jubilant modesty—if you harpoon a seal, exclaim "I almost missed it!" Carpentier, always missing, creates a jubilant rhetoric of disappointment that includes, as part of elegant mind-play, the fiction of a near-hit. Doomed, of course, to miss, and to omit, he makes the trajectory thrilling, so much so that one takes the rhetoric (the harpoon work), as one must, as an end in itself: the ineffable and finally not historical but cosmic mental adventure against whose ground the more overt "adventures" of his books—revolutions, pilgrimages, quests—are merely invitational tropes. The agon of an articulateness born incomplete; the flirtation with the ghost of an articulateness born complete: these are his preoccupations, much as Beckett's failure to express, aggravating the need to express, is his.

At its most obvious, *Reasons of State* is a portrait of a sybaritic, cultivated Latin American despot, an absentee totalitarian who sows his wildest oats in Paris, from time to time steaming home to quell the latest revolt. Rum, venery, and lush rhetoric compose his life style; opera and paintings finesse it; and he somehow contrives to stay in power; stifling dissent and confiscating "red" literature (including *Le*

Rouge et le Noir and *The Scarlet Letter*), at least until an uncurbable proletariat and some palace treachery dislodge him for keeps. He repines in Paris, wondering how single-mindedness, enforced by the military and a Model Prison full of electric chairs and wet-cement oubliettes, could have failed. "Yes," runs the hit tune of Jazz Age Paris, "We Have No Bananas." A banana republic has shed a skin and its naked-feeling despot dies, pulp for Eumenides of his own making.

But the novel is far from exclusively political or didactic: a big buzzing blooming confusion fills it, or at least a minor, fly-blown, withering chunk of window-dressing, in which Caruso, Nehru, Sarah Bernhardt, flit like contraband moths through the chromatic paroxysms of *señor presidente*'s vanity. Marble monuments, timely trains, imported squirrels and reindeer and North American firs, gala performances of *Marta* and *Rigoletto,* even Campaigns to Collect Funds for Reconstruction, are of no avail. Fornication goes on in the National Observatory; drunks invade the churches; skulls arrive in the mail and funeral wreaths at houses where no one has died; a Steinway ordered from New York arrives with a decapitated donkey inside it. The Republic of Nueva Cordoba disarranges and disorders itself like Rimbaud's mind, from stink bombs at the opera to a general strike led by a stereotypical energumen called The Student. The comeuppance is fizzy and satirically epitomistic.

But diverting and amusing as all this is, it isn't the novel's main impact or the source of its perceptual zeal. Life's heterogeneousness conducts us to intuitions of wholeness, and Carpentier, transcending satire even while he creates a near-documentary album, conducts us back— through and past matrices, regimes, credos, formulas, and codes, so familiar as almost to seem natural structures themselves—to an atavistic awe larded with unceremonious intrusions. Mind watches mind evolving, and distraction keeps it at full stretch, as in the long sortie that follows, characteristic of Carpentier's free-association anthems:

> Now the Consul is showing me a rare collection of root-sculptures, sculpture-roots, root-forms, root-objects—baroque roots or roots that are austere in their smoothness; complicated, intricate or nobly geometrical; at times dancing, at times static, or totemic, or sexual, something between an animal and a theorem, a play of knots, a play of asymmetry, now alive, now fossilized—which the Yankee tells me he

has collected on numerous expeditions along the shores of the Continent. Roots torn up from remote soil, dragged along, cast up, and again transported by rivers in spate; roots sculptured by the water, hurled about, knocked over, polished, burnished, silvered, denuded of their silver, until from so many journeys, falls, collisions with rocks, battles with other pieces of wood on the move, they have finally lost their vegetable morphology, become separated from the tree-mother, the genealogical tree, and acquired breast-like roundnesses, polyhedric arms, boars' heads or idols' faces, teeth, claws, tentacles, penises and crowns, or are intimately connected in obscene imbrications, before being stranded, after a journey lasting centuries, on some beach forgotten by maps. That huge mandragora with its fierce thorns had been found by the Consul at the mouth of the Bio-Bio, close to the jagged rocks of Con-Con, rocking in a hammock of blue waters. That other mandragora, contorted and acrobatic, with its fungus-hat and bulging eyes—rather like the "root of life" which certain Asiatic peoples put in flasks of aguardiente—had been found near Tucupita in the estuary of the Orinoco. Others came from the island of Nervis, from Aruba, from the rocks like basalt menhirs that rise amid the thunderous marine gorges near Valparaiso. And it was enough to mention the name of a port to the collector for him to pass from the root found there to the invocation, evocation, presentation of images brought to life by the syllables making up its name, or the proliferative activity of the letters— so he said—a process such as was foreshadowed in the Hebrew Cabbala. And merely by pronouncing the word Valparaiso there were plateaux of jurel-fish lying on seaweed, a display of fruit in the church porch, the windows of inns showing the whole counter covered in apocalyptic spider-crabs from Tierra del Fuego; and there were the German beer-shops in the main street, where reddish-black sausages spotted with bacon-fat lay beside warm strudels powdered with sugar; and there were the enormous public lifts, tirelessly moving parallel to each other, with orchestras of blind men playing polkas in the tunnels by which you reached them; and there were the pawnshops, with a broad-buckled belt, a reliquary made of shells, a scalpel with a jagged edge, a Negro figure from Easter Island, slippers embroidered with *Souv* (for the left foot) and *Enir* (for the right) which, when put endways on to the passer-by, illustrated with amazing eloquence Kant's Paradox of the Looking-glass.

What, that is radical in any sense, wouldn't fit into the contained ampleness of that? Delving into phenomena, Carpentier finds every sense-datum, every phoneme, a cross-roads, down each fork of which he ponders his way, aware that the time-traveller's very presence modifies the space he's in. That long prose journey from "Now" to "the Looking-glass" exemplifies his way of making something infinitesimal exemplify infinity, something natural counterpoint something manufactured, something almost sacred something vulgar. Yet you can lose the whole thing, responding only to swell's augmentations rather than to swell's meaning, if you don't follow the allusion to Kant which at once undercuts and makes a triumphant finale. The passage is a triumph of style, of course, enacting in its movements—playful, dawdling, side-spill and eddy and full halt—its theme. And this reminds us that style for Carpentier is more than embellishment or panache, but a means of participating anew in the universe through the fixed physical configurations of prose rather than in some unwritten reverie. He writes amazement, even through the stunted sado-misanthropic mind of his anonymous head of state, whose sense of wonder is shallow and arrested, yet nonetheless there, and especially visible when Carpentier vouchsafes him the use of the first person, occasions on which outrage and indignation lead even that unevolved hobgoblin to a wider view in which more things are possible than before. But his mind seals itself, clenched around a few treasured obsessions, and he seems finally less interesting than his shotgun-toting consort-housekeeper, his foul-mouthed and intricately self-willed daughter, his mandarin litterateur of a privy counsellor, even the part-Negro American consul who helps him escape. Behind them all, Carpentier the impresario of metaphors, the keeper of an entire zoo of assorted specificities, weaves and re-weaves complex patterns of transcendence which are like light streaming through a pornographic stained-glass window. Yet if this is a moralistic book, I didn't find it so; a saint would have looked just as ephemeral, stymied, flawed, as this mythic head of state. All one can do is reflect on the barrenness of demagogical thinking.

Scattered saliences linger on: the reek of the seaport, compact of brown sugar, hot furnaces, and green coffee; the skeleton found in a jar in a cave (the description of which occurs twice, with the wording only slightly varied, a *déjà vu* sponsored by Nemesis); the master driller and borer who carves mountains into animals (thus, in his view, releasing a whole trapped bestiary); the Little German Train on which the head of state dotes ("As if it had just come out of a Nuremberg toyshop, gleaming, repainted and varnished"); and his horse, Holofernes, to which he daily feeds a pail of best English beer. Scattered throughout these saliences, a series of epigraphs from Descartes hedge the telling about with dualisms: individual and public notions of reason; space occupied and space not; deliberate and automatic behavior; the certainty that one exists and the uncertainty about how long; all culminating in "And deciding not to seek more knowledge than what I could find in myself" and, atop the last page, ". . . stop a little while longer and consider this chaos. . . ."

Can we, the book implies, know what it is we do not know? There is no knowing that, but one lifetime's opportunity to observe acquaints us with the beguiling insufficiency of what we do know. As Carpentier proves, no matter how skilled we are at speculative hypothesis, our knowledge of our ignorance is mostly retrospective, except for the big, cosmic questions. In between, however, between what we do not know we do not know and, say, What created hydrogen? there's much that's feasible, much of it being observation such as yields thick description, at which Carpentier excels, perhaps because he knows how thin our attentiveness can become once we realize *we* are the thickness while the thickness lasts. "In the Kingdom of Heaven," as we read in Carpentier's *The Kingdom of this World*, "there is no grandeur to be won . . . the unknown is revealed, existence is infinite." Or, as John Wheeler of Princeton puts it, "In some strange sense, this is a participatory universe. What we have been accustomed to call 'physical reality' turns out to be largely a papier mâché construction of our imagination plastered in between the solid iron pillars of our observations. These observations constitute the only reality." Imagination's role is to serve itself, as Carpentier has his tyrant confirm in his dying words: *Acta est fabula* (the tale is told). The translation is a delight; the binding is abominable, half the pages having fallen out in a slab when I opened the book up.

Waldo Frank on Ricardo Güiraldes

Waldo Frank (1889–1967) is the United States writer who has been closest to Latin American letters. An international man of letters, his intellectual and political activities intersected all the significant artistic movements of the period from 1910 to 1950. With Van Wyck Brooks and Lewis Mumford, he spoke for the radical and aesthetic aspirations of a whole literary generation. His friendship with Victoria Ocampo, Jorge Luis Borges, and other Argentines during the 1930s and 1940s allowed for his work to become known in the Southern Hemisphere. Born in Long Branch, New Jersey, he was the child of Jewish immigrants. For a while Frank worked as a reporter for the *New York Times.* He published copiously in many genres: novels, essays, travelogues, biographies, historical studies, and dramas. His books include *The Dark Mother* (1920), *Dawn in Russia: The Record of a Journey* (1932), *Bridgehead: The Drama of Israel* (1957), *Chart for Rough Water: Our Role in a New World* (1940), and *The Jew in Our Day* (1944). On Spanish and Hispanic American themes, Frank wrote, aside from his introduction to Ricardo Güiraldes (1886–1927), *Virgin Spain* (1926), *America Hispana: A Portrait and a Prospect* (1931), *Birth of a World: Bolívar in Terms of His Peoples* (1951), and *Cuba: Prophetic Island* (1961), the latter a sympathetic view of Fidel Castro's revolution. This essay is Frank's introduction to *Don Segundo Sombra: Shadows in the Pampas,* by Ricardo Güiraldes (New York: Farrar and Rinehart, 1935).

The author of this story was born in Buenos Aires, February 8, 1886. He came of the large ranch-owning class that ruled the country until a short time ago, but in a benevolent, democratic way which it is hard for us to picture, whose notions about landlords have been gleaned mainly from Irish and Russian books. At the age of two the baby Ricardo was taken to Europe; and when he came back, four years later, he spoke French and German as fluently as Spanish. It may be said of his entire life that he "commuted" between his father's ranch, the national capital (of which his father at one time was Mayor), and Paris. He made a two years' trip around the world, visiting Egypt, Turkey, India, Ceylon, China, Siberia, and Russia. (It is interesting to note that he did not visit us.) But he always returned to his beloved

Argentina: and the intellectual and artistic training which he won from the old world he applied to the expression of the life of his own land.

As so often happens with American writers, Güiraldes received his first adequate recognition from Paris, where Valéry Larbaud wrote about his early books in *La Nouvelle Revue Française* of 1920. In 1924, with a group of Argentinian writers, he founded a magazine called *Proa* (which means the prow of a ship) whose program was to give expression to the national life with the aid of all the technical literary discoveries of post-war Paris.

In 1925, Güiraldes retired to his father's ranch, La Porteña, in the Province of Buenos Aires. There, all his life, he had known and loved a certain gaucho whom he was to immortalize as Don Segundo Sombra. (When I visited this ranch in 1929, the grand old man was still alive and I saw him dance and sing improvised verses, as it is described in this book.) On the ranch, not far from the main house, was a great *ombú*. This is a tree which, so far as I know, grows only on the pampa; and I can best picture it by saying that it looks like a cluster of huge elephants with all their legs and trunks rising into the air. Every day, Güiraldes climbed into a notch of this tree and wrote the story of Don Segundo Sombra. It was published in 1926, and made its author famous. Indeed, it was one of those rare books, like the great gaucho epic *Martín Fierro* (1872), that are read by everyone, intellectual and farmer, adult and child. Already when it was finished, Güiraldes was a sick man. He returned to Europe to seek the help of the greatest physicians; but they could not help him. He died in Paris on October 8, 1927.

Strange as it may seem, *Don Segundo Sombra* occupies in Argentinian letters a place not unrelated to that of *Huckleberry Finn* in ours. It, too, is the history of a boy, a waif who "on his own" wanders through the country. And that country, in both books, is the frontier—an old America that had already almost vanished when the two books were written. Both tell an exciting story of adventure from the standpoint of a boy, in the boy's own language; and both lads are typical products of their respective worlds. But the books are a great deal more than good adventure stories, being classic pictures of the traditions and ideas, the institutions and the folk of the two countries.

The differences of course are enormous; and are in a large part the differences between early North America and Argentina. The gaucho had received as his heritage the Catholic tradition of Spain; and although the life of these southern cowboys was primitive, it kept a humane quality from the culture of Spain. Huckleberry Finn floats blindly down a barbarous, anarchic world in which the traditions of Old England are broken up past recognition. His friend is a poor black fugitive slave; he finds literally no one and nothing to look up to. His Argentinian brother follows a man who not only teaches him how to rope cows, but becomes his spiritual father. In all the rough work, a real culture lives in the pampa; and one feels it not alone in the lives of the gauchos, but even in the attitude of the men toward their horses and their cattle.

These distinctions are carried into the minds of the two boys. Huck sees mainly the outside of events and is moved only by simple human feelings. The Argentinian lad, quite as naturally, is alive to the nuances in his adventures of color and emotion. Mark Twain's book is written in dialects that are no more complex than the waters of the Mississippi. The book of Güiraldes is in a prose that expresses the virile, rough life of the gaucho with the sensibility of a humane culture.

These distinctions may surprise the American reader who has been led to believe that ours is a more civilized world than Latin America. The reason for this is that we have a certain kind of order: industrial, commercial, and (as a reflection of these) political; and this order is the one that we are taught to praise. The order of Argentina is more inward, it is cultural rather than institutional. It is an order of human values, much more than of business and of public affairs. But it belongs to an old agricultural world which, even in Argentina, is fast disappearing. Which explains the social and political unrest in the Latin-American countries.

But the reader of *Don Segundo Sombra* need not bother about all this. He will learn, without knowing it, all the tricks of the noble art of bronco-busting and of cattle-wrangling. He will drink in, delightedly, the savor and rhythm of the pampa. He will read the story of a boy who, like boys the world over, learns to become a man by taking life humbly, and bravely.

Barbara Probst Solomon on Teresa de la Parra

Barbara Probst Solomon (b. 1930) is the author of two novels, two memoirs, including *Arriving Where We Started* (1972), which won the Pablo de Olavide Prize in 1979 in Barcelona, and the collection of essays *Horse-Trading and Ecstasy* (1989). A native New Yorker, she is a contributor to numerous journals in the United States and Spain, such as the *New Yorker, New Republic, New York Times,* and *Quimera,* and is cultural correspondent of *El País.* This essay, written in July 1994, first appeared in *DoubleTake.*

History as personal narrative, magic realism, eroticism, and female identity are stylist stuff north as well as south of the Caribbean, so it seems inevitable that Teresa de la Parra's classic novel *Iphigenia (the diary of a young lady who wrote because she was bored)* would at last be published in English. To my delight the University of Texas Press has published Bertie Acker's translation of it—de la Parra has always had a complicated geographical history. When *Iphigenia* was first published in 1924 in Paris as the winner of the Casa Editorial Franco-Americana prize for best Latin American novel of the year, it caused a scandal on both sides of the Atlantic. There were various attempts at an American edition, but a finished translation never materialized. By the early thirties de la Parra was critically ill with tuberculosis. After her death her work, in terms of a North American public, got lost in the tumult of the Spanish Civil War and World War II. When the Second World War was over the president of Venezuela, the writer Rómulo Gallegos, helped transfer her remains from Madrid to Caracas, where she was given an official burial. By the late 1950s her reputation as one of Latin America's most important writers was permanently assured, and succeeding generations have been influenced by her.

My own discovery of *Iphigenia* took place in the early fifties during a gray, wet Paris winter when I was reading lots of books in a hotel room short on heat. Some people fight with relatives—I fought with the novel. I was somewhat vaguely studying at the Sorbonne. The novel, not my parents, not men, seemed to constrict me, inflicting on me a musty morality. While men's fiction was expansive, inviting in the universe, women's fiction struck me as cramped. If the heroine needed more developmental space for her emotional growth than, say, the one bad love affair fictionally deemed her due, she was shifted to another genre, with other moral implications: she became the picaresque heroine of the picaresque novel. What made no sense to me was that females' language of sexuality was at times as blunt, as full of sexual words as their male partners, while in the novel, our sexual language was nonexistent, and our bodies, our partners' bodies, odorless.

One afternoon Paco Benet, also a student at the Sorbonne, and brother of the future novelist Juan Benet—also a student, but stuck in gloomy Franco Madrid—tired of hearing my *donc* this and *donc* that against the novel, gave me a copy of *Iphigenia*. I was stunned. It spoke directly to my obsession that a woman's reality, her shifting place in a fragmented society, couldn't be conveyed by a shapely short story or novel. De La Parra had split hers into four narrations. One operates through letters; the other three are different types of diaries, with a varied use of time present, past, and recollected, and an inclusion of the writer-as-narrator. Not until I read Doris Lessing's *The Golden Notebook*, though Lessing is less of a stylist, would I come across that ample a vision and generous structuring of the novel.

Combining the longeurs of Latin American history with the magic of "la naturaleza" came naturally to de la Parra. She saw history and nature as forever intertwined; they signified a permanent evocation of her lost paradise, her magical childhood at Tazon, the family sugarcane plantation near Caracas. Her use of the first person voice, whether Maria Eugenia in *Iphigenia* or the multivoiced women of succeeding generations in her other classic novel *Las memorias de Mamá Blanca*, was her way of melding the historic to the intimate.

Teresa de la Parra was the first Latin American woman novelist to introduce female eroticism and a strong feminist point of view into her fiction, but her political conservatism baffled her feminist followers. But what goes around, comes around. Ironically, her anti-ideological stance now makes her just wonderful for the postmodern world. Influenced by Ortega y Gasset's "Dehumanization of Art and Ideas on the Novel," she was highly critical of the Latin American habit of considering revolutions a solution to social problems. She felt stability was needed even more than reform. She rated the Russian Revolution, then admired by the intelligentsia, a bloody disaster, and startled her contemporaries by brushing aside the evils of the Spanish conquest. To further complicate matters, de la Parra had a strong anticlerical streak, she was a sort of jaunty free thinker—this scandalized the right—and an early follower of Freud. Her odd mixture of elitism and radical ideas about women made her a problematic model.

Though the Boom writers have liked the notion that they invented the literary wheel anew in Latin America, Latin American literature does have a continuum. I'm arguing against the idea that prior to the Boom there was *nada*. The intense Latin American need of European culture and vanguard techniques to enhance their literature, and their compensating obsession with their own country's history and identity, has been a constant. If one can imagine *Love in the Time of Cholera* written from a feminist point of view it bears an amazing resemblance to *Iphigenia*. Clearly Gabriel García Márquez is one of de la Parra's spiritual sons—she's a precursor to magic realism. De la Parra's observations on the sophisticated living conditions in convents during Sor Juana Ines de la Cruz's time and the origins of "pagan colonial Catholicism of the hammock" anticipate Octavio Paz's biography of the seventeenth-century Mexican poet. And her political thought resembles the ideas of Mario Vargas Llosa.

Rethinking Teresa de la Parra now, after reading *Iphigenia* in English, I wondered where I would place her among women writers. It occurs to me that she, Isak Dinesen, Anaïs Nin, Doris Lessing, and Marguerite Duras share a common trait. Relatively early in life they had abruptly shifted continents. In the case of Dinesen, Nin, and de la Parra language was also switched. Such displacement tends to produce an unnameable suffering, but it also can create a generic power. De la Parra, Nin, and Lessing were overtly interested in exploring female consciousness, sexuality, and social reality, which meant they had to introduce into their fiction some form of a love story. Romantic or sexual involvement reflected through larger, less personal concerns gains in intensity. The subterranean inclusion of an exile's heart, and an exile's heart, paradoxically, knows no gender, gave their work an awesome allure. Whether it is Lessing and Dinesen gazing at Africa from London and Denmark, or de la Parra and Duras gazing at Venezuela and Indochina from Paris, the need to collapse geography, to fuse the "other civilization" to their present, released these writers from the dictates of the conventional novel. Teresa de la Parra said that her habit of looking at Venezuela from afar made her understand it better than most Venezuelans. Like Nin and Lessing, she used a form of layered diaries to paste an intractable geography to previously unchartered truths about women's lives.

Teresa de la Parra was born in 1895 in Paris in the palmy beginning days of the *Belle Epoque*. Her family—her father was a diplomat—lived on the fashionable Avenue de Wagram. From the late nineteenth century until well into the 1920s, Paris was an essential venue for Latin Americans—the aristocratic Spanish colonial criolla society, the new rich, the writers and artists, all descended upon it. In addition to the tango, well-heeled Argentinians brought cows on their transatlantic voyage to France so that they would have the right kind of meat and milk to fortify them on their strolls through the Louvre. When Teresa was three the Santojo de la Parra family moved back to Tazon, their sugarcane plantation near Caracas. When she was eight her father died, and his estate was plundered by those in charge. Teresa's mother was left in diminished circumstances; her solution was to take her six children to live with Spanish relatives in Valencia.

Teresa was enrolled in a repressive religious order run by sisters. Everything familiar—her father, her landscape, culture, and economic ease had vanished. She responded to these losses by omnivorous reading, precocious writing, and a sharp observation of the world. At nineteen, after a short Paris detour, Teresa de la Parra arrived home with her literary suitcase stuffed with European goodies: in addition to an obvious grounding in Cervantes et al. she had acquired a taste for Voltaire, Rousseau, Flaubert, and Colette. Her first stories were published in France, not Venezuela, in a Parisian literary magazine, *La Vie Latine.*

After the First World War, after 1919, the world was never to be the same. The jolt of the modern—revolution, the machine age and jazz, and ideas of liberated sex and bobbed hair and silk lounging pajamas for women—had overtaken it. *Iphigenia* was published in 1923, one year after T. S. Eliot's *The Wasteland*. Paul Morand, de la Parra's exact contemporary, had published *Fancy Goods* and *Open All Night*. Proust, who enormously admired him, wrote the preface to the former. Ezra Pound set about translating the short novels into English. He felt that Morand had offered "the first clear eye that has been able to wander about both ends of Europe looking at wreckage."

De la Parra, who sounded like Morand in an early travel novela, was keenly aware that Venezuela was having its own special upheaval in addition to the worldwide tumult. Social cataclysm was the subject of her novel. Proust, whom she happened to have read early on, before most French writers had clued into him, informed her style of narration through memory.

Iphigenia begins with its rebellious heroine, María Eugenia Alonso, already having partaken of the Parisian-Latin American explosion of the early twenties. María Eugenia isn't on a quest. She merely wants to prolong her bohemian existence. "Just who, can forbid me on my twenty-first birthday to . . . get work in Paris, Madrid, or New York as a ballet dancer or a movie actress?" But in order to stay afloat in Venezuela's petroleum hard-money culture, Maria Eugenia must make a good marriage. She has the *trappings* of the sexual revolution—silk pants and animated talk—but no means of support. She's the spiritual sister of Tess Slesinger's heroine Elizabeth in *The Dispossessed*. Elizabeth also fails at Paris expatriate life and needs to return home: her lover, she says, "gave me back my own toothbrush, he gave me all he had to give and all he had was a bright red copy of *Ulysses* and my own American toothbrush."

From its beginning: "A very long letter wherein things are told as they are in novels" de la Parra makes clear that she is arguing against preexisting literary modes and the Latin American Bovarism stultifying middle-class women. Her much quoted remark "History, in truth, is a banquet made up only of men . . . simply rumors of false fiestas" explains the subtext of *Iphigenia*. In her lithe, sardonic, unfancy Spanish, she was wonderfully precise in describing love, money, and passion in a Caracas in social flux, a society caught between a disintegrated landed aristocracy and the new oil-rich bourgeoisie. "The city seemed bowed down by the mountain . . . by the telephone lines. . . . Caracas . . . turned out to be this flat town . . . a kind of Andalusian city, like a melancholy Andalusia, without a shawl or castanets, without guitars or music, without flowerpots and flowers on the balconies . . . a drowsy Andalusia that had dropped off to sleep in the sultry heat of the tropics!"

Despite her Uncle Panchito's advice: "Never look at silverware or anything else against the light," María Eugenia, as a means of defining herself, picks apart the Caracas she is stuck in. Her situation is lousy.

Her lover, the local *libre-penseur,* wants to make a swift fortune in petroleum deals more than he wants her. "Gabriel Olmedo . . . is a pretentious creature, full of himself, who talks about the importance of 'his freedom' as if he were some town or nation." But her rebellious utterings are only pin-pricks; the independence she longs for isn't available to her in Caracas. Her power consists only of words and thoughts. She shocks her grandmother by her wacky Cartesian observation that, given the Caribbean climate, it would make more sense to go naked wearing merely a straw hat as protection from the sun. "Clothing is the cause of immodesty. If doves wore clothes, we'd be scandalized with the movement of their wings, and this from below would make a very indecent impression."

The author's detractors in Latin America accused her of Voltairean ideas, of perniciously leading young women astray. Well, according to their lights, they had a point. *Iphigenia* was unparalleled in Latin American literature in its explicit eroticism. De la Parra had no model for writing so graphically about female sexuality, and certainly not in making her heroine the sexual initiator. Oddly enough, her interest in Freud, Proust, and states of consciousness, and her familiarity with religious mysticism, seems, as a solution for setting up the key erotic scene, to have led her to her discovery of magic realism.

Maria Eugenia and a good-looking younger male relative are in a tropical forest which ajoins her grandmother's country place. While nibbling on fruits and leaves—María Eugenia describes herself "as though I were under the influence of a hallucinogen"—she hears the river speak to her about her absent lover. Blame it on the river! It's the river which induces her rapture and urges her to write her wild "Song of Songs" to Gabriel, who has just jilted her for a petroleum heiress. "Gabriel . . . I love you because you live and move in me." Her river-induced rapture also causes her to use the boy with her as a stand-in for Gabriel. Her justification for her lack of fidelity to her absent amor is that religious ascetics embrace wooden images as a substitution for God.

My point is, while we North Americans frequently think of magic realism as exotic canaries flying through windows, its origins often had to do with displaced taboos and evasions.

Her detractors were also dismayed by de la Parra's view of women in the larger context of Venezuelan history. María Eugenia's uncle remarks: "In that hurly-burly of patriots leaving, of royalists coming in, the earthquake of 1812, the emigration of 1814, women were going one way and their husbands another and there were Mantuan women like the Aristeiguetas who had a lot of fun. . . . in the war of Independence, as in every truly important war, free trade was established. A proof of it is that since then the old convents that flourished so in Colonial times began to decline and it was rare for an old maid to survive the Independence without having some mysterious adopted child."

De la Parra's great love, the sophisticated Ecuadoran novelist-diplomat Gonzalo Zaldumbide, quipped in 1920s Parisian smart-assed cafe style: "Women don't narrate, they confess." But *Iphigenia* isn't disguised autobiography. Every choice of María Eugenia's, including her eventual pragmatic marriage to a local buffoon politician, has to do with the suffocating limits the social mores in the Caribbean capital imposed on women.

De la Parra's fiction and essays caused tremendous brouhaha in the Caribbean-Cuban-Parisian-Spanish literary circuit. In the late twenties, roughly the same time in which Virginia Woolf was writing *A Room of One's Own,* de la Parra, by then permanently based in Paris, went on two major tours to Havana, Bogotá, and Caracas. She was given the sort of reception we now reserve for super rock stars. Cars and trains were jammed with her fans en route to mobbed lecture halls. The Spanish philosopher Miguel de Unamuno adored her. The Chilean socialist poet Gabriela Mistral called her "that monstrously delicate and complicated being—that flower of the baroque."

By *baroque* Mistral didn't mean de la Parra's writing style but her interest in the Spanish colonial world. All this fuss was going on during Anaïs Nin's formative years. My hunch is that the Caracas-Parisian might have provided the Cuban-Parisian, who had such similar early losses, a literary legitimacy for insisting on the diary form, and a handle for conveying female sexuality—Nin's style of writing about sex has more to do with theatrical anti-Christ Spanish razzle-dazzle than it does with Henry Miller. In their body imagery both women owe a debt to good old Santa Teresa de Avila, the Spanish mystic poet. When defined as an American writer with vague international ties, Anaïs Nin seems an orphan, unclaimed by literary tradition. In a Spanish context she makes more sense.

On women's needs de la Parra was crisp. Unlike Woolf, the more worldly Venezuelan writer envisioned no five hundred pounds per annum plus a room of one's own handily coming to the rescue just around the bend. She warned her Caribbean middle-class female audience that unless they found authentic and remunerative work they would become an economically endangered species. Woolf was interested in androgyny, in the life of Shakespeare's imaginary sister. De la Parra was interested in the specificity of Latin American history; in women's concrete transaction with a society where "time was only ritual . . . the mixing of chocolate beans with vanilla."

"The Importance of American Women during the Conquest, Colonialism, and the Independence" and de la Parra's lecture on Simon Bolívar are gems of expository writing. Her innovative ways of thinking about the Spanish colonial period, including her insistence on the need for historical reconstruction of the lives of unknown women, is very much of the sort Braudel would later do. De la Parra came easily to her notion of history as an intimate business best handed down through feminine voices. Her Aunt Teresa Soublette was a direct descendant of General Carlos Soublette, who fought alongside Bolívar and later became president of Venezuela. Teresa de la Parra was working on a history of Bolívar, emphasizing his mistresses' political role, when she contracted tuberculosis.

She fought her illness for five years, seeking out the most progressive treatment in Europe for the disease. In the shaky Spanish spring of 1936, at the age of forty-one, she died in the sanatorium Fuenfría in the Sierra de Guadarrama, outside of Madrid. In her "Diary of Bellvue Fuenfría-Madrid" she reflected on the importance of those not yet too ill to not isolate themselves from the dying, and on Thomas Mann's occasional pomposity in *The Magic Mountain*. In July the Spanish Civil War erupted, and in August, four months after her death, the Spanish poet Federico García Lorca was murdered in the outskirts of Granada.

Robert Bly on Pablo Neruda

Born in Minnesota in 1926, Robert Bly has made his mark as a poet, translator, and the editor and sponsor of *The Fifties,* his own periodical, which has always kept its readers abreast of the latest developments in international literature while also publishing American authors. Bly has translated fiction by such writers as Selma Lagerlöf and Knut Hamsun and the poetry of Neruda, Lorca, Jiménez, Rilke, and Trakl. His thematic interests range from politics and the struggle for manhood to a very original mysticism. He has also written an interpretation of the work of Carl Jung, entitled *A Little Book on the Human Shadow* (1988). Firmly opposed to the Vietnam War, Bly donated the money he was awarded for a National Book Award to a political organization which was opposed to the draft. Among his most notable works, which include both conventional poems and prose poems, are *The Light around the Body* (1967), which earned him the National Book Award, *News of the Universe* (1980), *The Man in the Black Coat Turns* (1981), *Loving a Woman in Two Worlds* (1985), *This Body Is Made of Camphor and Gopherwood* (1977), and *Morning Poems* (1997). His book-long essay *Iron John* became a sensation and ignited the so-called Man's Movement. This review of *Pablo Neruda: Selected Poems* (New York: Delacorte Press, 1972) was first published in *Review* (fall 1972).

Several years ago, well before Neruda received the Nobel Prize, Nathaniel Tarn decided to put together a "Selected Poems of Neruda" translated by several hands in England. (The result of his work has been released here by Delacorte.) The English have been particularly resistant to Neruda. I remember in early '64, when Neruda was on his way to England to receive an honorary degree, he remarked: "You know, no book of mine has ever been published in England." He was sixty at the time.

So Tarn walked in where others refused to walk. The book has weaknesses, but it's a good job on the whole. The book is sizable, with about 115 poems. Seven poems from *Veinte Poemas de Amor,* translated by W. S. Merwin, open the book. Merwin's poems are colder than the originals; he is not as passionate and excitable as Neruda; but the translations are transparent and clear.

Merwin and Nathaniel Tarn have each done about half of the poems chosen from *Residencia I*. Here are four lines from "Arte Poética," with Tarn's translation:

como un camarero humillado, como una campana un poco ronca,
como un espejo viejo, como un olor de casa sola,
en la que los huéspedes entran de noche perdidamente ebrios,
y hay un olor de ropa tirada al suelo, y una ausencia de flores

like a humiliated scullion, a bell cracked a little,
a mirror tarnished, the fug of a deserted house
whose guests come in at night sloshed to perdition,
with a stench of clothes scattered on the floor
and a yearning for flowers—

Tarn is English, and somehow the language the English use is too colorless these days to translate Neruda. The words seem to lack energy and vowels, and the robustness of Neruda is missing entirely; "sloshed to perdition" and "fug of a deserted house" are too dry for Neruda.

Here are five lines from "Entierro en el Este" and Merwin's translation:

estridentes y finas y lúgubres silban
entre el color de las pesadas flores envenenadas
y el grito de los cenicientos danzarines
y el creciente monótono de los tamtam
y el humo de las maderas que arden y huelen.

strident and thin and lugubrious they whistle
amidst the colour of the heavy poisoned flowers
and the cry of the holy fire-dancers
and the growing monotony of the tom-toms
and the smoke of the different woods burning and giving off odours.

How much more sound! Merwin feels the rhythm of the original, and pays attention to the associations surrounding the English words he uses. I don't see how anyone could do better with that passage than Merwin does. His translation of "Tango del Viudo" is also brilliant.

With *Residencia 3*, Anthony Kerrigan enters, and most of the *Canto*

General selections are translated by Kerrigan, who did an immense amount of work. I'll quote the first six lines of "Amor América (1400)":

> Antes de la peluca y la casaca
> fueron los ríos, ríos arteriales:
> fueron las cordilleras, en cuya onda raída
> el cóndor o la nieve parecían inmóviles:
> fue la humedad y la espesura, el trueno
> sin nombre todavía, las pampas planetarias.

> Before wig and frockcoat
> were the rivers, the arterial rivers,
> the cordilleras, on whose scraped escarpments
> the condor or the snow seemed immobile,
> humidity and density, the thunderclap
> not-yet-named, the planetary pampas.

Anthony Kerrigan's weakness is using the cognate all the time. That's easiest, but the trouble is that, with Spanish, you end up with a Latinate word in English, for example, "immobile." If he had said "the condor or the snow seemed not to move," we would have felt Neruda's picture better, the bird high above peaks, floating. Similarly, "dampness and weight" give more of the sensual mood of Neruda's "la humedad y la espesura" than "humidity and density"; "arterial" doesn't work either to get the feeling of "ríos arteriales." It's very odd, but Neruda cannot be translated well in English using Latinates. I'm not saying Kerrigan's translation are bad—it's just that he doesn't do much work to pull them into strong English. Most of his translations are workmanlike and clear.

When we come to *Odas Elementales*, Nathaniel Tarn's translations immediately improve (bird-watching poem):

> leaves
> on the loose,
> stunt-riders
> of the air,
> petals
> of smoke,
> free,

happy,
flyers and singers,
airfree and earthbound,
wind navigators,
happy
constructors
of the softest nests

Partly I think this is because these brief lines make the elaborate Latinate words difficult to use—he goes primarily to Anglo-Saxon and does well.

With *Estravagario* Alastair Reid enters. His first translation, "Y Cuánto Vive?" is marvelous. He has a sure sense of what William Carlos Williams thought so important in poetry: how people talk. In the poem, Neruda has been saying that he got started asking some medical men questions; he was so startled by their answers that he turned to the gravediggers:

Me fuí a los ríos donde queman
grandes cadáveres pintados . . .
Cuando llegó mi oportunidad
les largué unas cuantas preguntas
ellos me ofrecieron quemarme:
era todo lo que sabían.

En mi país los enterradores
me contestaron, entre copas:
—Búscate una moza robusta
y déjate de tonterías.

Nunca vi gentes tan alegres.

Cantaban levantando el vino
por la salud y por la muerte.
Eran grandes fornicadores.

I went to the rivers where they burn
enormous painted corpses . . .
When I got the chance
I asked them a slew of questions.

They offered to burn me.
It was all they knew.

In my own country the dead
answered me, between drinks:
"Get yourself a good woman
and give up this nonsense."

I never saw people so happy.

Raising their glasses they sang
toasting health and death.
They were huge fornicators.

Alastair Reid also does most of *Las Piedras de Chile,* the selection from *Cantos Ceremoniales,* and all the seven poems from *Plenos Poderes,* always inventively, alertly, gently, with great charm. It's true the poems of Neruda are not so difficult to translate now—they do not have that heavy sensual anguish that the *Residencia* poems stretch the language with, but in any case, Reid does well.

In *Memorial de Isla Negra* Reid goes on working—how many poems he has done!—and does all of these too. So much work! But I don't think he's as interested in these poems as in the *Estravagario* poems. His translations are good, but much less inventive, more straightforward. Here are the first six lines of "Oh Tierra, Espérame":

Vuélveme oh sol
a mi destino agreste,
lluvia del viejo bosque,
devuélveme el aroma y las espadas
que caían del cielo
la solitaria paz de pasto y piedra,

Return me, oh sun,
to my wild destiny,
rain of the ancient wood,
bring me back the aroma and the swords
that fall from the sky,
the solitary peace of pasture and rock,

He's getting tired and using a few cognates. If he really wanted to bring this passage alive, he would have had to do something with "destiny," "ancient," "aroma," perhaps "solitary," and try to solve the problem of "oh sun." The rhythm is too flat also.

Nathaniel Tarn translated two poems from Neruda's 1966 book, *Una casa en la arena,* and the book ends with "La Barcarola Termina," an anti-Vietnam poem in which he recalls visiting Vietnam in 1928. Alastair Reid is not very interested in this poem either, but he makes the poem clear.

So what can we say at the end? Here are a few opinions.

Neruda's poems in the first half of the book are better than those in the second half. But the translations of the poems in the second half are better than those in the first half.

Also, Tarn bit off too much. He should, after having commissioned these 115 poems from himself and from others, thrown out the ones that did not have enough life as poems, in English. As it is, we have a book made up of half true translations, some brilliant, and half lifeless trots. That's OK, but it's not entirely fair to Neruda; it makes him seem more uneven than he is.

The greatest surprise to me in the book were Reid's translations of the *Estravagario* poems; they are so sprightly and lively. Some of Merwin's *Residencia* poems are beautifully done, but on the whole the turbid energy, the massive energy of *Residencia,* and its "dark sounds," is not caught in this book.

Canto General is very oddly represented, with almost all the poems on contemporary political life missing. I'm sure that was Neruda's idea, and not Tarn's: he said once that he was so tired of being regarded as a political poet that he longed to be thought of as just a poet.

All in all, it's a mixed bag. *Residencia* and *Canto General* are the weakest sections. Angel Flores' translations of *Residencia* poems, in the old New Directions book, long out of print, are still better than many of the *Residencia* translations here, and so are the few that H. R. Hays did years ago in *Twelve South American Poets.* I think some of Carlos Lozano's versions of the *Elementary Odes,* published by Las Americas ten years ago, are closer to the delicate mood of the originals than most of the *Odes* here. On the other hand, all of the translations here are better than Belitt's.

This book omits entirely the early poems, which Carlos Hagen and David Ossman translated well two years ago for New River's Press, so their book, *Neruda: The Early Poems* should be added by any library wanting to represent Neruda well.

Neruda has many good translators now, and the different eras of his poetry are fairly well covered. If we only had as many translations of Cardenal, or Mutis, or Velarde, or Lugones, or Darío, and younger ones, we'd be in good shape.

Kenneth Rexroth on Homero Aridjis

Poet and critic Kenneth Rexroth (1905–1982) was born in Indiana and moved to San Francisco after 1927. Orphaned during his youth, he is known primarily for his radical and antiestablishment social views, Objectivist poetry, and his place in the Beat movement. However, as is evidenced by his *Classics Revisited* (1960), Rexroth was also dedicated to the world's classical literature. A truly universal artist, he also did translations or adaptations from works written in Chinese, Japanese, and French. Among the collections of his own poems are *In What Hour* (1940), *The Phoenix and the Tortoise* (1944), *The Signature of All Things* (1949), and *Natural Numbers* (1963). His essays have been published in several volumes including *Bird in the Bush* (1959), *Assays* (1961), and *World outside the Window* (1987); he also wrote a play in verse form entitled *Beyond the Mountains* (1951). This brief piece was first published as "Homero Aridjis: Blue Spaces of Illumination," in *Review* (fall 1974).

Homero Aridjis, widely considered to be not only one of the best younger Mexican poets, but one of the best under forty now writing in Spanish anywhere, was born in Contepec, Michoacán in 1940. He was a fellow of Centro Mexicano de Escritores in 1959–1960, and a Guggenheim Fellow for 1966–1967. He was awarded the Xavier Villaurrutia Prize in 1964 for *Mirándola dormir.* He founded the review *Correspondencias* and was chief editor of *Diálogos* and is now at the Mexican Embassy to the Netherlands, in the Hague.

Aridjis's rise in the esteem of readers of Spanish poetry in less than ten years has been extraordinary. Few poets better demonstrate the spread of an international style throughout the world as well as the reduction and synthesis of the great writers of the heroic age of modern poetry to an international, negotiable idiom. Influence-hunters can find traces of San Juan de la Cruz, Luis de Góngora, and Eluard in the poetry of Aridjis, and behind them the mystical Nahuatl chants of the Aztec priests, and the contemporary initiation songs of the Huichol Indians; but they can also find Laura Riding, Gunnar Ekelöf, or Kathleen Raine, whom he has probably never read. This does *not* mean that he is only a bundle of influences, quite the opposite. It means that he is a visionary poet of lyric bliss, crystaline concentrations, and infinite spaces. It means that vision is the same for him as it was for a young Swede in Stockholm or a young English girl in the Lake Country. A poet like Aridjis moves confidently in a universe of discourse reached by Robert Desnos, for instance, only in the poignant illumination of his last two poems. I can think of no poet of Aridjis' generation in the Western Hemisphere as much at ease in the blue spaces of illumination—the illumination of transcending love. These are words for a new Magic Flute.

Robert Coover on Julio Cortázar

Born in Iowa in 1923, Robert Coover is a novelist who has ventured into genres of playwriting and screenwriting. He mixes both satire and fantasy in a narrative style which is both realistic and surreal. His prose demonstrates his concern with politics, human loneliness, black humor, and the juxtaposition of what appear to be contradictory elements. *A Night at the Movies, Or You Remember This* (1987) is particularly revealing in this regard since the book attempts to link fiction and film through the use of imagery. Other works, such as *Pricksongs and Descants* (1969), fuse legends with stories of his own invention. Coover's characters, such as the main character in *The Universal Baseball Association, Inc. J. Henry Waugh, Prop.* (1968), generally seek to escape their own realities; they create imaginary worlds in which they can lead the life that is denied to them by the human condition. His other works include *The Political Burning* (1977), *A Political Fable* (1980), *Spanking the Maid* (1982), *Gerald's Party* (1986), and *Pinocchio in Venice* (1991). Coover received the Faulkner Award in 1987. This book review of Julio Cortázar's *A Certain Lucas* (New York: Alfred A. Knopf, 1984), first appeared in the *New York Times Book Review*, 20 May 1984.

A curious book. Although it was first published in 1979, before Julio Cortázar's final illness, it reads as a kind of lighthearted, self-deprecating farewell. Cortázar, expatriate Argentine fabulator, died in Paris earlier this year, and this small volume would almost seem a last gift to his readers, a final testament, a surreal, whimsical text with which to celebrate, with a shrug and a wry smile, his wake.

This text is divided into three parts, a middle section of miscellaneous prose pieces bracketed by emblematic "episodes" from the life of this "certain Lucas," who is an Argentine writer living in Paris, "growing old," spending a fair amount of time in and out of hospitals, entertaining himself and alarming others with eccentric lectures, musing with nostalgia upon the past, even, in the penultimate piece ("Lucas, His Pianists"), providing instructions for his final hours: "At the hour of his death, if there is time and lucidity, Lucas will ask to hear two things: Mozart's last quintet and a certain piano solo on the theme of 'I Ain't Got Nobody.' If he feels that there won't be enough time, he'll only ask for the piano record. Long is the list, but he's already chosen. Out of the depths of time, Earl Hines will accompany him."

It is perhaps misleading to speak of the middle section as a miscellany (though Cortázar himself might have approved of the term, with its implication of a multitude of authors: "A Certain Lucas" opens with Lucas doing battle against his hydra-headed self). Rather, it is a kind of sampler of narrative ideas, a playful anthology of form, including everything from parables to parodies, folk tales to metafictions. It is as if to say: Here's Lucas, and here's how his funny old head works.

Formal innovation is at the heart of all of Cortázar's art, from his first big success, *Hopscotch* (first published in English in 1968), the book that launched the famous boom in Latin American fiction, through *A Manual for Manuel,* with its baby scrapbook collage of clippings, charts, signs, notes, poems, and communiqués scattered through a tale of revolutionary commitment inspired by a dream, and on to his most recent collections, including the virtuoso *We Love Glenda So Much* and now *A Certain Lucas.* Always this formal play—and more: the cataloguing of formal possibilities, argument, and demonstration, the illusionist exposing and enumerating his artifices, thereby astounding us with yet another illusion. Even critics who sometimes find his subjects frivolous and his philosophy banal remain dazzled by his inventiveness.

Dead forms, Cortázar believed, "rob us of identity," and it is art's task to disrupt and renew those forms so that man might find himself again. Sympathetic with the world's revolutions, he often found himself at odds with revolutionaries who wanted simple, familiar forms easily accessible to "the people." (Here, in the section "Lucas, His Partisan Arguments," he makes one last and no doubt futile effort to refute them: "What are you people so afraid of?") All the while, he himself remained convinced that "the truly revolutionary novel does not merely have revolutionary 'content,' but also seeks to revolutionize the novel itself, the novel form." Art, then, as a kind of redemption, an awakening and, above all, a pilgrimage, "an exploration."

This conviction he shared with—and perhaps learned from—the Surrealists, about whom he often wrote, so when he speaks here of the six men whose deaths stole a bit of his own life ("Steady, Steady, Six

Already"), it is not surprising to find that the first name on the list is that of Jean Cocteau. (The other five are Louis Armstrong, Pablo Picasso, Igor Stravinsky, Duke Ellington, and Charles Chaplin.) Cortázar's restlessly inventive, multifaceted ("polygraphic," as he would say—and he does, in a bemused meditation on Samuel Johnson), slightly airy, even sometimes goofy but always astonishing art is in the line of all those lifelong *enfants terribles* like Robert Walser, Cocteau, Robert Pinget—and including his own fellow Argentine and spiritual father, Macedonio Fernández, an early adversary of verisimilitude, linearity, and the integrity of "character."

That there are no more characters in fiction Cortázar was arguing as early as 1950: "There are only accomplices, who are also witnesses, witnesses who come forward to make statements which almost always condemn us. Once in a while one gives evidence in our favor and he helps us understand more clearly the nature of the human situation in our times."

Such a witness is Lucas, who comes forward to give evidence about aging, habit, memory, writing and communication, music, friendship, survival in a mechanistic universe, pedagogy, the pleasures of civilization, rhetoric, politics, duty and defiance, dreams, death and illusive love, and always with an edge of playful Surrealist irrationality. There are cats here who are telephones, tables that lift their legs, a bassoonist who keeps getting sucked into his instrument and blown out the other end.

Lucas, like Cortázar himself, is a kind of Zen master, entertaining us with the world's marvels and assaulting us with paradox and absurdity to provoke an epiphany of reality, of the Absolute, which either exists in our funny everyday world—where *"everything* is rubbing against something else and playing another game and scorching dictionaries"—or doesn't exist at all. He seems to be saying as death catches him "like a toad suddenly falling between your eyes," it's all laughable. It's wonderful.

Susan Sontag on Machado de Assis

Born in New York City in 1933, Susan Sontag grew up in Arizona and California. Primarily recognized for her literary criticism, Sontag has also met with critical success as a novelist, short-story writer, and essayist. Having completed her undergraduate career at the age of eighteen, she studied philosophy at Harvard University and settled in New York City in the 1950s. As an essayist, Sontag is both biographical and intimate with her reader. In *Against Interpretation and Other Essays* (1966), which turned her into an influential cultural critic, Sontag succeeds at making the most esoteric and obscure of artistic experiments into accessible material for a larger public. Much of her nonfiction work engages European subjects. Other works, such as *Styles of Radical Will* (1966) and *Trip to Hanoi* (1968), are devoted to the exploration of her political and artistic views. As a novelist, Sontag is anything but autobiographical. Her novels are often concerned with the exploration of philosophical and mythical concepts in a style which is both witty and uncanny. Her short stories combine both of the narrative interests, as they are often philosophical and profoundly intimate. Her other works include *The Benefactor* (1963), *Duet for Cannibals* (1970), *I, Etcetera* (1978), *Illness as Metaphor* (1978), and *The Volcano Lover* (1992). A member of the American Academy of Arts and Letters, she was named an Officier des Arts et des Lettres by the French government and received a five-year grant from the MacArthur Foundation. She has remained an active political commentator and has openly protested the treatment of writers and publishers in South Korea. This is Sontag's preface to *Epitaph of a Small Winner,* by José Joaquim Machado de Assis (New York: Noonday, 1990).

Foreword: Since it is only a completed life that reveals its shape and whatever meaning a life can have, a biography that means to be definitive must wait until after the death of its subject. Unfortunately, autobiographies can't be composed under these ideal circumstances. And virtually all the notable fictional autobiographies have respected the limitation of real ones, while conjuring up a next-best equivalent of the illuminations of death. Fictional autobiographies, even more often than real ones, tend to be autumnal undertakings: an elderly (or, at least, loss-seasoned) narrator, having retired from life, now writes. But, close as old age may bring the fictive autobiographer to the ideal vantage point, he or she is still writing on the wrong side of the frontier beyond which a life, a life story, finally makes sense.

I know only one example of that enthralling genre the imaginary autobiography which grants the project of autobiography its ideal—as it turns out, comical—fulfillment, and that is the masterpiece called *Memórias póstumas de Brás Cubas* (1880), known in English by the rather interfering title *Epitaph of a Small Winner*. In the first paragraph of chapter 1, "The Death of the Author," Bras Cubas announces gaily: "I am a deceased writer not in the sense of one who has written and is now deceased, but in the sense of one who has died and is now writing." Here is the novel's first, framing joke, and it is about the writer's freedom. The reader is invited to play the game of considering that the book in hand is an unprecedented literary feat. Posthumous reminiscences . . . written in the first person.

Of course, not even a single day, much less a life, can ever be recounted in its entirety. A life is not a plot. And quite different ideas of decorum apply to a narrative constructed in the first person and to one in the third person. To slow down, to speed up, to skip whole stretches; to comment at length, to withhold comment—these done as an "I" have another weight, another feel, than when said about or on behalf of someone else. Much of what is affecting or pardonable or insufferable in the first person would seem the opposite if uttered in the third person, and vice versa: an observation easily confirmed by reading aloud any page from this book first as it is, a second time with "he" for "I." (To sample the fierce difference *within* the codes governing the third person, then try substituting "she" for "he.") There are registers of feeling, such as anxiety, that only a first-person voice can accommodate. And aspects of narrative performance as well: digressiveness, for instance, seems natural in a text written in the first person, but a sign of amateurism in an impersonal, third-person voice. Thus, any piece of writing that features an awareness of its own means and methods should be understood as in the first person, whether or not the main pronoun is "I."

To write about oneself—the true, that is, the private story—used to be felt to be presumptuous, and to need justifying. Montaigne's *Essays*, Rousseau's *Confessions*, Thoreau's *Walden*, and most of the other spiritually ambitious classics of autobiography have a prologue in which the author directly addresses the reader, acknowledging the temerity of the enterprise, evoking scruples or inhibitions (modesty, anxiety) that had to be overcome, laying claim to an exemplary artlessness or candor, alleging the usefulness of all this self-absorption to others. And, like real autobiographies, most fictional autobiographies of any stylishness or depth also start with an explanation, defensive or defiant, of the decision to write the book the reader has just begun—or, at least, a flourish of self-deprecation, suggesting an attractive sensitivity to the charge of egotism. This is no mere throat-clearing, some polite sentences to give the reader time to be seated. It is the opening shot in a campaign of seduction in which the autobiographer tacitly agrees that there is something unseemly, brazen, in volunteering to write at length about oneself—exposing oneself to unknown others without any evident interest (a great career, a great crime) or without some documentary ruse, such as pretending that the book merely transcribes existing private papers, like a journal or letters, indiscretions originally destined for the smallest, friendliest readership. With a life story offered straight out, in the first person, to as many readers as possible (a "public"), it seems only minimal prudence as well as courtesy for the autobiographer to seek permission to begin. The splendid conceit of this book, that these are memoirs written by someone who is dead, just puts an additional spin on this regulatory caring about what the reader thinks. The autobiographer can also profess not to care.

Actually, writing from beyond the grave has not relieved this narrator from showing an ostentatious amount of concern about the reception of his work. His mock-anxiety is embodied in the very form, the distinctive velocity of the book. It is in the way the narrative is cut and mounted, its stop-and-start rhythms: one hundred sixty chapters, several as brief as two sentences, few longer than two pages. It is in the playful directions, usually at the beginning or end of chapters, for the best use of the text. ("This chapter is to be inserted between the first two sentences of chapter 129." "Please note that this chapter is not intended to be profound." "But let us not become involved in psychology," et cetera.) It is in the pulse of ironic attention to the book's means and methods; the repeated disavowal of large claims on the reader's emotions ("I like jolly chapters"). Asking the reader to indulge the narrator's penchant for frivolity is as much a seducer's ploy as promising the reader strong emotions and new knowledge. The autobiographer's suave fussing over the accuracy of his narrative procedures parodies the intensity of his self-absorption.

Digression is the main technique for controlling the emotional flow of the book. The narrator, whose head is full of literature, shows himself adept at expert descriptions—of the kind flattered with the name of realism—of how poignant feelings persist, change, evolve, devolve. He also shows himself understandably beyond all that by the dimensions of the telling: the cut into short episodes, the ironic, didactic overviews. This oddly fierce, avowedly disenchanted voice (but then what else should we expect a narrator who is dead to be?) never relates an event without drawing some lesson from it. Chapter 133 opens: "The episode serves to illustrate and perhaps amend Helvetius' theory that . . ." Begging the reader's indulgence, worrying about the reader's attentiveness (Does the reader get it? Is the reader amused? Is the reader becoming bored?), the autobiographer continually breaks out of his story to invoke a theory it illustrates, to formulate an opinion about it—as if such moves were needed to make the story more interesting. Bras Cubas's socially privileged, self-important existence is, as such lives often are, starkly uneventful; the main events are those which did not happen or were judged disappointing. The rich production of witty opinions points to the emotional poverty of the life, by exhibiting the narrator as seeming to sidestep the conclusions he might be drawing. The digressive method also generates much of the book's humor, starting with the very disparity between the life (modest in events, subtly articulated) and the theories (portentous, blunt) which the narrator invokes.

The Life and Opinions of Tristram Shandy is of course the principal model for these savory procedures of reader awareness. The method of the tiny chapters and some of the typographical stunts, as in chapter 55 ("The Venerable Dialogue of Adam and Eve") and chapter 139 ("How I Did Not Become a Minister of State"), recall the whimsical narrative rhythms and pictographic witticisms of *Tristram Shandy*. That Bras Cubas begins his story after his death, as Tristram Shandy famously begins the story of his consciousness before he is born (at the moment of his conception)—that, too, seems a homage to Sterne by Machado de Assis. The authority of *Tristram Shandy*, published in installments between 1759 and 1767, on a writer born in Brazil in the nineteenth century should not surprise us. While Sterne's books, so celebrated in his lifetime and shortly afterward, were being reassessed in England as too peculiar, occasionally indecent, and finally boring, they continued to be enormously admired on the Continent. In the English-speaking world, where in this century Sterne has again been thought very highly of, he still figures as an ultra-eccentric, marginal genius (like Blake), who is most notable for being uncannily, and prematurely, "modern." When looked at from the perspective of world literature, however, he may be the English-language writer who, after Shakespeare and Dickens, has had the greatest influence; for Nietzsche to have said that his favorite novel was *Tristram Shandy* is not quite as original a judgment as it may seem. Sterne has been an especially potent presence in the literatures of the Slavic languages, as is reflected in the centrality of the example of *Tristram Shandy* in the theories of Shklovsky and other Russian formalists from the 1920s forward. Perhaps the reason so much commanding prose literature has been issuing for decades from Central and Eastern Europe as well as from Latin America is not that writers there have been suffering under monstrous tyrannies and therefore have had importance, seriousness, subjects, relevant irony bestowed on them (as many writers in Western Europe and the United States have half enviously concluded) but that these are the parts of the world where for over a century the author of *Tristram Shandy* has been the most admired.

Machado de Assis's novel belongs in that tradition of narrative buffoonery—the talkative first-person voice attempting to ingratiate itself with readers which runs from Sterne through, in our own century, Natsume Sōseki's *I Am a Cat,* the short fiction of Robert Walser, Svevo's *Confessions of Zeno* and *As a Man Grows Older,* Hrabal's *Too Loud a Solitude,* much of Beckett. Again and again we meet in different guises the chatty, meandering, compulsively speculative, eccentric narrator: reclusive (by choice or by vocation); prone to futile obsessions and fanciful theories and comically designed efforts of the will; often an autodidact; not quite a crank; though sometimes driven by lust, and at least one time by love, unable to mate; usually elderly; invariably male. (No woman is likely to get even the conditional sympathy these ragingly self-absorbed narrators claim from us, because of expectations that women be more sympathetic, and sympathizing, than men; a woman with the same degree of mental acuity and emotional separateness would be regarded as simply a monster.) Machado de Assis's valetudinarian Bras Cubas is considerably less exuberant than Sterne's madcap, effusively garrulous Tristram Shandy. It is only a few steps from the incisiveness of Machado's narrator, with his rueful superiority to the story of his own life, to the plot malaise that characterizes most recent fiction in the form of autobiography. But storylessness may be intrinsic to the genre—the novel as autobiographical monologue—as is the isolation of the narrating voice. In this respect the post-Sternean anti-hero like Bras Cubas parodies the protagonist of the great spiritual autobiographies, who is always profoundly, not just by circumstances, unmarried. It is almost a measure of an autobiographical narrative's ambition: the narrator must be, or be recast as, alone, a solitary, certainly without a spouse, even when there is one; the life must be unpeopled at the center. (Thus, such recent achievements of spiritual autobiography in the guise of a novel as Elizabeth Hardwick's *Sleepless Nights* and V. S. Naipaul's *The Enigma of Arrival* leave out the spouses who were actually there.) Just as Bras Cubas's solitariness is a parody of a chosen or an emblematic solitude, his release through self-understanding is, for all its self-confidence and wit, a parody of that sort of triumph.

The seductions of such a narrative are complex. The narrator professes to be worrying about the reader—whether the reader gets it. Meanwhile, the reader can be wondering about the narrator—whether the narrator understands all the implications of what is being told. A display of mental agility and inventiveness which is designed to amuse the reader and purportedly reflects the liveliness of the narrator's mind mostly measures how emotionally isolated and forlorn the narrator is. Ostensibly, this is the book of a life. Yet, despite the narrator's gift for social and psychological portraiture, it remains a tour of the inside of someone's head. Another of Machado's models was a marvelous book by Xavier de Maistre, a French expatriate aristocrat (he lived most of his long life in Russia) who invented the literary micro-journey with his *Journey around My Room*, written in 1794, when he was in prison for dueling, and which recounts his diagonal and zigzag visits to such diverting sites as the armchair, the desk, and the bed. A confinement, mental or physical, that is not acknowledged as such can make a very funny story as well as one charged with pathos.

At the beginning, in a flourish of authorial self-knowingness that graciously includes the reader, Machado de Assis has the autobiographer name the eighteenth-century literary models of his narrative with the following somber warning:

> It is, in truth, a diffuse work, in which I, Bras Cubas, if indeed I have adopted the free form of a Sterne or of a Xavier de Maistre, have possibly added a certain peevish pessimism of my own. Quite possibly. The work of a man already dead. I wrote it with the pen of Mirth and the link of Melancholy, and one can readily foresee what may come of such a union.

However modulated by whimsey, a vein of true misanthropy runs through the book. If Bras Cubas is not just another of those repressed, desiccated, pointlessly self-aware bachelor narrators who exist only to be seen through by the full-blooded reader, it is because of his anger—which is by the end of the book full-out, painful, bitter, upsetting.

The Sternean playfulness is lighthearted. It is a comic, albeit extremely nervous, form of friendliness with the reader. In the nineteenth century this digressiveness, this chattiness, this love of the little theory, this pirouetting from one narrative mode to another, takes on darker hues. It becomes identified with hypochondria, with erotic disillusionment, with the discontents of the self (Dostoevsky's pathologically voluble Underground Man), with acute mental distress (the hysterical narrator, deranged by injustice, of Multatuli's *Max Havelaar*). To natter on obsessively, repetitively, used to be invariably a resource of comedy. (Think of Shakespeare's plebian grumblers, like the porter in *Macbeth;* think of Mr. Pickwick, among other inventions of Dickens.) That comic use of garrulousness does not disappear. Joyce used garrulousness in a Rabelaisian spirit, as a vehicle of comic hyperbole, and Gertrude Stein, champion of verbose writing, turned the tics of egotism and sententiousness into good-natured comic voice of great originality. But most of the verbose first-person narrators in the ambitious literature of this century have been radically misanthropic. Garrulousness is identified with the baleful, aggrieved repetitiveness of senility (Beckett's prose monologues that call themselves novels) and with paranoia and unslakable rage (the novels and plays of Thomas Bernhard). Who does not sense the despair behind the loquacious, sprightly musings of Robert Walser and the quirkily erudite, bantering voices in the stories of Donald Barthelme?

Beckett's narrators are usually trying, not altogether successfully, to imagine themselves as dead. Bras Cubas has no such problem. But then Machado de Assis was trying to be, and is, funny. There is nothing morbid about the consciousness of his posthumous narrator; on the contrary, the perspective of maximum consciousness—which is what, wittily, a posthumous narrator can claim—is in itself a comic perspective. Where Bras Cubas is writing from is not a true afterlife (it has no geography), only another go at the idea of authorial detachment. The neo-Sternean narrative hijinks of these memoirs of a disappointed man do not issue from Sternean exuberance or even Sternean nervousness. They are a kind of antidote, a counterforce to the narrator's despondency: a way of mastering dejection considerably more specialized than the "great cure, an anti-melancholy plaster, designed to relieve the despondency of mankind" that the narrator fantasizes about inventing. Life administers its hard lessons. But one can write as one pleases—a form of liberty.

Machado de Assis was only forty-one when he published these reminiscences of a man who has died—we learn at the opening of the book—at sixty-four. (Machado was born in 1839; he makes his creation Bras Cubas, the posthumous autobiographer, a full generation older, born in 1805.) The novel as an exercise in the anticipating of old age is a venture to which writers of a melancholy temperament continue to be drawn. I was in my late twenties when I wrote my first novel, which purports to be the reminiscences of a man then in his early sixties, a *rentier*, dilettante and fantasist, who announces at the beginning of the book that he has reached a harbor of serenity where, all experience finished, he can look back on his life. The few conscious literary references in my head were mostly French—above all *Candide* and Descartes's *Meditations;* I thought I was writing a satire on optimism and on certain cherished (by me) ideas of the inner life and of a religiously nourished inwardness. (What was going on unconsciously, as I think about it now, is another story.) When I had the good fortune to have *The Benefactor* accepted by the first publisher to whom I submitted it, Farrar, Straus, I had the further good luck of having assigned to me as my editor Cecil Hemley, who in 1952, in his previous incarnation as the head of Noonday Press (recently acquired by my new publisher), had brought out this translation of Machado's novel, which really launched the book's career in English. At our first meeting Hemley said to me, not implausibly: I can see you have been influenced by *Epitaph of a Small Winner*. Epitaph of a what? By, you know, Machado de Assis. Who, I said. He lent me his copy and several days later I declared myself retroactively influenced.

Although I have since read a good deal of Machado in translation, this book—the first of five last novels (he lived twenty-eight years after writing it) generally thought the summit of his genius—remains my favorite. I am told it is the one that non-Brazilians often prefer, although critics usually pick *Dom Casmurro* (1899). Now it is my turn to contribute to its life in English, in the form of a new Noonday paperback. I am astonished that a writer of such greatness does not yet occupy the place he deserves. Up to a point, the relative neglect of Machado outside Brazil may be no more mysterious than the neglect of another prolific writer of genius whom Eurocentric notions of world literature have marginalized: Natsume Sōseki. Surely Machado would be better known if he hadn't been Brazilian and hadn't spent his whole life in Rio de Janeiro—if he were, say, Italian or Russian, or even Portuguese. But the impediment is not simply that Machado was not a European writer. Even more remarkable than his absence from the stage of world literature is that he has been very little known and read in the rest of Latin America—as if it were still hard to digest the fact that the greatest author ever produced in Latin America wrote in the Portuguese, rather than the Spanish, language. Brazil may be the continent's biggest country (and Rio in the nineteenth century its largest city) but it has always been the outsider country—regarded by the rest of South America, Hispanophone South America, with a good deal of condescension and often in racist terms. A writer from these countries is far likelier to know any of the European literatures or literature in English than to know the literature of Brazil, whereas Brazilian writers are acutely aware of Spanish-American literature. Borges, the second greatest writer produced on that continent, seems never to have read Machado de Assis. Indeed, Machado is even less well known to Spanish-language readers than to those who read him in English. *Epitaph of a Small Winner* was translated into Spanish only in the 1960s, some eighty years after it was written and a decade after it was translated (twice) into English.

With enough time, enough afterlife, a great book does find its rightful place. And perhaps some books need to be rediscovered again and again. *Epitaph of a Small Winner* is probably one of those thrillingly original, radically skeptical books which will always impress readers with the force of a private discovery. It doesn't seem much of a compliment to say that this novel, written more than a century ago, is—well, modern. Isn't every work that speaks to us with an originality and lucidity we're capable of acknowledging something we then want to conscript into what we understand as modernity? Our standards of modernity are a system of flattering illusions, which permit us to selectively colonize the past, as are our ideas of what is provincial, which permit certain parts of the world to condescend to all the rest. Being dead may stand for a point of view that cannot be accused of being provincial. Surely *Epitaph of a Small Winner* is one of the most entertainingly unprovincial books ever written. And to love this book is to become a little less provincial about literature, about literature's possibilities, oneself.

Thomas Pynchon on Gabriel García Márquez

Born in Long Island, New York, in 1937, Thomas Pynchon graduated from Cornell University. Before becoming a novelist, Pynchon worked for Boeing Aircraft in Seattle and spent a year in Mexico. An experimental writer, Pynchon writes mystery stories and enriches them with elements of science fiction. His narrative style introduces the reader to a vast array of esoteric references and confusing clues which give his novels their intended ambiguity. However, these styles only serve as stepping stones for his larger reflections on entropy, timelessness, and the integration of order and chaos. His works reflect the strong influences that Wittgenstein, information theory, and physics have had on him. Among his works are *V.* (1963), *The Crying of Lot 49* (1966), *Slow Learner* (1984), *Vineland* (1990), and *Mason & Dixon* (1997). Pynchon received the National Book Award in 1973 for his novel *Gravity's Rainbow* (1973). This review of Gabriel García Márquez's *Love in the Time of Cholera* (New York: Alfred A. Knopf, 1988) was first published in the *New York Times Book Review*, 10 April 1988.

Love, as Mickey and Sylvia, in their 1956 hit single, remind us, love is strange. As we grow older it gets stranger, until at some point mortality has come well within the frame of our attention, and there we are, suddenly caught between terminal dates while still talking a game of eternity. It's about then that we may begin to regard love songs, romance novels, soap operas, and any live teen-age pronouncements at all on the subject of love with an increasingly impatient, not to mention intolerant, ear.

At the same time, where would any of us be without all that romantic infrastructure, without, in fact, just that degree of adolescent, premortal hope? Pretty far out on life's limb, at least. Suppose, then, it were possible, not only to swear love "forever," but actually to follow through on it—to live a long, full, and authentic life based on such a vow, to put one's alloted stake of precious time where one's heart is? This is the extraordinary premise of Gabriel García Márquez's new novel *Love in the Time of Cholera*, one on which he delivers, and triumphantly.

In the postromantic ebb of the seventies and eighties, with every-body now so wised up and even growing paranoid about love, once the magical buzzword of a generation, it is a daring step for any writer to decide to work in love's vernacular, to take it, with all its folly, imprecision, and lapses in taste, at all seriously—that is, as well worth those higher forms of play that we value in fiction. For García Már-quez the step may also be revolutionary. "I think that a novel about love is as valid as any other," he once remarked in a conversation with his friend, the journalist Plinio Apuleyo Mendoza (published as "El olor de la guayaba," 1982). "In reality the duty of a writer—the revolu-tionary duty, if you like—is that of writing well."

And—oh boy—does he write well. He writes with impassioned control, out of a maniacal serenity: the Garcimarquesian voice we have come to recognize from the other fiction has matured, found and developed new resources, been brought to a level where it can at once be classical and familiar, opalescent and pure, able to praise and curse, laugh and cry, fabulate and sing, and when called upon, take off and soar, as in this description of a turn-of-the-century balloon trip:

> From the sky they could see, just as God saw them, the ruins of the very old and heroic city of Cartagena de Indias, the most beautiful in the world, abandoned by its inhabitants because of the sieges of the English and the atrocities of the buccaneers. They saw the walls, still intact, the brambles in the streets, the fortifications devoured by hearts-ease, the marble palaces and the golden altars and the viceroys rotting with plague inside their armor.
>
> They flew over the lake dwellings of the Trojas in Cataca, painted in lunatic colors, with pens holding iguanas raised for food and balsam apples and crepe myrtle hanging in the lacustrian gardens. Excited by everyone's shouting, hundreds of naked children plunged into the wa-ter, jumping out of windows, jumping from the roofs of the houses and from the canoes that they handled with astonishing skill, and diving like shad to recover the bundles of clothing, the bottles of cough syrup, the beneficent food that the beautiful lady with the feathered hat threw to them from the basket of the balloon.

This novel is also revolutionary in daring to suggest that vows of love made under a presumption of immortality—youthful idiocy, to some—may yet be honored, much later in life when we ought to know better, in the face of the undeniable. This is, effectively, to assert the resurrection of the body, today as throughout history an unavoidably revolutionary idea. Through the ever-subversive medium of fiction, García Márquez shows us how it could all plausibly come about, even—wild hope—for somebody out here, outside a book, even as inevitably beaten at, bought, and resold as we all must have become if only through years of simple residence in the injuring and corruptive world.

Here's what happens. The story takes place between about 1880 and 1930, in a Caribbean seaport city, unnamed but said to be a composite of Cartagena and Barranquilla—as well, perhaps, as cities of the spirit less officially mapped. Three major characters form a triangle whose hypotenuse is Florentino Ariza, a poet dedicated to love both carnal and transcendent, though his secular fate is with the River Company of the Caribbean and its small fleet of paddle-wheel steamboats. As a young apprentice telegrapher he meets and falls forever in love with Fermina Daza, a "beautiful adolescent with . . . almond-shaped eyes," who walks with a "natural haughtiness . . . her doe's gait making her seem immune to gravity." Though they exchange hardly a hundred words face to face, they carry on a passionate and secret affair entirely by way of letters and telegrams, even after the girl's father has found out and taken her away on an extended "journey of forgetting." But when she returns, Fermina rejects the lovesick young man after all, and eventually meets and marries instead Dr. Juvenal Urbino who, like the hero of a nineteenth-century novel, is well born, a sharp dresser, somewhat stuck on himself but a terrific catch nonetheless.

For Florentino, love's creature, this is an agonizing setback, though nothing fatal. Having sworn to love Fermina Daza forever, he settles in to wait for as long as he has to until she's free again. This turns out to be fifty-one years, nine months and four days later, when suddenly, absurdly, on a Pentecost Sunday around 1930, Dr. Juvenal Urbino dies, chasing a parrot up a mango tree. After the funeral, when everyone else has left, Florentino steps forward with his hat over his heart. "Fermina," he declares, "I have waited for this opportunity for more than half a century, to repeat to you once again my vow of eternal fidelity and everlasting love." Shocked and furious, Fermina orders him out of the house. "And don't show your face again for the years of life that are left to you. . . . I hope there are very few of them."

The heart's eternal vow has run up against the world's finite terms. The confrontation occurs near the end of the first chapter, which recounts Dr. Urbino's last day on earth and Fermina's first night as a widow. We then flash back fifty years, into the time of cholera. The middle chapters follow the lives of the three characters through the years of the Urbinos' marriage and Florentino Ariza's rise at the River Company, as one century ticks over into the next. The last chapter takes up again where the first left off, with Florentino, now, in the face of what many men would consider major rejection, resolutely setting about courting Fermina Daza all over again, doing what he must to win her love.

In their city, throughout a turbulent half-century, death has proliferated everywhere, both as el colera, the fatal disease that sweeps through in terrible intermittent epidemics, and as la colera, defined as choler or anger, which taken to its extreme becomes warfare. Victims of one, in this book, are more than once mistaken for victims of the other. War, "always the same war," is presented here not as the continuation by other means of any politics that can possibly matter, but as a negative force, a plague, whose only meaning is death on a massive scale. Against this dark ground, lives, so precarious, are often more and less conscious projects of resistance, even of sworn opposition, to death. Dr. Urbino, like his father before him, becomes a leader in the battle against the cholera, promoting public health measures obsessively, heroically. Fermina, more conventionally but with as much courage, soldiers on in her chosen role of wife, mother, and household manager, maintaining a safe perimeter for her family. Florentino embraces Eros, death's well-known long-time enemy, setting off on a career of seductions that eventually add up to 622 "long-term liaisons, apart from . . . countless fleeting adventures," while maintaining, impervious to time, his deeper fidelity, his unquenchable hope for a life with Fermina. At the end he can tell her truthfully—though she doesn't believe it for a minute—that he has remained a virgin for her.

So far as this is Florentino's story, in a way his *Bildungsroman,* we find ourselves, as he earns the suspension of our disbelief, cheering him on, wishing for the success of this stubborn warrior against age and death, and in the name of love. But like the best fictional characters, he insists on his autonomy, refusing to be anything less ambiguous than human. We must take him as he is, pursuing his tomcat destiny out among the streets and lovers' refuges of this city with which he lives on terms of such easy intimacy, carrying with him a potential for disasters from which he remains safe, immunized by a comical but dangerous indifference to consequences that often borders on criminal neglect. The widow Nazaret, one of many widows he is fated to make happy, seduces him during a night-long bombardment from the cannons of an attacking army outside the city. Ausencia Santander's exquisitely furnished home is burgled of every movable item while she and Florentino are frolicking in bed. A girl he picks up at Carnival time turns out to be a homicidal machete-wielding escapee from the local asylum. Olimpia Zuleta's husband murders her when he sees a vulgar endearment Florentino has been thoughtless enough to write on her body in red paint. His lover's amorality causes not only individual misfortune but ecological destruction as well: as he learns by the end of the book, his River Company's insatiable appetite for firewood to fuel its steamers has wiped out the great forests that once bordered the Magdalena river system, leaving a wasteland where nothing can live. "With his mind clouded by his passion for Fermina Daza he never took the trouble to think about it, and by the time he realized the truth, there was nothing anyone could do except bring in a new river."

In fact, dumb luck has as much to do with getting Florentino through as the intensity or purity of his dream. The author's great affection for this character does not entirely overcome a sly concurrent subversion of the ethic of machismo, of which García Márquez is not especially fond, having described it elsewhere simply as usurpation of the rights of others. Indeed, as we've come to expect from his fiction, it's the women in this story who are stronger, more attuned to reality. When Florentino goes crazy with live, developing symptoms like those of cholera, it is his mother, Transito Ariza, who pulls him out of it. His innumerable lecheries are rewarded not so much for any traditional masculine selling points as for his obvious and aching need to be loved. Women go for it. "He is ugly and sad," Fermina Daza's cousin Hildebranda tells her, "but he is all love."

And García Márquez, straight-faced teller of tall tales, is his biographer. At the age of nineteen, as he has reported, the young writer underwent a literary epiphany on reading the famous opening lines of Kafka's "Metamorphosis," in which a man wakes to find himself transformed into a giant insect. "Gosh," exclaimed García Márquez, using in Spanish a word we in English may not, "that's just the way my grandmother used to talk!" And that, he adds, is when novels began to interest him. Much of what comes in his work to be called "magic realism" was, as he tells it, simply the presence of that grandmotherly voice.

Nevertheless, in this novel we have come a meaningful distance from Macondo, the magical village in *One Hundred Years of Solitude,* where folks routinely sail through the air and the dead remain in everyday conversation with the living: we have descended, perhaps in some way down the same river, all the way downstream, into war and pestilence and urban confusions to the edge of a Caribbean haunted less by individual dead than by a history which has brought so appallingly many down, without ever having spoken, or having spoken gone unheard, or having been heard, left unrecorded. As revolutionary as writing well is the duty to redeem these silences, a duty García Márquez has here fulfilled with honor and compassion. It would be presumptuous to speak of moving "beyond" *One Hundred Years of Solitude,* but clearly García Márquez has moved somewhere else, not least into deeper awareness of the ways in which, as Florentino comes to learn, "nobody teaches life anything." There are still delightful and stunning moments contrary to fact, still told with the same unblinking humor—presences at the foot of the bed, an anonymously delivered doll with a curse on it, the sinister parrot, almost a minor character, whose pursuit ends with the death of Dr. Juvenal Urbino. But the predominant claim on the author's attention and energies comes from what is not so contrary to fact, a human consensus about "reality" in which love and the possibility of love's extinction are the indispensable driving forces, and varieties of magic have become, if not quite peripheral, then at least more thoughtfully deployed in the service of an expanded vision, matured, darker than before but no less clement.

It could be argued that this is the only honest way to write about love, that without the darkness and the finitude there might be romance, erotica, social comedy, soap opera—all genres, by the way, that are well represented in this novel—but not the Big L. What that seems to require, along with a certain vantage point, a certain level of understanding, is an author's ability to control his own love for his characters, to withhold from the reader the full extent of his caring, in other words not to lapse into drivel.

In translating *Love in the Time of Cholera,* Edith Grossman has been attentive to this element of discipline, among many nuances of the author's voice to which she is sensitively, imaginatively attuned. My Spanish isn't perfect, but I can tell that she catches admirably and without apparent labor the swing and translucency of his writing, its slang and its classicism, the lyrical stretches and those end-of-sentence zingers he likes to hit us with. It is a faithful and beautiful piece of work.

There comes a moment, early in his career at the River Company of the Caribbean when Florentino Ariza, unable to write even a simple commercial letter without some kind of romantic poetry creeping in, is discussing the problem with his uncle Leo XII, who owns the company. It's no use, the young man protests—"Love is the only thing that interests me."

"The trouble," his uncle replies, "is that without river navigation, there is no love." For Florentino this happens to be literally true: the shape of his life is defined by two momentous river voyages, half a century apart. On the first he made his decision to return and live forever in the city of Fermina Daza, to persevere in his love for as long as it might take. On the second, through a desolate landscape, he journeys into love and against time, with Fermina, at last, by his side. There is nothing I have read quite like this astonishing final chapter, symphonic, sure in its dynamics and tempo, moving like a riverboat too, its author and pilot, with a lifetime's experience steering us unerringly among hazards of skepticism and mercy, on this river we all know, without whose navigation there is no love and against whose flow the effort to return is never worth a less honorable name than remembrance—at the very best it results in works that can even return our worn souls to us, among which most certainly belongs *Love in the Time of Cholera,* this shining and heartbreaking novel.

William Kennedy on Ernesto Sábato

Albany, New York, the birthplace of William Kennedy (b. 1928), has been the setting of all his books. Kennedy is an essayist, journalist, and novelist. His prose is imbued with a rather powerful realism and his characters are predominantly marginal. The most acclaimed of his works, *Ironweed* (1983), is particularly revealing in this regard, for in that novel Kennedy chronicles the return of Francis Phelan, an alcoholic bum who was formerly a major league pitcher, to Albany and the family he left behind. The most notable of his other works are his novels *Legs* (1975), *Billy Phelan's Greatest Game* (1978), and *Very Old Bones* (1992); his essay collection *O Albany!: Improbable City of Political Wizards, Fearless Ethnics, Spectacular Aristocrats, Splendid Nobodies, and Underrated Scoundrels* (1983). He is also responsible for *Quinn's Book* (1988), and *The Flaming Corsage* (1996). Kennedy was the recipient of both the National Book Award and the Pulitzer Prize in 1983. This essay was first published in *Review* (fall 1981).

In an author's note to his second novel, *On Heroes and Tombs,* Ernesto Sábato talks of a fictional narrative "whereby the author endeavors to free himself of an obsession that is not clear even to himself." He says that he has written countless "incomprehensible" stories but put few of them in print.

He published, in 1948, his first novel, *El túnel* (translated into English by Harriet de Onís as *The Outsider* in 1950), and in the thirteen years between that novel and his second, "I continued to explore the dark labyrinth that leads to the central secret of our life. I tried at one time or another to express in writing the outcome of my research, until I grew discouraged at the poor results and ended up destroying the majority of my manuscripts."

He says friends persuaded him to publish what survived, and *On Heroes and Tombs* is among the survivors. It is a very remarkable survivor, a book which derives its main motive power from incest, and which at the same time aspires to be a work of national significance: the Great Argentine Novel as of 1955, perhaps.

Helen R. Lane's translation does high justice to Sábato's prose, which ranges from syntax that is lush and fluid and baroque to dialogue that is irreducibly spare.

Sábato, born in 1911, has been active politically throughout his life: an early Communist, disillusioned; an editor, a polemical essayist, anti-Perónist; and so it is natural that politics plays a role in his fiction. In this novel politics is metaphorically central. He focuses the modern segments of his tale on the first Perón era (1946–1955) and also saves his most elegiac prose for a historical section set in 1841—the story of rebel soldiers in terminal retreat toward the Bolivian border, which powerfully and movingly captures the manic spirituality that in spite of temporary defeat eventually freed the nation from tyranny and shaped its democratic future. But tyranny returns under Perón, and Sábato explores its effect on the soul, but in a way which is open to myriad interpretations.

Principally the novel is the story of a young man named Martín del Castillo and his love for Alejandra Vidal Olmos, a young woman from a decadent aristocratic family which has been a part of the Argentine oligarchy that opposed Perón. Alejandra is living a secret life as a high-level prostitute for affluent Perónists. Her father, the third figure of significance, is a paranoid anarchist–bank robber named Fernando Vidal Olmos, with whom Alejandra seems to be having a prolonged incestuous relationship. A fourth character is Bruno Bassan, all but faceless, a childhood friend of Fernando, who narrates three of the novel's four sections and is Sábato's opinionated surrogate.

The novel, through Bruno, is a discursive, distracting, sometimes fascinating pastiche of Sábato's attitudes toward Buenos Aires as Babylon, toward Perónism, Marxism, the *Reader's Digest*, graffiti, Don Quixote, Jorge Luis Borges, the Argentine oligarchy, football, Patagonia, Italians, Jews, blacks, fascism, and much more.

Sábato reveals in a prologue that Alejandra shoots and kills her father in June 1955 (the year of Perón's overthrow) and then commits suicide by setting fire to herself and to the decaying Olmos mansion. He then opens the book with the young Martín encountering Alejandra at a public park. There is an immediate spark and after they talk and start to separate she says to him: "You and I have something in common, something very important. . . . Even though I think I shouldn't ever see you again. But I'll see you because I need you."

This meeting all but destroys Martín's young life. Lovesick, he moons insipidly after Alejandra, who keeps him at arm's length, tells him that she is "garbage" after she reluctantly makes love to him. Passion has nothing to do with why she likes him; neither he nor we ever learn precisely why she does, though he seems to be her lone link to innocence, to a healthy relationship with the male sex.

Martín follows her, begins to understand something of her secret life, but only dimly, then sees her with a man who seems to be her lover. "The man was cruel and capable of anything . . . reminiscent of a bird of prey." Martín suspects this is a cousin of whom she has spoken, and he confronts her with that notion. She is horrified at what Martín has seen (has he uncovered her incestuous passion?) and she angrily shakes him and tells him the man is Fernando, her father.

Sábato abruptly intrudes on this story with a discourse on the turbulent condition of Argentina under Perón, linking it to Martín's continuing quest for an absolute to cling to, "a warm cave in which to take refuge." But Martín, he concludes, had neither a home nor a homeland, "or what was worse, he had a home built on dung and disillusionment [he thinks of his mother as a sewer], and a tottering, enigmatic homeland." He had flung himself, like a shipwreck victim, on Alejandra: "But that had been like seeking refuge in a cavern from whose depths voracious wild beasts had immediately rushed forth."

Sábato follows this with an episode from June of 1955, when the Argentine navy rose against Perón in a coup d'état that failed, but led to Perón's overthrow three months later. In reprisal for the uprising, Perón's troops burned Catholic churches, since the church had sided against him. Martín moves through the debacle of church burnings, with Perón, in absentia, created in the image of a cruel Antichrist.

This concludes the first two sections, or half the novel. Sábato here imposes a novella, his 139-page, first-person *Report on the Blind*, written by Fernando, and recounting his paranoid fantasies about a conspiracy of blind people ruling the world "by way of nightmares and fits of delirium, hallucinations, plagues and witches, soothsayers and birds, serpents . . ." (Birds play a major role in the book; Fernando as a child put out the eyes of a bird with a needle, then released it inside a room.)

The *Report* is a tour de force which is brilliant in its excesses, a surreal journey into the depths of Fernando's personal Boschian hells, which, in their ultimate landscapes, are provinces of a "terrible nocturnal divinity, a demoniacal specter that surely held supreme power over life and death." This ruling specter is a faceless goddess with the wings and head of a vampire and a single gigantic phosphorescent eye shining where her navel would have been. Her realm is

> a charred museum of horrors. I saw hydras that had once been alive and were now petrified, idols with yellow eyes in silent abandoned dwellings, goddesses with striped skin like zebras, images of a mute idolatry with indecipherable inscriptions. It was a country where the one rite celebrated was a petrified Death Ceremony. I suddenly felt so hideously lonely that I cried out in anguish. And in that mineral silence outside of history my cry echoed and reechoed, seemingly down through entire centuries and generations long since gone.

Fernando realizes he must enter the giant vampiric goddess and he does enter what is clearly the vulva of the goddess:

> Something hideous happened to me as I ascended that slippery, increasingly hot and suffocating tunnel: my body gradually turned into the body of a fish. My limbs slowly metamorphosed into fins and I felt my skin gradually become covered over with hard scales . . . powerful contractions of that narrow tunnel that now seemed made of rubber squeezed me tightly but at the same time carried me upward by virtue of their incredibly strong, irresistible suction."

The consequence of this rising is a transcendent orgasm:

> I saw . . . afternoons in the tropics, rats in a barn . . . dark brothels, madmen shouting words that unfortunately were incomprehensible, women lustfully displaying their gaping vulvas, vultures on the pampas feeding on bloated corpses, windmills on my family's *estancia*, drunkards pawing through a garbage can, and huge black birds diving down with their sharp beaks aimed at my terrified eyes.

He awakens in the room of the Blind Woman, whom he has met almost at the outset of his descent and he perceives her to be the instrument conceived by the sacred Sect of the Blind to punish him. He anticipates the "most infernal of copulations" with her, which he senses will be the end of his lifelong quest for an unknown destiny. He imagines himself a centaur attacking the Blind Woman outside time and space, he becomes a lustful unicorn, a serpent, a swordfish, an octopus attacking her insatiable maw again and again, a giant satyr, a crazed tarantula, a lewd salamander. Excessive?

And again an orgasm:

> . . . men and beasts alike were swallowed up or eaten alive. Mutilated beings ran about among the ruins. Severed hands, eyes that rolled and bounced like balls, heads without eyes that groped about blindly, legs that ran about separated from their trunks, intestines that twisted round each other like great vines of flesh and filth, moaning uteruses, fetuses abandoned and trampled underfoot . . .

He awakens in his own room, finishes writing his *Report on the Blind*, hides it, and goes to meet his fate, "to the place where the prophecy will be fulfilled." He goes to his daughter's home, where she shoots him and then immolates herself.

What is one to make of such events? A sizable body of criticism and analysis of the novel, and of Sábato's other work has appeared in the Spanish language since the book was published in 1962. Sábato has also discussed its meaning in a dialogue with himself included in *El Escritor y Sus Fantasmas* (*The Writer and His Phantoms*) in 1963, but critics disagree on precise meanings. Sábato's own ambivalence contributes to the confusion, for instance his prefatory note about his "obsession" not being clear even to him. He has said that his questions to himself in the 1963 book were the synthesis of what many journalists and readers had asked him. Was the conflict in the novel representative of the actual conflict going on in Argentina? Was Alejandra an image of the country?

Sábato has said that this was "a curious hypothesis," and that such an idea about Alejandra had never occurred to him. But perhaps it is a valid idea, for he sought to create a "very Argentine woman," one for whom he had a passion: "A woman with whom I myself could have fallen in love."

One suspects that Sábato is being somewhat disingenuous here, for he has relied heavily on overt symbolic statement: the dates of Fernando's death and Perón's overthrow coinciding; and Martín saying after his first meeting with Alejandra that she was "a being he seemed to have been waiting a century for." The author has also seen to it that Alejandra looks like not only her own mother, Georgina, who was

Fernando's cousin, but also Fernando's mother, who was an object of Fernando's pubescent passion. Alejandra is thus the personification of womanhood in three generations (all targets of Fernando's lust) and the last female member of the aristocratic Olmos line.

But she also stands for Sábato's definition of the feminine principle. In a work called *Heterodoxia,* a collection of brief essays on life and literature, he wrote the following, under the title "Feminine-Masculine":

The principles coexist in each human being.

Feminine: night, chaos, unconsciousness, body, curve, softness, life, mystery, contradiction, indefiniteness, "corporal" feelings—taste, touch. Origin of the baroque, the romantic, the existential.

Masculine: day, order, consciousness, reason, spirit, rectitude, hardness, eternity, logic, definition, "intellectual" feelings—hatred, vision. Origin of the classical, the essential.

These feminine attributes apply perfectly and repeatedly to Alejandra, and the masculine attributes are parceled out, although sparingly, to the young, conscientious, and intellectual Martín, who in the final section of the book transcends his despair over Alejandra's death and becomes the spiritual inheritor of the future.

Further, Sábato links both male and female archetypes to Fernando and his unity with the demonic female goddess. The author has made Fernando a gangster, a cruel and violent child who grows into a cruel and violent man, a shrewd manipulator of people, power, and money, an anarchist, an autocrat, a tyrant, and ultimately a maniacal solipsist. Does the description fit Perón?

In 1956 Sábato wrote an open letter titled *The Other Mask of Peronism* and in it defined "Perónist" as a person whose basic doctrine was "the elevation of Colonel Perón by any method." He saw Perón as an "empiricist without scruples, an aeronaut disposed to throw any ballast overboard, any person, any theory, any promise, any system that obstructed his unbridled ascent."

He theorized further that Perón's ascent was not explainable by reason but by the passion of the masses who backed him. And the masses, he added, are feminine—that is to say, in his view, illogical, romantic, sentimental. Sábato feuded publicly with Borges in 1956 on the role the masses played in elevating Perón to power and maintaining him there, and at several points throughout his work he seems both accuser and apologist of the masses for what they did to the nation. They were wrong, but I understood them, is his tone.

His imposition of femininity on the masses has a historical counterpart, for Perón broke with Argentine political tradition, embraced feminism (however self-servingly), won for women the right to vote, and in 1951 they voted overwhelmingly for him. His wife Evita though heavily dependent upon Perón (a pussycat feminist herself) was also a powerful influence in attracting the masses to his cause. And as a postscript, when he returned to power in 1973 only to die a year later, his wife Isabel ran the government for two years.

Victoria Ocampo, the grand dame of Argentine letters, took exception to Sábato's views of women when he published an article, "Oh the Metaphysics of Sex," in her magazine *Sur*, in 1952. She argued convincingly that he was stereotyping women; he countered that she was a "furious priestess of Bacchus, ready to tear me apart alive and eat me raw," and insisted that feminism was really masculinism.

Whatever one thinks of Sábato's views of women thirty years ago, the point here is that they fused with his political views and his unconscious (which he felt was also feminine) and formed the ideological and phantasmagorical basis for *On Heroes and Tombs*. The politics are transformed into a paranoiac's incestuous cravings for his daughter, and hers for him; their coupling becomes a nightmarish trip into the vulva of the goddess, and the cloacal wasteland of Fernando's personal, private hell is a reflection of the tyranny, tortures, and killings of the regime.

Incest as the spiritual metaphor for politics is a striking invention, but Sábato is doing more than this. He has said that the novel's four main personages, Bruno, Martín, Alejandra, and Fernando, are all phases of himself. Their dialogue, he says, represents his own internal struggles. Martín is his innocent young manhood, Fernando his dark side. He is a strong proponent of a "national literature" which expresses the fundamental problems of the nation, but the fundamental problems of the human heart have equal primacy for him.

He believes a novel should reflect the fact that life is not explicable, that it is full of overheard whispers, fleeting visions, incomprehensible facts; and so he stocks his work with such characters, who pass through only to make a speech and move off to oblivion. The incest is never confirmed, only alluded to by Martín's glimpse of the passionate hand-holding by Fernando and Alejandra. Is Alejandra the Blind Woman of Fernando's paranoid fantasy? That would explain a great deal. But Sábato does not confirm this.

His aim, he wrote in *El escritor y sus fantasmas,* is to create "beings who can never decide from within if the changes in their destinies are the consequence of their efforts, their failures, or the course of the universe."

Why, for instance, should a spiritually cunning and promiscuous woman be drawn to an innocent like Martín? And why did Martín begin to behave like a paranoiac himself when speaking of Alejandra to Bruno, spewing out a flood of minute details as only madmen do? Was it because Alejandra's mind was ensnaring him as it had presumably ensnared Fernando's? Says Bruno: ". . . the pain born of a passion constantly confronted with obstacles, especially mysterious and inexplicable obstacles, is always more than sufficient reason . . . to cause the most sensible man to think, feel, and act like someone out of his mind."

The book, then, is a psychological melodrama as well as a work of politics, a cultural history as well as a bizarre dream of infernal order; and not least in Sábato's aesthetic priorities, it is a book of hope.

El Túnel was a cornerstone for *On Heroes and Tombs,* the story of a painter who falls in love with a married woman and then murders her when he discovers she has betrayed him. Prefigured are the paranoia, the love which becomes obsessive, the blindness (of the woman's husband), the violence. This book earned Sábato the praise of Thomas Mann, Graham Greene, and Albert Camus, and gave him instant international status as a novelist.

But Sábato saw *El túnel* as a work of his youth, a work that embraced only the negative side of his personality, his "black and hopeless side."

Martín comes to this sense of hope in the depths of his gloom after Alejandra's suicide. In an alcoholic stupor he stumbles onto Fernando's hellish terrain—"a vast swampy plain, amid filth and corpses, amid excrement and mire that might swallow him up . . . repellent landscape crawling with worms, running with his little crutch toward the place where the face seemed to be waiting for him . . ."

The face belongs to a woman, Hortensia Paz, who brings Martín to her home and helps him sober up from his despair. She is the mother of an infant, is living alone, is very poor and struggling, but insistent to Martín about the positive values: ". . . there are so many nice things in life." There's the baby, music, flowers, birds, dogs. "It's a shame the cat from the café ate my canary. It was such good company. . . . It's so beautiful to be alive!" Hortensia (her name means "Garden of Peace") succors Martín, draws him instantly up from the dismal swamp. He gives her his grandmother's ring as he leaves.

This lapse on Sábato's part, this ascent into the empyrean realm of Norman Vincent Peale, is repellent not in its Pollyanna hopefulness but in its absence of imagination and its facile reduction of 465 pages of dire complexity to a barrage of pop sloganeering. But Sábato means for Martín to come out of his depression alive and with a complete skin, and he recovers his stride effectively by giving Martín a ride to Patagonia with a trucker named Bucich.

This scene is largely dialogue and resembles Hemingway in its pithy understatement. Bucich, who has been on the Patagonia run for years, and who values the stars, wishes he'd been an astronomer. He's a realist, Bucich; he remembers his father's futile search for gold as far south as Tierra del Fuego, remembers an Englishman who told his old man: "Why don't you settle down here instead of wandering all over looking for gold? What's gold around here is sheep-raising, and I know what I'm talking about."

The message, of course, is not lost on Martín. The air on the southern pampa suddenly seems more decent to him. He feels useful. He is up from the sewer now and he sits by the fire waiting for the meat to cook. "The sky was crystal clear, and the cold intense. Martín sat there staring thoughtfully at the flames."

Counterpoint to Martín's Patagonia excursion is what I judge to be the best writing in the book, the conclusion of the final days of the retreat of General Juan Galo de Lavalle (an authentic figure) and his rebel forces, defeated in 1841 by the allies of Juan Manuel de Rosas, the caudillo who ruled Argentina from 1829 to 1852. An ancestor of the modern Olmos family rides with Lavalle, not only maintaining the historical thread, but also serving as a juxtaposed figure to Martín— two youths whose powerlessness in the face of oppressive life is told in parallel stories.

Lavalle dies a hero to revolutionary fervor, but Sábato wants us to see also his mundane side, and he ends the book with Lavalle's mythic figure appearing to an old Indian. Lavalle rides a white charger and wears a cavalry saber and a high-crested grenadier's helmet.

"Poor Indian," the narrator concludes, "if you only knew the general was only a man in rags and tatters, with a dirty straw hat and a cape that had already forgotten the symbolic color it once was. . . . If you only knew he was simply a miserable wretch among countless other miserable wretches!"

Wretches all, we read Sábato and we shudder, we exult, we are bewildered, fearful, mesmerized.

Acknowledgments

This anthology is made possible thanks to a generous grant from Amherst College. The editor wishes to express gratitude to Melissa M. Lorenzo, Jesse H. Lytle, José Matosantos, Laura Santiago, and the staff of *Hopscotch: A Cultural Review*, for the research and help provided. Gratitude is also due to the Institute of Latin American Studies at the University of London, where the editor was the 1998–99 Research Fellow during the completion of the manuscript. Rolando Hinojosa-Smith and Steven G. Kellman kindly agreed to read the manuscript and offered valuable comments.

Acknowledgment is made for permission
to reprint the following material:

John Barth: "The Literature of Exhaustion," in *The Friday Book: Essays and Other Nonfiction* (New York: Putnam's, 1984). © 1984 by John Barth. Reprinted by permission of The Waylie Agency, Inc.

Antonio Benítez Rojo: "Lafcadio Hearn, mi tía Gloria y lo sobrenatural." Translated by James E. Maraniss. © 1999 by Antonio Benítez Rojo. Used by permission of Antonio Benítez Rojo.

José Bianco: "The Sadism of Ambrose Bierce." Translated by Jennifer Radke. Originally used as the prologue to *Cuentos de soldados y civiles* (Buenos Aires: Jorge Alvarez, 1968). Reprinted in *José Bianco: Ficción y realidad* (Mexico City: Fondo de Cultura Económica, 1984). Used by permission of Fondo de Cultura Económica.

Robert Bly: "A Bell Cracked a Little." Printed in *Review* (fall 1972). Used by permission of the editors of *Review*.

Jorge Luis Borges: "Nathaniel Hawthorne." Lecture delivered at the Colegio Libre de Estudios Superiores, Buenos Aires, March 1949. Translated by Ruth L. C. Simms. Reprinted in *Other Inquisitions: 1936–1952* (Austin, Tex.: University of Texas Press, 1964). © 1964, renewed 1993. Used by permission of University of Texas Press.

Alejo Carpentier: "Herman Melville y la América Latina." Printed in *El Nacional*, Caracas, Venezuela, 4 February 1955. Used by permission of *El Nacional*.

Hiber Conteris: "A Long Good-bye to Raymond Chandler." © 1999 by Hiber Conteris. Used by permission of Hiber Conteris.

Robert Coover: "Parables and Parodies." Published in the *New York Times Book Review* (20 May 1984). © 1984 by Robert Coover. Used by permission of George Borchardt, Inc., for the author.

Julio Cortázar: "Poe as Poet and Story-writer." Translated by John Incledon. From the Introduction to *Edgar Allan Poe: Obras Completas,* translated into Spanish and edited by Julio Cortázar (Rio Piedras: Editorial de la Universidad de Puerto Rico, 1956). Printed in *Review* (spring 1976). Used by permission of Agencia Literaria Carmen Balcells.

Waldo Frank: "Introduction" to *Don Segundo Sombra: Shadows on the Pampas,* by Ricardo Güiraldes. Translated by Harriet De Onis (New York: Farrar and Rinehart, 1935). © 1935 by Waldo Frank. Used by permission of Farrar, Straus and Giroux.

Carlos Fuentes: "William Styron in Mexico." Translated by Margaret Sayers Peden. In *Review* (spring 1976). © 1976 by Carlos Fuentes. Used by permission of Brandt & Brandt Literary Agents, Inc.

Gabriel García Márquez: "William Faulkner, un Premio Nobel." Translated by José Matosantos. In *Textos costeños,* vol. 1 (Barcelona: Editorial Bruguera, 1981). Used by permission of Agencia Literaria Carmen Balcells.

William H. Gass: "Imaginary Borges and His Books." First published in 1981. From *Fiction and the Figures of Life* (New York: Vintage Books, 1972). Used by permission of William H. Gass.

Nicolás Guillén: "Conversación con Langston Hughes." Translated by Laura Santiago. *Diario de la Marina* vol. 98, no. 68 (9 March 1930). From *Langston Hughes in the Hispanic World and Haiti,* edited by Edward J. Mullen (Hamden, Conn.: Anchor Books, 1977). Used by permission of Anchor Books.

Pedro Henríquez Ureña: "Veinte años de literatura en los Estados Unidos." Translated by Melquíades Sánchez. © 1927 by Pedro Henríquez Ureña. In *Seis ensayos en busca de nuestra expresión, Obra crítica* (Mexico City: Fondo de Cultura Económica, 1981). Used by permission of Fondo de Cultura Económica.

William Kennedy: "Ernesto Sábato: On Heroes and Tombs." First published in *Review* (fall 1981). Collected in *Riding the Yellow Trolley Car: Selected Nonfiction* (New York: Viking, 1993). Used by permission of the editors of *Review.*

José Martí: "Walt Whitman." First published in *El partido liberal* (Mexico City, 1887) and *La Nación* (Buenos Aires, 1998). Printed in *Martí on the U.S.A.,* selected and translated with an introduction by Luis A. Baralt, foreword by J. Cary Davis (Carbondale, Ill.: Southern Illinois University Press, 1966). Used by permission of Southern Illinois University Press.

Ezequiel Martínez Estrada: "Taking Sides with Nature." Translated by Gregory Kolovakos. In *Review* (spring 1976). Used by permission of the editors of *Review.*

Pablo Neruda: "Robert Frost and the Prose of Poets." Translated by Margaret Sayers Peden. In *Passions and Impressions,* edited by Matilde Neruda and Miguel Otero Silva (New York: Farrar, Straus and Giroux, 1983). Reprinted by permission of Farrar, Straus and Giroux.

Victoria Ocampo: *"Las viñas de la ira"* and *"Sobre hombres y ratas,* de Stein-beck." Translated by Jesse H. Lytle. From *Testimonios. Quinta Serie: 1950–1957* (Buenos Aires: Sur, 1957). Used by permission from Editorial Sur, S.A.

Juan Carlos Onetti: "Lolita." Translated by José Matosantos. First published in *Marcha.* Reprinted in *Requiem por Faulkner y otros artículos* (Montevideo: Arca Editorial, 1975). Used by permission of Arca Editorial.

Grace Paley: "Introduction," *Soulstorm: Stories,* by Clarice Lispector (New York: New Directions, 1987). Used by permission of New Directions.

Octavio Paz: "William Carlos Williams: The Saxifrage Flower." Translated by Michael Schmidt. In *Of Poets and Others* (New York: Seaver Books, 1986). © 1986 by Octavio Paz. Translation © 1986 by Seaver Books. Reprinted by permission of Seaver Books.

Katherine Anne Porter: "Notes on the Life and Death of a Hero." Published as preface to *The Itching Parrot,* by José Joaquín Fernández de Lizardi. From *The Collected Essays and Occasional Writings of Katherine Anne Porter.* © 1970 by Katherine Anne Porter. Reprinted by permission of Houghton Mifflin Co. / Seymour Lawrence. All rights reserved.

Thomas Pynchon: "The Heart's Eternal Vow." Printed in the *New York Times Book Review* (10 April 1988). © 1988 by Thomas Pynchon. Reprinted by permission of Melanie Jackson Agency.

Kenneth Rexroth: "Homero Aridjis: Blue Spaces of Illumination." Published in *Review* (fall 1974). Used by permission of the editors of *Review.*

Barbara Probst Solomon: "Teresa de la Parra's *Iphigenia.*" © 1997 by Barbara Probst Solomon. First published in *Double Take* and *Quimera.* Used by permission of Barbara Probst Solomon.

Susan Sontag: Preface to *Epitaph of a Small Winner,* by José Joaquim Machado de Assis. Translated by William L. Grossman. New York: Noonday, 1952, 1990. © 1990 by Susan Sontag. Used by permission of the Wylie Agency, Inc.

Ilan Stavans: "Las Mariposas." Originally published in *The Nation.* © 1994 by Ilan Stavans. Reprinted in *Art and Angers: Essays on Politics and the Imagination* (Albuquerque: University of New Mexico Press, 1996). Used by permission of the University of New Mexico Press.

Mark Strand: "Nicanor Parra: Poems and Antipoems." Published in the *New York Times Book Review* (10 December 1967). Used by permission of Mark Strand.

John Updike: "The Great Paraguayan Novel and Other Hardships." First published in the *New Yorker.* Reprinted from "Resisting the Big Boys," in *Odd Jobs: Essays and Criticism* (New York: Alfred A. Knopf, 1991). © 1991 by John Updike. Reprinted by permission of Alfred A. Knopf, Inc.

Mario Vargas Llosa: "Hemingway: The Shared Feast." Translated by John King. In *Making Waves: Essays* (New York: Farrar, Straus and Giroux, 1997).

Index

Aristotle, 188, 231, 234n
Armstrong, Louis, 271
Arnold, Matthew, 20
Arrowsmith (Lewis), 23
art, 71–72, 158
Artaud, Antonin, 173
"Arte Poética" (Neruda), 261
As a Man Grows Older (Svevo), 276
Ascasubi, Hilario, 83
Asia, 6
"Asphodel" (Williams), 164
Asturia, Miguel Angel: *El Señor Presidente*, 117
Asunción (Paraguay), 192
Atherton, Gertrude, 14–15
athletic asceticism, 22
The Atlantic Monthly, 19
At Play in the Fields of the Lord (Matthiessen), 3
Atwood, Margaret, 10
Auden, W. H., 8, 102, 104
Aurelia (Nerval), 173
Auschwitz, 62
authors. *See* American writers; Latin American writers; writers
autobiography: defensiveness in, 273–74; fictional, 272–73, 274; narrator's solitariness in, 277; originality of, 22; plot in, 277; spiritual, 277
automatic writing, 156–57
Autumn of the Patriarch (García Márquez), 194
Aztec Indians, 62, 267

Babbitt, Irving, 22
Babbitt (Lewis), 23
Bacon, Francis, 175
Balzac, Honoré de, 134, 171, 181
bandits, mythical stature of, 3
"La Barcarola Termina" (Neruda), 265
Barlow, Joel, 4
Barnaby Rudge (Dickens), 169
Baroja, Pío, 27
Baroque style, 188
Barrenechea, Ana María, 189, 236n

Barth, John, 8; background / career of, 179; on Borges, 7; on García Márquez, 7; *Giles Goat-Boy*, 186; "The Literature of Exhaustion," 7; "The Literature of Replenishment," 7; on Machado de Assis, 7; *The Sot-Weed Factor*, 186
Barthelme, Donald, 233n, 278–79
Beach, Joseph Warren, 17
Beach, Sylvia, 145
Beat generation, 3
"Beautiful Women" (Whitman), 38
Beauvoir, Simone de, 140
Beckett, Samuel, 183, 187; first-person voice used by, 276, 278, 279; *Malloy*, 182; reductive extremism of, 243; as technically contemporary, 180, 181; *Watt*, 182
Beckford, William Thomas, 231
Beethoven, Ludwig van: Sixth Symphony, 180, 183
Being vs. Nothingness, 182
Belén (Mexico), 202
Belitt, Ben, 265
Bellow, Saul, 180
Benda, Julien, 70
Benedict XIV (pope), 214
The Benefactor (Sontag), 279
Benengeli, Cid Hamete, 186
Benet, Juan, 253
Benet, Paco, 253
Benítez Rojo, Antonio, 135
Benito Cereno (Melville), 57
Benjamin, Walter, 64
"Berenice" (Poe), 172
Beristain, Dr., 211, 220
Berkeley, George, 231, 233
Bernhard, Thomas, 278
Beyond a Boundary (C. L. R. James), 124–25
Bhagavad Gita, 110
Bianco, José, 129
Bible, 78
Bierce, Ambrose, 129–34; character development by, 130; "The Death of Halpin Frayser," 130; *Devil's Dictionary*, 131; disappearance of, 3, 4; "The Man and the Snake,"

130; military career of, 132; violence / horror in work of, 130
bilingualism, 195–96
biography, 272. *See also* autobiography
Bioy Cesares, Adolfo, 44, 233n.
Bishop, Elizabeth, 4
"The Black Hair" (Hearn), 136
The Black Jacobins (C. L. R. James), 124–25
Black Mask, 102
Black Mountain school, 160
Blacks: in Cuban literature, 151; Hughes on, 152–53, 154; *See also* racial prejudice
Blake, William, 276
Bloy, Léon, 231
Bly, Robert, 260
Boccaccio, Giovanni, 184–85
body, and will, 235
Bogart, Humphrey, 94, 95
bohemian lifestyle, 144, 146
Bolívar, Simon, 259
Bombal, María Luisa, 4
The Book of Imaginary Beings (Borges), 237–38
Boom writers, 59, 85, 254
borders, 1, 2
Borges, Jorge Luis, 228–38; *The Aleph,* 238; background / life of, 229–30; on Baroque style, 188; *The Book of Imaginary Beings,* 237–38; "Borges and I," 229n; *Evaristo Carriego,* 229n; *Ficciones,* 87, 182; on fictional aspect of existence, 187, 189; and Frank, 249; on Hitler, 236; influence / popularity of, 7, 66, 193, 280; influences on, 6, 230–31, 233, 238, 280; *Labyrinths,* 182, 186, 189–90; on memory, 229n; "The Modesty of History," 234; "Nathaniel Hawthorne," 6; on originality in literature, 187–88; *A Personal Anthology,* 238; on philosophy, 236n; "Pierre Menard, Author of the *Quixote,*" 182–84, 234; on reality / dreams, 185, 189; *regressus in infinitum* used by,

187, 188; and Sábato, 294; on Shakespeare, 188; sophistry in work of, 234–35; in *Sur,* 44; as technically contemporary, 180, 181; *Tlön, Uqbar, Orbis Tertius,* 184, 185, 187; on treachery, 234; Ultraism of, 236–37; *Universal History of Infamy,* 234n; on the universal Will, 238; writing in English, 4; writings on, 8, 10; Zeno's paradox used by, 189
"Borges and I" (Borges), 229n.
Bourne, Randolph, 21
Brackett, Leigh, 95, 96
Braithwaite, Edward, 27, 124
Brazil: as an outsider country, 280; borders of, 2; ethnicity / class in, 196–97; war with Paraguay, 192
Breton, André, 156–57; *First Manifesto of Surrealism,* 133–34
Brodsky, Joseph, 10, 119
Brontë, Emily: *Wuthering Heights,* 45, 183
Brook Farm (West Roxbury, Mass.), 82
Brooks, Van Wyck, 15, 21, 249; *The Flowering of New England,* 83–84
Browne, Sir Thomas, 60, 184, 185, 188, 231
Browning, Robert, 16
Bruno, Giordano, 184–85
"Brute Force," 52
Bryant, William Cullen, 14
Buchanan, Robert, 32
Buck, Pearl, 86
Buenos Aires, 192
Burgin, Richard, 229n, 231, 236, 238
Burnett, W. R., 103
Burns, Robert, 52
Burroughs, William, 3
Burton, Sir Richard, 183
Bustamante, Carlos María, 206, 207
Butterflies (Mariposas), 115–18

Cabbalists, 231
Cabell, James Branch, 24, 25, 27
Cabrera Infante, Guillermo, 4
Cain, James A., 103

"Calamus" (Whitman), 33, 38, 39
Calderón de la Barca, Pedro, 187
Calleja, Diego, 207, 208
Calvinism, 77
Campanella, Tommaso, 184–85
Campbell, George, 124
Campbell's Soup cans (Warhol), 183
Camus, Albert, 296; *L'Etranger*, 87
Canada, 2
Candide (Voltaire), 279
cannibalizing (plot-construction technique), 103
Canto General (Neruda), 261–62, 265
Cantos (Pound), 161, 162
Cantos Ceremoniales (Neruda), 264
Caracas, 256
Caribbean literature, 124
El Caribe, 116
Carlyle, Thomas, 20
Carpentier, Alejo, 5, 8, 242–48; appearance of, 242; background / career of, 56; *Explosion in a Cathedral*, 243–44; *The Kingdom of This World*, 248; *The Lost Steps*, 243–44; *Reasons of State*, 243, 244–48; *War of Time*, 243–44
Carriego, Evaristo, 229
Carrington, Leonora, 173
Carroll, Lewis, 82, 188–89
Carver, Raymond, 195
Casares, Julio, 171 n.
"The Cask of Amontillado" (Poe), 172
Castellanos, Rosario, 8, 10
Cather, Willa, 27; *My Ántonia*, 24; *The Professor's House*, 24
Catholic Church in Argentina, 291; vs. Freemasonry, 214; in Mexico, 215, 216–17
"The Cat's Testimony" (Fernández de Lizardi), 202
A Certain Lucas (Cortázar), 269–71
Cervantes, Miguel de, 255; *Don Quixote*, 72, 182–83, 186, 193
Chamoiseau, Patrick, 10
Champlin, Charles, 89
Chandler, Raymond, 87–106; atmosphere used by, 92; Auden on,

104; on detective / mystery writing, 104, 105; early mysteries / detective stories of, 102; education of, 103; *Farewell, My Lovely*, 104; goals as a writer, 102–3; influence / popularity of, 91–92, 102, 103; *The Little Sister*, 93; *The Long Goodbye*, 88, 96; MacShane on, 101; on Marlowe, 97–98; Marlowe character in novels of, 89, 90, 93, 94, 96–97, 101; on plot construction, 103; *The Simple Act of Murder*, 97–98; social criticism in work of, 104–5; Wilson on, 104
Chandler, Raymond (fictional character), 106
change, and language, 157
Chaplin, Charles, 271
Chartres cathedral, 180
Chekhov, Anton, 171–72
Chesterton, G. K., 69, 92–93, 231, 238
Chevigny, Bell Gale, 8
Chicago Poems (Sandburg), 28
Chicago poets, 29
Chicago police, 61
"The Children of Adam" (Whitman), 38
China, 77–78
Chinconcuac, 90
Chinese, 2
Chirico, Giorgio de, 121
cholera, 285
Chopin, Kate, 10
Christ, Ronald, 229n, 231n, 236–37
Christ, solitude of, 53
Christianity, 162. *See also* Catholic Church; Puritans
Christian love, 51
Christie, Agatha, 94
Cisneros, Sandra, 10
cities, American, 160–61
"The City in the Sea" (Poe), 170
civilization, debates over, 19
The Civilization of the United States, 19
Civil War (U.S.), 132, 133
Clare, John, 120
Clement XII (Pope), 214

de la Parra, Teresa (*cont.*)
Madrid," 259; as a free thinker, 254; on history, 259; illness of, 259; "The Importance of American Women during the Conquest, Colonialism, and the Independence," 259; influence / popularity of, 252, 257–58; influences on, 255, 256, 258; *Iphigenia (the diary of a young lady who wrote because she was bored)*, 252, 253, 255–58; magic realism of, 254, 257; *Las memorias de Mamá Blanca*, 253; on revolutions, 253–54; on Spanish conquest, 253–54; travels of, 258
DeLillo, Don, 8
democracy, 46, 161, 163, 200
De Quincey, Thomas, 80, 231
Désastres (Goya), 133
Descartes, René, 248; *Meditations*, 279
Desnos, Robert, 267
destiny, 134
detective novels: Chesterton on, 92–93; detectives in series of, 94; readers' participation in, 103–4; vs. serious literature, 102–3, 105
De Tribus Impostoribus, 184–85
Detroit, 61
Devil's Dictionary (Bierce), 131
"The Devil's Penitents" (Fernández de Lizardi), 202
The Dial, 19
Diálogos, 267
"Diary of Bellvue Fuenfria-Madrid" (de la Parra), 259
Dickens, Charles, 276, 278; *Barnaby Rudge*, 169
Dickinson, Emily, 10, 14
dictators, 117. *See also* Perón, Juan
Diego, Gerardo, 241
Díez-Canedo, Enrique, 27
Dime Detective Magazine, 102
Dinesen, Isak, 254
The Dispossessed (Slesinger), 256
Disraeli, Benjamin, 20
Divine Comedy (Dante), 69, 70, 161

Doerr, Harriet: *Consider This, Señora*, 3; *Stones for Ibarra*, 3
"The Dog in a Strange Neighborhood" (Fernández de Lizardi), 202
Dom Casmurro (Machado de Assis), 280
Dominican Republic, 2; history of, 115; literature of, 114; misogynistic / repressive society of, 116, 117, 118
Donne, John, 70
Don Quixote (Cervantes), 72, 182–83, 186, 193
Don Segundo Sombra (Güiraldes), 250
Doolittle, Hilda (H.D.), 28, 156
Dorfman, Ariel, 4
Dos Passos, John, 24, 27, 28
Dostoevsky, Fyodor, 181, 278
Doyle, Arthur Conan, 94
"Dreamland" (Poe), 170
dreams: and instinctive perception, 70–71; as literature, 67, 83; and reality, 185, 189; as theater, 67
Dreiser, Theodore, 24, 25, 27, 30
Drew, Bernard, 95
dualisms, 248
Duncan, Robert, 156, 160
Dunne, John William, 231
Dunsany, Lord, 174
Dupin, Auguste (fictional character), 94
Duras, Marguerite, 254
dust bowl, 47
Dutch, 2
duty, 130–31

"Earth's Holocaust" (Hawthorne), 76–77
Echeverría, Esteban, 83; "The Slaughterhouse," 4–5
economics, 109
The Education of Henry Adams: Study in the Multiplicity of the Twentieth Century (Adams), 17–18, 22
Eisenhower, Dwight D., 61
Ekelöf, Gunnar, 267
Elementary Odes (Neruda), 265

Eliot, T. S., 28, 155, 156, 244; *The Waste Land,* 161, 162, 255
elitism, fascist, 62
Ellington, Duke, 271
Ellison, Ralph, 10
Elmer Gantry (Lewis), 23
Eluard, Paul, 267
Emerson, Ralph Waldo: Borges on, 231; and Hawthorne, 82–83; "History," 77; North American spirit expressed in, 14; and Thoreau, 111; and Whitman, 2–3, 32
Emile (Rousseau), 210
England: imperialism of, 19–20, 121, 126–27; literature of exported to provinces, 122; pastoral culture of, 119–20, 121; power / morals of, 122; racial prejudice in, 127; spiritual / social life of, 20
English, 2
English Men of Letters booklet (H. James), 6, 84
The Enigma of Arrival (V. S. Naipaul), 10, 119, 120–24, 125–28, 277
"Entierro en el Este" (Neruda), 261
Epitaph of a Small Winner (Machado de Assis), 273, 274–78, 279–81
"Epithalamium" (Fernández de Lizardi), 216
equality, 200
Erasmus, 201
eroticism, 253, 257, 292–93. *See also* sexuality
El escritor y sus fantasmas (*The Writer and His Phantoms;* Sábato), 293, 296
Eskimos, 244
Esquivel, Laura: *Like Water for Chocolate,* 114
Essays (Montaigne), 273–74
Establecimiento Militar de Reclusión No. 1 (Military Institution for Confinement, Uruguay), 100–101
Estravagario (Neruda), 263–64, 265
Eternal Course to the Reader of These Pages (Puig), 4
Ethan Frome (Wharton), 17

ethics vs. aesthetics, 78–79
L'Etranger (*The Stranger;* Camus), 87
Eva Perón and the Killings in Trinidad (V. S. Naipaul), 127
Evaristo Carriego (Borges), 229 n.
"Even Though Robed in Silk, a Monkey Is Still a Monkey" (Fernández de Lizardi), 202
Everyman, 23–24
exhaustion, literature of, 179, 187, 189
existence, fictional aspect of, 187
Explosion in a Cathedral (Carpentier), 243–44

Facundo: Civilization and Barbarism (Sarmiento), 6
"The Fall of the House of Usher" (Poe), 174
Fancy Goods (Morand), 255
fantastic (supernatural) literature, 24, 138–39, 173–74
farce, 186
Farewell, My Lovely (Chandler), 104
A Farewell to Arms (Hemingway), 146
fascist elitism, 62
Faulkner, William: *Absalom, Absalom,* 60; brutality in work of, 83; influence / popularity of, 7, 85; Nobel Prize for Literature awarded to, 85–86; oeuvre of, 91; perversity in writing of, 49; *Sound and the Fury,* 87; style of, 116
female eroticism, 253, 257
"Feminine-Masculine" (Sábato), 294
feminism, 253, 295
Ferdinand VII (king of Spain), 209
Fernández, Macedonio, 271
Fernández de Lizardi, José Joaquín, 198–227; "Alacena de Frioleras," 210; appearance of, 205; background / life of, 198–99, 200–201; on Creoles, 209; criticism of, 225–26; "A Defense of the Freemasons," 214; on education, 210, 220; "Epithalamium," 216; excommunication of, 214–15, 217;

Hawthorne, John (an ancestor of Nathaniel), 67–68
Hawthorne, Louise (Nathaniel's sister), 68
Hawthorne, Mrs. Nathaniel (Nathaniel's mother), 68
Hawthorne, Nathaniel, 67–84; allegory used by, 68, 69, 76, 171; appearance of, 68; Bible read by, 68; Borges on, 6; at Brook Farm, 82; death of, 83; "Earth's Holocaust," 76–77; and Emerson, 82–83; fables / moralities by, 70–72, 79; Fuller on, 82–83; on his ancestors' guilt, 68; *The House of the Seven Gables,* 79; imagination of, 70, 80, 83; importance of, 14; influences on, 80; Henry James on, 82; journal kept by, 80, 82; and Longfellow, 68; *The Marble Faun,* 80–81; marriage of, 83; metaphor used by, 70; Lloyd Morris on, 21–22; "Mr. Higginbotham's Catastrophe," 82; on nude statues, 67; Poe on, 68; Puritanism of, 67, 70, 78; in Salem, 67; *The Scarlet Letter,* 72, 78, 79–80; seclusion of, 68, 76; situations as stimulus for, 72, 80; stories vs. novels of, 72; style of, 80; *Twice-Told Tales,* 72; Updike on, 6; visions of, 82; "Wakefield," 72–76; on writing as sinful, 78
Hawthorne, William (an ancestor of Nathaniel), 68
Hays, H. R., 265
Hearn, Lafcadio, 135–39; "The Black Hair," 136; on fantastic / supernatural writing, 138–39; "In a Cup of Tea," 136; influence of, 10; *Japanese Fairy Tales,* 135, 136
Hearne, John, 124
heart, and sin, 76–77
hedonism, 20
Helen's Husband (Moeller), 26
Hemingway, Ernest, 143–50; anti-intellectualism of, 149; in Cuba, 3; decline of, 147, 148; *A Farewell to Arms,* 146; horse-racing interest of, 145; imagination in work of, 25; lifestyle of, 143–45, 147; *machismo* / values of, 150; *A Movable Feast,* 143, 144, 147–50; oeuvre of, 91; racial prejudice of, 125; and Stein, 145, 148, 149; *The Sun Also Rises,* 145, 147; temperament / violence of, 145; understatement in work of, 297; writing passion of, 144–47
Hemingway, Mary, 148
Hemley, Cecil, 279–80
Henríquez Ureña, Pedro, 9, 13, 114
Herbert, Cecil, 124
Hergesheimer, Joseph, 24, 25, 27
Herman, Florence (Florence Williams), 156, 164
Hernández, José, 83
Herrick, Robert, 162
Hesse, Herman, 86
Heterodoxia (Sábato), 294
Hidalgo, Father Miguel, 201, 202, 203
Hijo de hombre (Roa Bastos), 192
Hinduism, 127
Hippodrome (Baltimore), 180
Hiroshima, 62
Hispanic hemisphere, 5
Hispanic literature. *See* Latin American literature
Hispanic phallocentrism, 116, 117
Hispanic writers. *See* Latin American writers
historical fiction, 192–93 n.
history: abolishment of, 77–78; accounts of events, 232–34; Benjamin on, 64; Khayyām on, 67; and nature, 253; as within people, 77; Schopenhauer on, 77
"History" (Emerson), 77
Histriones, 188
Hitler, Adolf, 236
Hobbes, Thomas, 231
Hoffmann, E. T. A., 80, 174
Hollander, John, 7, 141–42
Holmes, Oliver Wendell, 14
Holmes, Sherlock (fictional character), 94

U.S. literature read by, 4–5, 6, 9;
writing in English, 4
Laughlin, James, 156
Lavalle, Juan Galo de, 297, 298
Lawrence, D. H., 183; *Studies in
Classic American Literature,* 83–84
"A Leaf Treader" (Frost), 165
Leaves of Grass (Whitman), 2–3, 161
Lenin, Vladimir Ilyich, 49
Lessing, Doris, 254, 255; *The Golden
Notebook,* 253
"Letter to a Papist" (Fernández de
Lizardi), 215, 216
Lewis, Sinclair, 24, 27; *Arrowsmith,*
23; *Babbitt,* 23; *Elmer Gantry,* 23;
Main Street, 23
Lewis, Wyndham, 149
Lewisohn, Ludwig, 79–80; *Story of
American Literature,* 83–84; *Up
Stream: An American Chronicle,* 22
Lezama Lima, José, 8
The Liberator, 19
liberty, 36, 200
Lidice, 62
Lie Down in Darkness (Styron), 59–
60, 61, 62
life, inexplicability of, 295–96
*The Life and Opinions of Tristam
Shandy* (Sterne), 275–76, 277
Life of Reason (Santayana), 17
"Ligeia" (Cortázar), 6–7
"Ligeia" (Poe), 175
The Lightning Conductor, 211
Like Water for Chocolate (Esquivel),
114
Lima, 57
Lincoln, Abraham, 33–34
Lincoln Heights jail (East Los
Angeles), 90
Lindsay, Vachel: *The Congo and
Other Poems,* 29; *Going-to-the-Sun,*
29; *The Handy Guide for Beggars,
Especially Those of the Poetic Frater-
nity,* 29
Lispector, Clarice, 195–97
Li Su, 77–78
literature: for children, 68; dreams
as, 67, 83; of exhaustion, 179, 187,

189; fantasy, 24, 138–39, 173–74; as
a landscape, 232; North American
vs. Spanish-language, 83; original-
ity of, 22, 80, 187–88; picaresque,
220–22, 253; and social condi-
tions, 35; thematic, 171. *See also*
novels; poetry; short story
"The Literature of Exhaustion"
(Barth), 7
"The Literature of Replenishment"
(Barth), 7
The Little Sister (Chandler), 93
Little Theater of Maurice Browne
(Chicago), 26
Littmann, Enna, 229 n.
Lolita (Nabokov), 140–42
London, 88–89
London, Jack, 231
Londres, Alberto, 153
The Lonely Londoners (Selvon), 124–
25
Longfellow, Henry Wadsworth, 14,
68
The Long Goodbye (Chandler), 88, 96
The Long Goodbye (film; Altman),
88, 89–91, 92, 95–96, 98–99
The Long March (Styron), 59, 60, 61
López Velarde, Ramón, 157
Los Angeles, 90, 93–94, 104
The Lost Steps (Carpentier), 243–44
Louvain (Uruguay), 99
love: as a driving force, 287; fra-
ternal, 54; of humanity, 51; and
immortality, 282, 283–84; in nov-
els / stories, 254, 282–83; Whit-
man on, 33, 38
Love in the Time of Cholera (García
Márquez), 254
love stories, 254
Lowell, Amy, 28
Lowell, Robert, 14
Lowry, Malcolm: *Under the Volcano,*
4, 59–60
Lozano, Carlos, 265
"Lucas, His Pianists" (Cortázar),
269–70
"Lucas, Partisan Arguments" (Cor-
tázar), 270

Mexican Revolution (1910), 3, 199,
200
The Mexican Thinker (Fernández de
Lizardi), 204, 207, 208, 209, 210
Mexico: Catholic Church in, 215,
216–17; censorship in, 202–3, 210,
211, 212, 214; class / scholarship in,
199; Constitutionalists-liberals vs.
revolutionists in, 203, 211–12; education in, 210, 220; Federalists in,
215, 216–17; freedom of the press
in, 202, 203, 204, 214; independence of, 212–13; intellectual
renewal in, 13; political / clerical
corruption in, 199, 202–3, 204,
211, 214; secret political societies
in, 200; slavery in, 217; and the
United States, 1–2
Mexico City, 207–8
Mickey and Sylvia (singing duo),
282
The Middle Passage (V. S. Naipaul),
127
Midwest (U.S.), 28
migrant workers, 46n, 47
Milestone, Lewis, 54
Mill, John Stuart, 231
Millay, Edna St. Vincent, 26–27, 30
Miller, Henry, 258
Mills, Wright, 61
Milton, John, 119–20
Mir, Pedro: "Amén de Mariposas,"
115
Mirabal, Dedé, 115, 116, 117
Mirabal, María Teresa, 115–18
Mirabal, Minerva, 115–18
Mirabal, Patria, 115–18
Las Mirabal (Ferreras), 115–16
Mirándola dormir (Aridjis), 267
mirrors, 237
Les Misérables (Hugo), 49, 50, 53
misery. *See* suffering
The Misfortunes of Virtue (Sade), 133
Mishima, Yukio, 243
Mississippi region writers, 7
Mistral, Gabriela, 44, 258
Mitchel, Langdon: *The New York
Idea*, 26

Mitchell, Margaret: *Gone with the
Wind*, 60
Mitchum, Robert, 94, 95
Mittelholzer, Edgar, 124
Moby-Dick (Melville), 57, 193
modernism, 240–41
modernista movement, 5, 31
modernity, 61, 161, 255, 281
"The Modesty of History" (Borges),
234
Moeller, Philip: *Helen's Husband*,
26
Mohammed, 78–79
Monroe, Harriet, 27
Montaigne, Michel de: *Essays*, 273–
74
Monteagudo, Canon, 212
Montgomery, George, 94
Montgomery, Robert, 94
A Month of Sundays (Updike), 6
*Mont-Saint-Michel and Chartres:
Study in the Unity of the Nineteenth
Century* (Adams), 17–18
Moody, William Vaughan: *The
Great Divide*, 26
Moore, Marianne, 156
Morand, Paul, 256; *Fancy Goods*, 255;
Open All Night, 255
"Morelli" (Cortázar), 243
Morelos y Pavón, José María, 200,
201, 208, 210
Morris, Lloyd: *The Rebellious
Puritan*, 21–22
Morris, William, 20, 231–32n
Morrison, Toni, 10
mortality, 240
Moseley, Hardwick, 102
The Mosquito Coast (Theroux), 3–4
"Mother and Babe" (Whitman), 38–
39
A Movable Feast (Hemingway), 143,
144, 147–50
movement of characters, focus on,
133–34
"Mr. Higginbotham's Catastrophe"
(Hawthorne), 82
Multatuli: *Max Havelaar*, 278
Mumford, Lewis, 249

picaresque literature, 220–22, 253
Picasso, Pablo, 271
Pictures from Breughel (W. C. Williams), 156
Las Piedras de Chile (Neruda), 264
"Pierre Menard, Author of the *Quixote*" (Borges), 182–84, 234
Pinget, Robert, 271
Pirandello, Luigi, 71
"The Pit and the Pendulum" (Poe), 6
pity, 54
Plan of Iguala, 212, 213
Plato, 188, 236; *Republic*, 78
Playwright's Horizon (New York), 26
Plaza de las Tres Culturas massacre, 62–63
Plenos Poderes (Neruda), 264
plot, 67, 103, 277
Plotinus, 67
Poe, Edgar Allan, 10, 168–76; on allegory, 68; "Annabel Lee," 170; atmosphere created by, 171, 172; "Berenice," 172; "The Cask of Amontillado," 172; "The City in the Sea," 170; "The Conqueror Worm," 170; detective prototype created by, 94; "Dreamland," 170; "The Fall of the House of Usher," 174; "For Annie," 170; "The Haunted Place," 170; on Hawthorne, 68; "Hop-Frog," 172; "The Imp of the Perverse," 173; influence/importance of, 6–7, 14, 171, 231; "Israfel," 170; "Ligeia," 175; "The Man of the Crowd," 173; "The Masque of the Red Death," 174; mental condition of/substance abuse by, 173; "Murder in the Rue Morgue," 6; *The Narrative of Arthur Gordon Pym*, 174; "The Pit and the Pendulum," 6; as poet, 168–70; "The Raven," 34, 168, 169–70; *The Raven and Other Poems*, 168; realism vs. fantasy in work of, 173–74; "The Sleeper," 170; as story-writer, 171–76; *Tales of the Grotesque and Arabesque*, 174; "The Tell-tale Heart," 172; terror in work of, 174–75; thematic sources for, 172–73; "To Helen," 170; "Ulalume," 170
poetry: antipoems, 240–41; by Chicago poets, 29; content of, 27; as flourishing, 27; form in, 27; and imagination, 157–58, 164; Imagist, 27–28; importance of, 35–36; of liberty, 36; liveliness of, 162; and magic, 158; meaning in, 159, 160, 244; as metaphor, 160, 236; nationalist, 28; in New England, 28–29; New World, 162; and objects/things, 157, 158–59; Poe on, 168–69; protest in, 166–67; vs. short story, 173; and song/dance, 29; symbolist, 157, 159, 231; Ultraist, 236–37; of violence, 103; William Carlos Williams on, 263
Poetry magazine, 27
Point Counter Point (Huxley), 87
Poirot, Hercule (fictional character), 94
Ponge, Francis, 159, 160
Poniatowska, Elena, 8
Pop Art, 179–80
Pope, Alexander, 119–20, 232
Porter, Katherine Anne, 3, 198; on *The Itching Parrot*, 4
Portmanteau Theater, 26
Portrait of the Artist as a Young Man (Joyce), 185
Portuguese, 2, 280
Portuñol, 2
post-flashing, 90
postmodernism, 253
Pound, Ezra, 28, 145–46, 149, 155, 156, 255; *Cantos*, 161, 162
Powell, Dick, 94, 95
power, political, 62–63
Power Elite, 61
pragmatism, 16, 157
Pragmatism (W. James), 16
"Prayer for Columbus" (Whitman), 2–3
prejudice, racial, 125, 127–28, 280

Prescott, William H., 4, 14
Priestley, J. B., 102
Prisión de "Libertad" ("Liberty" Prison, Uruguay), 100–101
Prisma, 182
Proa, 250
The Professor's House (Cather), 24
progress, 200
propaganda, 46
prose, 27
Proust, Marcel, 17, 242, 255, 256
Provincetown Players (New York), 26
psychoanalysis, 134
psychological novels, 14
psychologism, 17
Puig, Manuel: *Eternal Course to the Reader of These Pages*, 4
Puritans, 20, 62, 70, 78
"The Pursuer" (Cortázar), 4
Pushkin, Aleksandr, 183
Pynchon, Thomas, 8, 282

Quechua, 2
Quevedo, Francisco Gómez de: *Sueño de la muerte*, 67
Quijano, Alonso, 186
Quiroga, Horacio, 8, 107

Rabelais, François, 278
racial prejudice, 125, 127–28, 280
Raine, Kathleen, 267
Randall, Margaret, 4
Rangel, Carlos, 192
Rauschenberg, Robert, 183
"The Raven" (Poe), 34, 168, 169–70
The Raven and Other Poems (Poe), 168
realism, 14; critical, 17; magic, 115, 254, 257, 287
reality: vs. art, 71–72; and dreams, 185, 189; as within one's self, 137–38
Reasons of State (Carpentier), 243, 244–48
rebelliousness of 1907–1927 period, 18–20
The Rebellious Puritan (L. Morris), 21–22

The Red and the Black (Stendhal), 24–25
reducciones, 192
Reed, John, 3
Reed, Rex, 95
regionalism, 14
regressus in infinitum, 187, 188
Reid, Alastair, 263–65
religious freedom, 199
Repertory Theater, 26
Republic (Plato), 78
Residencia 1 (Neruda), 261, 265
Residencia 3 (Neruda), 261–62
Reverdy, Pierre, 158
revolutions, 253–54
Rexroth, Kenneth, 267
Rhys, Jean, 124
Richards, Dick, 95
Richardson, Samuel, 186, 187
Riding, Alan, 2
Riding, Laura, 267
Rights of Man, 200
Rilke, Rainer Maria, 260
Rimbaud, Arthur, 169–70, 245
Rio Grande (Río Bravo), 1
Riopelle, Jean-Paul, 228
Roa Bastos, Augusto: in exile, 191; *Hijo de hombre*, 192; on historical fiction, 192–93n; *I, the Supreme*, 117, 191, 192–94
Roach, Eric, 124
Robbe-Grillet, Alain, 133, 134, 186, 243
Robinson, Edwin Arlington, 28–29, 30
Robinson Crusoe (Defoe), 121
Rodó, José Enrique, 3, 14
Roger's Version (Updike), 6
Romanticism, 169
Rome, 6
A Room of One's Own (Woolf), 258–59
Roosevelt, Franklin, 46n
Rosas, Juan Manuel de, 297
Roth, Philip, 59
Les Rougon-Macquart (Zola), 49
Rousseau, Jean-Jacques, 22, 110, 255; *Confessions*, 273–74; *Emile*, 210

Royce, Josiah, 16
Rulfo, Juan, 10; *Pedro Páramo*, 87
Rushdie, Salman, 6
Russell, Bertrand, 70
Russian Revolution, 253–54

S. (Updike), 6
Sábato, Ernesto, 289–98; background / life of, 290; and Borges, 294; *El Escritor y Sus Fantasmas*, 293, 296; "Feminine-Masculine," 294; on feminism, 294–95; *Heterodoxia*, 294; influence / popularity of, 296; and Ocampo, 295; *On Heroes and Tombs*, 87, 289–94, 295–98; *The Other Mask of Perónism*, 294; on Perón / masses, 294–95; political symbols in work of, 290–91, 293–94, 295; *El Túnel*, 289, 296
Sade, Marquis de: *The Misfortunes of Virtue*, 133
sadhus, 128
sadism, 48–49
Saint Bartholomew massacre, 62
Salem (Massachusetts), 67
Salmmaggi, Bob, 95
Sandburg, Carl, 29, 30; *Chicago Poems*, 28
Sandoe, James, 105
San Lázaro cemetery (Mexico), 219
Santa Ana, Antonio López de, 215, 217
Santayana, George, 16, 18; *Interpretations of Poetry and Religion*, 16; *Life of Reason*, 17; *Three Philosophical Poets*, 16
Sarmiento, Domingo Faustino, 10; *Facundo: Civilization and Barbarism*, 6
Sarris, Andrew, 90
Sayers, Dorothy, 94
The Scarlet Letter (Hawthorne), 72, 78, 79–80
Schneider, Pierre, 228
Schopenhauer, Arthur: on action / thought as voluntary, 76, 134; on body / will, 235; influence of, 189,

189, 231; influences on, 233n; on memory, 233; *Parerga und Paralipomena*, 77; on Zeno's paradox, 189
sculpture, 67, 79
"Selected Poems of Neruda" (Tarn), 260–66
Selvon, Samuel: *The Lonely Londoners*, 124–25; *Ways of Sunlight*, 124–25
El Señor Presidente (Asturia), 117
sensations vs. things, 157–58
Set This House on Fire (Styron), 59, 60
setting, focus on, 133–34
sexuality, 253, 254, 255, 256, 257, 258. *See also* eroticism
Shakespeare, William: Borges on, 188; on fictional aspect of existence, 187; *Hamlet*, 72, 119–20; imagistic thinking of, 70; influence / importance of, 76, 162, 276; *Macbeth*, 278; on the "milk of human kindness," 53; prejudice in work of, 125
Shaw, George Bernard, 15, 231
"The Shepherd's Calendar" (Spenser), 119
Sherman, Stuart Pratt, 22
Shklovsky, Viktor Borisovich, 276
short story, 171–72, 173
Simenon, Georges, 94
Simon, Claude: *Conducting Bodies*, 243
simony, 62
The Simple Act of Murder (Chandler), 97–98
sin, and the heart, 76–77
Sixth Symphony (Beethoven), 180, 183
"The Slaughterhouse" (Echeverría), 4–5
slavery, 63, 64, 71, 126, 217
"The Sleeper" (Poe), 170
Sleepless Nights (Hardwick), 277
Slesinger, Tess: *The Dispossessed*, 256
social criticism: by Brooks, 21–22; by Chandler, 104–5; of North

America, 60–61; by Styron, 60–61, 62, 63
Society of Guadalupe (Mexico), 208, 210
soldiers, barbarism / sufferings of, 130–33
solitude, 53, 277
Solomon, Barbara Probst, 252
Sombra, Segundo, 250
"Song of Myself" (Whitman), 37
"The Song of Songs," 38
Sonora, Bishop of, 216–17
Sontag, Susan, 7, 272; *The Benefactor,* 279
Sor Juana: The Traps of Faith (Paz), 254
Sōseki, Natsume, 280; *I Am a Cat,* 276
Soto, Father, 212
The Sot-Weed Factor (Barth), 186
Soublette, Carlos, 259
Soublette, Teresa, 259
Sound and the Fury (Faulkner), 87
Soupault, Philippe, 156–57
South (U.S.), 28, 60
South America, 6
south vs. north, 1
Southwest (U.S.), 28
Soyinka, Wole, 6
Spade, Sam (fictional character), 94
Spain, 192, 199, 202
Spanglish, 2
Spanish, 2, 262
Spanish Civil War, 259
Spanish Hapsburgs, tortures of, 62
Spanish-language writers. *See* Latin American writers
Spencer, Herbert, 231, 232n
Spenser, Edmund, 120; "The Shepherd's Calendar," 119
Spenser (fictional character), 94
Spillane, Mickey, 141
Spoon River Anthology (Masters), 29
Spring and All (W. C. Williams), 157–58
Stalinist purges, 62
Stavans, Ilan, 113

"Steady, Steady, Six Already" (Cortázar), 270–71
Stein, Gertrude, 145, 148, 149, 278
Steinbeck, John, 46–55; *The Grapes of Wrath,* 45, 46–47, 48–50; *Of Mice and Men,* 51–55; perversity in writing of, 48–49; Wells on, 55
Steiner, George, 7
Stendhal, 175; *The Red and the Black,* 24–25
Sterne, Laurence: influence of, 275–76, 278, 279; *The Life and Opinions of Tristram Shandy,* 275–76
Stevens, Wallace, 8, 30, 155, 156, 162
Stevenson, Robert Louis, 78, 231
Stone, Robert, 4
Stones for Ibarra (Doerr), 3
story, 171–72. *See also* short story
Story of American Literature (Lewisohn), 83–84
Strand, Mark, 239
Stravinsky, Igor, 271
Stroessner, Alfredo, 192
struggle, 61–62
Studies in Classic American Literature (Lawrence), 83–84
Styron, William: *The Confessions of Nat Turner,* 59, 60, 63–65; influence / popularity of, 59, 60; *Lie Down in Darkness,* 59–60, 61, 62; *The Long March,* 59, 60, 61; Lukács on, 60; *Set This House on Fire,* 59, 60; social criticism / activism by, 60–61, 62, 63; struggle in works of, 61–62
Sueño de la muerte (Quevedo), 67
suffering, 49–50, 130–33
The Sun Also Rises (Hemingway), 145, 147
supernatural, writing on, 138–39, 173–74
Sur, 44, 129, 141, 295
surrealist (metaphysical) painting, 121
Surrealists, 270–71
The Survey, 19
Svevo, Italo: *As a Man Grows Older,* 276; *Confessions of Zeno,* 276

Ilan Stavans teaches at Amherst College. His books include *The Riddle of Cantinflas* (1998), *The One-Handed Pianist and Other Stories* (1996), and *The Hispanic Condition* (1995). He has been a National Book Critics Circle Award nominee and the recipient of a Guggenheim Fellowship and the Latino Literature Prize, among many honors.

Library of Congress Cataloging-in-Publication Data

Mutual impressions : writers from the Americas reading one another /
edited by Ilan Stavans.

p. cm.

Includes bibliographical references and index.

ISBN 0-8223-2400-8 (acid-free paper). — ISBN 0-8223-2423-7 (pbk. : acid-free
paper)

1. American literature—History and criticism. 2. Latin American literature—
Appreciation—United States. 3. Latin American literature—History and
criticism. 4. American literature—Appreciation—Latin America.

I. Stavans, Ilan.

PS159.L38M88 1999

809'.897—dc21   99-34818